AF249148

Geometry in the Boudoir

Geometry in the Boudoir

CONFIGURATIONS OF FRENCH EROTIC NARRATIVE

Peter Cryle

Cornell University Press

ITHACA AND LONDON

First published 1994 by Cornell University Press.

Library of Congress Cataloging-in-Publication Data

Cryle, P. M. (Peter Maxwell), 1946–
Geometry in the boudoir : configurations of French erotic narrative / Peter Cryle.
p. cm.
Includes bibliographical references and index.
ISBN 0-8014-2913-7
1. Erotic literature. French—History and criticism—Theory, etc.
2. Sade, marquis de, 1740–1814—Criticism and interpretation.
3. Body, Human, in literature. 4. Narration (Rhetoric) 5. Sex in literature. I. Title.
PQ145.1.E65C79 1994
840.9′3538—dc20 93-40937

⊚The paper in this book meets the minimum requirements of the American National Standard for Information Sciences—Permanence of Paper for Printed Library Materials, ANSI Z39.48-1984.

Contents

Preface

It is not possible in our time to write about classical literature as if it provided the only texts worthy of critical attention. Nor is it really possible to write about erotic literature and pornography while simply forgetting that these texts are the site of an elaborate and oppressive politics of the sexual. It may well be possible, however, to pay tribute to these ethical and political concerns only episodically or parenthetically, so that one is not everywhere constrained by them. That is a worry I sometimes have about the work that follows here. By paying attention to erotic literature, am I not being drawn into a form of hermeneutic complicity with it? The struggle with this worry, and the energetic rejection of sympathetic closeness, tend to work themselves out in these pages as an exercise in humor, not to say derision. Reading carefully while reading-to-reject both produces and requires what I have called "attentive irony."

The narrowly tactical question I often had cause to ask myself was, and continues to be: is it helpful, or proper, or correct, to spend years of one's life as a teacher and researcher working over these highly schematic and sometimes outrageously inhumane representations of gender, pleasure, and time? My implicit, rationalist answer to this question is, of course, that these things need to be read and understood—understood not just in some broadly diagnostic and denunciative sense, but in the detailed workings of their thematic economy.

We can seek to turn away from this tradition and make local efforts to silence or interrupt it. We can refuse, as I now do, to include Sade and his colleagues in undergraduate programs. But at some point, we can also hope to gain some exegetical power over these monsters of erotic authority. This can be done, I hope to show, by attending to the inner tensions in their work, listening for the muttered avowals of disquiet that can be heard beneath the voice of the master libertines.

The texts studied here are classical in every sense. They are not read through modernist eyes, as celebratory outbursts of libidinal spontaneity. The Sade evoked in this book is not the Divine Marquess of post-Romantic fame: he is the late eighteenth-century libertine, put in his place within a long tradition. The striking thing, as I hope to demonstrate, is that the classical erotica studied here have remarkably little to do with such standardly modern notions as "desire," "climax," or "the sex act." Classical texts generally rehearse, and thereby enact, the teaching and learning of erotic "attitudes" as a set of venereal positions. In this way, they display the bodily discipline at work in an erotic culture. Read carefully—that is, without too much careless anachronism—they may help to give us room for maneuver with respect to routinely modern notions of the erotic. If we can (re)-conceive of eroticism without being overwhelmed by the thematics of desire in its radically subjective forms, then we may be better placed to understand the discursive authority at work in transmitting received notions of refined pleasure. That is, I submit, how a thematics of corporeal discipline can inform a critique of historically contingent regimens of the erotic. That is how a careful study of classical bodily geometry can lead to a clearer understanding of politics in the boudoir.

Earlier versions of portions of this book have been previously published. Parts of Chapter 1 appeared as "Erotic Literature: A First Essay in Improper Thematics," *French Forum* 13 (1988), 83–96. Chapter 5 was published as "Passing the Time in Erotic Narrative: Fictions of Power and Negotiation in Crébillon, Nerciat, and Sade," *Romanic Review* 70, no. 3 (1989), 371–90. Chapter 6 appeared under its present title in *SubStance* 64, no. 1 (1991), 91–113, copyright © 1991 by the University of Wisconsin, and is used here by permission of the University of Wisconsin Press.

My thanks are due to James Arnold, Ross Chambers, Anne Freadman, Meaghan Morris, and Ian Reid, who, at various times, read and commented on portions of the manuscript. A number of students, notably Jeannette Granfar, Yasmin Gunn, Amanda Macdonald, Natalie MacDonald, and Sandra Nicholls, made contributions to discussions that I found helpful. Lyn Wetzig did a very professional job of typing and retyping a demanding manuscript.

PETER CRYLE

Brisbane, Queensland

I

TRADITION

Chapter 1

Erotic Literature as a Field of Study: Canonical Thematics

It has long been the practice of critics addressing "erotic literature" to display their acumen by marking off literary erotica from vulgar pornography. Their first move is often to denounce the "slovenliness" (Storm Jameson)[1] of those who fail to make the distinction. We must try to overcome the habit of confusing the two, says Susan Griffin: "We have long been used to calling pornographic art 'erotic.' Yet in order to see our lives more clearly within this culture, we must question the meaning we give to certain words and phrases."[2] All around us, says Audre Lorde, "there are frequent attempts to equate pornography and eroticism, two diametrically opposed uses of the sexual."[3] To resist the habit of "confusion" is, among other things, to maintain certain literary values. Even as Steven Marcus condemns out of hand the vast bulk of shapeless "pornotopic" writing of the Victorian period, he does so in the name of a certain idea of literary form that allows one to redeem a handful of texts.[4] What makes the difference here, says Bradley Smith, is "sensitivity and talent."[5] Erotic writing in general may be "suggestive" by definition, but it must be tactfully, elegantly so in order to count as true literature. P. B. Gobin writes: "It is not what is said, but what is done, and sometimes even what is suggested that appear to characterize true erotic literature. And the suggesting draws one in."[6] [a] As J.-M. Lo Duca notes, "Eroticism holds sway when

[a] Ce n'est pas le dire, mais le faire, et parfois même le laisser-entendre qui semblent caractériser la véritable littérature érotique. Et ce laisser-entendre engage.

it takes the form of suggestion, allusion, and anticipation, sometimes even of an obsessive kind. As soon as sex turns up—and pornography makes its appearance for no reason—eroticism comes to an end."[7] [b] Erotic art depends on "secondary meanings," says one critic (Milan Chlumsky), while pornography harbors the illusion of uncluttered reference, of denotation.[8]

Yet such refusal by critics of the common habit is so widespread as to be itself a habit. Indeed, suggests Joan Hoff, the claim to make a clear distinction functions as social convenience, rather than as a genuinely analytical move:

> Beginning in the 1920s and 1930s, U.S. intellectuals began to make highly subjective distinctions between erotica and pornography that had no historical or etymological rationale. They automatically assigned a reputable (and primarily heterosexual) past to the former, but not to the latter. Although this attempt to distinguish between the two is at most an arbitrary and artificial product of three generations of writers, literary and theater critics, and journalists, it has so captured the imagination of the liberal establishment that its relatively recent arbitrary and self-interested origins have been obscured.[9]

Hoff is pointing here to the social position of intellectuals and to the power they gain by their distinction making, by their public exercises in subtlety.[10] The telling point she makes is essentially the one made, in recent years, against the eternal solidity of the literary canon. Aesthetic value is no longer to be understood as an immanent quality, but as a product of institutional politics. The "literary," in this view, is set in place by historically contingent acts of legislative inclusion and exclusion, its arbitrary choices being masked by the pomp of didactic arbitration.[11]

The self-conscious countermove against critics who insist on distinguishing between erotica and pornography is, of course, to insist that all fiction about sex be considered in the same terms. "Eroticism," says Angela Carter with telling simplicity, is "the pornography of the elite."[12] No privileged status is to be accorded to "elite" pornography: it is lumped in with its insignificant Other, the oft-reviled vulgar pornography, and the two are subject to the same critique, the same ethical and political strictures. Andrea Dworkin, in writing against pornography, is writing against erotic literature: "Intellectuals, especially, call what they themselves produce or like 'erotica,' which means

[b] L'érotisme règne quand il peut être suggestion, allusion, attente jusqu'à l'obsession. Dès que le sexe paraît—et la pornographie se manifeste sans raison—l'érotisme cesse.

simply that a very bright person made or likes whatever it is. [. . .] In the male system, erotica is a subcategory of pornography."[13] For Dworkin, to put it in the grammar of those French political slogans of May 1968, "Pornography, and eroticism: the same enemy!"

Between the two positions I have outlined—and blurring my own attempt to make a neat distinction opposing aesthetes and sociologists—there have been attempts to redraw the erotica/pornography divide by giving it new significance, attaching to it ethical rather than aesthetic value. A much-quoted comment by Gloria Steinem is characteristic of such terminological reformism: "Perhaps we could simply say that erotica is about sexuality, but pornography is about power and sex-as-weapon—in the same way we have come to understand that rape is about violence, and not really about sexuality at all."[14] A comparable, and even more explicit position is adopted by Diana Russell: "*Erotica* differs from pornography *by virtue of its not degrading or demeaning women, men, or children.*"[15]

My own position within the terrain I have just mapped out is not, I trust, unduly subtle or mobile. I can say from the outset that I do not intend to patrol the boundary between art and vulgarity. I shall, however, begin by talking largely about erotic literature, moving only subsequently to use "erotic literature" and "pornography" as approximately interchangeable terms. My reason for doing this has nothing to do with finding a gentle reformist tempo or espousing the rhetoric of insidiousness. I wish rather to consider more slowly and more fully the questions of canon formation raised in polemical fashion by Hoff, Dworkin, and others. The notion of canon formation is, after all, somewhat ambiguous—perhaps helpfully so. One can insist, as Hoff does in the passage cited above, on the highly contingent nature of judgments about what constitutes literature. It might well have been otherwise, suggests Dworkin, but for the dominance of some "very bright people." There is great political and rhetorical purchase to be had by insisting in this way on the relative newness of the canon and by pointing to the circumstances in which it has taken shape. In the mid-eighteenth century, as Joan De Jean shows, there were relatively unprecedented, but durably influential moves to exclude books by women writers from the canon on moral grounds.[16] Yet to speak of the "selection" of particular works, as Robert von Hallberg does,[17] or even to describe canon formation as a finite event may be misleading if it causes us to forget how the canon mediates, in an ongoing way, between past and present. Bound in dialectically with the "newness" of the canon is its powerful "oldness." By this I mean the way in which it tends to hold its "formation," confirming and consolidating its own shape, providing instructions for its proper use. Hoff talks of intellectuals "assigning a past" without any genuine historical support for their claims, but the role of literature at its most canonical is to provide this kind of support as internal evidence, progressively rewriting its own history, shoring up its claims to authority, and reinforcing its air of legitimacy by the play of intertextual reference. Canonicity is not produced just by repeated declarations on the part of overbearing critics, but by thematic and generic emulation of a textual sort.[18]

To study the canon *as such* is not necessarily to glorify it, or even to indulge it unduly. True, the politics of my writing can hardly be aligned with those of Dworkin, in that I am neither dismissing nor denouncing this set of texts. Yet in attempting to understand how "erotic literature" functions as a canonical tradition, I am also seeking to display its assumptions and to put pressure on its structural weak points, thus making it available to ethical and political attack. Setting out the regularities of erotic literature can amount to setting it up as a target, for those who wish to make it one. My practice of criticism could thus be called deconstructive, if that term were not so often the mark of self-conscious aestheticism. What I want to do is disturb the high seriousness of erotic literature by pointing up its very thematic insistence: its extraordinary stylizations of gender, of pleasure, and of time. My former teacher Georges Poulet might have seen this book, by contrast with his own writings, as an unsympathetic study in inhuman time. I shall take erotic literature seriously in order to expose its equivocations, to discern its muttered avowals of impotence. In that sense, the politics of my writing are those of an attentive irony.

If one seeks a theory of the work(ing) of tradition, it can be found in the writings of Hans-Georg Gadamer. Gadamer tries to account for the function of authority in the transmission/tradition (*Überlieferung*) that positions those who understand.[19] Tradition institutes a dialogue with works that speak to us out of the past: our being in a particular historical and linguistic environment makes of us the askers of certain questions. As readers, we are lined up by tradition in such a way as to know from the outset what a text is already about. In fact, there is really no "outset": we are always already caught up in the play of historical consciousness. Without tradition, we could not read, we could not say "we." I have tried elsewhere to show that this conception of tradition is strikingly thematic. The dialogue with works of the past functions compellingly because we know what is being spoken about—not as the Saussurian referent, but as what Gadamer calls the *Sache,* the thing about which the text speaks to us. In this sense, the theme is what is preknown and reknown in the circularity of interpretation: we are able to identify and understand it more fully because the theme is what we know already. Such (pre)knowing is what constitutes us as the readers we are.[20] Now Gadamerian hermeneutics may appear uncongenial to many, not least because of its tendency to preempt radicalism or modernism of any sort. There seems to be no room in Gadamer for a theory of contestation, of the kind found, for example, in Foucault. But his philosophy is not for all that an apology for conservatism, as he himself has pointed out: conservatism is an attempt to deny change, a pointless refusal to espouse the movement of historical transmission, which goes on in any case. The "truth" to which we are called in Gadamer's work is an authority that takes hold of our understanding, and the requirement, the achievement, the endowment of tradition are that we know what a canonical text is about.

Such an understanding of thematic canon formation has particular relevance here, precisely because it often seems difficult to articulate clearly what "erotic literature" is indeed about. What we know, with Denis Hollier, is that it is characterized largely by its aboutness, and not by more narrowly formal generic qualities:

> I shall speak first about what is conventionally called "erotic literature." The term refers to a genre of writing that is not defined according to formal criteria (as is generally the case when one seeks to characterize a genre), but merely according to the subject dealt with. Whether it be, as it is most commonly, novels, short stories, poems, or—more infrequently—plays, erotic literature is taken to include any text that describes, crudely or otherwise, those aspects of amorous behavior that are not generally mentioned in standard literature.[21] [c]

Furthermore, despite Hollier's reference to what is normally left unsaid in other texts, we have already seen that explicitness will not do as a criterion, when implicitness is so often adjudged to be the literary quality par excellence. It is tempting to shrug one's shoulders and say that erotic literature (or pornography) is implicitly (or explicitly) writing about sex. That is effectively what I did in passing a little

[c] Je parlerai d'abord de ce qu'il est convenu d'appeler littérature érotique. Cette désignation recouvre un genre d'écrits qui ne se définissent pas à partir de critères formels (comme c'est généralement le cas lorsqu'on veut caractériser un genre), mais simplement à partir du sujet qu'ils traitent: qu'il s'agisse, comme c'est généralement le cas, de romans, de nouvelles, de poésies, ou—ce qui est plus rare—de pièces de théâtre, appartient à la littérature érotique tout texte qui décrit, en des termes plus ou moins crus, ce qui des rapports amoureux est généralement passé sous silence par la littérature reconnue.

earlier, when I used the expression "fiction about sex," and when I referred uncritically to other texts using the same kind of talk. But that does not constitute any sort of progress, or even an effective sidestep. It would be foolhardy to suppose that "sex" is a reliably identifiable theme, functioning in some transhistorical or transcultural way. A few critics, such as John Atkins, do indeed seem prepared to shrug their shoulders, adopting a disarmingly commonsensical approach to the problem, and affirming that "everyone by and large agrees" as to what "is erotic literature."[22] But my assumption here is that of Foucauldian semiotics or Gadamerian hermeneutics: the subject of understanding is not universal, and the sense is not reliably common. "Agreement" itself has to be understood as a historical phenomenon. Sex, or eros, or eroticism, cannot simply be taken to be the same at all times and in all places. "It" is something that many English speakers, for example, claim to recognize instantly with massive confidence, but that very capacity to recognize I take as a mark of culture. What counts as erotic is likely to be culturally and historically specific.

Specific in principle, I must add quickly, but perhaps not always specified enough in modern practice to have a proper canonical-thematic shape. That is reason enough for some critics to declare "erotic literature" an ill-found or improper field of study. The phenomenologist Erling Eng suggests that making eros an object of attention—that is, I suppose, taking it as a thing, or as a theme—is somehow a mistake. "Acquaintance with eros," he says a little paradoxically, "is somehow excluded by its actual identification as such."[23] Simone de Beauvoir says much the same thing about the notion of "erotic literature": "We hated the notion of eroticism—used to the full by Malraux in *La Condition humaine*—because it implies a kind of specialization that both glorifies and debases sex."[24] [d] It is as if the very talk of eroticism, and of erotic literature in particular, were inappropriately, misleadingly analytical. The erotic may be ubiquitous, and in some sense fundamental, but for that very reason, can it be helpfully delineated as a "special" theme?

From a point of view informed by psychoanalysis, the whole "subject" seems even more problematic. To identify "erotic literature," says Horst Robert Glaser in effect, is to cleave it off from a putatively nonerotic literature, thus denying the element of the erotic in all aesthetic experience.[25] Barthes's version of the same point is typically

[d] Nous détestions la notion d'érotisme—dont Malraux usait abondamment dans *La Condition humaine*—parce qu'elle implique une spécialisation qui à la fois exalte exagérément le sexe et l'avilit.

corrosive. He envisages, with mock seriousness, the possibility of writing a thesis about pleasure in reading, and speaks of gathering together all the texts "that have at some time *given pleasure to someone,*" thereby producing a "corpus" resembling "the human erotic body."[e] But that, he says, would only be an attempt to "explain" these texts. It could not succeed in defining "pleasure," but could only "circle around the subject."[26] What threatens to occur in such a case is presumably the reification of pleasure: analytical earnestness might seek to produce the erotic as object, but for this very reason could not know the fullness—or at least the workings—of pleasure. An appropriately Gadamerian answer to this point is that "pleasure," and the pleasure of the text in particular, cannot provide us with an identifiable theme,[27] but that some specific topos may count, or have once counted, within a tradition, as the shared understanding, the *locus communis* of canonical eroticism.

Now Foucault, in his *Histoire de la sexualité,* addresses the question of shifts in the discursive formation of "sexuality." His broadest historical point is that, "historically, there have been two great procedures for producing the truth of sex":[f] *ars erotica* and *scientia sexualis.*[28] What Foucault calls "procedures" here are patently not just themes as things-to-be-found: they are articulated uses and exigencies of knowledge. But that is very much what is required or expected, in Gadamerian terms, of a canonical thematics. Although Foucault uses the term *thématique* quite diffidently (see, e.g., 9–11, 16, 109, 112)—perhaps for fear of echoing standard literary criticism—it seems fair to say that *ars erotica* and *scientia sexualis* are two rather different thematics whose succession or functional equivalence makes up, for Foucault, the broader historical thematics of "sexuality." To what extent can the two in fact be called equivalent? Foucault speculates about the possibility that our modern *scientia sexualis* might be the refined Western version of *ars erotica* (96). About *ars erotica* itself, he has tantalizingly little to say if one is interested in traditions of erotic literature. He does suggest that its knowledge is transmitted typically through a strict procedure whereby the disciple follows step by step a "keeper of the secrets" (77). But all this—whatever it is exactly—is lost to modern Europeans, he says: "Our civilization, on first examination at least, has no *ars erotica*" (77).[g] There may have once been an *ars erotica* in the West, but it is now a "tradition that is apparently lost" (96).

[e] auxquels il est arrivé de *faire plaisir à quelqu'un*/le corps érotique de l'homme

[f] Il y a historiquement deux grandes procédures pour produire la vérité du sexe.

[g] Notre civilisation, en première approche du moins, n'a pas d'*ars erotica*.

Ars erotica, then, is an old, nay, archaic name for an apparently lost thematic tradition. Yet there is a hermeneutical point to this observation, not recognized by Foucault. It is that the oldness, the very lostness of the tradition can have a canonical function. We can ask: is *ars erotica* not *referred to* as lost within a literary tradition? Does it serve in any way as a kind of distant authority, or as a mark of legitimacy? Given that Foucault has so little to say about the "it" of *ars erotica,* such question asking can hardly be based on his work, but I want to hold on to the term *ars erotica* precisely because it is a classical name for a thematics of erotic literature. A tautological one, of course, but the approximate circularity of an inquiry that goes from "sex" to "*ars erotica*" may be productive if we can find textual support for an established thematics, albeit a half-missing one. The lost classical may be made present in canonical tradition as the classically lost.

I propose, then, to look for traces of a vestigial but enduring *ars erotica,* as a mark—perhaps *the* mark—of canonical erotic literature. Yet before I embark on this, a further cautionary note is required. I do not wish, as I have my gaze fixed firmly on my archaeological enterprise, to deny the contingent nature of my own investigation. Many of the texts I shall discuss in this book have only become generally available to the academic community (scholars and students) in the last twenty years or less. A series of commercial operations undertaken in France by such publishers as Pauvert, Lattès, and Fayard has effectively produced works with a rather new status. Before that, such texts had largely been the preserve of those whom the French refer to elegantly as *les curieux:* learned bibliophiles and bibliographers in the lineage of Henry Spenser Ashbee, Louis Perceau, and Pascal Pia.[29] While referred to as books of the *second rayon,* these texts were nevertheless—and are still—in their privileged, "reserved" place in the great libraries of Europe: in the Private Case, or in the *enfer.* By a nice irony, certain notorious texts, like *L'Académie des dames* or *Portier des Chartreux,* have remained difficult of access until the last two or three years, even though their content is undoubtedly less offensive to modern readers than what we have come to call hard-core pornography. Were these texts confined because of their (canonical) prestige, or because they did not present sufficient commercial interest? As I write, Sade's work is appearing in the Pléiade series, and it may well be that the publishers' market is in the process of answering my question. Certainly, at least two French publishers have undertaken to present the "great classics" of eroticism in inexpensive editions, one of them effectively defining the works of value to be found in the *enfer* of the Bibliothèque Nationale.[30] This is a commercial dimension of so-called sexual liberation: it is the solemn revelation/publication of some notorious old secrets.

Another contingent factor in my investigation is the choice of national literatures. I shall be concentrating largely on French texts, for that is the literature I know best, although I shall be considering with some care the manner in which French writing refers back to Renaissance Italian texts, and texts in classical Latin. French, by a vast cultural habit particularly prevalent among Anglo-Saxons, is the best-established language of eroticism. With charming regularity, it serves phatically to titillate the non-French reader—French is risqué, and risqué is French—while at the same time helping, where necessary, to attenuate the obscenity of sexual description. Italian performed much the same function in eighteenth-century French writing, for example in Diderot or Nerciat, and Latin has done so over a wide historical range, from at least Aretino in sixteenth-century Italy, to Klossowski in twentieth-century France.

We will come to French literature, then, for reasons that are both contingent, and conveniently transcendent, but we will come to it via a Latin expression: *ars erotica.* That *ars erotica,* the (possible) name of our (apparently lost) theme, should be a Latin term is, as the linguists might say, thoroughly overdetermined. Latin is much more than a lexical convenience for avoiding obscenity. It is, in European writing since the Renaissance, the language of scholarly initiates; it marks so often a higher plane of learning to which one accedes on leaving the vernacular. In an important sense, when used this way, it can never be really obscene, or "vulgar." And in keeping with this function, but as an enhancement of it, Latin is the language whose every manifestation presents itself as rhetorical. To write in Latin is to be caught up in the world of learned disquisition, to be shaped by its traditional exigencies. Furthermore, for reasons intimately bound up with the above, the very use of Latin invokes an ancient culture in which art or knowledge, *ars* or *scientia* can be located as entities now half-lost. Latin refers us—classically—to a place and time invested with great cultural authority.

In the anonymous *Le Roman de Violette* (1883), the young Violette is undergoing erotic instruction at the hands of a benevolent and more or less serene narrator-hero. One of her learning experiences, in a straightforward *mise en abyme* that helps to identify and even define erotic literature, is to read Gautier's *Mademoiselle de Maupin* (1835). In Gautier's text, as all readers of true canonical worth will always already know, a moment of great erotic potential, an encounter between two women, is the subject of a teasingly imperfect narrative ellipsis. How are we to determine, in association with or instead of the fictional reader Violette, what transpired between the two? Not, as in Zola or Mirbeau, by checking the sheets or asking the maid: Gautier's narrator-hero tried that, and failed. Not even by letting our imagination run wild, whatever that might mean. If we are indeed worthy interlocutors for Gautier and for the narrator of *Le Roman de Violette,* we shall complete the ellipsis by referring to our classical knowledge, for the scene is "one of those ambiguous scenes that could only be explained through a perfect knowledge of ancient civilization."[31] [h] Armed with the perfect knowledge of classical (erotic) antiquity, we can read the implicit and the suggestive without crassness. But where exactly is that knowledge set out, and what constitutes its perfection?

There is at least one remarkably sustained and systematic attempt on the part of a classical scholar to answer these questions: Friedrich Carl Forberg's *De Figuris Veneris* (1824), now itself an eminent "erotic text." Forberg's work was translated into French in 1882 with the title *Manuel d'érotologie classique,*[32] the extraordinarily free translation of the title being justified in the following terms: "While reprinting this excellent study, which is thoroughly deserving of translation, we have given it a title that is much better suited" (I, xi).[i] "Erotologie" is presumably "better" because it is a more modern title: Foucault might have observed that it is closer to *scientia sexualis* than to *ars erotica.* There is, in any case, a marked ambivalence on the part of the disseminators of this text. *De Figuris Veneris* is valuable and prestigious because of its erudite and richly detailed account of the classical "figures of Venus," but it is perceived nonetheless to be in need of updating—despite its relatively recent production—in order to take its place in late nineteenth-century France. Between the recognition of a classical authority and the perceived need to adjust to modernity, we find the space of transmitted understanding. Such acceptance-and-rejection of the classical is exemplary of what Gadamer means by tradition.

Forberg's work sets about describing a set of figures (or erotic positions) in what the author himself seems to see as, at best, a broad taxonomic effort, for he concedes from the beginning that his classification cannot render the full range of human erotic possibilities. I quote in Alcide Bonneau's translation of the Latin: "We wish to review

[h] une de ces scènes ambiguës dont la parfaite connaissance de la civilisation antique pouvait seule donner l'explication

[i] En réimprimant cet excellent travail, qui méritait assurément d'être traduit, nous lui avons donné un titre qui lui convient beaucoup mieux.

the various metamorphoses of Venus. Not all of them, in truth: how could one hope to enumerate the thousand inventions, the thousand postures to which the ingenious satiety of pleasure dares to turn? But at least the ones that can be associated with specific kinds [he lists five], and lend themselves readily to methodical classification" (I, 3–5).[j] There is a sort of arithmetical tension here between the number one thousand, which is merely the routine rhetorical version of "infinity," and the numbered list of ninety figures that concludes Forberg's work and summarizes its classificatory achievement (II, 183–95). On the one hand, we must recognize that the nature of pleasure and human ingenuity makes an exhaustive inventory impossible. On the other hand, we are being shown that, once the categories are in place, a functionally complete list of positions can be drawn up.

Forberg's quotations of relevant classical texts include a reference in Suidas to ancient lists of figures: "Astyanassa, the servant of Helen, wife of Menelaus, the first one who imagined various ways of making love; she produced a treatise on erotic figures and poses. After her, and in her likeness, came Philaenis and Elephantina, who were reputed for impurities of that sort" (I, 7 n. 2).[k] This is an account of lost origins. It is also, I am going to argue, the closest thing we can know to an ancient *ars erotica.* It is the classical trace, not just of a theme, but of a kind of articulated thematics: the setting out of a range of erotic possibilities. When Forberg puts together his list of figures, he effectively retrieves (or mimics) a classical kind of knowing. His list making continues, in a half-apologetic way, the tradition of Astyanassa, Philaenis, and Elephantina or Elephantis.

Nicolas Chorier, in his *Satyre sotadique de Luisa Sigea* (1655) picked up the trace with some rather different detail attached to it. *La Satyre sotadique,* it should be noted, is the most notorious and covertly influential of seventeenth-century French erotic texts. Originally written in Latin, it was called variously, in translation, *L'Académie des dames, Les Dialogues de Luisa Sigea,* or *Le Meursius français.* Here is what Chorier has to say about ancient representations of the figures of Venus. They appear to be both descriptive and technical: "Elephantis, a Greek girl,

[j] Nous voulons passer en revue les diverses métamorphoses de Vénus, non pas toutes, à la vérité; comment serait-il possible d'énumérer les mille inventions, les mille postures auxquelles ose avoir recours l'ingénieuse satiété du plaisir? mais tout au moins celles qui, se rattachant à des genres déterminés [he lists five kinds], se prêtent facilement à la classification méthodique.

[k] Astyanassa, servante d'Hélène, femme de Ménélas, la première qui imagina diverses manières de faire l'amour; elle a composé un traité des figures et poses érotiques. Après elle et à son imitation vinrent Philaenis et Eléphantine, que des impuretés de ce genre ont fait connaître.

had outlined on painted wooden panels those [the positions] that she knew to be practiced by libertines, 'so that people could take pleasure in doing things according to the paintings.' Another woman put together twelve ways, likely to give pleasure to the contestant in coitus; it is called, accordingly, *Dodecamincanos*."[33] [l] Seen thus, erotic art is essentially a set of tableaux, setting out a range—or is it *the* range?—of venereal positions in such a way as to allow them to be studied and taught.

In the distant past, the half-lost story seems to go, there were women, apparently of rather inferior status: servants, young people, perhaps courtesans. They set out all that they knew, and conceivably all that there was to know, so that it could be understood and followed by others. And what might it mean, exactly, to "follow" Elephantis? Suetonius, in his *Life of Tiberius*, shows us how this knowledge was applied. In translating this, I have followed a French translation that seems less influenced by modern psychologism than Robert Graves's English version: "He adorned the different rooms with images and statuettes producing the most lascivious paintings and sculptures, together with the books of Elephantis, so that each accessory participant would always be able to find the model for positions he ordered them to adopt."[34] [m] The practice of this art as knowledge was, it seems, an imitative discipline. Here is another, quite different classical Latin text, following a French version by Bonneau:

> The tableaux taken from the obscene books
> Of Elephantis, to you, rigid God,
> Are dedicated by Lalagé, who asks you to determine
> Whether she is properly applying the painted figures.[35] [n]

Not only a (young) woman teacher, note, but a female pupil, practicing her skills under the aegis of a priapic god. What is more, the nature

[l] Eléphantis, jeune fille Grecque, avait tracé sur des panneaux de bois peints celles [les postures] qu'elle savait être pratiquées par les libertins, "pour qu'on s'amusât à besogner d'après les peintures." Une autre composa douze manières, propres à procurer le plus de plaisir au jouteur, dans le coït; on l'appelle pour cette raison *Dodecamincanos*.

[m] Il orna les chambres placées en différents endroits d'images et de statuettes reproduisant les tableaux et les sculptures les plus lascives, auxquels il joignit les livres d'Eléphantis, pour que chaque figurant trouvât toujours le modèle des postures qu'il ordonnait de prendre.

[n]
> Les tableaux tirés des livres obscènes
> D'Eléphantis, à toi, Dieu rigide,
> Les dédie Lalagé, et te demande d'éprouver
> Si elle pratique bien d'après les figures peintes.

and number of those skills appear quite finite. The set of postures is likely to be numerically precise—Chorier refers to the *dodecamincanos,* or *dodecamechanos*—as is the space of effort available to the learner. In fact Forberg, quoting Suidas again, suggests that *dodecatechnon* is the proper expression, used to refer to "a work that treats (the) obscene postures, twelve by number" (I, 11 n. 5).[o] *Dodecamechanos,* Forberg suggests, was the Greek term applied to a particular libertine woman because of her ability to practice all the positions (I, 11). The space of this applied erotic art appears, in any case, to have been bounded by the *technon* and the *mechanos.* It is hard to find room for the human ingenuity mentioned by Forberg in his introduction. And it is hard to see what inventive principle could generate positions by the thousand. Might Forberg's apology not have been part of his own acceptance-and-rejection of the tradition of *ars erotica*?

Brantôme, a contemporary of Chorier, gives in *Les Dames galantes* (1666) his own version of the trace of *ars erotica:*

> One reads of a great courtesan and procuress of ancient Rome, whose name was Elefantina, and who produced such figures of Aretino, even worse ones, which were studied as a very fine book by great ladies and princesses devoted to whoredom. And that good lady whore of Cyrenia, who was given the name "she of the twelve inventions" because she had found twelve ways to make pleasure more delightful and voluptuous![36] [p]

Once again, we find some interesting variations of detail, together with an Italianized version of the now familiar name of Elephantis, and the reference to the twelve *manières.* There is an Italian proper name added to the (Italianized) Latin one, that of Aretino. "Added to" is hardly the right expression for it, in fact, since there seems to be a perfect assimilation of Aretino's kind of art to that of Elephantis. Each is responsible for a set of erotic figures. Both, according to my hypothesis, are thus included within the tradition of *ars erotica.* Yet if we look closely at Brantôme's text, we see that Aretino's name is used generically to describe the kind of figures produced by Elephantis. Aretino is not just an author, but the name of the set of erotic figures,

[o] [un] ouvrage qui traite des postures obscènes au nombre de douze

[p] Il se lit d'une grande courtisane et maquerelle du temps de l'ancienne Rome, qui s'appelait Elefantina, qui fit et composa de telles figures de l'Aretin, encore pires, auxquelles les dames grandes et princesses faisant état de putainisme étudiaient comme un très beau livre. Et cette bonne dame putain cyrénienne, laquelle était surnommée aux douze inventions parce qu'elle avait trouvé douze manières pour rendre le plaisir plus voluptueux et lubrique!

as a genre. Presumably Astyanassa and Philaenis would also be said by Brantôme, if he had found their trace, to have produced "figures of Aretino." How can we account for this apparent looseness, this unthinking anachronism, if not by saying that Aretino's name has come to stand, in Brantôme at least, as a more recent version of what I am calling *ars erotica*?

It is around the time of Aretino that some historians locate the "emergence" of modern erotic literature (or pornography). David Foxon, in his detailed and helpful study of libertine literature in England, writes: "The story for our purposes begins with Aretino."[37] His purposes are not mine, however, and the story he tells is not the kind I wish to write here. A concern with the canon has led me to espouse first of all a movement backward, rather than a progression toward the present. We can never arrive at the beginning, I would claim with Foucault and Gadamer, but we can note what is said to have gone before. We cannot claim to apprehend the new as it "emerges," but we can understand the play of antecedence, and observe change, despite Poulet and Bachelard, as a property of elapsed time. Those who do talk of emergence, however, seem close to agreeing on the timing of the event they narrate. Morse Peckham writes: "About a third of the way through the sixteenth century pornography as we know it emerged in the form of the *Ragionamenti* and the *Sonnetti lussuriosi* of Aretino and of Giulio Romano's *Posizioni*, engravings of sexual positions with stimulated genitals fully displayed in genital activity and behavior preparatory to it."[38] What makes Aretino count as having "emerged" so decisively, I want to suggest, is the legitimacy given to his work by the half-lost tradition of *ars erotica*.

Aretino's production as an author of erotic literature can seem out of keeping with his reputation. It amounts to two texts, the first of these being the *Sonnetti lussuriosi* (1524), written to accompany a set of engravings by Giulio Romano entitled *I sedici modi.*[39] The second is the *Ragionamenti (Dialogues)* (1534–39), which belong to a somewhat different, though closely related subgenre of erotic literature, to which I shall turn in the next chapter: the intimate dialogue between two women. The sonnets are associated, as one can see immediately, with the usual numbered set of figures (in this case, sixteen). While the number may not be constant, the fact of numbering does seem to be. The *Ragionamenti,* too, are (mis)remembered as describing a set of positions. For Chorier, Aretino deserves the epithet "divine"—an epithet that was already his, in any case, doubtless for quite other reasons[40]—because he has so enhanced the genre begun by Elephantis and her colleagues: "In our time, a man of divine genius, Pietro

Aretino, has represented a great number [of positions] in a lively manner, in his Satirical Dialogues; after him, Titian and Carrachio, those masterly artists, have reproduced some in paintings" (III, 190).[q]

Are Aretino's texts worthy, indeed, of this great reputation? Richard Lewinsohn, having examined the sonnets critically, can do no more than express his dismay: "The sonnets contain not a trace either of the wit of the Pompeian *Positiones* or of the poetry of the Kâmasûtra or the late Indian *Anangaranga.* Aretino gives, so to speak, a dynamic explanation of each drawing. He describes the whole course of the *modo* in question, but apart from a few mythological allusions each poem is merely a coarse enumeration of the most vulgar expressions for the genitals and the sexual act."[41] But this disappointment at the vulgarity of the poems—at their lack of distinction—is answered by the defenders of the "true" person of Aretino. Louis Perceau, in his introduction to Nogaret's *L'Arétin français,* expresses irritation that Aretino's name should have been so widely misused, and in particular that he should have been spoken of as the author of a set of figures.[42] The anonymous presenter of a French translation of the *Ragionamenti* (probably Bonneau) makes the same point with even more vigor:

> Read all the historians or chroniclers, from Brantôme to Michelet; read all the bibliographers, all our critics of art and literature, from Bayle, La Monnoye, and Félibien to Libri and Brunet [. . .]; read all the Italians [. . .], everywhere you will find that Aretino owes most of his bad reputation to these two works [the set of engravings and *La Puttana errante,* neither of which is by him]. If a circumlocution is needed to refer to him, he is indiscriminately called the man of the positions or the author of *La Puttana errante.*[43] [r]

My diagnosis of the opinions of Lewinsohn, on the one hand, and Perceau and Bonneau on the other, is that they display a symmetrical failure to comprehend the semiotics of canonical tradition. The first deplores the fact that the work is unworthy of its reputation, while

[q] De nos jours, un homme d'un génie divin, Pietro Aretino, en a figuré un grand nombre [de postures] avec sel, dans ses Dialogues satyriques; après lui, le Tiziano et le Carrachio, artistes souverains, en ont reproduit dans la peinture.

[r] Lisez tous nos historiens ou chroniqueurs, de Brantôme à Michelet; lisez tous nos bibliographes, tous nos critiques littéraires et artistiques, de Bayle, La Monnoye et Félibien à Libri et à Brunet [. . .]; lisez tous les Italiens [. . .], partout vous trouverez que l'Arétin doit le plus clair de sa mauvaise renommée à ces deux ouvrages [les gravures et *La Puttana errante,* ni les unes ni l'autre nétant de lui]: si l'on a besoin d'une périphrase pour le désigner, on l'appelle indifféremment l'homme aux postures ou l'auteur de la *Puttana errante.*

the second and third are indignant that the reputation should be in any way disjunct from textual scholarship. What none of them recognizes is that the "content" of Aretino's work is not made available in a way that allows us to take that old metaphor of containment seriously. What Aretino's work is "about" is determined and regularly confirmed by the way in which his name is referred to and deferred to. Its theme can be understood, more or less, as the function of the work: how it counts, or what it is equivalent to. For Brantôme and Chorier, the name is equivalent to that of Elephantis. And that same "deplorable" periphrasis whereby Aretino is called "l'homme des postures" is merely the inverse of a thematically powerful reduction of *ars erotica* to the name "Aretino." His reputation is, in that sense, fully canonical, and can function as part of a remarkable thematic economy, authorizing and compelling the traditional interpretation of his works. There may be some error of judgment here, in Lewinsohn's terms. There are certainly errors of scholarly attribution involving *La Puttana errante* and the *Dialogua tra Maddalena e Giulia,*[44] but the durability of such error, as a historical and hermeneutical phenomenon, must be considered in approximately the same terms as its notional opposite. As Gadamer might say, misunderstanding is a form of understanding.

The name "Aretino" becomes, as I have suggested, something other than the name of an author: it is the name of an erotic genre, the name of a thematics. Thus, Brantôme speaks of "un Aretin en figure" (26), meaning not a statuette of the author, but a concrete representation of one or more sexual positions. When, in the late eighteenth century, an anonymous text was published seeking to "draw up the inventory of women of pleasure in the capital,"[s] it was entitled *Chronique Arétine, ou Recherches pour servir à l'histoire des mœurs au XVIII*[e] *siècle.*[45] The text is recognizably "Aretine" because it presents an erotic inventory. In the narrower acceptance of the term, an Aretino, or Aretine art, should contain visual representations of the range of positions. Perceau, in his modern introduction to Nogaret's *L'Arétin français* of 1787, gives some idea of the strength and breadth of the tradition in Italy and France:

> Other engravers followed in the steps of Marcantonio [Raimondi]: Rosso, Caraglio, and Perino del Vaga circulated a set of *Metamorphoses of the Gods;* Giulio Bonasono made fourteen etchings of the *Lovemaking of the Gods;* and Annibale Carrachio, toward the end of the sixteenth century, drew a new set of sixteen positions.

[s] dresser l'inventaire des amoureuses de la capitale

In the following century, Petre de Jode engraved twenty plates that were sold as "postures of Aretino." These are the ones that Coiny engraved again in 1798 under the title *The Aretino of Augustin Carrache,* and that were called, in a new edition, *The Lovemaking of the Pagan Gods.*[46] [t]

In this list of works, the name Aretino is roughly equivalent to that of a pagan god. Both have the same classical, legitimizing function.

Yet even as Perceau provides documentary evidence of the historic importance of Aretine erotica, he does so in terms that appear hermeneutically insensitive, not to say brashly anachronistic: "The title *The French Aretino* is reminiscent of the trend that, for more than three centuries, had favored collections of amorous positions, which were wrongly attributed to Aretino" (7).[u] Can a "trend" (*vogue*) last three hundred years? To speak that way is surely a grudgingly post-Romantic view of the classical, a submodernist trivialization of tradition.[47]

By a coincidence that is somehow both frustrating for scholars and an aesthetically pleasing *retouche* of history, the engravings accompanying the *Sonnetti lussuriosi* had themselves become lost by the late eighteenth century.[48] They—that is, "Aretino"—still stood as the model, but only in principle. Their "imitation" by other artists was itself an imitation, and their modeling a generic practice—just as it must have been classically with Astyanassa, Philaenis, and Elephantis. None of this "lostness," in fact, amounted to an explicit break with the past. The rhetoric was so often that of continuity, fidelity, and respect for the "divine" example. In literary contexts, the Aretine models were often *invoked* as an example, rather than actually displayed. Thus the first edition (dated 1642) of Pallavicino's *Retorica delle puttane* has no engravings printed with it, but the Aretine figures, presumably not lost yet, although not graphically present either, are nonetheless taken as a point of reference. An old woman, instructing a young one in the art of being a successful whore, teaches her pupil to apply this art in the shaping of her own body: "The figures of

[t] D'autres graveurs suivirent les traces de Marc-Antoine [Raimondi]: le Rosso, le Caraglio et Perino del Vaga mirent en circulation une suite de *Métamorphoses des Dieux;* Giulio Bonasono grava quatorze estampes des *Amours des Dieux;* enfin Annibal Carrache, vers la fin du XVIe siècle, dessina une nouvelle suite de seize postures.

Au siècle suivant, Petre de Jode grava vingt planches qu'on vendit comme postures de l'Arétin. Ce sont celles qu'en 1798 Coiny devait graver de nouveau sous le titre *L'Arétin d'Augustin Carrache,* et qu'on intitula, dans une nouvelle édition, *Les Amours des Dieux Païens.*

[u] Le titre de *L'Arétin français* rappelle la vogue dont jouissaient, depuis plus de trois siècles, les recueils de postures amoureuses que l'on attribuaient improprement à l'Arétin.

Aretino referred to above are exemplary, and when someone has a whim for extravagant behavior, take them as a model."[49] [v] The examples are there to be imitated, and they continue to be made present by the ongoing practice of postural modeling as erotic learning. Later, when the originals are lost, this procedure will continue of itself. For where imitation as performance is the primary value, such Romantic themes as originality and authenticity are unlikely to be a major concern.

In the evaluation and propagation of Aretine art, there seems to be no effective distinction between quantity and quality. Whether the range of bodily positions corresponds to the fullest extent of human possibilities is not really the point: they represent a *theatro bastevole,* says the old woman in *La Retorica delle puttane,* a practically "adequate" range of what will be required in a lifetime of erotic performance. They provide, in effect, the formal thematic definition of variety, the full postural specification of a predictable erotic diversity:

> The figures of Aretino gathered together in one frame will be a sufficiently large theater, and desires will find there all the scope they need to draw a full bounty of pleasure. Moving over these images, one will be able to play a toccata on the organ of the senses, and varying the tone accordingly will cause the variety of images to produce most harmonious music. In the pleasure that is always the same, you will have the only possible diversity, the sole spice of earthly delights. (E2)[w]

The following extract from a seventeenth-century French poem, by Pierre Motin, is less elaborate, but it shows an easy familiarity with the same theme:

> It is all for some robust lover,
> With strong back and august prick,
> Whose fortune is to fuck well
> That their lustful suppleness
> Takes pleasure in practicing
> The positions of Aretino.[50] [x]

[v] Le figure sopra accennate dell' Aretino sono l'esemplare, e quando tal'uno s'incapricciarà di stravaganze imitisi il modelo.

[w] Le figure dell' Aretino in unico quadro raccolte saranno theatro bastevole, e havranno ivi largo campole le cupiditadi per fondare copiose le rendite dei piaceri. Scorrendosi questi imagini, si farà une toccata sù l'organo dei sensi, e variansi i registri conforme la varietà di quelle si farà un suono molto armonioso, et nel diletto ch'è sempre lo stesso, havrassi la diversità unico, e solo condimento delle dolcezze terrene.

[x] C'est pour quelque ami robuste,
Aux reins forts, au vit auguste,

The performance referred to here is summarized in general (and generic) terms. It is to be carried out at some time by "quelque ami," some lover or other, using a set of figures that is culturally available, although not literally to hand. Its performers are required to know the paradigm already, to be able to imitate its particular elements, and to have the capacity to play over its range. The role of erotic art is therefore not only to enumerate the erotic, but to represent and thus determine its own full and proper use.

As Elephantis gave way to Aretino, the range of figures and the art of imitating them were not lost. Yet something else does appear to have disappeared: the notion that women were at the origin of *ars erotica*. What happened, then, to female authorship? The quick, polemical answer is: exactly what happened to it everywhere else. Where women produced erotic art and instructed other women in it, there must have been a feminine initiatory tradition. The secrets taught, while eventually disseminated by emperors, might nonetheless have appeared disturbingly independent of patriarchal authority, functioning effectively as a kind of didactic lesbianism, binding teachers and pupils in an erotic chain. Indeed, if one attends to the classical resonance of "lesbian," one cannot fail to think of Sappho and her legendary *gynaikeion*. Was that perhaps a (lost) place of instruction, a theater for the disciplined performance of *ars erotica*? The written traces of the tradition would suggest not, in fact. Sappho's name is not taken as equivalent to that of Elephantis or Aretino, nor is it associated with a set of positions. Thus, if one seeks the trace of what Diane Crowder calls "a tradition of autonomous female culture preserved by outlawed lesbians,"[51] then *ars erotica* cannot be the answer, or even the proper form of the question. Far from being "outlawed," Elephantis and her line of pupils have long signified the ritual integration of lesbianism into a dominant erotic culture. Women are here represented, so to speak, in series—as the teachers and learners of a certain erotic order. Elaine Marks, in her discussion of the Sappho model, sees at least this particular aspect of Sapphic lesbianism as thoroughly integrated into a patriarchal code, in the theme of "the gynaeceum, ruled by the seductive or seducing teacher."[52] In some later fictional texts concerned with female homosexuality, there seems to be a lingering notion that ritual initiation is attached to the practice of lesbianism. *La Secte des anandrynes* (1789), by Pidansat de Mairobert, is a case in point,[53]

Dont bien foutre est le destin,
Que leur souplesse lubrique
Se plaît à mettre en pratique
Les postures d'Arétin.

and so is Renée Vivien's *Une Femme m'apparut* (1905).[54] But the general function of *ars erotica* as tradition is surely to keep feminine erotic pedagogy in its (privileged but narrow) place, preventing it from becoming autonomous, or even unduly mysterious, by subjecting it to an imitative erotic discipline.

In the Aretine phase of the tradition, the practitioners of erotic art continue to be preeminently women. In Chorier's text, their authorial role is still able to be retrieved and defended by the fictive attribution of the *Satyre sotadique* to the famous classical scholar Luisa Sigea. Are there readers, asks the (male) editor/presenter, who doubt the authority of women to teach this subject? The doubters are answered, and any general wavering of confidence dealt with, by a firm reminder of Luisa Sigea's classical antecedents: "But it should be no surprise that a woman might have set about discussing matters like these. Elephantis, who was a girl, and some others as well, became famous for producing works of the same kind" (I,1xxxii).[y] In other seventeenth-century texts of this sort, women may have lost authorial status, but they are still represented as teachers and learners. This is what gives rise to the subgenre referred to by Lo Duca as "the eternal conversation between the expert woman and the *novia*"[55] [z]—although it is not, of course, eternal, merely traditional. The conversation—or rather, the ordered, usually numbered series of dialogues—can take place between a mother and a daughter, as in the *Ragionamenti,* between a young woman and an old, experienced one, as in *La Retorica delle puttane,* or between two young women separated by an age difference of only a few years: *L'Académie des dames, L'Escole des filles* (1660), or *Vénus dans le cloître* (1682). Of these, *La Retorica delle puttane* is the most stiffly didactic. It is in fact a series of lectures, delivered in order and without interruption, across the space that separates age from youth. The other texts, however, follow more closely the example of the *Ragionamenti* in representing teaching as conversation. Intimacy between mother and daughter is strongly marked in Aretino's text, and the two women retire to bed together at the end of a day's exchanges. *L'Académie des dames, L'Escole des filles,* and *Vénus dans le cloître* all develop the intimacy of the teaching relationship, so that the manner of teaching becomes itself explicitly erotic. In *L'Académie des dames,* Tullia and Ottavia do most of their conversing in bed: "Tonight, so that I can endoctrinate you about everything while speaking more freely, we

[y] Mais on ne doit pas s'étonner qu'une femme se soit appliquée à traiter de semblables matières. Eléphantis, une jeune fille, et quelques autres encore, se rendirent célèbres par des compositions du même genre.

[z] l'éternelle conversation entre la femme experte et la *novia*

will lie together in my bed, about which I should like to say afterward that it was the sweetest jousting-place of Venus" (I, 24).[a] Tullia's pedagogy, we see, is anything but abstract. She refers to the ancient classics in the appropriate fashion, for she is very much a scholar, but does so with her pupil pressed against her. The "furieux assauts" (I, 42) and the "violentes irruptions" (I, 44) that take place during these sessions are not a diversion, nor even a genuine interruption: they prove that the content of what is being taught here cannot be separated from its style.

At its most ceremonious, *ars erotica* is likely to include pictorial representations, especially mural ones in temples of Venus. Here the young woman can be initiated formally into a range of (formal) pleasures, with all the support of pedagogical figures, to be designated with the wave of a teacherly hand and espoused with a twist of the pupil's body. From the boudoir to the *pavillon* to the temple, such richly contrived environments abound in erotic literature, although they tend to be more prevalent in texts of the later eighteenth century, which often display great architectural consciousness. In Mairobert's *La Secte des anandrynes,* the anonymous *Le Rideau levé, ou l'Education de Laure* (1786), Nerciat's *Les Aphrodites* (1793), and even Musset's *Gamiani* (1833), the traces of *ars erotica* are inscribed on the walls—not just as fading graffiti, but as finely constraining detail. Most often, however, especially in texts of the seventeenth and eighteenth centuries, the chain of teaching and learning is established and reinforced by the handing on of books. Within erotic literature, we thus find represented the dynamics of its own canonical perpetuation. Aretino's Nanna, while still a youthful nun, receives the didactic gift of a "missal" that is actually an anonymous set of positions, while Agnès, in *Vénus dans le cloître,* is offered, among other books, *L'Académie des dames* and *L'Escole des filles.*[56] Thérèse, in *Thérèse philosophe,* is let loose in an erotic library for two weeks as an initial phase in her training,[57] and the heroine of Nerciat's *Mon Noviciat* has as bedside books *L'Education de Laure, Portier des Chartreux,* and *Thérèse philosophe* itself.[58] Tradition functions thus as a gift bestowed compellingly on the pupil. One could continue at length what I have begun to do here, joining up the dots in the line of succession, tracing the regular movement whereby the canon holds its shape.

To the extent that women come to be seen more as readers and

[a] Cette nuit, pour que je puisse t'endoctriner sur tout d'une langue plus libre, nous coucherons ensemble dans mon lit, dont je voudrais pouvoir dire qu'il aura été la plus douce lice de Vénus.

less as authors of *ars erotica,* they can no longer be held responsible for the demanding range of positions to which they—especially, but not exclusively, as courtesans—are required to apply themselves. In *La Retorica delle puttane,* which is in many ways a more "traditional" (though less dynamically canonical) text than the earlier *Ragionamenti,* the pupil is still being told that bodily versatility is required of her by the goddess of love. Venus demands that she have all the flexibility of an eel, twisting, turning, stretching, contracting, pushing forward or leaning backward, in order to assume whatever position of pleasure is required by these divine "precepts" (E7). Aretino's Nanna, however, has no thought for the traditional erotic authority of women, with its corollary moral responsibility. She insists that men are responsible, both for inventing positions and for attributing their inventions to women. In particular, all those poses that appear undesirable or uncomfortable can be seen as having their origin in quite another place than in the mind of Elephantis or the will of Venus. They are born of male desire, and executed by women in response to male power. If we are whores, says Nanna, that is because we are forced into it: "They are the ones who've made whores out of us and [. . .] taught us their filthy tricks. Our science comes from the imaginings of this pimp or that one, and only a liar, a damned liar, would dare to say that the first person who got the idea of using us like boys [. . .] did not do so by forcing us to consent" (V, 179–81).[b] That is why Pippa may well prefer lackeys, as future customers, to gentlemen, precisely because they do not imagine, and consequently impose, an exhausting variety of positions: "They do not spend four hours working your body over, breaking your bones and dislocating your joints by making you take up those positions where you have to hold your legs up in the air while being screwed. Those are positions that men dream up, that they have dreamed up in the past, and that they will always dream up just to make life hard for us all" (V, 179).[c] No, it is not women, she says, who elaborate and maintain this discipline. It is men who impose it on them:

> They turn us around, up and down, this way and that, day and night, and anyone who does not consent to all the filthy tricks men dream up

[b] C'est eux qui ont fait de nous des putains et [. . .] nous ont appris leurs cochonneries. *Notre science,* nous la tenons des fantaisies de tel ou tel putassier, et c'est un menteur, un archimenteur, celui qui oserait dire que le premier qui imagina de se servir de nous comme de garçons [. . .] ne nous y fit pas consentir de force.

[c] Ils ne te restent pas quatre heures sur le corps à te briser les os et à te disloquer pour te faire prendre ces postures où il faut lever les jambes en l'air et se laisser cheviller

> ends up dying on the job; one of them prefers it boiled, another roasted; they have invented screwing with your beaver at the back, with your legs around your neck, the ironing board manner, the crane, the tortoise, the church and steeple, the stirrups, the grazing ewe, and other positions more bizarre than the gestures of a goblet trickster. (IV, 117)[d]

This list of positions describes the scope of the whore's knowledge, but also the extent of her oppression. *Ars erotica,* thus recast, becomes a target opportunity for feminist critique: it gives an elaborate inventory of the poses of subjection and abjection.

Most of the time, as part of its ongoing thematic consolidation, and its sustained masking of sexual politics, erotic literature avoids this kind of tirade, even if it does happen to provide ammunition for a feminist Nanna. Chorier's characters are content to recognize an acceptable range of pleasurable positions. The erotic imagination (gender unspecified) may conceive all sorts of things, but the (woman's) body does not always bend that way: "But there are many [positions] that could not be executed, even if the joints and back of those coupled in the mysteries of Venus were more flexible than one might suppose. By dint of meditation and reflection, many ideas come into the mind that are impossible to put into practice . . . it is not so easy for the body to bend to what thought, good or bad, can conceive" (III, 190–92).[e] In place of the tortured flexibility mentioned in Aretino and Pallavicino, Chorier's Tullia is content to advocate a kind of routine suppleness: "Everything your husband demands of you as a favor you should do; let nothing that seems enjoyable to him appear shameful to you. Transform yourself, like Proteus, into all kinds of figures, if he orders you to" (II, 122).[f] Attentive obedience to the male works

---

en même temps, postures que les hommes imaginent, qu'ils ont imaginées et qu'ils imagineront toujours pour tourmenter le pauvre monde.

[d] On nous tourne et on nous retourne par tous les bouts, de jour et de nuit, et qui ne consent à toutes les saletés que l'homme peut imaginer, meurt à la peine; l'un préfère le bouilli, l'autre le rôti; ils ont inventé de baiser la motte en arrière, les jambes sur le cou, à la jeannette, à la grue, à la tortue, à l'église sur le clocher, à franc étrier, à la brebis qui broute et autres postures plus bizarres que ne sont les gestes d'un joueur de gobelets.

[e] Mais il y en a beaucoup [de postures] qu'on ne peut mettre à exécution, quand même les articulations et les reins de ceux qui s'accouplent pour les mystères de Vénus seraient flexibles au-delà de ce qu'on saurait supposer. A force de méditer et de réfléchir, beaucoup d'idées tombent dans l'esprit, qu'il est impossible de réaliser. . . il n'est pas aussi facile au corps de se plier à tout ce que la pensée, bonne ou mauvaise, conçoit.

[f] Tout ce que ton mari exigera de ta complaisance, fais-le; que rien de ce qui lui semble doux, à lui, ne te paraisse honteux, à toi. Change-toi, comme Protée, en toutes sortes de figures, s'il l'ordonne.

itself out as studied postural diversity. *Ars erotica* is exercised submissively, within the space of the marriage bed.

The supposed threat of lesbian autonomy melts away to nothing when feminine erotic instruction is so tightly constrained. Not only is it hedged about with exemplary figures—that is, after all, the nature of classical instruction—but it now appears limited in *time,* framed by the need to prepare for marriage or at least for the decisive encounter with the male. Aretino's Nanna spoke directly to her daughter and considered marriage as one unappealing option. Chorier's Tullia was delegated by the mother (I, 102) to provide instruction during the days (or nights) immediately preceding Ottavia's marriage. *L'Escole des filles,* however, moves even further away from the classical thematics. While continuing to call on women's knowledge, it does so very much for convenience, and with minimal respect, so explicit is the text about locating feminine dialogue within the context of male discipline. While *L'Escole des filles* is recognizably, as Pascal Pia says, "a slightly cynical manual of practical erotology,"[59] [g] we can no longer be sure of the voice providing the instruction. There is from the outset, if not an absolute ambiguity of destination, at least a multiplicity of address in *L'Escole des filles,* for the text contains both a "Letter of invitation to girls" and a "Notice to ladies."[60] [h] On the face of it, the book itself might be taken as a message, a written example of feminine pedagogy, although there is no indication that the *je* who speaks to the *filles* and the *dames* is feminine. Indeed, it is hard to see how the authorial voice could be identified as feminine without a dramatic loss of consistency for the text. More than once, we are told that the maternal voice, in particular, is not to be trusted. Whereas Nanna spoke as a mother and Tullia on behalf of one, the pupil in *L'Escole des filles* is told that mothers are a fount of sexual ignorance: "That is what comes of always listening to one's mother and never attending to the words of men" (5).[i] To read the dialogue is not simply to be informed, at second hand, by the words of a learned woman (as written by a male author). Rather, what we read, the very dialogue between women, must be framed by male wisdom in some identifiable way, so as to avoid passing on errors.

The thematic exigency of the enunciation in *L'Escole des filles* manifests itself quite clearly in the plot. The motivation, the raison d'être of the dialogue is not in the first instance some traditional rite of

[g] manuel un peu narquois d'érotologie pratique

[h] Epître invitatoire aux filles/Avertissement aux dames

[i] Voilà ce que c'est d'écouter toujours une mère et ne prêter jamais l'oreille aux paroles des hommes.

passage, or the older woman's desire, or even the younger woman's curiosity. It is the desire of Robinet, the male character, to seduce the young Fanchon. Unable to win her directly, he seduces the more experienced and measurably less attractive Susanne, who is then sent to carry out the seduction on his behalf. It is not that Susanne has no valuable knowledge—she gives Robinet tactical instructions about where to be and how to behave after she has spoken—but the very fact that the dialogue is established through intrigue serves to deny its ritual, traditional nature. And if we wish to test the history inscribed in the text by regressing to the origin of the teacher Susanne's knowledge, we find once again, not the mother, or the aunt or the older cousin, but the male lover. When Fanchon expresses astonishment at her teacher's skill and knowledge, Susanne replies: "My lover it was who was pleased to instruct me, for his great enjoyment" (115).[j]

Insofar as *L'Escole des filles* marks a further shift in the tradition of *ars erotica,* it would appear to represent, beyond the loss of fictive womanly authorship, the further loss of feminine erotic authority. In *L'Académie des dames,* the woman teacher knows her place, as she knows her time. She is present as a first stage in her pupil's initiation: "Afterward, you will have a man who will be better in bed than I am" (I, 24).[k] And Ottavia shows her new learning when she interposes: "I presume that it is only in the arms of men, when they sleep with us, that we can enjoy solid sensual pleasure" (I, 48).[l] That is indeed how it works. Marriage comes after lesbian initiation, moving quickly and decisively beyond it. In *L'Escole des filles,* however, female instruction is locked into a much narrower circuit of male pleasure. The man is visibly first and last, origin and conclusion, and women's knowledge is the instrument of his seductive activity.

Brantôme observes that, in his time, classical erotic books appear to have been made redundant because husbands themselves now undertake to instruct their wives in the art of pleasure: "Today there is no need for books or paintings, for husbands teach them so much: that is what husbands' schools lead to!" (30–31).[m] It is the husbands who now teach "those outrageous [*énormes*] figures of Aretino," with the most disturbing consequences. For women might no longer be authors, and they may not even be commanding teachers, but they

[j] C'est mon ami qui a pris plaisir à m'instruire, pour son grand plaisir.

[k] Après, tu auras un meilleur coucheur que je n'aurai été une bonne coucheuse.

[l] Car, je le présume, c'est seulement dans les bras des hommes, quand ils couchent avec nous, que nous pouvons goûter une solide volupté.

[m] Aujourd'hui n'en est besoin de ces livres ni de ces peintures, car les maris leur en apprennent prou: et voilà que servent telles écoles de maris!

are, he notes, remarkably good learners: "So that, for every ember they have in their bodies, [the lessons] produce a hundred more, thus turning them into loose women. And when they have been trained in this fashion, they cannot resist leaving their husbands and turning to other suitors" (26).[n] Should we declare this, with Brantôme, to be the effective end of *ars erotica*? No, the end is not yet, for *ars erotica* seems to go on aging, rather than come to a dead stop. Canonical aging—indeed, a kind of orderly decay—seems to defer almost indefinitely the end of the tradition, the death of the theme.

Vénus dans le cloître (1682), the next in historical succession of the much-quoted works of erotic literature, is a fine example of this thematic undoing-as-becoming. Its events take place entirely, as the title suggests, within a closed, feminine space. The book consists of a numbered set of dialogues, most of them between the young Agnès, aged sixteen, and the youthful but adequately experienced Angélique, aged twenty. The age difference is the same as that in *L'Académie des dames,* but here it is measured somewhat apologetically. "My child," says Angélique, "you may be surprised by the lessons I am going to give you, and you will be astounded to hear a girl of nineteen or twenty sounding so learned" (28).[o] Whatever the possible doubts, Agnès's very enthusiasm seems to invest Angélique with authority: "My dear Angélique, please go ahead with your teaching; I am overcome with impatience to hear what you have to say. You have never had a pupil more attentive than I shall be as I listen to all your instruction" (28).[p] Yet Angélique's authority is more than a by-product of Agnès's enthusiasm: despite the convent walls and the youth of the protagonists, their feminine space has already been broached by male teaching. Angélique—and this is the source, indeed the very definition of her greater experience—has had occasion to learn from a Jesuit with a particular fondness for her, who sought to "open up" her mind and "make it capable of speculation of this sort" (30).[q] From this priest, she appears to have learned a kind of critical libertine spirit, one that includes the philosophical, the political, and the erotic (see 67–68,

[n] De telle sorte que, pour un tison de feu qu'elles ont dans le corps, elles y en engendrent cent, et les rendent ainsi paillardes; si bien qu'étant de cette façon dressées, elles ne se peuvent en garder qu'elles ne quittent leurs maris et aillent trouver autres chevaliers.

[o] Mon enfant, tu vas peut-être être surprise des leçons que je vais te donner, et tu seras étonnée d'entendre une fille de dix-neuf à vingt ans faire la savante.

[p] Ma chère Angélique, commencez, je vous prie, vos instructions; je languis dans l'impatience où je suis de vous entendre. Vous n'avez jamais eu d'écolière plus attentive que je le serai à tous vos discours.

[q] le rendre capable des spéculations présentes

185). She and Agnès spend much of the time embracing in cloistered intimacy, but the cloisters are permeable to male desire, and the cells are filled with libertine books (see 79–82, 183). The two women can lend themselves to lesbian play, but their ultimate erotic destiny, even as nuns, is to give themselves to male lovers: "It is a perfect concert of tenderness that arises from the charming harmony or the sweet understanding of two hearts closed to all but each other, even though it is ultimately only a frail image, a pale shadow and a vain ghost of the love one finds between two people of different sexes" (223).[r] Moreover, while lesbian caresses clearly have a teacherly function, they are not even, strictly speaking, a prelude. Agnès has two encounters with men quite early in the story: they are simply not narrated in any detail. Only with the story of Cornélie (149–52), and that of Angélique and Don Gracio (156–58) do we attend more closely to male-female intercourse. It even transpires that there is a young man loose in the convent, disguised as a nun (180ff.). But that is where the plot makes its thematic point. These cloisters are never effectively closed to men; they are both shaped and traversed by the requirements of a male-centered discipline.

In *Les Amours du chevalier de Faublas* (1787), feminine instruction scenes are invaded or mimicked by a male in disguise. The young Faublas, dressed as a girl, finds himself in bed with the experienced Mme de B***, aged twenty-five, and there learns his first erotic lesson: "She helped my timid inexperience . . . With as much astonishment as pleasure, I received a charming lesson, repeated more than once."[61] [s] It seems to him that there is nothing complicated to be learned—just one lesson to be repeated *ad libitum*. Later in the same story, Mme de B*** comes to him disguised as a man (I, 157–58), reminding us no doubt that intrigue and adventure can triumph at every point over the solemnity of ritual gender roles. Whatever is left of *ars erotica* in this text is heartily exploited and undermined by Faublas's comic energy. Eventually, in disguise once again, he finds himself employed as a *lectrice* by the comtesse de Lignolle, whose husband is impotent. This provides Faublas with the opportunity of passing on what Mme de B*** has taught him: "I found myself in M. de Lignolle's place, teaching the pretty comtesse the rudiments of the noble science I had

[r] C'est un concert parfait de tendresse qui résulte de la charmante harmonie ou de la douce sympathie de deux cœurs fermés l'un pour l'autre, quoique après tout ce ne soit qu'une faible image, qu'une ombre légère et qu'un vain fantôme de l'amour qui se retrouve entre deux personnes d'un sexe différent.

[s] Elle aida ma timide inexpérience. . . Je reçus avec autant d'étonnement que de plaisir une charmante leçon que je répétai plus d'une fois.

learned from the beautiful Mme de B***, under the auspices of the marquis" (II, 63).[t] Husbands are fools and cuckolds, just as Brantôme feared. And the ancient chain of feminine knowledge even appears to function independently of them. But only in the most derisory fashion: at every point, women's teaching and learning is inhabited by transvestite male pleasure.

It might be said that the thematics of *ars erotica* tend to lose their richness—or at least their range—shrinking progressively to the scale of a lesbian instruction episode contained in a much broader narrative. It is as if an atrophied, more or less singular theme were surviving beyond its maturity and thus enduring disjunctively in a wider thematic context that I have yet to describe. In *Thérèse philosophe* (1748), the heroine finds herself, at a crucial point in her development, being instructed by a retired prostitute, Bois-Laurier, in the range of male erotic whims.[62] The scene has its full, canonically predictable, erotic conclusion: "I had to sleep with her—one must howl with the wolves—and we did and said all sorts of indiscreet things" (II, 51).[u] Of course Thérèse enters into intimacy, but only to humor the older woman, she says. Yet it is "fortunate" for the sake of her erotic career that she meets her *cher comte* the very next day: "It was, my dear Comte, on the next day, following that libertine night, that I spoke to you for the first time. O fortunate day! Without you, without your advice, without the tender friendship and happy warmth that bound us at first, I would have slid by degrees to my ruin" (II, 51–52).[v] Just when one might have thought women's teaching had lost its force, just when you thought it was safe to go out, Thérèse runs into a female wolf, for the temporary lack of proper male guidance. But sighs of relief are in order, because she has now been saved from lesbianism, just as the text has been saved from an enduring preoccupation with *ars erotica*. As a consequence of this male tutelage, and the proper refocusing of pleasure that it brings, Thérèse is able to continue her lessons, but the style of instruction is no longer erotic: "After some words from Bois-Laurier, which were meant to serve as lessons instructing me about the different types of male character, we went to

[t] Je me trouvais à la place de M. de Lignolle, enseignant à la jolie comtesse les premiers éléments de l'auguste science que j'avais apprise de la belle madame de B***, sous les auspices du marquis.

[u] Il fallut coucher avec elle: on hurle avec les loups, nous dîmes et nous fîmes toutes sortes de folies.

[v] Ce fut, mon cher comte, le lendemain de cette nuit libertine, que je vous parlai pour la première fois. Jour fortuné! sans vous, sans vos conseils, sans la tendre amitié et l'heureuse sympathie qui nous lia d'abord, je coulais insensiblement à ma perte.

bed and, once we were there, our former indiscretions gave way to reasoned discussion" (II, 55).[w] Erotic madness gives way now to reason, and women's initiatory knowledge-as-practice to the "philosophy" of the novel's title. Just as in *Vénus dans le cloître,* women are called on to move beyond those intimations of pleasure—the ancient memory or the vague foreshadowing—to be found in lesbian instruction, so as to reach a balanced libertine wisdom. This they can do, we (and they) are told repeatedly, only under the guidance of men.

The narrowly instrumental view of women's erotic teaching tends to prevail over the richer, classical one, and this may be a thematic reason for the fact that the series of teaching dialogues, as a subgenre of erotic literature, recedes in importance during the eighteenth and nineteenth centuries. One still finds such late and surprisingly classical examples of it as *L'Ecole des biches* (1868), or even Monnier's *Deux Gougnottes* (1864), but women's initiation tends to become just a thematic set piece, embedded in narration and description, as in Gervaise de Latouche's *Portier des Chartreux* (1741), Choiseul-Meuse's *Amélie de Saint-Far* (1802), or her *Julie, ou J'ai sauvé ma rose* (1807). Instead of occupying the bed in her own right, or even as a brief prelude to copulation with a man, the woman teacher tends to be more self-effacing, less self-embodying. In *Julie, ou J'ai sauvé ma rose,* the youthful-but-experienced Céline refuses to play the role of initiator made available to her by thematic tradition. She defers to an older man, Saint-Albin, in the name of didactic efficiency: "Listen, my dear, Saint-Albin is much more valuable for clearing up your uncertainties, because he can follow up theory with practice, and that form of teaching is surely the best; everything he demonstrates to you will be engraved indelibly in your memory, whereas I could only struggle in vain to give you an understanding of the delightful mysteries of love."[63] [x] Céline cannot fulfill the role because there is no recognized erotic *pratique* between women: the exchange could only be abstractly theoretical. What she *is* able to teach, in the absence of a full-blown *ars erotica,* is the art of feminine seduction: "I am giving you lessons in coquetry; I am teaching you how to please others, and I am being so

[w] Après quelques discours de la Bois-Laurier, qui visaient à me servir de leçons, propres à m'apprendre à connaître les différents caractères des hommes, nous nous couchâmes, et dès que nous fûmes au lit, nos folies firent place au raisonnement.

[x] Tenez ma chère, Saint-Albin vaut infiniment mieux que moi pour éclaircir vos doutes, car il peut joindre la pratique à la théorie, et cette manière d'enseigner est certainement la meilleure; tout ce qu'il vous démontrera se gravera dans votre mémoire, en traits ineffaçables, au lieu que ce serait peut-être vainement que je m'efforcerais de vous faire comprendre les délicieux mystères de l'amour.

generous as to pass on good taste to you" (I, 138).[y] Even in *L'Ecole des biches,* whose title links teaching and lesbianism, we find a form of deference, and deferral, to the encounter with a male. Since contact between women gives only a feeble idea of the encounter to come, the older woman can only appeal to a sense of anticipation: "You see, my dear; if I, as a woman, can have such an effect on your senses, what would have happened if your male suitor had been more bold?"[64] [z] Her pedagogy is that of the ersatz, performed by a self-deprecatory teacher: "Wait there. I shall try to give you a vague idea of it using my fingers" (206).[a] All that is left here is a "faible idée" of *ars erotica:* the weakness of the theme is reflected, as one might expect, in the theme of weakness.

The final *reductio ad rationem* of *ars erotica* is doubtless to be found when its knowledge is displaced by scientific discourse, represented as the special property of male subjects. Nowhere is this more explicit and more urbanely systematic than in *Le Roman de Violette* (1883). The narrator-hero of that text has the role of erotic tutor in relation to the beautiful, innocent, and willing Violette. He has something of an ongoing struggle with a still-young-but-more-experienced lesbian widow who is determined to play the initiatory role to the full. But the man is there first and last, even if the older woman is allowed a part with his voyeuristic indulgence. Christian's great advantage over his lesbian rival, Odette, is founded not merely on his genital morphology, but on the power and precision of his technical knowledge of sexuality. For as it happens, he lectures at the Ecole de médecine in Paris (57), and is thus perfectly qualified to instruct his pupil in the anthropological foundation of gender difference (37), in addition to providing a series of lessons, each more apposite than the preceding one, in descriptive anatomy (55–57). Concurrently, *Le Roman de Violette* continues to lay claim, in the self-consciously literate way we noted earlier, to the perfection of classical knowledge. Yet the knowledge that really tells in the story, that which makes of the narrator a pedagogical hero in every sense, is eminently progressive rather than classical.

The lingering trace of *ars erotica* has not gone in *Le Roman de Violette.* This is, after all, where we came in, the point at which I proposed to enter the circle of traditional understanding. The broad-based the-

[y] Je vous donne des leçons de coquetterie, je vous enseigne l'art de plaire, je pousse les bons offices jusqu'à vous donner du goût.

[z] Tu le vois, ma chère amie; si moi, une femme, je produis sur tes sens un tel effet, que serait-il donc arrivé si ton amoureux eût été plus téméraire!

[a] Attends, je vais essayer de t'en donner une faible idée avec mes doigts.

matic assurance of the novel is such, indeed, that it can eventually allow the standard demonstration scene of lesbian teaching to take place, in good time, and under strict supervision (120ff.). Entertaining the old theme can only serve, however, to highlight its thorough narrative submission. *Ars erotica*—or its asthenic and vaguely titillating trace—is invoked in order to be dealt with, summoned in order to be properly, rationally, dismissed.

Did women ever really have special power or authority as teachers and learners of the art of pleasure? Was their supposed power anything more, in fact, than a semiotic arrangement serving the interests of men? Such questions cannot be pursued through the kind of study I am attempting here—if they can be helpfully pursued at all. What I have tried to make clear is that a tradition of erotic literature shows women as having first had the power to know and teach the art of pleasure, then having gradually lost that power. Classical erotic literature, then, is not a vehicle for the unrelieved assertion of patriarchal dominance. It represents a kind of hazardous transfer: the laborious and perhaps incomplete shift of erotic authority from women to men.

The very slowness of change here should be read as the mark of canonicity. *Ars erotica,* as a lingering, defective, even archaic theme, serves to associate newly appearing pornographic texts with a long and somewhat obscure tradition. In this way, pornography lays claim to literary status. The enduring paradox is that the homocentric rituals of later erotic writing may continue to depend, for their cultural legitimacy, on maintaining the trace of something they might otherwise have happily effaced, as they practice forms of stylized and half-respectful allusion to a tradition of feminine knowledge and power.

Chapter 2

Conversation and Confession: The Secrets of Femininity

I referred in the previous chapter to a "subgenre" of erotic literature: the courtesans' dialogue. To make a separate place for such dialogues within the domain of erotic literature is something of an analytical contrivance, and I have already had to pick my way around them for fear of untimely complications. The clearest symptom of expository artifice is that some texts I wish to consider first as part of this subtradition have in fact been discussed, or at least mentioned, in Chapter 1: Aretino's *Ragionamenti,* Pallavicino's *Retorica delle puttane,* and the anonymous *Dialogua tra Maddalena e Giulia,* often called in error *La Puttana errante.* If Gadamer is right about the thematically inclusive and confirmatory nature of tradition, then the very notion of a subtradition may be somewhat problematical. It does seem helpful, nonetheless, to resituate the texts mentioned above in a rather different historical lineage, even if the final point of the exercise is to assimilate the separate themes within a broader thematics. Indeed, one of the things I hope to achieve in this chapter is to account for elements of canonical erotic literature that appear to wax stronger as classical *ars erotica* goes on waning through the seventeenth and eighteenth centuries.

The most visible literary antecedent for the courtesans' dialogue is the second-century *Hetairikoi Dialogoi* by Lucian of Samosata. According to Gilbert Lély, Lucian's work was first brought to Italy from Constantinople in 1425, and was translated into French in 1582.[1] That makes it, in a sense, a (classical) contemporary of Aretino: not a lost antecedent like the works of Astyanassa, Philaenis, or Elephantis, but a happily found one. Is it for that very reason that it is not referred to solemnly and regularly, as Elephantis was? Is it because the genre itself displays vulgarity of all kinds and has no claim to nobility, or even legitimacy? Could it be that these texts are "pornographic"? Courtesans' dialogues certainly cannot be simply opposed to *ars erotica* by reference to the etymology of *pornographia* (*porné*, "prostitute," + *graphein*, "to write"), for *ars erotica* was also sometimes said by tradition to have been composed by courtesans. It may be, however, that the courtesans' dialogue was closer to what our aesthetes would call pornography in that it actually described prostitution, using its crude language and representing it as a trade in deception. Prostitution was seen as an exercise in forward defense for women with no other means, certainly, but it was also presented as a set of petty subterfuges whose purpose was narrowly economic.

La Retorica delle puttane (1642) raises all the vulgar questions in the most explicit way. To call it a handbook for vocational guidance would be whimsically anachronistic, but it does address, in a manner so explicit as to appear rather rigid, the question of a young woman's choice of profession (or estate). The young woman in the text has an unimpressively limited range of options: she has no dowry to enable her to marry, and no gift (*genio*) for monastic life. She can therefore remain shut up in her house, imprisoned in poverty, or choose "the whore's profession," which is presented by the old woman as "virtually the only solution" for her situation (A10).[a] The self-styled therapeutic instructor does not seem fully qualified to provide a recipe for success: she was once wealthy, but has now been reduced to begging. That very defeat has, however, taught her the ways of the world, so that she is now ready to teach the secrets of nonfailure. Whatever authority she has is of a vulgar kind, quite without prestige. And the wisdom she makes available is less an initiatory art than a set of clever tricks. "Retorica" is used early on as a synonym for "artificii" (A2, A14), providing a formal reminder that whores trade in artifice, in "fintioni" and "furberie," lies and deceptions (E3).

The knowledge involved here may not be such as to lend itself to a proper taxonomic description. Should we take as a sign of relative disorder the fact that there are fifteen lessons, rather than the twelve or sixteen we have been led to expect of *ars erotica*? The "lessons" (A13) or "talks" (B3) are delivered on separate "days" (E3)[b] but do not correspond on any one-to-one basis to a formal set of erotic posi-

[a] il mestiere della Puttana/quasi l'unico rimedio

[b] lettioni/discorsi/giornate

tions—not even to a set of particularly deceptive ones. Indeed, the very definition of the whore's artfulness seems to be her capacity *not* to be held to a strict erotic order. The essence of her art is persuasion or seduction, and what is recommended for her is a rhetorical application of the positions of Aretino. The old woman speaks of the "laws for coupling, in which consists the better part of feminine persuasive art" (D8).[c] The laws are there, apparently inescapable, but they must be applied with skill and a measure of tactical freedom: "The whore is not obliged to follow any strict order in this, since she is only bound to observe one rule, the one that exactly strikes the fancy of the man whom she has to persuade" (D8).[d] It is thus entirely inappropriate to rehearse a classical order in liturgical fashion or to practice a range of positions *as range,* for its own sake. It is a matter of finding the position that works best to manipulate the other: "Arrange yourself in such a way as to display your limbs in that part of the proceedings where they will be shown to best effect, and will give greatest pleasure to the man" (D8).[e] The position itself is a trick, a rhetorical device.

It should be quite clear that this kind of seductive flexibility still supposes a bodily *grammatica* (see A13) in the form of Aretine training, but the point of such training is to be prepared for every eventuality, having discerned one's strengths and weaknesses and being ready to fall back to the tactical position. The history of accidents and difficulties encountered in the past or identified by others in the same trade has to be superimposed on the more abstract (classical) range of possibilities: "You must be practiced enough in yourself to discern the best [ways], and respond to the imagination of the proposer with exquisitely appropriate attitudes. I should add, to complete this lesson, that, whatever other thoughts you may have, you should always keep clearly in mind the image of any accidents that may have happened to others, or indeed to yourself" (E2).[f] Worldly wisdom consists here in defining a narrower range of positions and working within it, both in order to avoid being hurt and to exercise maximum seductive power: "When you have practiced many positions, and experienced the requirement to vary your treatments, you will remember to count as eligible those

[c] leggi per lo congiungimento, in cui consiste l'ultima parte della persuasiva feminile

[d] Non s'astringe quivi la puttana ad alcun ordine, come obligata al l'osservare quel solo, che maggiormente colpirà nei capricci di chi s'hà de persuadere.

[e] Offervi solo di porre i membri in quella parte del periodo, in cui faranno migliore effetto, e riusciranno più aggredevoli all'huomo.

[f] In tu te dovrà esser esercitata per discernere le migliori [maniere], e incontrare il genio di chi propone con la esquisitezza dei medesmi diportamenti. Aggiungo per fine di questa lettione, ch'in altro sentimento conservar dovete buona memoria con le imagini delli accidenti occursi in altri, o pur anche in voi stessa.

that gave pleasure to others. The positions that displeased them you will set aside in your mind, and make a point of not using them" (E2).[g] It may well be, according to Elephantis or Aretino, that there are twelve or sixteen figures of Venus, but each prostitute needs to know how many "eligible" ones there are for her. *Ars erotica* maintains a kind of authority here, of course, and Aretino's name is mentioned with due solemnity as the model (E9). Yet the classical knowledge seems to be coming undone at the point of its bodily application, as it is revised with a view to feminine survival and reconceived as feminine persuasive artifice. That is, it would appear, the social definition of the whore in a text such as this: the woman who practices an initially defensive and ultimately lucrative seduction—seduction being understood not as a general style of deportment in some loosely modern sense, but as a comprehensive set of rhetorical tricks and positional maneuvers.

La Retorica delle puttane ought to be read not only for the lessons it claims to teach, but for the fictive enunciation framing the whole. There is in fact an opening address to whores as a class, announcing that the text will contain "[the] artifices that are proper to your profession" (A2).[h] This is not, of course, the voice of the old woman, but that of an author/presenter. The same voice, presumably, passes judgment from time to time on what the old woman says, declaring it to be exaggerated or tendentious. All this helps one to construct an authorial subject whose role, despite the apologetic tone of the initial address to the courtesans, is to be complicitous, certainly, with the old woman's teaching, but also to reveal the secrets being taught, by making them available to all of his readers. That, I suppose, is the second-order rhetoric of the text: it reveals, incidentally but explicitly, the vast array of tricks practiced by whores. By intercepting the dialogue of worldly women, *La Retorica* effectively puts their artifices on display and thus makes a kind of prophylactic contribution to the worldly wisdom of those men who are their customers and potential "victims." Women can be readers here by occupying the teacher's or learner's position, aligning themselves with whores in space and time, but men who read are participating in the subversion of courtesans' knowledge. They are learning the truth about this kind of venal seduction and its feminine lies.

[g] Quando havrete pratticati molti [diportamenti], e nella moltiplicita dei capricci havrete conosciuto l'obligo di variare trattamenti, vi rammentarate come eleggibile quelle delle quali altri si compiace, e quelle onde altri prese disgusto, riserbarete a parte per haver nella mente, e tener a cuore l'obligo di non usarle.

[h] [li] artificii propri della vostra professione

The interception of women's teaching occurs in many more texts than the *Retorica,* which actually handles the whole matter a trifle inelegantly, being narratorially intrusive about its narrator's thematic intrusion into a feminine world. The *Ragionamenti* (1534–39) perform the whole voyeuristic operation more engagingly, sustaining the fiction of a lively and spontaneous exchange between the two women (Nanna and Antonia, Nanna and Pippa) present at any given time. "We," as male readers, are not just lectured to about how these women lecture each other: we are taken through the rhythms of their intimate conversation, gleaning the secrets and tricks as they come to light. Instead of a structural contradiction between orderly presentation and statements about the need to resist order, as in *La Retorica,* we find a thematic conflict within Aretino's text between, on the one hand, notions of a taxonomy helping to shape the text as a whole, and on the other, spontaneous outbursts—displays of curiosity, impetuosity or indiscipline—that interrupt the flow of exposition, but do so in such a way as to reveal all sorts of things in passing. The text moves dialogically, almost dialectically, between instruction and disarming revelation, between the systematic unmasking of the whore's trickery and the charm of passing insights made available in the frankness of these (fictively) private exchanges.[2]

The question of a woman's choice of estate gives to the *Ragionamenti* what one might call its external or explicit shape. The dialogues occur at the "crossroads" (I, 11) where a young woman's options are visible as a range, and three days (*giornate*) of exchanges correspond respectively to the standard roles: nun, wife, and whore. These taxonomic headings act as a constraint on Nanna's narrations and tirades. At times she may forbear from telling a particular tale because it belongs in another place, as on the occasion when there is mention of one character's widowhood. Why she remained a widow will not be told just then but at another time, since "the life of widows is such that it requires a chapter all to itself" (II, 83).[i] Yet the spontaneity of her conversation is such that broad paradigms are not allowed to dictate the syntagmatic workings of the text in any reliable way. Still present in the whore's knowledge, but in no way helping to segment the text or establish order in Nanna's discourse, is, of course, the "Aretino," the range of positions. Knowing the full set is vital for the learner—but is it not principally for fear of being caught short in some way? "Try to ensure that it is not possible to imagine any caresses that you

[i] la vie des veuves est telle qu'elle exige un chapitre à elle seule.

don't engage in with the person you're sleeping with" (IV, 39).[j] Within the range of positions, certain ones are to be preferred, not just for defensive reasons such as protection from discomfort, but for tactically aggressive ones. Getting on top of the male—in the literal sense, of course—has much to recommend it (IV, 49). Indeed, the list of positions has to coexist for Nanna with other, less canonical inventories, such as a characterization of types from different foreign countries and of the best ways in which to deal with them (IV, 121–45). *Ars erotica* here has been rehashed and served up among a great variety of helpful hints for intending prostitutes. Ritual solemnity, in whatever vestigial form, has been assimilated into a mobile and resourceful worldly wisdom.

The *Ragionamenti,* like many later texts in the canon of erotic literature, represent feminine intimacy in conversational rhythm. The characters in this work may be prepared to rehearse the figures of Venus as bodily discipline for the sake of survival or material gain, but their theoretical commitment is disturbed by the play of desire, by impatience, curiosity, and forgetfulness—all represented as somehow feminine. Disturbing the *giornate* as lectures but helping to give them rhythm as dialogues is an explicitly recognized source of disorder, namely, that of the simmering, inconsistent mind of the female teacher: "I am trying to think," says Nanna. "The truth is, my brain is all awash; it is simmering on the stove; it is only fit for shucking beans, due to my habit of hopping from topic to topic."[3] What could be more suitable, at the end of such a day's talk, than to retire to bed together (IV, 269)? Nanna's "rhetoric" is finally indistinguishable from pillow talk.

If, in pursuit of classical antecedents, we ask about the place of Lucian's *Dialogues,* there may not be very much to say. The sixth of his short dialogues does involve a mother-daughter conversation in which the mother seeks to convince the daughter of the financial value of becoming a courtesan, and then begins to train her in seductive etiquette without mentioning erotic positions. More typically, the dialogues seem to turn on some form of misapprehension. Their conversation is effectively problem-solving, or indeed a way of showing that what appeared to be a difficulty was not really one at all, merely the product of misunderstanding. In that sense their local hermeneutics consists in revising the question rather than providing some revealing

[j] Tâche qu'il ne se puisse imaginer de caresses, que tu ne fasses avec qui couche avec toi.

answer. Unlike Aretino's text, which outweighs it immeasurably in canonical influence, Lucian's seldom brings together the didactic and the intimate.[4]

A more significant contribution is made by the *Dialogua tra Maddalena e Giulia* (c. 1531). The form of exchange here equivocates profoundly between the didactic and the personal. Maddalena, the older of the two whores, begins her discussion of the range of "pleasures" with some general, taxonomic comment—there are relations between women, between men, between men and women, as well as solitary pleasure—although she has no rhetorical commitment to any *discorsi* or *giornate* organized under the various headings. Indeed, it is remarkable that all there is to know is included within her narration of personal experience. Instead of a reminder that the perfect whore will need to know all the tricks, as in the *Retorica,* we have here an active remembering that seems to coincide happily with a full erotic knowledge, retrieving standard models from a subjective past. This has presumably become the definition of a literary whore: not a "composer" of erotic art like Elephantis, but one who has lived the full range of erotic attitudes, one who has adopted them all. When such a woman recounts her life, she cannot fail to be instructive—both intimately and formally. At the outset, Maddalena expresses just a modicum of doubt as to the completeness of her experience: "I doubt whether I shall recall all the conjunctions that occur, because I may not perhaps have experienced all of them, although I believe there are hardly any about which I could not speak knowledgeably."[5] [k] To which Giulia replies, providing whatever reassurance is necessary: "You can tell me the ones you have experienced, and how; if I have tried a few more than you, I shall tell you of them. In that way, we shall find them all" (11).[l] "Who is being taught here?" one might ask. The two experienced women are shown to be rehearsing their knowledge for the pleasure of recalling it, and for the satisfaction of completeness. So it is that Maddalena relates her first four sexual experiences, which correspond with compelling nicety to a first set of (vertical) positions. The young couple of which she was part was presumably restricted by circumstance to making love standing up, but the narrator feels no need, apparently, to justify this coincidence of the classificatory and experiential orders. It is Giulia, in fact, who provides the summary and the

[k] je doute si je me ressouviendrai de toutes les conjonctions qui se font, parce que peut-être je ne les ai pas toutes éprouvées, quoiqu'il n'y en ait guère, à ce que je crois, dont je ne puisse parler pertinemment.

[l] Tu diras celles que tu as éprouvées, et comment; et si j'en ai essayé quelques-unes plus que toi, je te les dirai: ainsi nous les trouverons toutes.

classification: "I do not think that there are other kinds of conjunctions in which the man is upright, beside those four" (25).[m] There lies the irony of this conversational mimicry of the instruction theme: Giulia, as taxonomist, actually knows more at the end than she was taught by Maddalena in the course of the dialogue. When Maddalena, in conclusion, puts on a show of pedagogical severity—"Now repeat your lesson for me to hear" (54)[n]—she is answered by Giulia with a list of all the modi, including numbers and names that did not appear in the initial narration. Giulia is not revealed to be the one who really knew all along, presumably because all whores "really know" in this way. She is merely congratulated at the end on her good "memory" (56). The notion of memory here is richly complex: it alternates dialogically between recollections (especially Maddalena's) and taxonomic retrieval (especially Giulia's). Memory may thus happen as a series of subjective events, but it is supported by something transcendentally collective: the always already known of an *ars erotica.*

Foucault, examining the discursive history of sexuality, suggests that confession—as both art and discipline—became established in Europe during the seventeenth century as the privileged modern form of a *scientia sexualis.* I mentioned this in Chapter 1, noting Foucault's suggestion that *scientia sexualis* may have taken the place of a now lost *ars erotica.* What I want to suggest here is that a thematics closely akin to that of confession is at work in the genre of the courtesans' dialogue, serving both to integrate and to break down *ars erotica.* Foucault's primary concern in *La Volonté de savoir* is with nonliterary texts, and especially pastoral ones: training manuals for confessors. My response to this, as in the first chapter, will be to modulate Foucault's analyses by giving them a more Gadamerian inflexion. In particular, I want to suggest that the discipline of confession is given thematic and generic support by a literary tradition representing feminine conversational intimacy as a revelation of the erotic. In other words, my claim is that canonical erotic literature not only includes the traces of an ancient *ars erotica,* but negotiates its thematic displacement by a more confessional understanding of sexuality as intimate truth. Aretino's Nanna, who speaks of crimes she has committed in the past, is able to say toward the end of the dialogues: "I confessed them, without actually going to confession" (IV, 119).[o]

Insofar as the secrets of whores are simply revealed as a set of tricks,

[m] Je ne crois pas qu'il y ait d'autres sortes de conjonctions, l'homme étant debout, que ces quatre-là.

[n] Répète donc ta leçon: que je t'écoute.

[o] Je m'en suis confessée, sans aller à confesse.

they are secrets without intimacy, and their revelation is a rhetorical gesture that has nothing to do with confession as an art. On the other hand, where these women are represented in dialogue with each other, drawing out each other's experience of such tricks, a distinctive shift has occurred. In the *Ragionamenti* and the *Dialogua tra Maddalena e Giulia* those very women whose success depends on their being seductive liars are shown revealing to each other the true nature of their professional tricks. To represent their dialogue is therefore to play a trick on them on behalf of all men, but this trick is, somewhat like their own, a seductive one. It is a way of allowing them to perform—to perform their whoredom, to show the truth behind their lying, the truth *of* their lying—without the readers being deceived by them. "Oh heavens!" says Maddalena in the next to last paragraph of their dialogue, "someone has been listening to us!" (67). No character emerges from hiding, and none needs to for the sake of the story, for this is presumably how the text inscribes its own enunciation. Whether the author/voyeur is actually sighted or not, the same nasty surprise must be waiting just round the corner at the end of every courtesans' dialogue.

In the history of *ars erotica,* we saw that the threat of feminine initiatory knowledge was eventually neutralized and domesticated by the tutelary presence of the male. What the woman teacher said to the woman pupil was not only set out in advance, then, but governed by the seductive purposes of men. The courtesans' dialogue, however, does not attempt to eliminate the secret as such. Rather, it cultivates the theme in order to reveal the secrets more seductively. *Ars erotica* invests women with authoritative knowledge but makes of that knowledge an iconographic display, available as a paradigm to all. The courtesans' dialogue posits a more resistant secrecy, in the form of active feminine deception, but then proceeds to represent those secrets as they are being passed on in unguarded moments. Yet this semiotic triumph over feminine knowledge is based on doubtful premises. What if women's talk, when not overheard by men—when not represented as if overheard by them—were somehow indescribably different? What if whores, as a class of seductive liars, did not stand reliably for all women? These and some related questions will continue indefinitely to threaten patriarchal mastery of the "secrets" insistently attributed to women by a long tradition.

Canonical thematics can have as their function to help preempt such disturbing questions by keeping others to the fore. In this instance they provide reassurance as to just what constitutes feminine intimacy. All sorts of private conversations can be represented as overheard in such a way that their secret content is continually known and revealed to be the same "thing." Thus, when the whores' dialogues we have discussed so far are followed by nuns' dialogues, for example, that very extension can be a confirmation of the theme. Such texts as *Vénus dans le cloître* (1682) and *Thérèse philosophe* (1748) take part in the productive consolidation, within erotic literature, of a thematics of feminine conversation-as-confession.

Vénus dans le cloître begins at the moment when Angélique enters Agnès's room, invading her privacy: "Oh Lord, Sister Angélique! Don't come into my room. I'm not fit to be seen right now" (17).[p] The novice asks what appears to be a rhetorical question: "Ought people to be caught out in the state I'm in?" (17).[q] But the context seems to call for the answer she did not expect: yes, there is a kind of thematic necessity here requiring a young woman's privacy to be invaded. Not by brutal penetration, mind, but by the most ingratiating feminine gentleness. Angélique has, as it happens, observed Agnès through the keyhole and seen her caressing herself. She could have remained in the voyeur's role, but clearly has no wish to. Her most urgent desire is to share with Agnès the secret she has witnessed, as if the sharing finally mattered more, for the pleasure it gave, than the caress, or the bodily position: "I only said that to you because I plan to say other things in confidence about myself" (22).[r] Such secrets are of the greatest erotic value, for amorous friendship means hiding nothing from the other:

> Good friends must not hide anything about themselves from one another. (17)
>
> Dissimulation has no place in a friendship as strong as ours. Let me embrace you, so that our hearts can speak to each other in the midst of our kisses. (20)
>
> You must not conceal anything from me, and I must not keep anything hidden from you. (22)[s]

[p] Ah Dieu! sœur Angélique, n'entrez pas dans ma chambre; je ne suis pas visible à présent.

[q] Faut-il surprendre les personnes dans l'état où je suis?

[r] Je ne t'ai dit cela que dans le dessein de te faire bien d'autres confidences de mon côté.

[s] Les bonnes amies ne se doivent aucunement cacher les unes aux autres.

> La dissimulation n'a point de part à des amitiés aussi fortes que la nôtre. [. . .] Permets que je t'embrasse, afin que nos cœurs se parlent l'un à l'autre au milieu de nos baisers.
>
> Tu ne me dois rien celer, et je ne dois rien avoir de caché pour toi.

Indeed, as a later dialogue confirms, *confidences* are not just a way of referring to erotic themes: they are the theme itself, the very currency of amorous exchange between women, equivalent to kisses and caresses in every way. Here is how Séraphique greets Virginie: "Alas! How long I have had to wait since our last chat to be able to spend time with you, delighting in your tender caresses and listening to your intimate secrets! Come here, my sweet child. Unveil your heart to me, and lavish your caresses on me" (219).[t] For Angélique, to act as teacher is to pass on her most secret principles, no doubt, but it is, most dramatically, to reveal her private habits: "I want to share my most secret habits with you, and give a perfect idea of the conduct of a well-behaved nun" (20).[u]

As Agnès responds to these seductive revelations, she can only do so in kind. Having appeared momentarily as a victim of Angélique, she now becomes a kind of penitent, entering with her older sister into the profound complicity of a confessional relationship: "not only shall I teach you what you wish to know about me, but I shall even take real pleasure in passing on to you my most secret thoughts and actions. This will be a general confession" (24).[v] Such talk is thoroughly liturgical, but it has none of the ceremonious quality of a ritually applied *ars erotica:* its erotic quality lies in the fact that these are Agnès's innermost thoughts and deeds, the deepest (sexual) secrets dwelling at the heart of a general confession. At this point, the confession of pleasure and the pleasure of confession would appear to be identical. Confession is not the exteriorization of an inner monologue, but a reflexive exchange between the two: it is a form of dialogic play.

Nuns can only dream of what it would be like to be a sanctified confessor, having in one's charge the most delightful young female penitents: "As for me, I think I should find that occupation a rather enjoyable one, provided I was allowed to choose my own penitents. I should take pleasure in listening to them, and my imagination would be deeply impressed by the stories they told of their indiscretions. That could only lead to great satisfaction on my part" (122–123).[w]

[t] Hélas! qu'il me tardait, depuis notre dernière entrevue, de te joindre à souhait pour jouir de tes tendres embrassements et recevoir tes intimes confidences! Viens çà, ma belle enfant, me dévoiler ton cœur, et me prodiguer toutes tes caresses.

[u] Je veux te faire part de mes plus secrètes habitudes, et te donner une idée parfaite de la conduite d'une sage religieuse.

[v] non seulement je vous apprendrai ce que vous souhaitez savoir de moi, mais même je veux me faire un sensible plaisir de vous communiquer jusqu'à mes plus secrètes pensées et actions. Ce sera une confession générale.

[w] Pour moi, je trouverais, ce me semble, cette occupation assez divertissante, pourvu qu'il me fût permis de faire le choix de mes pénitentes: je prendrais plaisir à les entendre,

Within the church hierarchy as it stands, their role is, of course, quite other, and Angélique provides Agnès with advice about what to say in formal confession so as to protect her secrets and avoid difficulties with the father confessor (118–20). Nanna herself could not have offered a more apposite lesson in the art of deception.

Now the result of this arrangement is that there are two parallel rites of confession: a truly erotic one, between the women, and a defensive one, for dealing with the church hierarchy. There are, however, within the world of *Vénus dans le cloître,* as we noted earlier, men who know all there is to know about pleasure. They are not just masters of eroticism, but ipso facto master confessors. Of the two priests with whom Agnès has had sexual relations, Angélique says: "They are perfectly well informed about all the sweetest and most appealing ways of those who know how to make love passionately" (140).[x] To be properly equipped to hear confession, they must know all the *manières* of making love, all the figures of Venus, all the *scientia sexualis,* "for they are clearly required, as confessors, to have a perfect knowledge of evil, in order to identify it with certainty" (140–41).[y] These males have the world of feminine eroticism within their full control precisely because they are able to discern its most intimate secrets through the art of confession. Angélique has her nasty surprise, just as Maddalena did, when she fears her dialogue with Agnès has been overheard: "Oh heavens! I'm in despair! I'm sure we have been overheard because I just heard someone up on the roof" (110).[z] Yet the function of a truly "general" confession should be to take away such surprises, for the role of the master is to know in advance all the possible secrets, such that none can be kept from him. In general confession, as in the courtesans' dialogue, the *confidences* are always already overheard.

Unlike the texts discussed so far in this chapter, *Thérèse philosophe* is not a simple dialogue, or set of dialogues. It is, above all, a lengthy written *confidence* tenderly addressed by the heroine to her *cher comte.* Thérèse writes, as we can infer from the first paragraph, in response to a series of questions. The broadest one is a call for a general

---

et mon imagination serait vivement frappée par le récit qu'elles feraient de leurs sottises: ce qui ne pourrait être sans une grande satisfaction de mon côté.

[x] Ils sont parfaitement instruits de toutes les manières les plus douces et les plus engageantes de ceux qui savent passionnément aimer.

[y] car il est certain qu'ayant la direction des âmes, ils doivent avoir une parfaite connaissance tant du bien que du mal, pour en faire un juste discernement.

[z] Ah! ciel! je suis au désespoir! Assurément on nous a écoutées, car je viens d'entendre quelqu'un sur les montées.

autobiography: "Really, Sir, do you seriously want me to write my story?" (I, 1).[a] Immediately following this, and effectively included within it, are other questions, other desires expressed by her (now silent) interlocutor. They involve the stories of two couples, each composed of a priest and a woman: "You want me to relate the mystical scenes of Mademoiselle Eradice with the Very Reverend Abbé Dirrag, and inform you about the adventures of Madame C . . . with Abbé T . . . " (I, 1–2).[b] There is every indication that the practice of confession will be a key erotic theme of the forthcoming confidential narration. The reader is entitled to expect, indeed, that the stories of the two couples will be closely bound in with Thérèse's own story. The count, and anyone else who might occupy the inscribed reading position, can thus expect to learn the details of the heroine's erotic development: "No, you will never have to put up with a refusal on the part of your loving Thérèse: you will see into the recesses of her heart from the time of her earliest childhood; her soul will develop in full through the details of the small adventures that have led her step by step, as if in spite of herself, to the height of sensual pleasure" (I, 3).[c] This is what Thérèse has in common with the whores Nanna and Maddalena: the story of her encounter with other characters is by necessity the story of her own sexuality. Adventure, for the whores of narrative, is always a form of intimacy, and first-person narration always a form of confession.

Of the confessional couples whose story is promised by Thérèse, the more spectacularly scandalous is also, in a sense, the more straightforward. Alluding to the notorious Girard-Cadière affair, and using transparently anagrammatic names, Thérèse recounts the exploitation by an unscrupulous priest of a young woman's (problematic) innocence. Thérèse is doubly qualified to tell the tale: not only was she a close friend of Eradice, but she was actually invited by Eradice (I, 35) to witness the holy rites that led to such a state of ecstasy. Thérèse's narrative proceeds thus from shared *confidence* to descriptive voyeurism. As a fellow half-innocent of Eradice, she did not exactly recognize the confession scene at the time as sexual intercourse, although her

[a] Quoi, Monsieur, sérieusement vous voulez que j'écrive mon Histoire?

[b] Vous désirez que je vous rende compte des scènes mystiques de Mademoiselle Eradice avec le très-révérend Père Dirrag; que je vous informe des aventures de Madame C. . . avec l'Abbé T. . .

[c] Non, vous n'essuyerez jamais un refus de votre tendre Thérèse: vous verrez tous les replis de son cœur dès la plus tendre enfance; son âme toute entière va se développer dans les détails des petites aventures qui l'ont conduite, comme malgré elle, pas à pas, au comble de la volupté.

mature understanding frames it retrospectively, while her narration makes it available in lurid detail both to the *cher comte* and to the reader. What is demonstrated to all is that the rite of confession can be the theater for activity of the most lascivious kind. Furthermore, the libidinal dynamics of confession, for Eradice, seem to be such that she can only be freed of her bond to Dirrag by finding another confessor to play the same role. She discovers the erotic secret at the heart of her mystical ecstasy when a "lascivious monk" renews and extends the experience, adding a more varied, more explicit series of lessons (I, 67). By a kind of thematic short-circuit, the intercourse of confession, for Eradice, seems to have become compulsively genital.

More circuitous—and more canonically so—would appear to be the relations of the other couple, Mme C. . . and Abbé T. . ., for their bonds serve eventually to bind the heroine herself in a more enduring fashion than with Eradice and Dirrag. Having been exposed, at least in theory, to the disturbingly unorthodox influence of Dirrag (I, 66–67), Thérèse appears to be in need of some other spiritual tutelage and is actually ordered by her mother to take Mme C. . . as a guide. But just what kind of a guide is Mme C. . .? "Alas! The poor woman hardly suspected what kind of lesson I was to receive from that lady, who happened to enjoy a fine reputation" (I, 75).[d] Has the worthy mother not stumbled unwittingly into the old practice of *ars erotica,* by delivering the daughter into the hands of an older woman who will now proceed to instruct her in the art of pleasure? Of course she has, for the fatality of erotic literature seems to be that libertine mothers can do that sort of thing on purpose, or virtuous ones by mistake, without in either case disturbing a predictable course of events. Yet Mme C. . . 's role is enriched here, beyond what we might expect, by the thematics of confession. Her first private talk with Thérèse takes place in a "charming little cabinet beside the sea" (I, 78). There the two begin by discussing Thérèse's religious practices and the possible influence on them of Père Dirrag. In particular, Mme C. . . asks about the appearance of (unorthodox) stigmata: "Come, my dear," she says. "Don't hide anything from me. Explain to me how and when these wounds appeared. You must be assured that I shall not betray your trust" (I, 78–79).[e] The older woman is intervening here, rather in the manner of Angélique in *Vénus dans le cloître,* between the young woman

[d] Hélas! la pauvre femme ne soupçonnait guère la nature des leçons que je devais recevoir de cette Dame, qui jouissait en effet de la plus haute réputation.

[e] Allons, ma chère petite, dit-elle, ne me cachez rien: expliquez-moi de quelle manière et quand ces plaies ont paru: vous devez être assurée que je n'abuserai pas de votre confiance.

and the bad father confessor. In order to do so successfully, she uses the means available to her for learning secrets: those of feminine *confidence*. It is all done through the gently seductive play of champagne and curiosity: "While women are curious, they also love to talk. I had a little of this fault myself, and besides a few glasses of wine left me feeling rather flushed. I had been suffering a great deal, and this was more than I needed to make me tell all" (I, 79).[f]

Yet this exchange is not a decisive moment of truth, and certainly not a triumph of female over male. It simply leads Mme C. . ., the next day, to refer Thérèse to a specialist, in the form of her own confessor, Abbé T. . . : " 'What you confided to me yesterday,' she said, 'is of greater moment than you think. I felt I should tell Monsieur T. . . about it, and he is presently waiting for you in his confessional. I insist that you go and see him there, and that you repeat word for word what you said to me' " (I, 87).[g] In the name of feminine intimacy, the young woman is sent to a good father confessor. What makes Abbé T. . . so good, exactly? In the first place, it is no doubt his gentleness and tolerance (see I, 92–93). In the second, as Thérèse eventually finds out, he is Mme C. . . 's erotic tutor, her kindly, all-knowing master in the art of love. He lends her books such as *Portier des Chartreux,* discussing them with her afterward (I, 130). He is quite simply her lover, as Thérèse discovers when she overhears an intimate exchange between them (I, 100). It follows naturally enough, then, that the teacherly chain should lead Abbé T. . . to provide some erotic instruction to Thérèse herself, since he is the true master. Mme C. . ., who occupies the place of the female instructor with the mother's unconscious complicity, accepts in turn a form of complicity in the erotic relationship between father confessor and young woman: "Out of the goodness of your heart or just to please Thérèse, you are the kind of man who would give a short lesson in voluptuousness, a friendly little intervention that, according to you, would make no difference to me. Go ahead then, dear Abbé, I gladly give my consent" (I, 106–7).[h] This embedding of *confidence* and confession—this bed-

[f] Si les femmes sont curieuses, les femmes aiment aussi à parler: j'avais un peu de ce dernier défaut; d'ailleurs quelques verres de vin de champagne m'avaient chauffé la tête, je souffrais beaucoup, il n'en fallait pas tant pour me déterminer à tout dire.

[g] Ce que vous m'avez confié hier, me dit-elle, est de plus grande conséquence que vous ne pensez. J'ai cru devoir en parler à Monsieur T. . . qui vous attend actuellement à son confessionnal. J'exige de vous que vous alliez le trouver, et que vous lui répétiez mot à mot tout ce que vous m'avez dit.

[h] Par bon cœur ou pour faire plaisir à Thérèse, vous seriez homme à lui donner une petite leçon de volupté, un petit clistère amiable, qui, selon vous, ne me ferait ni bien ni mal. Va, mon cher abbé, continua-t-elle, j'y consens avec joie.

ding down together of the female and male instructors—represents a kind of marriage of the feminine *ars erotica* tradition with the theme of patriarchal confession. As long as we do not forget that these confessions are being passed on in Thérèse's narrative to the count, and to any other who may be listening in: "Remember at least [says the authoritative Abbé T. . .] that everything said in the tribunal of penitence must be as sacred for the penitent as it is for the confessor, and that it is a dreadful sin to reveal any aspect of it to anyone" (I, 93).[i] But if Thérèse does remember this sacred law, she does so only in order to violate it quite systematically during her narration. Just as every *confidence* is likely to become a confession to the ear of the father confessor, so every confession can become a *confidence* on the lips of the playful sister.

Thérèse's narrative does not stop at this elaboration of the *confidence*-confession theme: it moves on to something else. Despite the firm promise of an elaborate initiation for Thérèse, she finds herself whisked away by her mother, who then dies and leaves her without support—without mothers, *confidantes,* or confessors. She has a degree of formal instruction, including the erotic kind, but now finds herself thrown into the domain of the picaresque, and dangerously lacking in worldly wisdom: "There I was then in the middle of Paris, left to myself, without relatives, without friends, pretty, so I had been told, having been taught many things, but without any knowledge of the ways of the world" (I, 161).[j] Will she be condemned to learn only by cruel experience, without the guidance of teachers? In the event, she meets with Bois-Laurier, a former prostitute now acting discreetly as a procuress. This woman draws Thérèse, by feminine complicity, into recounting her story: "Giving in to my agitation, I related to her what I had seen of Abbé Dirrag and Mademoiselle Eradice, and the lessons I had been given on that subject by Abbé T. . . and Madame C. . . One thing led to another, and that cunning Bois-Laurier woman managed to draw my whole story from me" (I, 180).[k] Bois-Laurier is a skilled confessor, for she actually inveigles Thérèse into an exchange

[i] Souvenez-vous au moins que tout ce qui se dit dans le tribunal de la pénitence, doit être aussi sacré pour le pénitent que pour son confesseur, et que c'est un péché énorme que d'en révéler la moindre circonstance à personne.

[j] Me voilà donc au milieu de Paris, livrée à moi-même, sans parents, sans amis, jolie, à ce qu'on me disait, instruite à bien des égards, mais sans connaissance des usages du monde.

[k] Emportée par mon agitation, je lui contai ensuite ce que j'avais vu du Père Dirrag et de Madamoiselle Eradice, les leçons que j'avais reçues à ce sujet de Monsieur l'abbé T. et de Madame C. Enfin de propos en propos, la rusée Bois-Laurier sut tirer de moi toute mon histoire.

of stories, and thence into a lesson on whores' seductive ruses. "I owe you a secret for each of yours," she says, "and a lesson for each lesson" (I, 181).[l] Through the play of confidential exchange, Thérèse now finds herself embroiled in a full-scale courtesans' dialogue, positioned as a whore by the dynamics of intimacy. It is almost as if *Thérèse philosophe* were committed overall to displaying not the full range of positions, but the full set of thematic variations on eroticism that we have identified so far. Formal instruction, intimate conversation, and religious confession are bound together as mutually supportive and approximately equivalent ways of exchanging sexuality as knowledge.

One literary text that Foucault mentions, in his *Histoire de la sexualité* is *Les Bijoux indiscrets* (1748). He goes so far as to suggest that Diderot's text is emblematic of a modern discourse about sexuality: "What is this series of studies about?" he says of his own work. "Transcribing into history the fable of *Les Bijoux indiscrets*" (101).[m] What allows Diderot's fable to stand for something quite general, says Foucault, is "(the) sex that speaks" (101):[n] the articulation of sexuality and speech in the production of truth as avowal. When the sultan Mangogul, in Diderot's story, receives a magic ring from the genie Cucufa, he is able to provoke immediate feminine confession of the most voluble kind. By pointing the ring at a particular woman, he compels her *bijou* to recount its organic history, evoking its experiences more or less in narrative order. Women have never been known to tell the truth about themselves, says the genie at the outset: "why expect women to confess their adventures? They never have done and never will" (8).[o] He does not seem to know—presumably for the lack of canonical reading—that women can be drawn into revealing their secrets or their conversations overheard. Mangogul does not know this either, for he now takes to himself the most imperious power over the whore's rhetoric: the power to compel vaginal speech. The net effect of his magic device is, more than anything, comic embarrassment. There is no subtle insinuation, no play of conversational intimacy. Neither the art of the Father confessor nor the ruses of women count for anything here. Sexual truth is manifested instantly, poured forth as unrestrained monologue—blurted out rather than simply overheard. Mangogul can move in imperial triumph through the spaces of feminine intimacy, but the

[l] Je te dois confidence pour confidence, leçon pour leçon.

[m] Ce dont il s'agit dans cette série d'études? Transcrire en histoire la fable des *Bijoux indiscrets*.

[n] le sexe qui parle

[o] vouloir que des femmes confessent leurs aventures, cela n'a jamais été et ne sera jamais.

very ease with which he does so makes for an impoverishment of the confession theme. Eventually, even the sultan himself comes to admit that the whole thing is too repetitive. This male's trick overshoots the mark because it is too clever (or too fantastic). When the man has absolute and immediate power over feminine sexuality, confession no longer functions as discursive intercourse.

Another text by Diderot, *La Religieuse* (1760), while decidedly less ribald, is more closely aligned with such canonical erotic works as *Vénus dans le cloître,* whose subtitle was *La Religieuse en chemise.*[6] It might be said, in fact, that *La Religieuse* establishes a form of moral seriousness precisely by going to the verge of confessional eroticism, then pulling back from it in a polemical affirmation of virtue. The young nun has to deal with a seductive mother superior who seeks to turn their ostensibly spiritual dialogue into a more sensual one, directing confessorial questions toward her charge's secret pleasures. The young heroine, who recounts this, so to speak, through a veil of innocence, is unable and unwilling to enter into such *confidences.* Invited to speak of her "excitement," or her "senses," she declares that she does not know "the language of the senses."[7] [p] Unlike Pippa, Ottavia, or Agnès, the young Suzanne has none of the familiar eagerness to learn that would allow the older woman to retrieve the delights of classical erotic instruction: "No, dear Mother, no. I know nothing, and I would rather not know than acquire knowledge that might make me more unfortunate than I am at present. I have no desires and no wish at all to seek desires that I could not satisfy" (351).[q] The old game may be there, ready to begin, but Suzanne has no desire to play—not even a desire for desire.

Having failed thus in an attempt at seduction, the mother superior tries to block any formal religious confession on Suzanne's part, trivializing as she does so what has passed between them: "'Well,' she said, 'I am your superior, you owe me obedience, and I order you not to speak to him [the father confessor] of those indiscretions. It is of no use for you to go to confession if you have only trifles to tell him'" (365).[r] When required to confess, and yet enjoined by the mother not to speak of their exchange, Suzanne is quite unable to do what

[p] trouble/sens/le langage des sens

[q] Non, chère mère, non. Je ne sais rien; et j'aime mieux ne rien savoir, que d'acquérir des connaissances qui me rendraient peut-être plus à plaindre que je ne le suis. Je n'ai point de désirs, et je n'en veux point chercher que je ne pourrais satisfaire.

[r] Eh bien! me dit-elle, je suis votre supérieure, vous me devez obéissance, et je vous ordonne de ne lui point parler de ces sottises. Il est inutile que vous alliez à confesse, si vous n'avez que des bagatelles à lui dire.

Angélique and Agnès presumably did with ease: "I confessed, then fell silent; but the confessor asked questions, and I hid nothing" (367).[s] The father confessor moves in with all his pastoral skill, and all his sexual knowledge: "He questioned me on a thousand strange things, which are still incomprehensible to me even as I recall them now" (367).[t] Having discovered the secret—which is, predictably for him and for readers in the tradition, that of sexual desire between women—he gives Suzanne strict orders to avoid all intimacy with the superior. " 'But Father,' I said to him, 'she is my superior; she can come into my room, or call me to hers, whenever she wishes' " (367).[u] This may be true—the young woman's privacy is there to be entered, as it was for Agnès—but her strict religious duty, made clear by the confessor, is to avoid the play of feminine *confidence.* The only hope of relief, given this severe constraint, is for some kind of spiritual intimacy, some sharing of secrets that would not be tainted by feminine seduction. This is provided by a second confessor—a kind one, as opposed to the earlier, severe one—who moves with Suzanne from the confessional to the *parloir.* Between them, there is a pleasurable form of confidential conversation: "He finished confiding in me about his life, and I confided in him. There were ever so many circumstances that made for points of contact and resemblance between us" (379).[v] The mirror image of two lives and two souls is thus seen, for once, as something binding a man to a woman: "the story of moments in his life was my story; the story of his feelings was the story of mine; the story of his soul was the story of my own" (379).[w] During this short interlude in Suzanne's pathetic story, she seems to find a passing synthesis of confession and conversation, of a virtuous kind uncharacteristic of erotic literature. Hounded as she is by bad mothers and bad fathers, she finds briefly a father who is transformed into a brother.

It could be said, in summary of my efforts to trace a shifting thematics of the erotic, that confession-as-conversation tended, from Renaissance times until the eighteenth century, to provide a more dynamic and more apparently spontaneous representation of sexuality than

[s] Je me confessai, et je me tus; mais le directeur m'interrogea, et je ne dissimulai rien.

[t] Il me fit mille demandes singulières, auxquelles je ne comprends rien encore à présent que je me les rappelle.

[u] Mais, mon père, lui dis-je, c'est ma supérieure; elle peut entrer chez moi, m'appeler chez elle quand il lui plaît.

[v] Il acheva de me confier de sa vie, moi de la mienne, une infinité de circonstances qui formaient entre lui et moi autant de points de contact et de ressemblance.

[w] l'histoire de ses moments, c'était l'histoire des miens; l'histoire de ses sentiments, c'était l'histoire des miens; l'histoire de son âme, c'était l'histoire de la mienne.

the aging tradition of *ars erotica*. This shift, as I have tried to show, was anything but a revolution: it was simply a slow reworking of the thematic economy, a continual adjustment of that which was taken as known. There are signs, however, as we have just seen in examining the two texts by Diderot, that confession itself, and notably the feminine dialogue subgenre in which it took shape, was tending by the mid-eighteenth century to lose some of its force. *Tableaux des mœurs du temps* (1750), attributed to Crébillon fils, begins with a series of three dialogues that can be read as a set of variations on feminine intimacy. In the first, a young woman on the eve of marriage, but still in a convent, is talking to the mother superior. In the second, she is talking to the *gouvernante,* who acts as a kind of lay confessor, and in the third to her mother. Subsequently, the text moves on to other things—as if one of the marks of an old theme were precisely that it might serve to establish canonical legitimacy at the outset, and then fade from view.

The written *confidence,* or the marking of first-person narration as confidential, does tend to become an identifiable subgenre. We saw it in *Thérèse philosophe,* and it is also present in such later texts as *La Secte des anandrynes* (1789) and *Le Rideau levé, ou l'Education de Laure* (1786). The heroine of *La Secte des anandrynes,* Mlle Sapho, at the time when she was being initiated into ritual lesbianism, promised solemnly never to betray the secrets of this cult: "with her hands on me, I made an oath that I would give up intercourse with others and reveal nothing of the mysteries of that assembly."[8] [x] The letters we read amount, then, to a sustained breach of this confidence and draw much of their erotic interest from that very fact. In *Le Rideau levé,* the fiction of interception is itself quite elaborate. The main body of the text is a written *confidence* sent by one woman to another. What makes it available to be read is that a third woman has stolen it and sent it to a male friend, saying, "It is a trifle produced by the fair hand of one belonging to my sex; and it is a chatty piece of writing meant to while away the hours in a cloister."[9] [y] The kind of "chat" involved here is partly a recollection of erotic play between the two women. Laure reminds the younger Eugénie of "ta curiosité, tes désirs," and recounts the erotic demonstration that passed between them (440–41). Embedded within the written *confidence* is reference to confidential dialogue, but girlish intercourse is dealt with in a few pages. Whatever constitutes

[x] Je prêtai entre ses mains le serment de renoncer au commerce et de rien révéler des mystères de l'assemblée.

[y] C'est une bagatelle sortie d'une jolie main de mon sexe: et c'est un délassement badin adressé dans un cloître.

"education" for Laure is patently more than cloistered feminine instruction.

A thoroughly urbane and secular version of confidence-as-confession occurs in a noticeably later text, *Entre chien et loup* (1807), by Choiseul-Meuse. *Entre chien et loup* is presented as a series of twilight stories, told by mature women to one another. There is a time of day, says the narrator, suited to *confidences* and to discreet signs of love. The time is "between sunset and nightfall":[z] "Everyone knows that this hour is suited to confiding secrets and to love; even the most severe mothers let themselves go somewhat and unblushingly relate little events from their youth, things they would not have dared to admit in the light of midday. Young people gently pressed each other's hands, and slipped each other love letters."[10 a] The role of the narration is not, of course, to direct a brutal spotlight onto these little events: "let us not reveal what the twilight has hidden so well" (I, 3).[b] A sensitive narrator may simply find the propitious time, and the appropriate half-light, for the communication of erotic truth. In the story, eight women are alone together in a country house, while their husbands are away hunting for a week. Having had a certain amount to drink, they settle down in the salon, delighting phatically in their intimacy: "we are in the country, all women, all friends" (I, 14).[c] The proper thing to do at this time, for women looking back on the day and on their lives, is to tell stories of a confessional kind: "but I would wager that each of us had some little sin on her conscience. So let each tell her story in turn, with utter frankness . . . " (I, 15).[d] Instead of the whores' *giornate,* there will be a series of pleasant *soirées:* eight in number, occupying a whole French week. The first story, told by Mme de Marsan, recounts in part her intimacy in a convent, while still a girl, with one of her girl companions (I, 19), but does not dwell on it, for the point of her story is her relationship with the companion's brother (I, 20–22). The stories told by the other women deal with rather different events, but what they have in common is the same tone, or rather the same hue. Youth lies far behind for Mme de Marsan and her companions: they can only look back with quiet indulgence on

[z] entre chien et loup

[a] Et qui ne sait pas combien cette heure est favorable à la confidence et aux amours; les mamans les plus sévères, s'oubliant un peu, racontaient sans rougir de petits événements de leur jeunesse, qu'elles n'eussent pas avoués en plein midi, les jeunes gens se pressaient doucement la main, ou se glissaient un billet doux.

[b] ne révélons pas ce que Chien et Loup a si bien caché.

[c] nous sommes à la campagne, toutes femmes, toutes amies.

[d] mais je gagerais que chacune de nous a bien quelque petit péché sur la conscience, et bien racontons-nous, chacune à notre tour, avec une entière franchise. . .

the erotic eagerness that led to their little sins. The true object of their *confidence,* the basis of their sharing, is a warmly distant recollection. It is as if Choiseul-Meuse's text, in thematizing maturity, sought to deal reflexively with the aging of our theme. Feminine intimacy as the shared avowal of desires seems to have become an occasion of quiet indulgence rather than a theater of urgent passion.

Chapter 3

Number and Singularity

At one point in the *Ragionamenti,* Nanna describes an orgy, characterizing it as a kind of ensemble performance of pleasure. According to her story, there were eight people present, and their eight sighs, emanating from the liver, lungs, heart, and soul of each, produced a blast of such force that it could have blown out eight torches. On hearing this, Antonia interrupts the telling of the tale, not with a sigh of her own, but with a humdrum, though eminently reasonable, question: "How were you able to count the eight sighs?" (I, 59).[a] How, indeed? What kind of arithmetical awareness could possibly be maintained in the midst of all this erotic excitement, even by a close observer? Yet Antonia's kind of psychological concern is not allowed to tell against the force of Nanna's story: it is brushed aside with the remark that Antonia is too fussy (I, 59). Why is the interruption not more embarrassing, not to say thoroughly disabling? Why is Nanna able to continue without any loss of narratorial authority? How can she be so confident about the number? The answer, I suggest—the solid basis of confidence—lies in the tradition of erotic literature. To Antonia's rather modern question, whenever it might be asked, there is a preemptive classical answer, and it is that the number given here is properly thematic. Thematic in a fully Gadamerian sense, in that it is always already known, and does not need to be arrived at by a local act of counting. My claim is that number, in classical erotic literature, is not an epiphenomenon of description: it is bound in with tradition, as a vehicle or a locus of authority.

[a] Comment as-tu pu compter les huit soupirs?

If my hypothesis is correct, the number eight, in the *Ragionamenti* and elsewhere, is not produced or reached by counting: it is a kind of given. There need be no psychological fiction, no phenomenology of counting as subjective process, since the number is canonically thematic. Not that the number eight recurs unvaryingly: that would be more like the conservatism characterized by Gadamer as defying the life of tradition. Rather, there is a set of numbers that, even as they change, appear to maintain many of the same arithmetical properties. They display a kind of thematic insistence, an open-ended stability. David Foxon observes both the change and the continuity, noting that Aretino's sixteen positions were disseminated and elaborated throughout the following centuries as sets of twenty-four or thirty-six. "Where did it all begin?" asks the critic:

> There is no completely satisfactory explanation for the numbers involved: Giulio Romano's original sixteen and the twenty-four and the thirty-six of the seventeenth and eighteenth centuries. It is tempting to associate them with the fact that the normal small format of the books they illustrated changed from 8° to 12° between these times. R. H. van Gulik [. . .] relates that the albums of erotic prints which were produced in China between 1570 and 1640 most commonly showed twenty-four postures; twenty, thirty, and thirty-six are also found. It is by no means impossible that such albums could have found their way to Europe, but the number of months makes good round figures in East or West.[1]

Foxon's search for an origin is brave but disheartened from the outset: the answer, for him, could lie anywhere between the technical exigencies of formatting and the secrets of a mystic Orient. All that can be recognized with certainty are these "good round figures." My procedure here, in keeping with that followed earlier, will be to take the problem not as a clue, but as a kind of vade mecum. Valuing the guide rather than the destination, we can hold to these numbers as a theme. Giving up on the search for an explanatory origin, we can observe their elaboration, their consolidation—and indeed their eventual devaluation.

Through the play of classical reference, we have already become familiar with the twelve positions of the *dodecatechnon,* as well as with the sixteen of Aretino. By persistent association, we may even have learned to regard these numbers (3 × 4 and 4 × 4) as roughly equivalent—not so much for their "roundness" as for other geometrical qualities. They seem to stand squarely for an orderly paradigm. For *ars erotica,* each position in the set must have its own recognizable shape, as we know, but the function of numbers is to give shape to the set as such. In a sense, then, the numbers twelve and sixteen (and their later variants) can be seen as equivalent to the thematic names "Elephantis" and "Aretino."[2] Not only do they transmit the canonical theme: they describe its conformation, invoking, if not actually rehearsing, a particular thematic order.

It is no doubt for this transcendent reason, and not for some fictively subjective one, that Aretino's Nanna can hear eight sighs without counting them. Are the eight sighs distinctly recognizable as elements of the erotic chorus? That is not the point, and it is unlikely to trouble a narrator as fast and loose as Nanna. She knows by a habit proper to classical erotic literature that there are not going to be seven or nine. And when one is confident of the shape of events, fussiness has no place. As Nanna says to Pippa on another occasion: "if you are not an algebrist, you can calculate it approximately" (III, 39).[b] There is no need for any mystical calculation, or even any liturgical counting. We all know that the figures will come out more or less the same: eight, or twelve, or sixteen.

So it is that, paradoxically, a certain looseness with number can become integrated into the dynamics of numerical stability. The *Dialogua tra Maddalena e Giulia,* for example, is said by Pierre Bayle in his dictionary (under the entry "Pierre Arétin") to contain thirty-five *congiugamenti,* while Forberg also notes that the so-called *La Puttana errante* contains "up to thirty-five ways of making love"[3] [c] The two editions of the dialogue that I have been able to consult, however, list in one case thirty-six positions, and in the other, thirty-two. In order to maintain classically geometrical numbers, they appear in fact to fudge the count. One of them has Giulia conclude, after describing position number thirty-six: "I shall not talk of the other ways of doing it, whether between the thighs, between the tits, or under the armpits."[4] [d] In other words, there are thirty-six, plus a few indeterminate leftovers. The other edition of the dialogue, also an early French translation, has thirty-two, maintaining its proper shape by including several different positions under the final number.[5] The voice of Nanna can still be heard: "you can calculate it approximately."

By a now familiar feature of canonical erotic texts, classical number seems to persist in authority beyond the time of its greatest vitality, and this very looseness of counting allows it to do so. Nogaret's *L'Arétin*

[b] si tu n'es pas algébriste, tu calculeras par à peu près.

[c] jusqu'à trente-cinq manières de faire l'amour

[d] Je ne parle pas des autres manières de le faire, soit entre les cuisses, entre les tétons ou sous les aisselles.

français (1787) has seventeen figures, but does not actually attach a number to each, perhaps in the expectation that readers will not notice the discrepancy.[6] *Les Quarante Manières de foutre* (c. 1790) maintains geometricality, in turn, by dint of loose counting: there are in fact forty-one *manières* described in the text.[7] Yet how much more telling is the play of reference when the number is nicely square! Restif writes of "la fouterie ordinaire": "It is the best of the Forty ways!"[8] [e] Only foursquare numbers deserve to be spelled with capital letters. The same ever-shifting stability, the same confidence and looseness, appear in a still later text, *Les Dames de maison et les filles d'amour* (c. 1830), where the skills learned by young whores are described as "fucking in forty ways, according to Aretino."[9] [f] As long as geometrical numbers hold their shape, they are equivalent to the name Aretino. Bandied about or fiddled with, they maintain the function of approximate canonical reference.

In the course of such continual adjustment, the number of positions is subject to a kind of historical inflation. New arithmetical heights are reached in *Les Quarante Manières de foutre,* which serves as a benchmark for Restif, but does not become a secularly enduring standard. As if the very increase in number corresponded to a progressive loss of canonical value, one finds in the late eighteenth and early nineteenth centuries an exponential growth that effectively ruins the classical paradigm. The heroine of *Mon Noviciat, ou les Joies de Lolotte* (1792) finds herself in a space that bears all the marks of traditional iconographic instruction: "More than two hundred little black frames, very simple ones, displayed against a background of green wallpaper everything that is known about fucking, and all kinds of oddities."[10] [g] Reaching and passing the number two hundred might well be seen as progress, the cumulative achievement of ongoing erotic enlightenment, but only at the expense of a classically thematic understanding of pleasure. What do the two hundred illustrations say to the female pupil? They act as a *general* invitation to copulate: "In a word, everything in this den of lubricity said to people: 'Go ahead and fuck!'" (201).[h] Far from proposing a disciplinary range, as Elephantis or even Aretino did, the little black frames melt together into one urgent imperative, their vast array being summed up in the singular force of one verb, one erotic action.

[e] C'est la meilleure manière des Quarante!

[f] foutre de quarante manières, d'après l'Arétin

[g] Plus de deux cents petits cadres noirs, très simples, étalaient sur un fond de papier vert tout ce qu'il y a de connu en fait de fouterie et de toutes sortes de caprices.

[h] En un mot, tout dans ce repaire de lubricité disait aux gens: "Foutez donc!"

In that sense, very large numbers—greater, say, than thirty-six or forty—would appear to be part of a quite different thematic economy. *Ars erotica* begins with a small, square number, applying, maintaining, and even expanding it in an orderly way. The kind of erotic profusion found in Nerciat's texts and others of the same period seems to begin (and end) with a notion of singular pleasure able to be expanded indefinitely into vast numbers, yet still reducible to a single verb. Indeed, the title of *Les Quarante Manières de foutre,* examined closely, reveals the same undoing of classical number. Aretino and his successors spoke of modi, *postures, façons* or *manières* without attaching a verbal complement. That they should have done so was not merely a matter of politeness, for to say that the sixteen modi are forms of the same action is effectively to change their thematic nature. In the *ars erotica* tradition, the theme *is* the set of variations, but Nerciat's contemporaries seem to take *foutre* "itself" as the underlying theme, and regard the set of positions as a potentially infinite set of variations on it.

Variation now appears as a process, and an erotically driven one at that. The concern is not with number as such, but with plurality, and with multiplication. Nogaret's *L'Arétin français* expresses just this erotic ambition, albeit in it most modest form:

> To the greatest of pleasures give yourself to the full:
> Let us caress each other in more than one fashion. (21)[i]

By a kind of upward spiral of desire, the greatest pleasure may lie precisely in enjoying more than one mode of pleasure: plurality is of erotic value in itself. Sade, the compulsive arithmetician and the arithmetician of compulsion, has his erotic heroes talk of doubling their pleasures. Let us put two women side by side, says Rodin in *La Nouvelle Justine* (1797): "that will double the sum of our pleasures."[11] [j] In much the same way, although with less precision, *Les Quarante Manières de foutre* talks of "reproducing pleasure, which is basically always the same, in a thousand different forms" (43).[k] "Reproduction" here, far from being biological, is what mathematicians call algorithmic, for *doubler* is likely to be followed by *redoubler* (see, e.g., Sade, *Histoire de Juliette, Oeuvres completes,* VIII, 177). By beginning with the simplest pleasure, one can repeat indefinitely the operation of

[i] Au plus grand des plaisirs livre-toi toute entière:
Caressons-nous de plus d'une manière.

[j] cela doublera la somme de nos jouissances.

[k] reproduire le plaisir, au fond toujours le même, sous mille formes différentes

doubling, thereby producing a dizzying multiplication. When Sade's Juliette defines wisdom as the desire to "double the sum of her pleasures" (*La Nouvelle Justine,* VI, 34),[l] she utters a rallying cry for those who seek the infinitely erotic.

For lovers of the infinite, the practice of finite number can appear as the very antithesis of passionate multiplication—although Sade, as we shall observe later, is a fascinating exception. *Ars erotica* might then be seen, in opposition to the classics, as a calculating division of pleasure. Sade's contemporary and fellow prisoner Mirabeau, in his *Erotika biblion* (1783), pays studious attention to ancient and exotic works that, for us, bear many of the marks of *ars erotica,* yet he cannot conceal his distaste at their unspontaneous practice of number. Of a Turkish erotic poem, he writes:

> I shall not try to translate these lines into French; they were not written by a poet. That arithmetical calculation, those thirty qualities solemnly cut up into threes would chill anyone's enthusiasm. One does not calculate the charms one adores; one grows drunk on them, one catches fire, one covers them with kisses; only then is one attractive. The fair woman who saw the charms that adorned her being counted on someone's fingers could only consider the one who did the calculations to be a fool, and would hardly cut a fine figure herself. There are more than thirty charms; there are more than a thousand. Can it be that someone seeing Helen naked can think so clearly? . . .[12 m]

There are not just thirty qualities in a beautiful woman, any more than there are thirty positions for making love to her! True passion will always soar beyond a thousand—that is, in effect, beyond number.

Variation, then, can be understood either as applied diversity within a closed paradigm, or as a way of going beyond previous experience, giving new forms to pleasure that remains the same in principle. Accordingly, the historical erosion of *ars erotica* can be seen in part as a shift from the first to the second, from theme-as-variations to variation-as-theme. There is in fact a slow drift from ceremony to psychology, subjecting erotic literature to an increasing concern with diversion

[l] doubler la somme de ses plaisirs

[m] Je n'essaierai point de traduire ces vers en français; ils n'ont point été faits par un poète. Ce calcul arithmétique, ces trente qualités coupées gravement trois à trois glaceraient toute verve. On ne calcule point les charmes qu'on adore; on s'enivre, on brûle, on les couvre de baisers; ce n'est qu'alors qu'on est intéressant. La belle qui verrait compter par ses doigts les attraits dont elle est ornée prendrait le calculateur pour un sot, et ferait elle-même une pauvre figure. Il y en a bien plus de trente; il y en a plus de mille. Quoi! lorsqu'on voit Hélène nue a-t-on la tête si nette? . . .

or entertainment. Rather than simply rehearsing a paradigm and advancing a number as the mark of its closure, narrators and other writerly voices tend to be expressly preoccupied with avoiding repetition, so that monotony becomes a kind of contrapuntal antitheme of erotic writing. The rather flamboyant narratorial courtesy practiced by Crébillon fils and Diderot, and indeed by so many of their contemporaries, takes on a particular thematic significance here. In exercising the art of narratorial seduction, they playfully but insistently "entertain" the possibility of readerly boredom, while even the overbearing Sade poses the problem from time to time.[13] *Les Quarante Manières de foutre* is remarkably civil in this regard: "People may complain about the monotony of the text: always putting it in the cunt, then coming! I admit that is so, but that is not the aim of all the imaginable positions. Some are for slowing down pleasure, others for speeding it up: the final outcome is the same . . . One day perhaps, if I think of it, I shall turn this into some more concrete and stylish tableaux. Meanwhile, as compensation, may you ever put it in the cunt, and come!" (34).[n] Precisely because the erotic can be summed up in one or two verbs, the specter of monotony will linger indefinitely around erotic narrative. Avoiding fatigue in *L'Académie des dames* was not a matter of tone or style, but of bodily technique. New positions allowed the participants to overcome their tiredness: "By changing position, you will whet your fading appetite, for you are languid and tired. One must add spice to voluptuousness, so that pleasure can be endlessly born of pleasure" (III, 72–74).[o] The kind of "spice" added by changing positions is what generates further desire, making it possible to begin again on a round of *volupté*. But where *volupté* becomes an action verb, to be conjugated in the imperative, there is always the possibility that a character or a "reader" will make the witheringly thematic observation "plus ça change, plus c'est la même chose."[14]

In response to this threat, so often quoted apologetically or disarmingly within erotic literature itself, one does not find, of course, an appeal to canonical oldness, for that would only compound the difficulty, but a celebration of the new. Erotic value lies in going beyond

[n] On se plaindra peut-être de la monotonie du texte: toujours enconner, décharger! j'en conviens; mais ce n'est pas aussi le but de toutes les postures imaginables; les unes sont pour ralentir, les autres pour précipiter le plaisir: le terme en est le même. . . Un jour peut-être, en y pensant, ferai-je de tout ceci des tableaux ornés d'un style plus soigné. . . En attendant, pour vous dédommager, puissiez-vous toujours enconner et foutre!

[o] En changeant de posture, tu exciteras ton appétit languissant; car tu languis, tu es fatiguée. Il faut assaisonner de la sorte la volupté, pour que de la volupté renaisse, sans fin, la volupté.

the already described, adding to the stock of established knowledge. Aretine eroticism still has a place, and still serves indeed as a kind of standard, but all that is most valuable exceeds it by an incalculable supplement of unprecedented pleasure. The notion of supplementary delights, beyond the list of positions, was invoked as early as the *Dialogua tra Maddalena e Giulia,* but there it was a matter of some diffuse quality. Something resembling a general amorous style, not able to be counted in a list: "You should know that there is an infinite number of flirtatious gestures, caresses, and kisses that go with true love, but I have not spoken of them because one cannot give a full account of them" (53).[p] From the mid-eighteenth century onward, however, there is continual reference to the actual invention of new positions, as if to account step by step for the broad inflationary trend of literary history. In *Thémidore* (1745), we find what may be the weakest form of invention, in which the young hero boasts of striking an *attitude* he had not previously encountered: "An imagination like yours, my dear Marquis, will easily be able to picture the humorous attitude in which we found ourselves. I have many ribald etchings, but none of mine copies a situation according to that taste."[15] [q] Are we to suppose that this is a genuine achievement—or merely the reflection of youthful ignorance, and a deficient collection of libertine etchings? In any case, the *cher marquis* addressed here is known to be capable of representing the new position in his imagination. Such novelty, and the new surge of desire it ought to provoke, will presumably be the very source of his readerly pleasure.

It may well be that the novelty alluded to in *Thémidore* is simply circumstantial, rather than a confident imaginative addition to the established set of figures. *Portier des Chartreux* (1741), however, leaves us in no doubt at all as to its audacity, by speaking in terms of the "discovery" of a new position. This position is taught within a monastery, in the most classical way, but it is one that has only just been given a name. Its teachers did not learn it from Elephantis or Aretino but from "nature": "Our praise of this manner of enjoying pleasures aroused the monks and sisters. They made it their duty to fuck in quatrains (that is the name we gave to the position) and we set about giving them an example. Thus the finest discoveries are due to

[p] Tu peux croire qu'il y a une infinité de badineries, de caresses et de baisers qui accompagnent le vrai amour, desquels je ne t'ai pas parlé parce que cela ne se peut tout dire.

[q] Une imagination comme la vôtre, cher Marquis, se représente aisément combien était plaisante notre attitude. J'ai beaucoup d'estampes très gaillardes; mais aucune des miennes ne copie une situation dans ce goût.

nature."[16] [r] Mirabeau, in *Ma Conversion* (1783), claims the capacity to invent new positions as a distinctive quality of his erotic writing. He is currently producing a novel whose thematic content is described, quite classically, as "subjects for etchings": "I am producing for this novel, which is absolutely new, and which, if I were a bookseller, would make my fortune, subjects for etchings that will not resemble any other and that will be, I like to think, very pretty" (*OE*, 25).[s] Later in the same text, he gives details of his inventions: "Two kinds of fucking gave special entertainment to my princess, and as I am the inventor of them, I want to describe them to you in detail" (135).[t] The postural detail is of less interest, I suggest, than the pomp that surrounds its presentation. Is it possible, asks the authorial voice, that posterity might fail to remember me for my contribution (135–36)? There really ought to be an academy created: "I therefore propose an academy, as one who lives only for the glory of my country. Each recipient must be the inventor of at least one position. [. . .] each year there will be a prize granted to the most beautiful manner of fucking, and a gold medal for the one who has used it best" (136–37).[u] Sade's Madame de Saint-Ange has actually endowed her own prize for just such a purpose,[17] and Saint-Fond in *Histoire de Juliette* uses his ministerial powers to ensure that "in this way, there will be prizes awarded to every inventor of new forms of lubricity, every author of unprincipled books, and every libertine known for taking vows in that order" (VIII, 348).[v] There is no need for an *académie des dames*, then, nor for an *école des filles*. Whether through Mirabeau's Académie française of eroticism or Sade's Ministry of the (Libertine) Interior, there is evidence of eager commitment on the part of certain writers in the late eighteenth century to the progress of positional science.

[r] Notre éloge sur cette façon de goûter les plaisirs excita les moines et les sœurs. Ils se mettent en devoir de foutre en quatrain, c'est le nom que nous donnâmes à cette posture, et nous à leur donner l'exemple. Ainsi les plus belles découvertes sont dues à la nature.

[s] Je fais pour ce roman, qui est absolument neuf, et qui, si j'étais libraire, ferait ma fortune, des sujets d'estampes qui ne ressembleront à aucunes, et seront, je m'en flatte, très jolies.

[t] Deux manières de foutreries divertissaient surtout ma princesse, et comme j'en suis l'inventeur, je veux te les détailler.

[u] Je propose donc une académie, moi qui ne respire que la gloire de ma patrie. Chaque récipiendaire doit être inventeur d'une posture au moins. [. . .] chaque année il y aura un prix accordé à la plus belle manière de foutre, et une médaille d'or pour celui qui l'aura le mieux employée.

[v] On accordera, de même, des récompenses à tout inventeur de lubricités nouvelles, à tout auteur de livres cyniques, à tout libertin connu pour être profès dans cet ordre.

The true erotic point of inventing new positions—as Mirabeau knows perfectly well, but pretends to forget for the purpose of humor—is not to establish new academies, but to recognize the spontaneous creations of desire. Elsewhere in *Ma Conversion,* the narrator-hero describes his participation in an orgy that rehearses all of the Aretine set, only to go beyond it. Imagine his surprise when his partner discovers another, new position: "One day when, in our sensual madness, we really had done all the wild things that the good Aretino depicted in his thoroughly religious book, suddenly I found the marquise taken with a love for my posterior" (71).[w] Two things are remarkable here: the continuing force of the classical—allowing *délire* (madness) to include a full recollection of the Aretino—and the compelling need to generate new forms of pleasure. Where positions are called *folies,* the most amorously insane of all is, by definition, the noncanonical one. Passionate ingenuity, at its most radical, appears to recognize the classical only in order to move beyond it, gesturing toward the old in order to highlight the new, supposing the academic stability of the Aretino, and yet effectively shutting down its authoritative transmission. *Margot la ravaudeuse* (1750) does not just add one or two positions, but more than doubles the Aretine number: "Aretino and Clinchetel, with all their knowledge, were never able to invent half the attitudes and positions that he made me adopt."[18] [x] Mr. Aretino and his fellow academicians are called into question as *authors* of the set of positions. Their imaginative invention is measured and found wanting, by comparison with that of a modern hero. In their defense, the logically minded might want to object that a claim to double the number makes little arithmetical sense when the given number is itself unstated, but the point of the passage quoted seems to be exactly the opposite: when the movement of expansion and innovation is so powerful as to lead to a doubling of numbers, the exact extent of the original seems to matter less and less. When, in *La Secte des anandrynes* (1789), Mlle Sapho learns "a lesson such that the positions of Aretino give no idea of it" (85),[y] the classical reference is routinely paradoxical. And when Sade's Juliette speaks of Aretino as one who "would only give an imperfect description of the inconceivable delights in which we in-

[w] Un jour que, dans le délire des sens, nous avions fait ma foi toutes les folies que le bon Arétin a dépeintes dans son livre si religieux, la marquise ne prend-elle pas subitement de l'amour pour mon postérieur?

[x] Jamais Aretin ni Clinchetel avec tout leur savoir, ne furent capables d'inventer la moitié des attitudes et des postures qu'il me fit tenir.

[y] une leçon dont les postures de l'Arétin ne donnent pas une idée

dulged in this sacred refuge" (VIII, 588),[z] the name "Aretino" gives us some sense of a number and an erotic capacity that fall short. It gives us an idea of that which fails to give us an idea. Invoking the classical only serves to show how far it is left behind, in quantity and quality.[19]

Musset's *Gamiani* (1833) quotes the classical at some length, but only dwells on it in order the better to rise above it. The book's heroine tells of her apprenticeship in a convent fitted with all the trappings of *ars erotica.* She describes a carpet that represents a set of twenty aphrodisiac variations, remedies for erotic fatigue: "One could see represented there, in absolutely magical colors, twenty groups of lovers, adopting lascivious attitudes apt to rekindle desires that had gone cold."[20] [a] But the very measure of erotic vigor is the capacity to go beyond the classical by the creative surge of imagination. Of the nuns we are told: "They varied things infinitely. Deprived of men, we were in fact all the more ingenious at inventing extravagant things. All the priapic texts, all the obscene stories ancient and modern were known to us. We had gone beyond them. Elephantis and Aretino had less imagination than we" (128).[b] In this context, all those old discussions of technique, including the tricks of the trade, appear unworthy of narration: "It would take too long to tell of our tricks, our ruses, our wonderful potions for reviving our strength, awakening our senses and satisfying them" (128).[c] Various positions may occur, but the point of practicing them is to find the one that is truly superlative: "We looked at each other with eyes of fire, and it was a struggle to see who could adopt the most lascivious, the most seductive [pose]" (127).[d] The range of erotic knowledge is insignificant when compared with the power and excitement of the new. All that matters, finally, is what matters most. All that counts is the singular.

To declare classical eroticism clinically dead at this point, to suppose that its corpse will now be swept away by the torrent of Romantic

[z] ne peindrait qu'imparfaitement les inconcevables luxures où nous nous livrâmes dans cet asile sacré

[a] On y voyait représentés, avec une magie suprenante de couleurs, vingt groupes amoureux, dans des attitudes lascives bien propres à rallumer les désirs éteints.

[b] Elles variaient à l'infini. Privées d'hommes, nous n'en étions que plus ingénieuses à inventer des extravagances. Toutes les priapées, toutes les histoires obscènes de l'antiquité et des temps modernes nous étaient connues. Nous les avions dépassées. Eléphantis et l'Arétin avaient moins d'imagination que nous.

[c] Il serait trop long de dire nos artifices, nos ruses, nos philtres merveilleux pour ranimer nos forces, éveiller nos désirs et les satisfaire.

[d] On se contemplait avec des yeux de feu, et on luttait à qui prendrait la [pose] la plus lascive, la plus entraînante.

passion, might well provide a kind of relief. Yet this, I maintain, would still be too quick for a Gadamerian hermeneutics—too Romantic an account of the triumph of Romanticism. For even as the old authorities have been slighted, and the old numbers belittled, something else has tended to persist: the notion that positions are the basic units of erotic knowledge. Counting them, multiplying them to infinity, and inventing the position to surpass all others are, in that sense, different aspects of the same thematic game. Could we perhaps establish the figure/model/position as the minimal form of our theme, present throughout the historical range of French erotic literature? If so, it might at least provide, in the absence of some unvarying unity, the kind of vade mecum I mentioned a little earlier. In effect, I have supposed that such was the case, since the notion of the erotic position is precisely what has endured throughout the first three chapters of this study, while so much of *ars erotica* has tended gradually to fade from view. Having said this, I shall now move relentlessly to suggest that there is a historical shift in the very notion of the position.

An instruction scene in *Thérèse philosophe* (1748) seems to take place at a thematic crossroads. Bois-Laurier proposes to tell Thérèse the tricks of the profession, but in doing so she distinguishes between two things I have until now taken as equivalent: *caprices* and *attitudes galantes.* Rather than rehearse the Aretine set of *attitudes,* which can be taken as known—even to the young Thérèse!—she proposes to recount her own adventures:

> So you understand that when I told you my adventures would teach you about the fancies of men, I did not mean the different attitudes that pleasure leads them to vary, so to speak infinitely, when they actually have women in their embrace: all the nuances of libertine attitudes were discussed by the famous Pietro Aretino, who lived in the fifteenth century, and discussed with such energy that there is nothing left to add today. All that I shall be teaching you here will be those whimsical tastes, those bizarre indulgences that are demanded of us by a great number of men. Whether by predilection on their part or some defect in their natural shape, these things, for such men, take the place of perfect pleasure. (II, 3–4)[e]

The point of this narrative lesson is to highlight the bizarre aspects of male behavior, the unpredictable, the imperfect, the oddly individual

[e] Tu comprends donc que lorsque je t'ai dit que mes aventures t'instruiraient des caprices des hommes, je n'ai pas entendu parler des différentes attitudes que la volupté leur fait varier, pour ainsi dire à l'infini, dans leurs embrassements réels avec les femmes: toutes les nuances des attitudes galantes ont été traitées avec tant d'énergie par le

shapes of pleasure or desire. Note that this is a proper lesson, and not just a rambling series of recollections. Thérèse is being presented with a *tableau,* albeit an incomplete one, of singular tastes: "I would never come to an end if I described all the bizarre tastes and the weird things I have encountered in men, not considering the different positions they demand of women in coitus" (II, 25).[f] The knowledge being imparted here is likely to be both narratively diverting and tactically useful. Substituting adventure for ritual, it identifies unusual forms of erotic behavior as the property of individual clients. Each unit of narration, each transaction with the whore is defined by its singular nature, by its difference from the corpus of other bodily pleasures.

After the mid-eighteenth century, what we might first recognize as "positions" are just as likely to be called *goûts,* or *caprices,* or *folies.* They can proliferate as objects of narrative interest—and arise disconcertingly as new situations for the apprentice whore—without any apparent principle of closure to bring their narration to an end. Newness may appear at every point, at the entrance of every new character. And if it does not appear, then there is nothing much to tell. Thus Sade's Juliette: "Since all these devirginators went about it rather clumsily, I shall spare you the details, and focus on the duc de Stern, whose mania was more unusual" (*Histoire de Juliette,* VIII, 147).[g] We can observe that only the "unusual," the singular, is worth recounting, and that the duc is defined as character by the singularity of his "mania." The *manie* or the *goût* is likely to be the property of episodic characters, whose passing adds one more oddity to the whore's narrative list. Thus, when Sade, in *Les Cent Vingt Journées de Sodome* (1785), lists six hundred passions, he is setting out what purports to be the comprehensive set of singularities, built up through the experience of four different whores. The number is not given by tradition, although it does remain strictly geometrical: it is reached by manic accumulation, and by the accumulation of manias. Sade is able to count to six hundred, rather than twelve or sixteen, not just by dint of

---

célèbre Pierre Arétin, qui vivait dans le quinzième siècle, qu'il n'en reste rien à dire aujourd'hui. Il n'est donc question, dans ce que j'ai à t'apprendre, que de ces goûts de fantaisie, de ces complaisances bizarres, que quantité d'hommes exigent de nous, et qui, par prédilection ou par certain défaut de conformation, leur tiennent lieu d'une jouissance parfaite.

[f] Je ne finirais pas, si je te faisais le tableau de tous les goûts bizarres, des singularités que j'ai connu [*sic*] chez les hommes, indépendamment des diverses postures qu'ils exigent des femmes dans le *coït.*

[g] Comme tous ces dévirgineurs s'y prirent assez lourdement, je vous ferai grâce des détails, et ne m'arrêterai qu'au duc de Stern, dont la manie fut plus singulière.

"imagination," but because his narrator-whores are no longer counting the same things that Aretino did. They are committed to counting difference as essentially erotic, and to recounting each manifestation of it. Sade assigns, as we shall see, a rather different task to square numbers: to bring order to the profusion of singular desires, to glorify their array—what he calls the "buffet"—and somehow to call it to account at the same time: he classifies the unpredictable, and codifies the bizarre.

By the late eighteenth century, the numbers have changed, and the units are somewhat different. Yet the arithmetic lingers on, like the instruction scene and the intimate dialogue between women, as one of the more persistent traces of a dislocated tradition.

II

GRADATION

Chapter 4

Toward the Learner-Centered Boudoir

Classical erotic texts, as we have seen, are characterized by the *mise en abyme* of instruction. While fulfilling for readers the broad didactic function of listing and transmitting the standard figures of eroticism, they regularly dramatize the teaching of these figures to young pupils. For doing that they can be deemed unspontaneous or abstractly inhuman by the post-Romantics among us, but their very didacticism, I suggest, ought still to be valued, if only because it foregrounds the *cultural* nature of eroticism. The objects of desire, seen in this way, are not uniquely individual, or even radically contingent: they are conceived in tradition and given shape through discourse.

What may be quite uncongenial to almost all modern readers, however, are the binarisms that inform classical notions of instruction: from innocence to knowledge, from childhood to adulthood, there appears to be only one giant step, to be taken always as a kind of initiation. The narrative of learning, if such it is, follows the ritual whereby a young person, usually a woman, changes her estate. Whether she now becomes a whore or marries, the transformation is effected in the space of a few days, and the substance of what she needs to know presumably assimilated in that time, as the set of positions (or tricks) is passed on to her. Instantaneous transfer is not possible, of course, precisely because the knowledge involved is not a simple call to action—not some imperative utterance of a singular desire—but rather an extensive paradigm, to be passed on item by numbered item, figure by figure, anecdote by anecdote.

Insofar as teaching and learning are taken to be unproblematically symmetrical in this way, any modern thematics of learning is thoroughly preempted. Where the learner is a mere receptacle, albeit a willing and even eager one, learning is not thought of as a subjective process. *Bildung,* maturation, the long and fruitful growth of understanding cannot take place narratively because there is no time for them to do so. Aretino's Nanna would no doubt be impatient with educational psychology as we know it. She says things to her daughter Pippa in order to have done with them, so that she will not have to say them again (*Ragionamenti,* IV, 172). Each piece of instruction can therefore be counted, in principle, just as Giulia counted Maddalena's experiences during their dialogue.

Those metaphors of vegetable growth so dear to modern discourses on learning do appear occasionally in classical eroticism, as when Nanna says how much pleasure it would give her if the words she has just uttered were to bear fruit in the brain of Pippa like grain sown in the fields (IV, 267–69). The activity represented in the *Ragionamenti* may indeed be spoken of as sowing, but the comparison itself does not bear fruit in the long run: there is no question of extending the metaphor (in time) by watching the seed grow into a plant. Similarly, the male teacher of Pallavicino's *Alcibiade fanciullo a scola* (1642) is utterly determined to plant his doctrinal seed in the pupil: "I shall introduce into the receptacle of your intelligence seeds of fertile and pleasant doctrines that will seem to you supernatural."[1] [a] There will be quite a delay before his desire is fulfilled, but that delay—equal to the extent of the story—is the time of teacherly seduction. It is the space of the teacher Philotime's rhetorical achievement, rather than the period of Alcibiade's growth. The end point of the dialogue is the bodily confirmation of the seed-planting metaphor (120), showing that teaching is something done to the pupil by the master. Instruction is an event to be witnessed, whereas growth as such can only be the object of hopeful allusion. Whether growth happens under the ground or inside the mind, it is out of sight—and effectively out of the field of representation. *Ars erotica* claims to display all there is to know about the erotic, but can only do so in the closure of its thematic self-confirmation. All there is to show or tell here is the teacherly showing and telling of *ars erotica.*

To represent learning in a properly modern way is not to dramatize instruction, but to thematize durative time—observing the passing of the seasons, rather than just numbering the days. In keeping with this, eighteenth-century erotic texts often replace the fiction of ritual

[a] J'introduirai dans le réceptacle de votre intelligence des semences de doctrines fécondes et agréables qui vous paraîtront surnaturelles.

transmission with that of gradual acquisition. As if to evoke and espouse the dynamics of learning, they tend to shift their rhetorical attention from the paradigmatic to the syntagmatic, from the set of figures as such to the order of their discovery. Instead of being a pointless contingency, or a mere formal necessity, the linear unfolding of the text may now appear germane to the process of teaching and learning. By taking its time in this way, the text also takes (and gives) the time of learning. To varying degrees, *Thérèse philosophe, Félicia, Mon Noviciat, La Secte des anandrynes, Le Rideau levé, Illyrine, Portier des Chartreux, Thémidore, Les Amours du chevalier de Faublas,* and many other eighteenth-century novels do the same thing. All the texts I have listed are retrospective first-person narratives recounting a transition from sexual ignorance to knowledge. What their heroines and heroes know is what they have learned in time, and that cannot be readily told in the space of four days, or eight nights, or twelve dialogues.

What I am calling the "modern" view of learning appears to be a corollary of the broad historical shift described by Philippe Ariès in his study of childhood and family life under the ancien régime. Ariès shows convincingly that childhood does not stand as a fixed notion throughout western European history. According to him, the medieval conception of the stages of human life limits childhood to a very short span (the time of not speaking, of the *in-fans*), followed by full participation in adult life. It is only with the establishment of public schooling that childhood is allowed (and required) to be drawn out in time. The medieval program of study, as exemplified by that of John of Salisbury, appears not to be a program at all in the modern sense, in that it is not chronologically ordered: "During his many years as an artist, John of Salisbury did not follow any plan. There is no sign of any gradation: dialectics, grammar, revision of the *trivium, quadrivium,* revision of rhetoric, logic. The order might have been different. It does not correspond to any habitual order of succession."[2] [b] From the seventeenth century, says Ariès, we see the emergence—Foucault might have said, the production—of education as a gradual leading-out of the child toward mature adulthood. For "child" here, we must remember to read "boy." As Ariès himself points out, growth appeared an exclusively male activity: "While schooling in the seventeenth century may not have been monopolized by one class, it was in fact monopolized by one sex. Women were excluded

[b] Pendant ses longues années d'artiste, Jean de Salisbury n'a suivi aucun plan, on ne relève aucune gradation: dialectique, grammaire, révision du *trivium, quadrivium,* révision de la rhétorique, logique. L'ordre eût pu être différent. Il ne correspond à aucune succession coutumière.

from it. Thus, where they were concerned, the habits of precocity and short childhood went unchanged from the Middle Ages through to the seventeenth century" (371).[c] Girls, in this context, may be condemned to precocious adulthood, and therefore to a dramatic shift from innocence to adult awareness, rather than enjoying any progression from ignorance to knowledge. Yet the eighteenth-century novels I listed above give much the same temporal shape to female as to male learning, although they tend to confine female knowledge more narrowly to the sexual domain. According to a conventional view, girls are kept in convents, preserved in childhood innocence until the eve of their marriage, then plunged at one organic stroke into womanhood. But that was never the story told by erotic literature of the sixteenth and seventeenth centuries. The convent was always seen as inhabited by teachers—father confessors, mother superiors, and older sisters—who continually provided sexual instruction. By the time the young woman reached the verge of adulthood, innocence had already been lost. What the eighteenth century adds to this is a new understanding of *ignorance* as something partial. There is consequently no ritual "loss" of innocence, but rather the gradual displacement of ignorance in the positive acquisition of sexual knowledge.

To understand learning as a process, as something more than a creeping accident, is to see it as driven in some way. We know that the pupils of *ars erotica* were always eager for instruction, but there is more to eighteenth-century erotic learning than eagerness, or even curiosity. Sexual knowledge is now often shown to be naturally conceived, so to speak, rather than culturally transmitted. There seems to develop, in fact, a culture that denies itself as culture,[3] locating its origins in nature and seeking in the hero's or heroine's very desire for knowledge the key to an understanding of desire as a natural phenomenon of bodily imagination. The earliest example of this that I have found occurs in *Portier des Chartreux* (1741). The narrator-hero of that novel learns actively, through a kind of reflexive voyeurism. When he sees mature adults in sexual play, he turns back on himself to explain what he has observed: "I examined all their actions with no guide other than nature, and no form of instruction other than their example, and, in my curiosity to know what could be giving rise to these convulsive movements in the father, I sought the cause in

[c] Si la scolarisation n'était pas encore au XVIIe siècle un monopole de classe, elle restait le monopole d'un sexe. Les femmes en étaient exclues. Aussi chez elles les habitudes de précocité et d'enfance courte se trouvent inchangées du Moyen Age au XVIIe siècle.

myself."[4] [d] Finding the cause of these convulsive movements is a matter of physiological introspection, and growing in understanding means re-cognizing the natural knowledge that already dwells within: "The knowledge that nature had put in my heart had just come to light. The clouds with which it had naturally been covered had now blown away" (I, 14).[e]

Where women characters are concerned—and women's erotic learning is more canonical in erotic literature than men's—the notion of a natural aptitude for knowledge is an object of increasing narrative attention. It is as if the thematics of teaching were now torn between two forms of (male) pleasure: the old satisfaction of imparting a body of knowledge to a virginal innocent and the somewhat newer excitement of imagining the young woman as riddled with desire from the outset. The most common eighteenth-century name for a natural predisposition to erotic learning in women is *le tempérament*. The empress Messalina might well be remembered classically for the sum of her achievements in a life of debauchery, but in the description of *Margot la ravaudeuse* (1750) the name Messalina stands for a remarkable *potential:* "Margot was born with a temperament like Messalina's" (141).[f] Lolotte, the heroine of *Mon Noviciat* (1792), starts out with much the same gift, and intends to enrich it through variation—or rather variety: "You should know that I have done, or at least aimed to do, everything required by a superlative temperament, and everything that is taught by perfecting the practice of the most varied frolics" (10).[g] Under the "command" of temperament, the heroine is driven to fuller erotic awareness. Illyrine, the narrator-heroine of *Illyrine, ou l'Ecueil de l'inexpérience* (1799), tells early in her story of what she "already" knew. Her knowledge is a development, an unfolding of her natural temperament, as potential is enhanced by practice: "I was already familiar with love: the two nights spent with my lover had developed my temperament".[5] [h] A nun seduced by the narrator-hero of *Le Tartuffe libertin* (c. 1830) quickly comes to display "consummate

[d] J'examinais tous leurs mouvements sans autre guide que la nature, autre instruction que l'exemple, et, curieux de savoir ce qui pourrait occasionner ces mouvements convulsifs du Père, j'en cherchai la cause en moi-même.

[e] Les connaissances que la nature avait mises dans mon cœur venaient de se développer, les nuages dont elle les avait couvertes s'étaient dissipés.

[f] Margot [. . .] est née avec un tempérament de Messaline.

[g] Sachez que j'ai fait, ou que j'ai du moins ambitionné de faire tout ce que peut commander un tempérament superlatif, et tout ce qu'enseigne la pratique perfectionnée des ébats les plus variés.

[h] Déjà je connaissais l'amour; les deux nuits passées avec mon amant avaient développé mon tempérament.

experience."[i] This is not because the hero himself has a special gift for rapid instruction, but because "love and temperament are the two great teachers for exercises with the cunt, and for everything to do with fucking."[6] [j] In *ars erotica,* the set of positions functioned as cultural foreknowledge of the erotic, binding the theme into hermeneutic circularity, and making of it something always already known. Here, it is *le tempérament* that performs the thematic function of foreknowledge, suggesting that these young women are so ready to learn because of what each of them naturally knows, or wants to know, already. The narrator-heroine of *Félicia* (1776) describes herself early in the story as "already knowledgeable (*savante*),"[7] while Illyrine regularly refers to herself, in times of considerable impropriety, as "still innocent." The space of gradual erotic learning, for women, lies in fact between being *déjà savante* and *encore innocente*—not of course as some kind of compromise, but as a highly constrained movement through time. The present is closely bounded by continual reference to the *déjà* and the *encore.*

By understanding erotic foreknowledge as *tempérament,* eighteenth-century novels give it a psychological dimension not present in *ars erotica.* If the heroine was born with this predisposition, when and how was it first revealed, for example? Under what circumstances is it likely to be most visible? Such questions can lead to a fuller characterization, and to narrative inquiry outside the standard age range for characters in erotic stories, thus disturbing one of their most durable canonical elements. We have already noted that the classical women's dialogue occurs between a girl of about fifteen and a woman of eighteen or twenty. With the fading of the *ars erotica* tradition, the eighteen-year-old may be only present episodically, or may even be replaced by a man, but the heroine on the verge of sexual experience is still usually aged about fifteen, from *Thérèse philosophe* to *Le Roman de Violette* and beyond. The tendency for characters to appear on the scene only when they have reached the age of fifteen gives support to Marcel Hénaff's claim, apropos of Sade, that "the character never has a childhood."[8] [k] This is in many ways an acceptable generalization about a range of erotic narratives, but I want to hedge it around with an understanding of the temperament theme. When the bishop in *Les Cent Vingt Journées de Sodome* (1785) finds himself responsible for the education of two orphans, he cannot (or does not) make a place

[i] une expérience consommée

[j] l'amour et le tempérament sont les deux grands maîtres pour les exercices du con et tout ce qui tient à la fouterie.

[k] le personnage [. . .] n'a jamais d'enfance.

for his erotic interests within their childhood world. They are four or five when they come under his power, and he simply waits until they turn thirteen before torturing and destroying them, as is his wont (I, 31–32). There is nothing else to be done during the intervening years, even for one so perverse as this, but to wait—at least until within two years of the normal time. Childhood, here, is an enduring delay in the libertine's program. Erotically, it is quite literally a nonevent, and one of the heroines of *Entre chien et loup* (1809) must speak for many of her sisters and brothers when she says, "I reached fifteen years of age without the slightest event" (II, 146).[l]

The notion of natural temperament threatens this pattern—without finally disturbing it unduly—by making of childhood a time of greater erotic value. The childlike and the childish may still be quite without interest, but early manifestations of desire can be read as precocious signs of a remarkable future adulthood. In *Thérèse philosophe,* the heroine's childhood masturbation is less noteworthy for any introspective knowledge it yields her, than for the narrative promise it holds out to the reader. Here, we are being told, is a really strong temperament:

> My mother asked me where I had learned the horrible things she had just witnessed. I replied, in tears, that I did not know what I had done to anger her, and that I did not know what she meant by the terms *touching myself, immodesty,* and *mortal sin* that she was using. The naïveté of my replies convinced her of my innocence, and I went back to sleep, which led to more titillation by me, and more complaints from my mother. Finally, after some nights of attentive observation [not on Thérèse's part], noone doubted that it was the strength of my temperament that led me to do in my sleep what so many poor nuns do for relief when they are awake. They decided to tie my hands firmly.
>
> [. . .] I lost the habit, but my temperament grew stronger. At the age of nine or ten, I felt a kind of disturbance, and desires that led I knew not where. (I, 9–10)[m]

Locating desire in the "child" might be seen, in eighteenth-century terms, as a kind of hyperbole, rather than a fundamental relocation

[l] Je parvins à quinze ans sans le plus petit événement.

[m] Ma mère [. . .] me demanda de qui j'avais appris les horreurs dont elle venait d'être témoin? Je lui répondis, en pleurant, que j'ignorais en quoi j'avais pu la fâcher, que je ne savais ce qu'elle voulait me dire par les termes d'*attouchements*, d'*impudicité*, de *péché mortel* dont elle se servait. La naïveté de mes réponses la convainquit de mon innocence, et je me rendormis: nouveaux chatouillements de ma part, nouvelles plaintes de celle de ma mère. Enfin, après quelques nuits d'observation attentive, on ne douta plus que ce ne fût la force de mon tempérament, qui me faisait faire, en dormant, ce qui sert à soulager tant de pauvres religieuses en veillant. On prit le parti de me lier étroitement les mains.

of narrative interest. In pushing back the time of sexual awakening to a point before the standard age of fifteen, *Thérèse philosophe* further undoes any notion of original purity, representing youthful beings as a mixture of "innocence" and "temperament"—still ignorant, certainly, but already "commanded" by precocious adult desire.

No heroine in erotic literature is more extraordinarily beyond childhood from the outset than Sade's Juliette. At nine, she has "already" learned to masturbate: "Gifted with the most active temperament, I had accustomed my fingers from the age of nine to responding to the desires of my head, and my only thought from that time on was of the happiness I should find when the opportunity came to gain instruction, and plunge into a career whose doors were already being indulgently opened for me by precocious nature" (VIII, 54).[n] *S'instruire,* for Juliette, is a reflexive action, a reflexive verb of which she is the subject. Nature is on her side and in her body, propelling her into the search for knowledge. Her quest for erotic opportunity is already under way six years before its time. Throughout her career, this rhythm of learning will be maintained: Juliette will always be in advance of the libertine standard, more aware, further down the path than any of her age group. Observing Delbène's injustice toward her, she quickly learns from that example. Morally, she is "astonishingly corrupt already" (VIII, 145).[o] When encouraged to commit theft by her slightly older companion, Fatime, she says: "Oh wicked woman, you will finish off my corruption. I already find myself far too strongly disposed toward such horrible deeds" (VIII, 150).[p] The process of her corruption is not yet finished, and will endure almost for the length of Sade's interminable novel, but we are continually invited to wonder at this gifted learner of vice. Instruction is meted out to her in large doses, of course: there are lectures, and long sessions of practical work. Yet through it all, her teachers never cease to delight in and appeal to her temperament. She is called on, in the most classical manner, to imitate the attitudes of her masters, but often with an explicit reminder of how naturally ready she is to do so: "Imitate me, Juliette," says Saint-Fond, "it is the way of your natural inclinations"

[. . .] L'habitude se perdit, mais le tempérament augmenta. A l'âge de neuf à dix ans je sentais une inquiétude, des désirs dont je ne connaissais pas le but.

[n] Douée du tempérament le plus actif, dès l'âge de neuf ans j'avais accoutumé mes doigts à répondre aux désirs de ma tête, et je n'aspirais, depuis cet âge, qu'au bonheur de trouver l'occasion de m'instruire et de me plonger dans une carrière dont la nature précoce m'ouvrait déjà les portes avec autant de complaisance.

[o] étonnamment corrompue déjà

[p] O scélérate, [. . .] tu achèveras de me corrompre: je ne me sens déjà que trop de dispositions à toutes ces horreurs.

(VIII, 366).[q] Bending with her *penchants,* oriented by her natural *dispositions,* Juliette is always equal to the temporal demands of ongoing corruption, ready to follow the lead almost before it is given. In the company of Clairwil, she finds herself "led on by the frightful example of this wild woman," and drawn along "even more by my cursed imagination" (VIII, 390).[r] Juliette moves through the learning process with a force and a sureness that themselves become the object of erotic fascination in the telling.

Another Sadian heroine shares Juliette's gift for rapid learning: Eugénie de Mistival, the fifteen-year-old pupil of *La Philosophie dans le boudoir.* Dolmancé, the accomplished libertine, wonders at her temperament: "What excellent dispositions!" (III, 395).[9] [s] Yet her learning does not take place in a long narrative of sexual growth. It occurs in the time span of classical instruction: "we shall spend two days together . . . two days of delight; the greater part of the time I shall spend educating this young woman" (III, 387).[t] In just two days (seven dialogues) of intensive tuition, Eugénie will be taught the essentials of Sadian erotic knowledge. Saint-Ange and Eugénie had met the previous autumn in a convent, but were too closely watched there to take any great sexual liberties (III, 387). Now, however, Saint-Ange has changed the scene from convent to boudoir, and has organized a ritual seminar in which she will act as convener and guide: "you know, do you not, that it is in this interview that I am to initiate you into the most secret mysteries of Venus?" (III, 391).[u] Dolmancé has been chosen by Saint-Ange as a masterly accomplice, a kind of keynote speaker whose presence will mark the central part of the program. As it happens—and it always seems to happen this way in erotic literature when women seek to exercise power independently—Dolmancé is already there, waiting in the boudoir when Saint-Ange enters with Eugénie. No further preliminaries will take place in the absence of the master: he has been informed by Saint-Ange's brother that lessons will be given, and that his presence is likely to be required (III, 393). From the first, even before Saint-Ange expected and planned it, the woman's activities as tutor will be subject to male supervision. Eugénie,

[q] Imite-moi, Juliette, tes penchants t'y portent.

[r] entraînée par l'affreux exemple de cette sauvage/plus encore par ma maudite imagination

[s] Quelles excellentes dispositions!

[t] nous passerons deux jours ensemble. . . deux jours délicieux; la meilleure partie du temps, je l'emploie à éduquer cette jeune personne.

[u] ne sais-tu pas que c'est dans cette entrevue que je dois t'initier dans les plus secrets mystères de Vénus?

as the willing pupil who says to Saint-Ange, "you know that you would never have a more submissive pupil than I" (III, 418),[v] thus sees her allegiance transferred to Dolmancé, passed on by the older woman to the man called "your master and mine" (III, 398).[w] Saint-Ange it is who provides the model and says to Eugénie, "Imite-moi," but her demonstrations are framed by Dolmancé's lectures.

It is hard to avoid the impression that *La Philosophie dans le boudoir,* for all its taming of female autonomy, constitutes a kind of thematic regression, a late flowering of *ars erotica.* Yet that is only true to a degree, for the classical notion of instruction is kept under continual pressure here by the newer theme of learning. Saint-Ange is concerned about the passage of time in a way unknown to her more classical colleagues. She fears there will not be time to cover the course material: "How brief this period is, my sweet angel!" (III, 391).[x] At certain moments, she urges her companions to press on: "Let us begin our lesson, or the short time we have available will be spent in preliminaries and the instruction will not be carried out" (III, 396).[y] At other times, she asks Dolmancé in particular to forbear, fearing that his desire for immediate gratification may distract him from his teacherly responsibilities: "Just be patient for a little longer. The education of this girl should be our sole occupation! . . . How pleasant it is to teach her!" (III, 401).[z] The pleasure of teaching referred to here is not simply that of watching the pupil grow rapidly in understanding. Indeed, libertine instruction for Sade, by contrast with Aretino and Pallavicino, is not seed-planting, but seed-suffocating: Saint-Ange plans to "stifle within this young heart every seed of virtue and religion planted by her tutors" (III, 388).[a] What Dolmancé will place inside Eugénie will be the enemy of growth: "Notify Dolmancé, explain everything to him immediately he gets here, so that the poison of his immoralities, circulating in this young heart together with the venom I shall inject, will rapidly destroy all the seeds of virtue that, but for us, might germinate there" (III, 388).[b] *Déraciner* (literally, uprooting) can take

[v] va, tu n'aurais jamais une écolière plus soumise que moi.

[w] notre maître à toutes deux

[x] Que cet intervalle est court, mon cher ange!

[y] Commençons notre leçon, ou le peu de temps que nous avons à jouir d'Eugénie va se passer ainsi en préliminaires, et l'instruction ne se fera point.

[z] Encore un moment de patience. Que l'éducation de cette chère fille nous occupe seule!. . . Il est si doux de la former!

[a] étouffer dans ce jeune cœur toutes les semences de vertu et de religion qu'y placèrent ses institutrices

[b] Préviens Dolmancé, mets-le au fait dès qu'il arrivera, pour que le venin de ses immoralités, circulant dans ce jeune cœur avec celui que j'y lancerai, parvienne à

place in a few moments, or at least in two days, whereas the slow germination of virtue is likely to take much longer. The very nature of Sade's "philosophy" seems to make rapid instruction not only possible, but somehow necessary.

In response to the speed and intensity of Dolmancé's and Saint-Ange's teaching, Eugénie displays not some capacious receptiveness, but a splendidly proportionate speed of assimilation. Confident of her achievements to date, she can ask Dolmancé: "Tell me, master, are you content?" (III, 465).[c] The question is a rhetorical gesture on the part of the gifted learner, answering and even provoking the rhetoric of her teachers. Of course they are happy with her, even if further progress is still possible in the remaining scenes. As Saint-Ange says, "I am exceedingly pleased with my Eugénie; she shows the happiest predispositions" (III, 465).[d] The pupil asks about her achievement, and is answered with talk of her promise, but there is hardly any space between promise and achievement, so quick is Eugénie's progress. Before long, the teachers themselves will be moved to echo her rhetorical question. Dolmancé says to Saint-Ange: "Well, Madame, are you content with your student? Is she making sufficiently rapid progress?" (III, 483).[e]

The learning program for Eugénie, as Sade's title reminds us, is more than a set of positions, and Dolmancé's particular role is to train her in "philosophy": he is, says Saint-Ange, "at just the right level of philosophy that we require for your education, [. . .] of all the men in the world he is best able to instruct you, and guide you in the career of happiness and pleasures that we wish to undertake together" (III, 394).[f] Eugénie is said to be embarking on a *carrière* through which she is to be guided: she is not just taking a single decisive step as a rite of passage. Yet she is able to be so quickly transformed precisely because she meets eroticism not as an art or a trade requiring a long apprenticeship, but as a philosophy driven by a few essential principles: "Fuck, in one word, fuck: that is why you are brought into the world" (III, 416).[g] If there is a further maxim necessary to guide

---

déraciner dans peu d'instants toutes les semences de vertu qui pourraient y germer sans nous.

[c] Eh bien, mon maître, es-tu content?

[d] Je suis fort contente de mon Eugénie; elle annonce les plus heureuses dispositions.

[e] Eh bien, madame, êtes-vous contente de votre élève? ses progrès sont-ils assez rapides?

[f] précisément du degré de philosophie qu'il nous faut pour ton instruction, [. . .] l'homme du monde le plus en état de te former, et de te conduire dans la carrière du bonheur et des plaisirs que nous voulons parcourir ensemble.

[g] Fouts, en un mot, fouts; c'est pour cela que tu es mise au monde.

Eugénie, it is the following: "in the interests of your education, let me compress what has been said into one single word of advice: never listen to your heart, my child; it is the most untrustworthy guide we have received from nature" (III, 536).[h] The very fact that all these discourses can be summed up so pithily is no doubt to be taken as proof of their rational coherence. Eugénie's rapid learning is a glorious product of the encounter between temperamental psychology and systematic philosophy, for the very "nature" to which Dolmancé appeals is that which compels Eugénie to understand him. The culmination of it all is the pupil's delight at the perfection of her own learning: "Here I am: at one stroke incestuous, adulterous, sodomite, and all that in a girl who only lost her maidenhood today! . . . What progress, my friends! . . . With what rapidity I'm advancing along the thorny path of vice! . . . Oh! I am a doomed girl! . . ." (III, 554).[i]

It is intriguing to note that Juliette's learning is much more protracted than Eugénie's, without being visibly slower. While still in the convent, Juliette is exposed, in every sense, to the influence of a libertine mother superior, Mme Delbène, who takes her through a drastically intensive program of instruction. Together with her fellow pupil, Euphrosine, aged fifteen, Juliette, at thirteen (VIII, 54)—two years early—is invited to begin a libertine career: "As I said to you, my dear, I am taking you on as a pupil; your candor and naïveté prove that you are in great need of a guide along the thorny pathway of life, and it is I who am going to play that role" (VIII, 60).[j] In no time at all, Juliette is participating resourcefully in libertine orgies, has rid herself of her virginity, and can take an active part in the ritual murder of a girl younger than herself. "Where to from there?" we might ask. Nancy Miller points out that "She performs the permutations of sexual exercises with astonishing skill and advances so rapidly, in fact, that after her first indoctrination the reader might well wonder how the remaining volumes can be structured convincingly upon a developmental premise."[10] It must be the case, as Miller goes on to suggest, that a broader process of philosophical learning is taking place in the novel. For Barthes and Miller, the one who really needs

[h] résumons pour votre éducation l'unique conseil qu'on puisse tirer de tout ce qui vient d'être dit: n'écoutez jamais votre cœur, mon enfant; c'est le guide le plus faux que nons ayons reçu de la nature.

[i] Me voilà donc à la fois incestueuse, adultère, sodomite, et tout cela pour une fille qui n'est dépucelée que d'aujourd'hui!. . . Que de progrès, mes amis!. . . avec quelle rapidité je parcours la route épineuse du vice!. . . Oh! je suis une fille perdue!. . .

[j] Je te l'ai dit, ma chère: je t'entreprends; ta candeur et ta naïveté me prouvent que tu as grand besoin d'un guide dans la carrière épineuse de la vie, et c'est moi qui t'en servirai.

to go on learning is the reader,[11] but it is important to note that Juliette's own learning can be almost perfect at every step, while still not measuring up definitively to the escalating standards of Sadian libertinism. Indeed, the more the heroine learns, at least in the first half of the novel, the more her teachers seem to insist on going further: "Listen to me, Juliette . . . " says Delbène. "You have a quite extraordinary need for training . . . " (VIII, 143).[k] Perhaps this continual need for education can be seen as the consequence of Juliette's talent: her achievements increase her potential, and any new knowledge tends to open her up to further learning.

As if to temper the exultation and astonishment that mark Juliette's learning achievements, there are occasional reminders of what is yet to be done. Having begun with "an awareness of philosophy that is far beyond her age" (*La Nouvelle Justine,* VI, 33–34),[l] and moved speedily to the point where she is "astoundingly corrupt already" (VIII, 45),[m] she notes that a severe apprenticeship still lies ahead: "I no doubt had a severe apprenticeship ahead of me; this unfortunate beginning was to finish off the corruption of my habits" (VIII, 145).[n] Beyond Delbène, she finds a succession of masters and mistresses; among them is Clairwil, who acts as one of the most advanced guides and draws from Juliette the learner's declaration of allegiance: "You can be sure that you will not find anywhere a more submissive pupil than I. There is nothing I should not take on with you, nothing I could not imagine, if guided by your counsel" (VIII, 312).[o] When initiated, under Clairwil's sponsorship, into the *Société des Amis du Crime,* Juliette has occasion to be quite humble: "I thought I knew everything in the way of libertine behavior, but that evening convinced me that I was still only a novice" (VIII, 462).[p] In advanced crime, she is still a virtual beginner, as Clairwil and Noirceuil continue to point out to her some time later: "You still need some encouragement; you must reduce the sensitivity that ruins you" (VIII, 493).[q]

Ahead of Juliette lies not organic growth, but its exact opposite:

[k] Ecoute-moi, Juliette. . . Il est inouï le besoin que tu as d'être formée. . .

[l] une philosophie très au-dessus de son âge

[m] étonnamment corrompue déjà

[n] J'avais sans doute un rude apprentissage à faire; ces malheureux débuts devaient achever de corrompre mes mœurs.

[o] Sois sûre que tu ne trouveras nulle part une plus soumise écolière. Il n'est rien que je n'entreprenne avec toi, rien que je n'imagine, guidée par tes conseils.

[p] Je croyais tout savoir en libertinage, et cette soirée me convainquit que je n'étais encore qu'une novice.

[q] Vous avez encore besoin de quelques encouragements; il faut diminuer cette sensibilité qui vous perd.

diminuer cette sensibilité. Enthusiasm and invention come naturally to her, as does passionate cruelty, but she has to learn to carry out the same criminal actions in a progressively more dispassionate way. It appears to be a matter, as with any truly learner-centered education, of learning how to learn. Delbène speaks to her of the importance of gradually developing crime as a habit: "Oh Juliette, if, like me, you wish to live happily in crime—and I commit a lot of crimes, my dear—if you wish to find the same happiness in this as I do, try to turn crime, in due course, into an easy habit, so that it becomes impossible for you to go on living without committing one, and [. . .] so that your flexible yet quite resistant soul gradually becomes accustomed to turning human virtues into vices, and making virtue out of crime" (VIII, 66).[r] Repetition and multiplication are thus the keys to a long, slow acquisition of insensitivity. To commit just one crime, as Juliette explains much later to her own pupil, Donis, is to remain static, exposed to remorse: "Don't just go part of the way. You would be the most unhappy of women if you were to commit only one misdemeanor. Either refrain completely, or plunge into the abyss as soon as your foot reaches the edge of it. Only the sheer quantity of your misdeeds will stifle remorse. It will give rise to the gentle familiarity that dulls them so thoroughly, and will guarantee that your face holds the mask that is needed to deceive others" (IX, 40; cf. VIII, 199).[s] Crime might be an "abyss," but there is no free fall: the pupil's role is continually to descend below the previous stage, finding in that very moving-beyond the dynamics of an insensitive pleasure. The teacher's role here is somewhat paradoxical. "Let us begin by hardening ourselves," says Delbène to Juliette (VIII, 142); "become used to it," says Juliette to Donis (IX, 39); "ripen [the mind]," says Dolmancé to Eugénie (III, 539).[t] As simple imperatives, all of these teacherly maxims cannot guarantee any immediate effect: they are pointless unless taken up and applied at length by disciplined pupils. For the learner's role is

[r] O Juliette, si tu veux, comme moi, vivre heureuse dans le crime. . . et j'en commets beaucoup, ma chère. . . si tu veux, dis-je, y trouver le même bonheur que moi, tâche de t'en faire, avec le temps, une si douce habitude, qu'il te devienne comme impossible de pouvoir exister sans le commettre; et [. . .] que ton âme flexible, et malgré cela nerveuse, se trouve imperceptiblement accoutumée à se faire des vices de toutes les vertus humaines et des vertus de tous les crimes.

[s] Ne restez donc point en chemin: vous seriez la plus malheureuse des femmes, si vous ne commettez [*sic*] qu'un seul délit. Ou ne commencez pas, ou plongez-vous entièrement dans l'abîme, dès que vous avez mis le pied sur le bord. La multitude seule de vos forfaits étouffera le remords. . . fera naître la douce habitude qui les émousse si bien, et assurera à votre physionomie le masque nécessaire à tromper les autres.

[t] Commençons par nous endurcir/accoutumez-vous/mûrissez [l'esprit]

to describe herself as *corrupted,* or *dulled* (VIII, 433), or *hardened* (VIII, 469),[u] using past participles to mark the finished quality of her achievement, while all along knowing that they represent no more than stages in the lifelong development of a habit of insensitivity. It is always necessary to be even more *endurcie,* and libertines who cannot shrink and desiccate their hearts in this way are eventually doomed to failure, no matter how strong their natural temperament. That is the case with Olympe, for example: "Olympe, princess of Borghese, was a sweet, loving woman, carried away during pleasure, libertine by temperament, full of imagination, but she had never fully examined her principles. She was timid, still clung to her prejudices, and was therefore susceptible to being converted at the first sign of adversity. For this very weakness, she was unworthy of two women as corrupt as we" (IX, 414–415).[v] For failing to go further and deeper, for failing to stay on the pace despite her early start, Olympe is ruthlessly destroyed by Juliette and Clairwil. In the long run, she is just another murder victim, just one more small step in the development of Juliette's mature callousness.

Maurice Blanchot calls *Histoire de Juliette* a bildungsroman precisely because of its narration of this process: "*Juliette* is a kind of bildungsroman, a book of apprenticeship in which we learn to recognize the slow education of an energetic soul. On the face of it, Juliette is entirely depraved from the outset. But in fact she only has a number of inclinations, and her head is still intact; a gigantic effort remains to be made."[12] [w] Again, however, it might be more appropriate to speak of anti-*Bildung,* if we suppose with Franco Moretti that *Bildung* is the making of personality, and in a sense the very opposite of initiation.[13] Juliette's life's work is seen by Blanchot as a labor of self-destruction: "Such a transformation, such a labor of self-destruction can only be brought off with extreme difficulty."[14] [x] This may be, after all, the only kind of *Bildung* available to women characters. Elizabeth Abel,

[u] corrompue/engourdie/endurcie

[v] Olympe, princesse de Borghèse, était une femme douce, aimante, emportée dans le plaisir, libertine par tempérament, pleine d'imagination, mais n'ayant jamais approfondi ses principes; timide, tenant encore à ses préjugés, susceptible d'être convertie au premier malheur qui lui serait arrivé, et qui, par cette seule faiblesse, n'était pas digne de deux femmes aussi corrompues que nous.

[w] *Juliette* est une sorte de *Bildungsroman,* un livre d'apprentissage où nous apprenons à reconnaître la lente formation d'une âme énergique. En apparence, Juliette est, dès le début, entièrement dépravée. Mais, en réalité, elle n'a encore que quelques penchants et sa tête est intacte; un effort gigantesque lui reste à accomplir.

[x] Une telle transformation, un tel travail de destruction de soi ne s'accomplit pas sans d'extrêmes difficultés.

Marianne Hirsch, and Elizabeth Langland speak of the exclusion of women from the genre: "Even the broadest definition of the Bildungsroman presupposes a range of social options available only to men."[15] Not only are women shut out of certain social spaces: they are generally denied the privilege, as Ellen Morgan points out, of the progressive time in which personality might develop dynamically.[16] Juliette's self-destruction can always be seen with David Williams as a pathetic "loss" of human qualities: "By [her] becoming one with the predatory world around her, [. . .] her femininity has been cauterized, and a loss of human identity has taken place."[17] But this makes learning sound too much like a wound or a disfigurement. This kind of interpretation is a humanist refusal to read the time of Sade's text and leads only to hopeful affirmations of a natural childhood quality that is everywhere denied by the narrative. Juliette's temperament spurred her toward cruelty from the moment the first opportunity presented itself. Her great accomplishment, in Sade's terms, has been to "ripen her head" through philosophy (IX, 211), while progressively hardening her heart—growing thus to full status as a natural destroyer of all that grows.[18]

When women become established in erotic narrative as active learners, the teacher's role is brought under pressure. As long as instruction was the norm, teaching was essentially a matter of performance—rhetorical and gymnastic. Now, however, it becomes appropriate to think in terms of *training,* as an attentive management of the learning process. How can the young woman be kept under control while she learns, so that the process itself is mastered? The teacherly control envisaged by erotic narrative must not be some medieval constraint: locking the young woman in a tower is a rigidly spatial approach to the problem. It takes no cognizance of development and makes of the woman a simple victim. In that situation, as Boccaccio and Chaucer show, the main narrative possibility lies in the woman's taking revenge, that is, in an equally simple role reversal, which hardly constitutes any sort of progression in or through pleasure. For more modern purposes, the heroine—and, for that matter, the young hero—must be disciplined without being stunted in her growth. Temperament must be harnessed by narrative—not locked up in a chastity belt.

Restif's *L'Anti-Justine* (1798) tells as its main story the sexual growth of two sisters maturing into promiscuous adult sexuality. Their father, Cupidonnet, the narrator-hero, sees it as his responsibility to provide close erotic supervision throughout the whole process. His teaching program, conceived for and imposed on the young women, is based on a carefully graded curriculum, in which the different *fouteries* are ranked according to complexity and intensity. As narrator and teacher, he fulfills two sets of duties simultaneously, shaping his daughters' future and organizing the order of events in so doing. Here we see him warming to the task, savoring his responsibilities in advance:

> We now come to the supreme fuckings: those that will strengthen my delicious Conquette-Ingénue and my delightful Victoire-Conquette, making their fortune and mine by taking away any false delicacy, and uncovering something admirable that will only be seen at the end. The road I am going to follow in order to train these two beauties and their lady friends may appear startling at first. But in all things one must wait for the final outcome.[19] [y]

"Forming" or educating his daughters means strengthening them through practice (*aguerrir*), and revealing their hidden potential only in the fullness of time. Paternal tyranny in *L'Anti-Justine* is in no way pompous or distantly authoritarian. It is insistent and cajoling, attending so closely to the young women's bodies as to shape them without and within.

Cupidonnet is in fact the first to penetrate one of his daughters sexually, as well as being in charge of the ongoing bodily development of both. Maturation here is defined, in a narratively convenient and tyrannically reductive way, as the progressive widening of the vagina. The father's attitude is one of domineering modesty, for his claim is not ultimately to satisfy his daughters, but merely to lead them through his pleasure and theirs to the promiscuity of a whore's adulthood: "I am no longer at the age where I can leave you satiated with sensual pleasure. So, I shall arrange for you to be laid by handsome young men, graduating the size of their pricks" (356).[z] Paternal domination lies precisely in this mastery over time, and in the claim to measure growth with intimate precision. Consistent with this role—and required indeed by narrative order—is the fact that the father does not have a large penis: "I took hold of her cunt (as well as having a keen desire to possess her, I wanted to make her bolder and prepare her

[y] Nous en sommes aux fouteries par excellence, à celles qui vont aguerrir ma délicieuse Conquette-Ingénue, ma ravissante Victoire-Conquette, faire leur fortune, la mienne, en leur ôtant une fausse délicatesse, et découvrir une chose admirable, qu'on ne verra qu'à la fin. La route que je vais prendre, pour former ces deux belles et leurs compagnes, étonnera d'abord. Mais en toutes choses il faut attendre le dernier résultat.

[z] Je ne suis plus d'un âge à te rassasier de volupté. Ainsi, je te ferai mettre par de jolis jeunes gens, graduant la grosseur des vits.

jewel to receive a bigger member than mine)" (363).[a] Or more precisely, in order to make the best of a double constraint whereby the father must be first, but not later be cast aside, his penis is long without being thick: "fortunately my father's dick was not fat, but it was long. It gave me complete pleasure, because it went in so far that it tickled the end of me, and seeing as how I was so narrow, it filled me up as if I'd had a mule's dick in there . . . That's how I lost my maidenhead" (440).[b] After the father may come the uncle, or another who has been carefully chosen, followed by the father's former secretary: "After him, I'll get Traitdamour, my former secretary, for you. He is a handsome lad who will finish widening you for the member of whatever paying customer you prefer" (362).[c]

As we see, phallic dimensions in Restif are not just a reflexion of the kind of priapic splendor found in Sade and others. Penis sizes are assessed, first of all, according to their place in the narrative of vaginal *Bildung*. There is a class that includes Cupidonnet and the young lover Timori, whose members are suited to gentle deflowering: "After me, you will seem like a maiden to your fiancé, or anyone else who fucks you" (441). Timori has "a maidenhead prick smaller than mine" (350).[d] The second class is that of the *fouteurs préparatoires* (355), including no doubt Traitdamour: "Neither Timori nor I would be enough for you. We don't have big enough pricks: ours are only maidenhead pricks" (355–56).[e] An ill-defined third class would seem to include such organs as that of the "customer with the large dick"[f] who bears the functional name of M. Lélargisseur (Mr. Widener) (360). Beyond them are the giants destined to appear in the *grandes fouteries*, but also the much-feared sons-in-law, Vitnègre and Guaé, whose dimensions threaten irreparable damage to the narrator's daughters. Clearly, virility is defined and measured by its place in the woman's pattern of growth—but only because sexual growth is itself defined as readiness

[a] Je lui pris le con (outre que je désirais vivement sa possession, je la voulais enhardir et préparer son bijou à l'admission d'un plus gros membre que le mien).

[b] heureusement le vit de mon père n'était pas gros, mais il était long. Il me donna un plaisir complet, car il pénétra si avant qu'il me chatouilla le fond, et au moyen de ce que j'étais très étroite il m'emplissait le con comme si j'avais eu un vit de mulet. . . Voilà comment je fus dépucelée.

[c] Après lui, je t'aurai Traitdamour, mon ancien secrétaire, un joli garçon qui achèvera de t'élargir pour l'engin du payeur que tu préfères.

[d] Après moi ton futur, ou tout autre fouteur, te trouvera comme pucelle./un vit à pucelage plus petit que le mien

[e] Ni moi, ni Timori ne te suffirions point: nous n'avons pas le vit assez gros, ce ne sont que des vits à pucelage.

[f] payeur à gros vit

for penetration. Orifice enlargement is practiced as educative technique in a number of quite modern stories, such as *Histoire d'O*[20] and *Trois Filles de leur mère.*[21] Yet nowhere is it taken quite so "regularly" and simplistically as equivalent to erotic maturation.

Le Rideau levé, ou l'Education de Laure (1786), attributed to Mirabeau or to Sentilly, has much in common with *L'Anti-Justine.* It, too, narrates the sustained use of a father's power in a program of incestuous education. Power, in this more applied and diffuse sense, is not synonymous with sexual potency, any more than it was for Cupidonnet. Laure's father "fits" equally well into the deflowering role: "my rapture came," says Laure, "from nothing more than this charming, pointed, snub-nosed, not very potent prick belonging to a man [the father] whom I adored."[22] [g] Furthermore, this father has the capacity to manage gradual change in the midst of intense erotic activity. A young man, Vernol, is quite disoriented during a particular session of debauchery, but the father, as supervisor, knows what stage has been reached: "Vernol did not know what stage he was at: my father was calculating the gradation" (403).[h]

Laure herself is subject to a special regimen whose explicit purpose is to lead her to erotic maturity. The father provides instruction in the form of caresses and occasional sexual demonstrations, interspersed with periods during which Laure must wear a chastity belt. This is not old-fashioned oppression, we must understand, but a solicitous alternation, an ongoing attempt to espouse the natural rhythms of growth. The problem is, you see, that Laure has a very strong temperament, and is in danger of developing too quickly. Just how great and how immediate is the danger can be seen in the fate of two other women characters. Lucette, a young woman close to the heroine, dies an early death after leading a life of unbridled pleasure (360), and Laure is "bridled" by her father precisely so that she will not develop too quickly:

> My dear Laurette, I'll be frank with you. I don't trust you, nor any of us; your temperament is not yet sufficiently trained for me to be able to leave you to your own devices, and you are so dear to me that I must look after you and conserve you with all the care of which I am capable. Nonetheless, you will enjoy our caresses, and caress us in turn; you will not be stopped from enjoying our pleasures in certain ways, and from

[g] je ne [. . .] devais [mes transports] qu'à ce vit charmant, pointu, retroussé et peu puissant, porté par un homme [the father] que j'adorais.

[h] Il [Vernol] ne savait lui-même où il en était. mon papa calculait la gradation.

time to time we shall arrange a night like this for you. You will find it all the more pleasant for having had time to look forward to it. (359)[i]

The father of Laure is more subtle than Cupidonnet, and in a sense more invasive still, in that he seeks to manage temperament itself, cultivating future promise and containing the threat of premature eruption. Rose, a coeval of Laure, becomes a victim of immature debauchery. She and her brother Vernol are exciting erotic companions because they hurl themselves into every conceivable excess—minus a few hundred of Sade's, of course—but they are erotic orphans. They lack a father, Laure is told, to manage the stages of their growth: "My dear Laure, Rose will be the victim of her passion and her temperament. There is nothing to hold her back; she gives in to it wildly, without moderation or care. You can be certain that she will pay for her rashness, as will Vernol, whom she has pushed into the same excesses. But I want to take advantage of that to work out my purposes" (399).[j] In yielding rashly to desire, Rose and Vernol go far beyond what is reasonable: "Rose was dying: pleasure was dear to her, and was never far away. She felt its effects three or four times for every one that we did. Her cunt was a spring trickling with sperm" (412).[k] Dying metaphorically of pleasure too early and too often leads, in this story, to dying *tout court:* "Rose, given over unrestrainedly to the wild passion that was her dream of happiness, finally succumbed to it" (422).[l] What is the cause of death, exactly? Precocity: Rose dies because she has plunged into adulthood ahead of time. Between her child's body and the demands of adult eroticism, the disparity is presumably too great: "Her periods had not appeared. Before long, she suffered from total exhaustion, followed by dreadful vapors. Her eyesight deteriorated, and she looked like a walking shadow. Her exuberance disap-

[i] Ma chère Laurette, je ne te le cache pas, je me défie de toi, de nous tous; ton tempérament n'est pas encore assez formé pour que je t'abandonne à toi-même, et tu m'es trop chère pour que je ne cherche pas à te ménager avec toute l'attention qui peut dépendre de moi. Cependant, tu jouiras de nos caresses, tu nous en feras; sans gêne avec toi, tu partageras en quelque façon nos plaisirs; et de temps en temps nous te réserverons une nuit pareille, que tu trouveras d'autant plus agréable que tu l'attendras avec impatience.

[j] Ma chère Laure, Rose sera la victime de sa passion et de son tempérament; rien ne la retient; elle s'y livre avec fureur, sans mesure ni ménagement; sois assurée qu'elle paiera de sa personne cette imprudence, ainsi que le pauvre Vernol qu'elle a jeté dans le même excès: mais je veux en profiter pour remplir mes desseins.

[k] Rose se mourait: si elle chérissait le plaisir, celui-ci ne la fuyait pas; elle en ressentait les effets des trois ou quatre fois contre nous une; son con était une source de foutre.

[l] Rose, livrée sans frein à la passion furieuse dont elle faisait l'idole de son bonheur, à la fin y succomba.

peared completely, and a slow, debilitating fever led her to the grave" (422–23).[m]

Waiting for the daughter's first period, respecting the natural ripening of her body is, in *Le Rideau levé,* a fundamental principle of teacherly erotic management. When the right time finally comes, both father and daughter are ready to seize the opportunity with delight. Laure runs to her father, saying, "Here I am now at the time at which you wanted me!" (350).[n] *L'époque où tu me désirais* is ambiguous, in fact: this is the time when he is free to desire her, but it is also the time he has been wanting her to reach. Both maturity and maturation, the product and the process are the objects of his desire. That this is the decisive time is readily apparent to Laure herself, so carefully has she been trained to understand her body as existing in time. The teacher has done much more, in this case, than plant the seed. He has tended the plant during its growth. As tutor and violator, he achieves the perfect synchronization of flowering and deflowering: "this very day I want to have your maidenhead, and pluck the flower that has just bloomed" (350).[o]

Despite the precision of this narrative focus, deflowering is not the culmination of *L'Education de Laure.* As with *L'Anti-Justine, dépucelage* is not *the* erotic event—just one of a series. Indeed, for Restif, one of a very long series of relative *dépucelages.* Any sudden transformation—ritual or otherwise—is effectively anticipated and smoothed out by teacherly gradation. There is therefore no need, in this context, to plumb the psychological or spiritual depths of an inner feminine mystery. All that is required for patriarchal mastery is an indwelling, coercive attention to the processes of change shaping the girl's body into a woman's. By recognizing and cultivating temperament, the teacher can do far more than instruct his pupil: he can apprehend the dynamics of growth as the impulsion of burgeoning desire.

[m] Ses règles n'avaient point paru; elle ne fut pas longtemps sans essuyer un épuisement total, suivi de vapeurs affreuses. Sa vue s'en ressentit, elle ne ressemblait plus qu'à une ombre ambulante. Sa gaieté fut totalement perdue et un dépérissement, produit par une fièvre lente, la conduisit enfin au tombeau.

[n] Me voilà donc enfin à l'époque où tu me désirais!

[o] aujourd'hui même je veux avoir ton pucelage et cueillir la fleur qui vient d'éclore.

Chapter 5

Measured Pastimes, Graded Narratives

Va. Et ne reviens plus mesurer l'ampleur des effets d'un amour.
—Irigaray, *Passions élémentaires*

In the eighteenth century, it is seldom the case that a set of positions is simply displayed or rehearsed in fiction as the paradigm of pleasure. Whatever is left of *ars erotica* tends to be worked out novelistically, so that time becomes the key dimension of pleasure, and syntagmatic gradation the essential shape of erotic textuality. Thus, in the stories of Crébillon, there is a concern with the quality of delay, as dalliance itself achieves thematic status. Learning about sex, for the young hero of Crébillon's *Les Egarements du cœur et de l'esprit* (1736), is a graded introduction to *les gradations* as such:

> She added to that many delicately conceived things, and gave me a glimpse of the need for gradations. This word, and the idea it contained, were totally unknown to me. I took the liberty of saying so to Madame de Lursay who, smiling at my simplicity, was prepared to take the trouble of teaching me. I put each precept into practice as she gave it to me, and the important study of gradations could have led us a very long way, had we not heard a noise in the antechamber that forced us to interrupt the lesson.[1] [a]

[a] Elle ajouta à cela mille choses finement pensées, et me fit enfin entrevoir de quelle nécessité étaient les gradations. Ce mot, et l'idée qu'il renfermait, m'étaient totalement inconnus. Je pris la liberté de le dire à Madame de Lursay, qui, en souriant de ma simplicité, voulut bien prendre la peine de m'instruire. Je mettais chaque précepte en pratique à mesure qu'elle me le donnait, et l'étude importante des gradations aurait

A woman's practice of gradation during amorous encounters, in Crébillon's civilized world, must be morally and aesthetically sensitive, that is, it must be based on a fine sense of timing. If the woman is too fast, she will be considered unseemly; if she is too slow, she will be called a prude: "continual easiness and unrelenting virtue are two things that ought to be feared by a woman" (128).[b] Finding the right pace is a matter of seductive tact. It is possible for Versac, the older libertine in *Les Egarements du cœur et de l'esprit,* to admire the alacrity of response he finds in one of the women characters, crediting her with some of the qualities later to be found in Sade's Juliette and Eugénie: "What a charming woman Madame de Senanges is! With her, there is no fear of foolish remarks or affected delays. In an instant, her mind has noticed everything, her heart has felt everything" (148).[c] But Versac, for saying this, is subject to polite rebuke by the hero, Meilcour: "For me, that is not a reason to like her better. A little hesitation, when it comes to choosing a lover, appears to me more proper in a woman than the hasty response you so appreciate in Madame de Senanges" (148).[d] Indecision and hesitation, in the proper doses, ought to be tastefully integrated into the gentle progress of seduction.

That Versac and Meilcour should disagree about what is proper, even if Meilcour clearly has the last word, points to a fundamental difficulty. In Crébillon, *les gradations* are not so well codified as to be unambiguous. They are presumably always in the process of being elaborated and refined through social intercourse. That may take a long time, of course—just about the time of Crébillon's texts.[2] In *ars erotica,* time was counted out ceremoniously as scenes or tableaux or *giornate,* whereas here it is being transformed into a succession of subtle forward moves. Dalliance thus becomes the very stuff of narrative, as the time of erotic progress coincides, in Crébillon, with the time of the text. *Les gradations,* it must be observed, are anything but pointless delay: they are the graceful constitution of erotic time as seductive extension.

---

pu nous mener fort loin, si nous n'eussions entendu dans l'antichambre un bruit qui nous força de l'interrompre.

[b] une facilité continuelle et une vertu qui ne relâche jamais rien de sa sévérité, sont deux choses à craindre pour une femme.

[c] C'est une femme charmante que Madame de Senanges! On n'a jamais avec elle, ni sottes réflexions, ni lenteurs affectées à craindre. En un instant, son esprit a tout aperçu, son cœur a tout senti.

[d] Ce ne serait pas, repris-je, ce qui me la ferait aimer davantage. Un peu d'indécision, quand il s'agit du choix d'un amant, sied, je crois, mieux à une femme que cette précipitation dont vous savez si bon gré à Madame de Senanges.

Articulating such novelistic time with the vestiges of *ars erotica* was no easy matter and appears to have led to explicit conflict between the narrative-progressive construction of time and the ritual counting of it. Some later eighteenth-century texts seem in fact to display an ambivalent attitude to dalliance. For them, the subtle maneuvering would appear to be too protracted. Will she really yield to him? Can he overcome her resistance? Is she worthy of him, and he of her? How much more incisive and telling it would be to cut through the equivocation, and gauge what is happening in concretely physiological terms! Texts such as those of Diderot and Nerciat sometimes give thematic status both to the equivocation and to the cutting-through. In one anecdote in *Les Bijoux indiscrets* (1748), set in a utopian context, the (half-) seductive ambiguity is overcome by a kind of whimsical rationalism. Two people on the eve of marriage are assessed in order to determine their suitability for each other, but not by the exercise of someone's fine psychological judgment. They are instrumentally measured in a sacred laboratory:

> The two priests spread one of the girls out on the altar, and a third placed the sacred thermometer in her. The great pontiff observed closely the point to which the liquor rose in six minutes. Meanwhile, the young man had been spread out on another bed by two priestesses, and a third had placed the thermometer in him. When the great priest had observed how high the liquor had risen over the same period, he declared the marriage to be valid, and sent the couple off to be joined together in the father's house.[3] [e]

The humor of Diderot's anecdote derives no doubt from the very straightforwardness of the method used. Despite the combined authority of science and religion, we can only look with irony on the claim to measure *tempérament* with a thermometer. The irony, it must be noted, is anything but gratuitous. It derives from a kind of thematic short-circuit, from a desire both to apprehend and expedite the gradual in nature. Instrumental measurement is comic when applied to eroticism precisely because it involves such a literal-minded notion of "degree." At this point in our historical thematics, we witness a conflict,

[e] Alors deux prêtres étendirent une des filles sur l'autel: un troisième lui appliqua le thermomètre sacré; et le grand pontife observait attentivement le degré où la liqueur monta en six minutes. Dans le même temps, le jeune homme avait été étendu sur l'autre lit par deux prêtresses; et une troisième lui avait adapté le thermomètre. Le grand prêtre ayant observé ici l'ascension de la liqueur dans le même temps donné, il prononça sur la validité du mariage, et renvoya les époux se conjoindre à la maison paternelle.

or at least an enduring equivocation in erotic narrative, between straightforward measurement (of stages, of positional scenes, of temperament) and seductive indulgence in gradation-as-delay.

In Nerciat's *Le Diable au corps* (1803), there is an episode in which two kinds of time, gradual negotiation and graded measurement, are considered side by side, and judged on their relative merits. The marquise, the novel's most central character, declares that she is having her period and will thus be unavailable for a planned orgy (III, 159). The tréfoncier (landholder), a senior libertine, is quite undeterred. He proceeds to check her pulse, while subjecting her to stimulation in the form of certain general words (*plaisir, morale*) and proper names like that of Aretino (III, 162). The conclusion he draws from his measurements is that her body is eminently ready for the orgy. He presents her with the evidence of her desire: "At the word *pleasure* your blood began to bubble; the word *morality* straight away made it coagulate. Which leads me to conclude, without being a great sorcerer, that you are obviously in need, in great need of a priapic remedy administered in the most vigorous manner" (III, 166–67).[f] Now this may be read as a touching moment in the literary history of behaviorism, but it is of particular interest to me because of the tréfoncier's self-conscious choice of method. He could have attempted to convince the marquise through discussion, but this would have been complicated and unreliable: "If I had just asked you the question flatly, you would undoubtedly have said: 'I know, I don't want anything; I don't need anything; it's revolting.' I should then have contradicted you, and then it would have become a matter of stubbornness. Instead of helping you to decide to do something pleasurable, I should have put you in a bad temper" (III, 165–166).[g] The tréfoncier, by a second-order measurement, determines that measurement is preferable.

The method set aside here is essentially the one we find in Crébillon: it is that of conversation and negotiation. The method preferred is recognizably that of Diderot's priests, but more pertinently that of Sade: a hand thrust under a dress, a mensurative look at a penis, and so on. And the difference between them is essentially one of power,

[f] Au mot *plaisir* votre sang a bouilli; celui de *morale* a failli le coaguler tout de suite. De quoi, sans être un grand sorcier, j'ai pu conclure qu'[. . .] il est évident que vous avez besoin. . . je dis, grand besoin d'un bon confortatif priapique des plus vigoureusement administré.

[g] Si j'en avais fait tout platement la question, vous n'auriez pas manqué de dire: "Oui, je ne veux rien; il ne me faut rien; c'est une horreur." J'aurais contredit; l'entêtement, pour lors, s'en serait mêlé; et, au lieu de vous déterminer à quelque chose d'agréable, je vous aurais donné de l'humeur.

of efficacity, of speed. By taking hold of the other's body, the libertine master exercises preemptive control, bypassing those endless exchanges in which desire strolls down the wandering paths of seductive elegance. The use of reason, for the tréfoncier, consists in appealing to the physiological authority of nature, and grasping natural processes through their measurable effects. This is how narrative itself can get on with the job. Masculine vigor no doubt requires the master narrator to turn away from what Sade calls the lingering "hypocrisy" of Crébillon's pale-faced *petits-marquis.*[4] Yet this apparently simple move may not guarantee the powerful, direct outcome Sade often supposes. Its cost to narrative seductiveness, as Nerciat notes with perfect ambivalence, may indeed be too great.

Nerciat attempts to measure one kind of gradation against another, while at the same time dallying with both. On occasion, he allows measurements and figures to be the neatest representation of facts: at the end of an elaborate and potentially confusing description, we are promised a "recapitulation" (*Le Diable au corps,* VI, 184). The salient features are in fact "accounted" for efficiently in terms of the number of erotic bouts in which each character has been involved (VI, 184–87). Elsewhere, however, it is measurements themselves, as part of the content of a description, which are said to be long-winded: "the reader's drudgery is at an end. He will not hear any more talk, at least in regard to this place, about height, width, inner walls, or diameters" (*Les Aphrodites,* I, 170n).[h] The trouble is that, if the action of measurement is a sign of power, its products are likely to be signally boring. In *Le Diable au corps,* we find an approximately Sadian set piece, in which two libertines compete to see who will be faster to deflower ten virgins in succession. The challenge as such may not be Sadian, but the whole disposition of the orgy most certainly is. What is the yield, in terms of narrative interest, of this profligate expenditure of virginity? Remarkably little, as the narrator himself suggests: "No, dear readers, I shall not set out for you in detail the circumstances of their maneuver. The description, while no doubt original, would be monotonous, and lacking vitality in the opinion of most of you. The brutal folly of continually repeating a selfish act, and thereby displaying one's vigor, can hardly count as interesting, and still less as moving" (VI, 147–48).[i] Whatever is of greatest erotic value could

[h] la corvée du lecteur est faite. Il n'entendra plus parler, du moins quant à ce lieu-ci, de hauteur, largeur, parois et diamètre.

[i] Non, chers lecteurs, je ne vous ferai point le minutieux détail des circonstances de leur manœuvre. Ce tableau, bien qu'original, sans doute, serait monotone et manquerait

be found only in the vicinity of this orgy, by one who wandered around its edges: "Undeniably more gay for you, and much more interesting, would be a description of some of the sweet little affairs that were going on parallel to the serious and lasting scene involving the wagerers" (VI, 148).[j] All that can be found *in* the orgy is the mechanical application of a kind of sexual algorithm—something which has little to do with truly aesthetic libertinage: "One loves the description of pleasures, and even of odd fancies; but the task undertaken by two depraved men who are very far from knowing what is *truly beautiful* about libertinage (for it does have its own beauty) can only give rise to astonishment if they succeed, or utter ridicule if they fail" (VI, 148; his emphasis).[k] The libertine tyrant is caught in this dilemma: there is nothing, for him, between the simply impressive and the simply ridiculous.

On occasion, measurement signifies the presence of a whole erotic order, entailing erotic practices, indeed full-blown orgies, that are perfectly organized and sustained. Trottignac, a Gascon, is introduced into the secret society that is in principle the subject of *Les Aphrodites,* and the source of its title. As part of his induction into the role of what Sade would have called a *fouteur,* his virility is measured by the attachment of weights to his erect penis. Célestine, the servant, conducts the experiment with care, as if the care were what mattered most: "The detail of this experiment reveals one part of the internal administration of the Aphrodites' guesthouse" (I, 112).[l] At the same time in the story, Mme Durut, the chief administrator, is in the countinghouse, counting out her money (I, 160–62). When she says "sept, huit, neuf, dix . . . " (I, 162), we hear the voice of an order that is capable of existing parallel to and in defiance of dominant social norms. When an orgy is planned, we are privileged—reassured, even—to read in advance the table that shows, for each woman participant, the list of her seven male partners, in order (I, 181–82n).

Yet the narrative and aesthetic value of tabulation, enumeration,

---

de piquant aux yeux de la plupart de vous. La brutale folie de multiplier un acte égoïste et d'y signaler sa vigueur, ne peut intéresser, encore moins émouvoir.

[j] Plus gaie sans contredit et beaucoup plus intéressante serait pour vous, la description de nombre de jolies passades qui se faisaient parallèlement à la sérieuse et durable scène des parieurs.

[k] On aime la peinture des plaisirs et même des caprices; mais la tâche que se sont donnée deux dépravés, bien éloignés de connaître le *vrai beau* du libertinage (car il a le sien aussi) ne peut qu'étonner s'ils la remplissent, ou paraître dans l'autre cas, du dernier ridicule.

[l] Le détail de cette expérience sert à faire connaître une partie de l'administration intérieure de l'hospice des Aphrodites.

and measurement in Nerciat remains doubtful. In *Le Diable au corps,* we find the most precise "account" of a libertine exploit, rendered to the unappealing but naturally vigorous Hilarion by the servant Nicole on behalf of her mistress. A full page of text is taken up by the list of fourteen numbered "inoculations" undergone by the marquise, each marked with an epithet and a sum of money corresponding to its erotic value (IV, 230–31n). The servant describes it all as *plaisant:* she is presumably amused not so much by the evaluation of any particular event as by the fact of doing the formal accounting. It serves to illustrate the fragility and potential inadequacy of a virile quantitative eroticism, all the more so because the quantity of pleasure involved tends to diminish with each successive event. The marquise is "dissatisfied with herself, not that she could have wanted, from the point of view of quantity, anything more than what had been done for her . . . but this long, hot scene had been so monotonous! . . . so unexciting! . . ." (IV, 228–29).[m] All of this serves to highlight the difficulty of choosing comfortably and surely between seduction and measurement as erotic pastimes. Instead of following some march of progress that might have led from Crébillon's elegant hesitation to Sade's vigorous mensuration, Nerciat seems to find himself entertaining both, dancing from one position to another, and making ironic narrative capital out of a broad thematic opposition.

The problem is that not only measurement, but speed and power themselves deserve to be considered ambivalently from the point of view of narrative, for very quick stories are hardly stories at all. As Peter Brooks has shown convincingly, narrative depends for its very existence on a certain kind of delay, or of middleness. Narrative must be understood, he says, in terms of plotting: "the middle as detour, as struggle toward the end under the compulsion of imposed delay, as arabesque in the dilatory space of the text."[5] Can such a principle of delay be maintained in stories that are committed to a strong notion of libertine mastery? Can there be a delay that, conceived in masculinist terms, does not just give itself up, through dilatoriness, to feminine power as coyness, or coquetry? Are there principles of delay that can maintain the time of the story in the absence of the sustained, playful talk that is the very stuffing of *Le Sopha,* without lapsing into the mechanics of tiresome repetition? Crébillon's sultan is happy when Zulica finally yields to her suitor's entreaties: "That's very good, very

[m] peu satisfaite d'elle-même, non qu'elle eût pu désirer, quant à la quantité, quelque chose de plus que ce qu'on avait fait pour elle. . . mais cette chaude et longue scène avait été si monotone!. . . si peu piquante!. . .

good! You've brought me great relief. Indeed, I was beginning to fear that it would never take place. What a foolish creature that Zulica was, with all her shilly-shallying!" (215–16).[n] Had this listener not experienced the "fear" of the nonevent, he could not have known the relief of the denouement. Is that not superior in quality to the "relief" posited by Nerciat at the end of a period of readerly "drudgery" (*Les Aphrodites,* 17On)? Are there in fact ways in which the erotic could be spun out, made to last long enough actually to constitute a proper narrative, other than through the deviousness and the relative imprecision of fictive seduction?

As if to escape this dilemma, Nerciat makes plots out of the negotiation of obstacles to eroticism. Continually, the characters in his stories are faced with difficulties arising within the domain of their own erotic practices, so that it is largely the overcoming of these difficulties that constitutes the story of pleasure, and doubtless the pleasures of the story. As Suzanne Giroux de Morency says in *Illyrine* (1799), which proceeds in much the same way as Nerciat's narratives, "How exciting it is to have to overcome these little obstacles!"[6] [o] Erotic narrative is thus able to adapt to its purposes certain elements of the novel of adventure. Such old peripatetic favorites as smallpox can be put to work in a somewhat different way. In *Les Liaisons dangereuses,* smallpox functions antierotically, as the *fléau* that destroys Mme de Merteuil's power to seduce. In *Julie, ou la Nouvelle Héloïse,* it has a sustained, almost tutelary impact on the story: as Julie and Saint-Preux heal slowly from it, they are seen to heal, in part, from their passion for each other. But in *Illyrine* and *Le Diable au corps,* smallpox is more or less mastered by erotic intrigue. In both of these stories, like a true adventure, it simply comes and goes. Illyrine goes dramatically from being beautiful to being unattractive, but then returns to her original state (160, 190). The marquise, in *Le Diable au corps,* is struck down with the illness, but being "down" in this way is also an erotic position, as it happens. The monk Hilarion, who is ostensibly at her bedside in order to minister to her spiritual needs, yields to temptation by entering the bed himself. Of this event, we are told that it is extraordinary, but also that it is the mark of a certain quality of erotic *attentiveness:* "That was how far things had gone, when a particularly bizarre set of circumstances gave rise to these extraordinary events, which proves how much some people, whose temperament has its chains,

[n] Fort bien cela, fort bien![. . .] vous me tirez d'une grande peine. Ma foi! Je commençais à craindre que cela ne fût jamais. Ah! la sotte créature que cette Zulica, avec ses façons!

[o] Que ces petits obstacles à vaincre sont piquants!

are alert to the opportunity of breaking loose" (IV, 106).[p] Is it as a reward for temperament and resourcefulness or simply by coincidence that the marquise recovers from the illness virtually unmarked (IV, 141–42)? The narrator does not know the answer to this question, but there is at least a possibility that a certain adventurous attitude has allowed the heroine to eroticize the obstacle itself, and ultimately to triumph over one of the dark bodily enemies of pleasure.[7]

Le Diable au corps manages, in fact, to deal successfully with a whole series of narrative difficulties that are more or less germane to erotic behavior, and whose very appearance, in another context, might have compelled restraint, or abstinence. We have already noted that the marquise's period is said by her to be an obstacle. All that remains to be seen, in this regard, is how the tréfoncier's desire plunges him into the very substance of interdiction: "With a roar, the virtuoso plunges [his prick] in with one thrust, and drowns in a stream of blood: that is his fancy" (IV, 28).[q] More durably, the marquise's pregnancy, after her recovery from smallpox, effectively disqualifies her from orgies in the last month: "She was resolute enough at that time to abstain from any libertine caprices" (VI, 4).[r] Yet she has not really "fallen" pregnant, in the fullest narrative sense. She goes *through* her pregnancy without falling into motherhood, since the twin babies are kind enough: (a) to be ugly and (b) to die (VI, 11). More dramatically still, perhaps, we see the return to combat of one of the characters after he has suffered a bout of venereal disease and undergone a severe operation. As he copulates with the marquise, by now quite recovered from her smallpox (V, 123), the story enacts the triumph of erotic activity over those things that might elsewhere have brought it to a sudden stop.[8]

Laughter often appears in libertine stories as a sign of the antierotic, the mark of something that must be overcome if erotic narrative is to proceed. It tends often, in fact, to be a symptom or a by-product of male impotence. Laughter can be thought of as a privileged form of *badinage,* precisely the form of feminine teasing that holds sway in the absence of male triumph.[9] The woman's laughter sometimes appears as a kind of punctuation marking the end of the act. When the man is exhausted, he can be mocked in the name of what he was so shortly

[p] Les choses en étaient là, quand une circonstance, des plus bizarres, fit naître un de ces événements extraordinaires, qui prouvent à quel point certaines gens, dont le tempérament a des chaînes, sont attentifs à saisir la moindre occasion de les briser.

[q] Le virtuose rugissant plonge [son vit] impitoyablement d'un seul coup de reins, et se noie dans des flots de sang: c'est son caprice.

[r] Elle eut pour lors, le courage de s'abstenir de toute folie galante.

before: "The mischievous servant girl, as she moves away from the exhausted tréfoncier, cannot refrain from laughing insultingly at the sight of his deeply humble weapon, which only a short time before had looked so boastfully proud" (*Le Diable au corps,* IV, 78).[s] What is so narratively amusing is that the man is unable to continue, having just spent himself. Here is an example from *Thémidore.* The narrator-hero has already made love to two courtesans when the woman who really interests him arrives unexpectedly to join the group:

> I was humiliated, I must confess. Argentine and Laurette were gloating inwardly. My eyes turned to Rozette, begging her pardon for what was happening to me, or rather what was not happening. She appeared touched by that: a misfortune that happened in her company almost seemed to include her.
>
> They taunted me, and poked fun at me. (12)[t]

In *Le Sopha,* by a kind of sceptical, even scornful inversion, it is the man who laughs at his own impotence, and the woman who is offended by his lack of rhetorical seriousness in the seductive enterprise: "On hearing this well-placed exclamation, Mazulhim could not help but burst out laughing, and Zulica, who knew how dangerous laughter sometimes is, was seriously upset with him for laughing" (167).[u] Zulica is right: laughter is indeed dangerous. As we shall see, in Sade it is likely to lead to death or damnation, but here it simply threatens the conclusion of erotic narrative. The resourcefulness of Nerciat's libertine storytelling, in particular, consists in raising it as obstacle in order to work around it, filling out the story with that which threatens the story.

The key thing about laughter seems to be its timing. Nerciat's writing recognizes an essential seriousness in the commitment to intense pleasure,[10] but this seriousness is something that comes on his libertine characters at certain moments: "The seriousness that is always brought on by supreme pleasure finally overcame the marquise's levity. She

[s] L'espiègle soubrette ne peut, en s'écartant de l'épuisé Tréfoncier, s'abstenir d'insulter par des ris, l'humilité profonde du braquemart naguère si fanfaron.

[t] Je fus humilié, je le confesse. Argentine et Laurette triomphaient intérieurement. Mes yeux se tournèrent du côté de Rozette, et lui demandaient pardon de ce qui m'arrivait, ou plutôt de ce qui ne m'arrivait pas: elle en parut touchée; un malheur qui arrivait en sa compagnie l'en rendait presque participante.

On me badina, on me tourna en ridicule.

[u] A cette exclamation si bien placée, Mazulhim ne put s'empêcher d'éclater, et Zulica, qui savait combien quelquefois il est dangereux de rire, se fâcha fort sérieusement de ce qu'il avait ri.

gave up, caught fire with passion, lost control, and came" (*Le Diable au corps,* VI, 29).[v] Laughter can be a powerful weapon, when used against the desire of the other: "as soon as there is ridicule about, all desire disappears" (*Les Aphrodites,* I, 41).[w] In *Félicia,* Monrose tells of attempts by male teachers to seduce him, provoking Félicia and Sylvina to laughter: "The poor young man was so nonplussed that he did not dare look at us. We realized just how impertinent we had been" (202).[x] But it is not reliably the case that laughter kills pleasure. The marquise in *Le Diable au corps* is left in the spectator's position, while the tréfoncier sodomizes her servant. She responds, not only with *badinage,* but with outright *persiflage,* and yet still the force of laughter is less than the strength of desire:

> *The Marquise:* That's enough my dear Comte: you are no longer concentrating on the conversation; and . . . it actually looks as if he is feeling pleasure! . . . It's utterly laughable! Can you believe it? Look at his eyes fluttering . . . Is it not true, Comte, that it is coming on?
> *The Tréfoncier* (flushed): No, my dear . . . It is just leaving me . . .
> (*Le Diable au corps,* II, 119)[y]

Symmetrically, the marquise, having engaged her friend the comtesse with the help of an enormous, nay, ridiculous *godemiché* (VI, 31–32), reaches a state of satisfaction where she cannot be assailed by the tréfoncier's mockery: "Does the handsome prelate think he can ridicule me? Let him try. I have just taken my pleasure, and I am still in its afterglow. No one can upset me" (VI, 36).[z] Laughter, in Nerciat, happens around the central seriousness of pleasure—most dangerously beforehand, and most naturally afterward[11]—but it is finally made to serve the purposes of erotic narration.

All this thematic dalliance with stories of illness and impotence must appear from a Sadian point of view as a denial of the truly erotic.

[v] Le sérieux, qu'occasionnent toujours les approches du plaisir suprême, succède enfin chez la Marquise à l'enjouement; elle est résignée, s'enflamme, s'égare et jouit.

[w] dès que le ridicule s'en mêle, tout désir disparaît.

[x] Le pauvre petit, déconcerté, n'osait plus nous regarder; nous sentîmes toute l'étendue de notre impertinence.

[y] *La Marquise:* C'est assez, mon pauvre Comte: vous n'êtes plus à l'entretien; et. . . l'on dirait, en vérité, qu'il a du plaisir!. . . C'est à mourir de rire! Tout de bon! Voilà ses yeux qui clignotent. . . N'est-ce pas, Comte, que cela vient?
Le Tréfoncier, avec agitation: Non, ma chère. . . Cela s'en va. . .

[z] Il croit me persifler, ce beau prélat? A son aise. Je viens de m'en donner: je suis encore dans le crépuscule du plaisir. On ne peut me mettre de mauvaise humeur.

Sade's work does actually contain one or two rare incidents resembling those described routinely in Nerciat, such as the following from *Les Infortunes de la vertu:* "With these cruel words, Dalville lunged toward me . . . but I was so revolted by him, and his dreadful maxims filled me with such hatred that I pushed him away strongly. He had to resort to force, and I felt the strength of his blows, but he did not conquer me. His frantic passion died without success, and the tears he shed then were my revenge for his assault on me" (II, 359).[a] Justine fails here to play her normal role as victim. She does not laugh, of course, but she does not cry either. Only the would-be rapist is left to cry at the fiasco. How fragile and ineffective Dalville is when he encounters determined resistance! He certainly does not provide us with a full-fledged example of the Sadian tyrant, but he *is* profoundly Sadian, at least, in not finding the obstacle in any way *piquant.* Indeed, it could be said that, for Sade, the erotic obstacle is a contradiction in terms.

Before we move to further considerations of Sadian narrative time, there is more to be said about the role of negotiation within more complicated erotic encounters. In texts like those of Nerciat, we find a politics of the orgy very far from that of Sade. In the first place, there is actually intrigue *within* orgies: tricks are played by one partner on another, particularly in relation to sodomy. On one occasion, in *Les Aphrodites,* a woman preempts a ruse by her partner: "being easily annoyed, she struggled and pulled free, thus frustrating the grand vicar at the key moment, and left him with the disappointment of firing his shot into the air" (II, 84–85).[b] In *Le Diable au corps,* Chiavaculi, a devout sodomist, is tricked—literally manipulated by the comtesse into vaginal sex. Everyone present laughs at him as he cries out to be released, protesting that he has been betrayed. He appears perfectly ridiculous at this point—"Priape, whose ridiculous situation made everyone laugh" (VI, 203)[c]—but is soon won over to pleasure by the art of the comtesse: "she triumphed over the most vice-laden and stubborn of men" (VI, 204).[d] That women should be the tricksters in each case seems not to be a coincidence: they exercise this form of

[a] A ces mots cruels, Dalville se précipita sur moi. . . mais il me faisait une telle horreur, ses affreuses maximes m'inspiraient tant de haine que je le repoussai durement; il voulut employer la force, elle ne lui réussit pas, il s'en dédommagea par des cruautés, je fus abîmée de coups, mais il ne triompha pas; le feu s'éteignit sans succès, et les larmes perdues de l'insensé me vengèrent enfin de ses outrages.

[b] très aisée à se fâcher, elle se débat, se dégage, frustre tout net le grand vicaire au plus beau moment, et lui donne le chagrin de tirer son coup en l'air.

[c] Priape, dont le ridicule faisait rire tout le monde

[d] Elle triomphait du plus vicieux et du plus entêté des hommes.

diverting or deflecting power against senior dominant males in the libertine herd.

In Nerciat, the very mechanics of the orgy, always brought off without incident in Sade, are themselves a source of narrative interest. Two people wishing to join the Société des Aphrodites simply fail the practical section of their entrance examination in the most risible fashion, despite having begun promisingly as a couple (II, 204). The problem is that they emerge from ritual anonymity only to find that they are opponents in a lawsuit, about which they begin to quarrel noisily. They are soon excluded from the society for their own failure to exclude outside considerations (II, 204). Elsewhere in Nerciat, there are problems with the mechanics of joining an already functioning erotic tableau. A comte wishes to join a duchesse and a chevalier, but fails to time his entry correctly: "He walked toward the bed, but that was just when the chevalier and the duchesse reached a critical point. Their excitement, the tone of their voices, their passionate words of endearment were such that the comte felt more humiliated than aroused. He slumped into a chair, nonplussed, pensive, ill at ease, somber, with his head down and sighing in pain" (*Les Aphrodites,* I, 47).[e] In fact, this is not a simple failure, or a definitive exclusion: it is eventually shown as the source of delay in constituting more elaborate erotic scenes. Yet it is delay made out of, or made within, a malfunctioning erotic order—the kind of delay that would be unacceptable to Sade.

There is a general tendency for Nerciat's orgies to be broadly collaborative, rather than ruled by tyrannical masters of ceremonies, as in Sade. The rhythm of simultaneous pleasure is not achieved merely by the uttering of commands, but by a whole series of exclamatory exchanges whose function is a kind of urgent negotiation:

> *The Marquise:* Fuck . . . what delight . . . Ah! . . . Ah! . . . The pleasure is killing me . . . stop for a while . . .
> All three, at the same time, slow down their movement.
> (*Le Diable au corps,* I, 114; cf. I, 175)[f]

[e] Il marche vers le lit, mais c'est tout juste le moment où le chevalier et la duchesse tombent en crise. Leurs agitations, leurs accents, leurs mots caressants, passionnés, sont de nature à ce que le comte soit plus humilié qu'enflammé. Il se jette sur un siège, confus, pensif, embarrassé de sa contenance, l'oeil sombre, la tête baissée et soupirant avec douleur.

[f] *La Marquise:* Foutre!. . . quelles délices. . . Ah!. . . ah!. . . le plaisir me tue. . . suspendez. . .
Tous trois, à la fois, ralentissent leurs movements.

Collaborative restraint is required when, by a contingency almost unknown in erotic literature, there are uneven numbers of would-be participants in a major erotic event: "It is unfortunate, noted the chevalier, having counted us with his eyes, that there should be seven men here, while we have only five women. If the numbers were even, we would get drunk on purpose so as not to be guilty of any premeditated act toward a sex that deserves our infinite respect. Each one of us then, being out of his senses, would marry the woman next to him" (*Mon Noviciat,* 166).[g] The obstacle is overcome by having one of the men dress as a woman, and play a dual role, while two men together engage the servant Félicité. The most striking example of collaboration occurs when a carefully planned orgy, whose preparations had occupied a good deal of textual space, actually fails to take place. This is the ultimate erotic *péripétie,* more than deserving, surely, of the narrator's mild exclamation, "quel dommage!" (*Les Aphrodites,* VI, 101). What brings about this hiatus is that someone has denounced the organizer, Mme Couplet, to the police. In response to this, there is a spontaneous assembly, in which organizational decisions are taken more or less consensually. The option of nudity or disguise is exercised, with a clear majority in favor of the latter (VI, 131). A new venue is proposed and accepted by acclamation (VI, 114); they will repair to the tréfoncier's place, where the original M.C. can no longer preside: "Here, the ingenious Couplet would not have the honor of officiating during the ceremony" (VI, 129).[h] Their provisions will be leftovers, but they will have a perfectly satisfactory, two-star orgy: "We shall make our supper out of the banquet's debris. It is true that we shall not have colored lights, fireworks, or music, but we shall enjoy ourselves without all that" (VI, 113–14).[i]

Now even to contemplate such carefully negotiated pleasures is thoroughly anti-Sadian. Sade not only rejects the eroticism of the obstacle but, beyond and behind it, a whole tradition of narrative seduction. To return to the thematic watershed with which we began this chapter, it is possible to understand Sade as going through with the choice that Nerciat was unwilling to make in a definitive way,

[g] Il est malheureux, s'avisa de dire le chevalier, nous ayant comptés de l'œil, que nous soyons ici sept hommes, tandis que nous n'avons que cinq femmes. En nombre égal, nous nous enivrerions exprès afin de n'être coupable de rien de prémédité envers un sexe à qui nous devons infiniment de respect; chacun alors en véritable insensé, épouserait sa voisine.

[h] Ici, l'ingénieuse Couplet ne devait point avoir l'honneur de régler le cérémonial.

[i] Des débris du banquet nous souperons: nous n'aurons, à la vérité, ni lampions, ni fusées, ni musique; mais nous nous amuserons bien sans tout cela.

resolutely choosing the time of measurement, for its power and its efficacy, over that of negotiation. Sade has no tolerance for the feints of the seducer, no patience with his endless games, no respect for his show of weakness. He scorns courtly seductive behavior as pointless, shapeless waiting: "Those spineless adorers of women: I shall leave them at the feet of their insolent Dulcineas, still awaiting the sign that is to make them happy" *(La Philosophie dans le boudoir,* III, 542).[j] As Marcel Hénaff says, Sade sets up the machinery that will allow desire to be followed by satisfaction, without delay.[12] There should be no pining, no pleading, no *badinage.* Instead of striptease, with the feminine power that implies, we have instantaneous nudity, so that any delay is not the sign of indulgence, but a symptom of clumsiness: "'Undress her, undress her!' he said to Marie in a fury. 'She should be naked already'" (*Les Cent Vingt Journées,* I, 119).[k] In *La Nouvelle Justine,* undressing takes place with an instantaneous violence akin to murder: "And straightaway throwing her skirts up over her head, he slashed them with his knife in such a horrible manner that it seemed for a moment as if the scoundrel had cut open the poor girl's belly. In a trice, the most beautiful body in the world was exposed for the second time to lasciviousness at its most monstrous" (VI, 76).[l] By its brutally efficient functioning, erotic action must preempt what Hénaff calls "the old threat that spoils libertine desire: a refusal on the other's part, or doubt that is allowed to hang over her/his reply, thus necessitating the quest, the wait, the digression and, in spite of everything, the risk of failure."[13] [m]

All this is not just a matter of temperament, but of conviction, for Sade's philosophy specifically requires the psychology of impetuousness. Desires come from nature and should not be resisted, as a matter of principle: "These inclinations were given to me by nature, and I should be provoking nature were I to resist them" (I, 27).[n] The

[j] Plats adorateurs des femmes, je les laisse, aux pieds de leur insolente dulcinée, attendre le soupir qui doit les rendre heureux.

[k] Déshabillez donc, déshabillez donc! disait-il à Marie, en fureur, elle devrait déjà être nue.

[l] Et lui passant aussitôt ses jupes par-dessus la tête, il les fend, avec son couteau, d'une si horrible manière, que l'on crut un moment que c'était le ventre de cette malheureuse que le coquin partageait en deux. En un instant le plus beau corps du monde fut une seconde fois exposé à tout ce que la luxure peut avoir de plus monstrueux.

[m] la vieille menace qui gâte le désir libertin: le refus opposé par l'autre ou le doute qu'il laisse planer sur sa réponse, donc la nécessité de la quête, de l'attente, du détour, avec malgré tout le risque de l'échec.

[n] C'est de la nature que je les ai reçus, ces penchants, et je l'irriterais en y résistant.

libertine who takes his own desires seriously should not allow them to be obstructed or diverted in any way. It may even be the case, as Durcet argues to the duc de Blangis, that happiness does not lie in mere satisfaction, but it certainly lies in the breaking out and the breaking through of desire: "Happiness is not found in the enjoyment of sensual pleasure, but in desire" (I, 181).[o] If the obstacle has a role, it is precisely in being destroyed—not toyed with, displaced, or even overcome. When the duc de Blangis wishes to disparage a particular "passion," he says of it: "it is more diverting than lubricious" (I, 308).[p] For Crébillon, these two epithets might have been approximately synonymous: for Sade, there is a qualitative, hierarchical difference between them.

It is not that we never hear of seduction or negotiation in Sade's fiction. There is occasional mention, for example, of the activity whereby young people are seduced into a life of vice. This is what Curval does, rather exceptionally, with Adonis, the son of a colleague: "he was the one who had provided the necessary means and information for corrupting the boy" (I, 57).[q] But *débaucher,* as we saw in *La Philosophie dans le boudoir,* need not take very long. It is hard to notice any difference, in this regard, between the time of seduction and that of abduction: the "information" possessed by Curval would appear to be circumstantial, rather than subtly psychological. In general, the task of recruiting youthful partners/victims is menial enough to be delegated to lesser people. It can in fact be a more or less full-time job, as the following example indicates:

> No other person had a more remarkable talent than this man for leading young girls into vice, and since it was his most sublime skill he made of it his one and only pleasure. All his satisfaction came from uprooting childhood prejudices, pouring scorn on virtue, and presenting vice in the most appealing light. Nothing was left out: seductive descriptions, flattering promises, delightful examples. Everything was deployed and skillfully ordered, artistically proportioned according to the age and mind of the child, and he never failed to bring it off. (I, 138)[r]

There is definite artistry involved here, but the narration of *Les Cent Vingt Journées* does no more than summarize it in passing as a particu-

[o] Ce n'est pas dans la jouissance que consiste le bonheur, c'est dans le désir.

[p] elle est plus divertissante que lubrique.

[q] c'était lui qui avait donné et les moyens et les renseignements nécessaires pour le débaucher.

[r] Aucun être dans le monde n'avait un talent plus singulier que cet homme pour entraîner de jeunes filles dans le vice, et comme c'était son art le plus sublime, il en

lar, relatively minor passion. There is no time to enter into the process of seduction as such, with all its wandering complications.

It is tempting to conclude, in view of Sade's constant temptation to conclude, that Sadian eroticism amounts to a refusal of plot, in Peter Brooks's sense. In the very haste with which transformations are effected, there is a threat of narrative short-circuit—something much like the premature ejaculation that affects some minor Sadian libertines.[14] In order to make time for his novels while still maintaining the urgent tyranny of desire, Sade must practice measure itself as an *art.* At least one model for such an art can be found in Sade's fiction, in the person of someone who is herself a storyteller: Duclos, in *Les Cent Vingt Journées.* Duclos, we are told more than once, is an outstanding *branleuse.* This is how she practices her skills on the duc de Blangis:

> Grasping his lordship's enormous instrument, she began to shake it, keeping its head uncovered, and moved it with such art. She agitated it with strokes so swift and simultaneously so perfectly attuned to the state she observed her patient to be in, that the bomb finally exploded over the hole it was to cover, flooding it. The duc shouted, swore, and stormed. Duclos did not lose her rhythm; her motion was regulated by the degree of pleasure it produced. (I, 120)[s]

What is most impressive about Duclos's technique is that it combines urgency (*secousses rapides*) with a sense of proportion, and a fine judgment as to the state of her patient. Each time that she is described as masturbating others, we are reminded of her remarkable sense of erotic *timing* (I, 143, 329, 330). It is a matter not of leaping to the point of greatest intensity, but of reaching it by gradation: "While frigging him, I had to strike him in a graded way, that is, gently at first, then a little harder as his prick took on some consistency, then finally with bone-shattering blows when he ejaculated" (I, 265).[t] What

---

faisait aussi son seul et son unique plaisir. Toute sa volupté consistait à déraciner les préjugés de l'enfance, à faire mépriser la vertu et à parer le vice des plus belles couleurs. Rien n'y était négligé: tableaux séduisants, promesses flatteuses, exemples délicieux, tout était mis en oeuvre, tout était adroitement ménagé, tout artistement proportionné à l'âge, à l'espèce d'esprit de l'enfant, et jamais il ne manquait son coup.

[s] Empoignant l'énorme instrument de monseigneur, elle se met à le secouer, la tête toujours découverte, à le remuer avec tant d'art, à l'agiter par des secousses si rapides et en même temps si proportionnés à l'état dans lequel elle voyait son patient, qu'enfin la bombe éclate sur le trou qu'elle doit couvrir. Il s'en inonde; le duc crie, jure, tempête. Duclos ne se démonte pas; ses mouvements se déterminent en raison du degré de plaisir qu'ils procurent.

[t] Il s'agissait, en le branlant, de le souffleter par gradation, c'est-à-dire doucement d'abord, puis un peu plus fort à mesure que son vit prenait de la consistance, et enfin à tour de bras lorsqu'il déchargeait.

precedes the final climax is not a detour, or a struggle, or even suspense, but a measured buildup.

It is not hard to see the general value of this model for Sadian narration: it enacts a form of mastery that is mastery over its ultimate object, mastery both in and over time. What is known at the outset, as Brisa-Testa says on one occasion to his companions in *Histoire de Juliette,* is that "we have a long time ahead of us for pleasure, and consequently gradations to observe" (IX, 314).[u] Precisely because there are no real obstacles, no negotiations, no doubt whatsoever about the final outcome, it is possible to measure off the proceedings as a controlled, ascending series. This is how time is materialized in erotic terms: the libertine who is "irritated" by unsatisfied desire, and committed in principle to going through with his actions may learn thus to hold back—avoiding premature ejaculation at all costs—in order to enhance his very irritation, and with it his drive toward the most drastic libertine acts.[15] Saint-Fond arrives for a night of murderous debauchery, saying to Juliette: "I have not ejaculated for a week. No one can equal me in the art of sharpening his passions by industrious abstinence. I do not miss out on my pleasures for that: I have been fucked perhaps two hundred times, and seen a hundred or a hundred fifty individuals of all sexes while on this regimen, without losing a drop of spunk" (VIII, 341).[v] So it is that Sade considers *not* ejaculating, in a situation of powerful stimulus, to be near the height of erotic mastery. Such is the physiology of virile delay—as opposed to pale, seductive waiting—experienced by the duc in Duclos's school for *branleuses:* "It cost him an unbelievable effort of control in order not to lose his spunk there, but he had enough self-mastery to be able to hold it in and came back in triumph to boast of having resisted such an assault. He defied his friends to go through it all with the same self-control" (I, 125).[w] Durcet, at the end of a similar experiment, actually makes of his impotence a kind of triumph (I, 136). Despite having spent some time with the girls, he has not finished with them, and is all the more severe for that.

Erotic measure can be understood as practicing both urgency and delay at the same time, *as* the same time. This is Jérôme, at his most deliberate, in *La Nouvelle Justine:*

[u] nous avons longtemps à jouir, et, par conséquent, des gradations à observer.

[v] Il y a huit jours que je n'ai déchargé; personne ne possède comme moi l'art d'aiguiser ses passions par une abstinence industrieuse; je n'en jouis pas moins: j'ai peut-être été foutu deux cents coups, et vu cent ou cent cinquante individus de tout sexe pendant ce régime, sans perdre une goutte de foutre.

[w] Il lui fallut d'incroyables efforts sur lui-même pour n'y pas perdre son foutre, mais

> *Urged on* by the need to lose my spunk, I obliged my victim to hold her lover's prick in her mouth, and buggered her in that position. I had a dagger in my hand; I was planning to kill her at the moment of my discharge . . . That moment was getting closer; I delayed my strokes; I wanted the last one to come slowly. Meanwhile, I quietly delighted in the pleasurable idea of mingling the divine surge of my discharge with the last sighs of the person I was fucking. (VII, 15)[x]

Slowness flourishes, so to speak, in the midst of haste, expanding in the murderous certainty of the outcome. In quite the same way, narration itself can be measured and masterly by the way in which it refrains from blurting out its strongest episodes, being content to work toward them by degrees. To let it all come pouring out might be to confess the truth in a moment, in some garrulous, no doubt childish or feminine way. "Don't oblige him to make his confession, my lord. He'd tell things we must not hear yet" (*Les Cent Vingt Journées*, I, 149).[y] To resist this temptation and practice the discipline of "not telling yet" is to hold out the promise of steadily increasing intensity.

Les Cent Vingt Journées de Sodome is arguably the best example of measured narration in Sade, since the "plot" itself is virtually without obstacles or adventures, taking the form of a pact of violence *and* restraint. This pact, frequently renewed, is to be confirmed and justified in the eventual fullness of pleasure: "But we must behave ourselves: by having to wait like this for our pleasures, we shall make them much more delightful. [. . .] But patience . . . everything will come in good time, you will see" (I, 308).[z] In dealing with a regally impatient audience, Crébillon's Amanzéi had to respond by being constantly diverting, but Sade's Duclos can answer in the name of the pact: "but have a little patience, and we shall gradually come to what you are referring to" (I, 187).[a] Libertine patience and libertine *sagesse* have nothing to do with virtue, of course, they are merely techniques

---

assez maître de lui, il sut se contenir et revint triomphant se vanter qu'il venait de supporter un assaut qu'il défiait ses amis de soutenir avec le même flegme.

[x] Pressé du besoin de perdre mon foutre, j'oblige ma victime à prendre dans la bouche le vit de son amant, et je l'encule en cet état. J'avais un poignard à la main; je lui réservais la mort à l'instant de ma décharge. . . Elle approche; je fais devancer mes coups; ce n'est qu'avec lenteur que je veux lui faire recevoir le dernier. Je caresse en attendant avec délices la voluptueuse idée de mêler aux divins élans de ma décharge les derniers soupirs de celle que je fouts.

[y] Ne lui faites pas faire sa confession, monseigneur; il nous dirait des choses que nous ne devons pas encore entendre.

[z] Mais il faut être sage: en attendant ainsi nos plaisirs, nous les rendrons bien plus délicieux. [. . .] Mais patience. . . tu verras que tout viendra avec le temps.

[a] Mais un peu de patience, et nous arriverons par degrés à ce que vous voulez dire.

for inscribing vice in time. After all, on the face of it, the one hundred twenty days might have been constituted simply as a space in which the range of "passions" could be deployed, as the ultimate *ars erotica*. Its distributive, paradigmatic dimension is visible enough, with the broad division into four classes of passion, each class containing, in principle, one hundred fifty items. But, as Leo Bersani and Ulysse Dutoit point out, "the work is organized in order to produce a certain type of narrative progression which is itself erotically stimulating. The purpose of the book is, we might say, to create its own narrative."[16] The initial project attributed to the four friends is apparently to develop a taxonomy, and then to add narrative interest to it: "It would thus be a question of finding some individuals capable of providing an account of these processes, of analyzing them, of graduating them, and of running a story through it all, for interest's sake" (I, 46).[b] This is broadly consistent with the banquet metaphor—the spread of passions made available to the reader—found in the authorial presentation (I, 79). Yet in (syntagmatic) practice, the unfolding of the list becomes of itself the point, or the sense of the text. Joan De Jean notes the tension between these two kinds of textual organization: "As the narrator of the *120 journées* constantly proclaims, the building blocks of his text cannot be shifted or interchanged, for they possess a developmental logic all their own: Sade uses a fixed mathematical schema, a narrative accountability, to make parataxis the narrative equal of unfolding."[17] The "table" as model for the space of the text comes under pressure from the notion of measure, which provides, so to speak, a paradigm of the syntagmatic. The novel rehearses the full set of passions, but it also moves through them with increasing intensity, enacting their gradation as something erotic in itself. In the terms of Bersani and Dutoit, "the pacing [. . .] is more deeply characteristic of Sadean sex than the sexual content of any one day's adventures" (28).[18]

Reading this gradation, we can infer a hierarchical order of pleasure constraining the narrative. The most fundamental rule, stated explicitly in the text, is, of course, the one that guards against anticlimax: "you must not go from the stronger to the weaker" (I, 361).[c] Without this, erotic narrative might fall back into some sequence of adventures, and Sade is resolutely, powerfully set against the vicissitude as such. It does not suffice, however, to know that the erotically weak must precede the erotically strong: we have to note what, in Sade's world,

[b] Il s'agissait donc d'abord de trouver des sujets en état de rendre compte de tous ces excès, de les analyser, de les étendre, de les détailler, de les graduer, et de placer au travers de cela l'intérêt d'un récit.

[c] il ne faut pas aller du fort au faible.

counts as strong, stronger, strongest. The rules for this are simple enough to determine, being not only inscribed narratively but enunciated "philosophically" with the greatest vigor. Indeed, the most powerful stricture on Sadian narrative—its self-confirming destiny—is said to be a law of nature: "the priority of the strong over the weak was ever among the laws of nature" *(Les Infortunes de la vertu,* II, 352).[d]

Predictably enough, Sade's laws of gradation inflect the natural according to philosophical conviction: it seems to be a general rule that acts involving females (choice of victims, training of libertines, copulation, cruelty) precede those involving males, and that *le con* everywhere precedes *le cul* in a respectfully self-effacing way. Where torture is concerned, the dosage of cruelty can presumably be measured quite accurately by counting blows, mutilations, and the like. Murder poses a particular problem for narration since it takes place at the drastic meeting point of life and death. Libertine effort and skill consist nonetheless in producing gradation within it. Here are Dolmancé's instructions to his fellow libertines for dealing with Mme de Mistival: "During our pleasure, each one is invited to decide for himself what torture he wishes to inflict on her; but bear in mind that the suffering must increase gradually, so as not to kill her off straightaway" (III, 553).[e] Saint-Fond somehow always hopes, unreasonably, to do better than he has done before, to kill for longer—more intensively and more thoroughly. Clairwil calls him to reason: "do not try to kill a single person for a long time: that is impossible. Murder many others: that is perfectly feasible" (VIII, 420).[f] But the dream of ultimate gradation remains, as a tempting alternative to Clairwil's endless multiplication. Chantal Thomas discusses the point with care:

> From the libertine's point of view, one single victim whose death was made to go on indefinitely would be preferable to a multitude of victims, even if their number were endless, since the art of dosage and measurement would then be applied with the greatest precision. But "the slow, rigorous anguish" of torture, even if it does lead to death, encounters insurmountable resistance: the atemporal, unanalyzable, incalculable passage from life to death. That is why he utters this cry of impotence:

[d] la priorité du fort sur le faible fut toujours dans les lois de la nature.

[e] Pendant la jouissance, chacun sera maître de la condamner à tel supplice que bon lui semblera, en observant d'aller par gradation, afin de ne la point crever tout d'un coup. . .

[f] ne tue pas plus longtemps un même individu, ce qui est impossible, mais assassines-en beaucoup d'autres, ce qui est très faisable.

"If only there could be gradations in the so-called crime of murder." The individual nature of death eliminates the pleasure of gradation, which the libertine can never give up without regret.[19] [g]

The challenge for Sadian measure is to undo such binarisms as life and death, transforming them as far as possible into a range of sensations that can be followed, implacably, from lowest to highest. Instead of indiscriminate brutality, or innumerable horrors, Sade works to make narrative by discriminating between murderous atrocities, counting the horrors in order to align them crescendo.

In practice, *Les Cent Vingt Journées* could not really be regarded as a straightforward exercise in narrative mastery. Not that it runs into any impasses—avoiding them is, after all, its overriding purpose—but it does produce some rather disturbing side effects. The first of these is a kind of uneasy reflexivity that bears on the initial stages of the story. *Early* passions, minor orgies tend to be regarded as mediocre ones. They can be dealt with, comfortably enough, by forms of narrative ellipsis, such as the following: "The evening meal [. . .] was followed by orgies in the course of which many little infamies were perpetrated" (I, 134).[h] Narratorial tact—for some tact *is* required—must consist then in not burdening us with unworthy anecdotes and tiresome descriptions: "I shall omit mention of several not very interesting episodes dating from my childhood, for they would only be tedious repetitions of what you have already heard" (I, 147).[i] Yet while the actual repetition of minor perversions might reasonably be avoided, it is a requirement of graded narration that we progress *through* the whole range: to leave out the lesser is potentially to abolish the time of the novel, and thereby to diminish the impact, the advent of the greater. The *historienne* who bears the particular burden of having to recount whole series of mediocre episodes is, of course, the first one, Duclos. She cannot help exclaiming in the midst of her own narration at the miserably inadequate passions she is currently

[g] Du point de vue du libertin, une seule victime que l'on ferait périr indéfiniment serait préférable à leur multiplication [celle des victimes], même illimitée, car l'art du dosage et de la mesure s'y exercerait avec une plus grand exactitude. Mais "les lentes et rigoureuses angoisses" d'un tourment, si elles mènent à la mort, ouvrent sur une résistance irréductible, celle atemporelle, et par conséquent inanalysable et incalculable du passage vie/mort. D'où ce cri d'impuissance: "S'il pouvait y avoir des gradations dans le prétendu crime de meurtre." L'individualité de la mort supprime le plaisir de gradation, auquel le libertin ne renonce jamais sans regret.

[h] Le souper [. . .] fut suivi d'orgies où l'on fit beaucoup de petites infamies.

[i] Je passerai sous silence plusieurs anecdotes peu intéressantes de mon enfance, qui ne vous offriraient que des répétitions monotones de ce que vous avez déjà entendu.

describing: "But what mild stuff! What lack of imagination!" (I, 122).[j] The tiny sexual organs, the narrow, withered imaginations, the miserable lack of detail! "His prick struck me as paltry and mean, all his person rather puny, and his discharge was as mild as his proceedings were benign" (I, 129). "He pulled out a little old organ, pale and shriveled like the divinity he worshiped [. . .] he lost two or three miserable drops of sperm responsible for all of his ecstasy" (I, 167).[k] It is not hard to understand the storyteller's reluctance, when she has to deal with "a prick whose incredible littleness is not worth the bother of describing" (I, 140).[l] How can such hardened libertines as Curval and Durcet respond to this kind of insipid narration? "They agreed that what they needed were scenes less sweet and delicate to stir their old, worn-out souls, for all these winsome frolickings were only good for youngsters" (I, 333–34).[m] How can the reader who is capable of reaching the twenty-seventh day still respond to such things? How can the narrator be bothered? These are the points at which the novel fails to master its own drive toward intensity, rounding on itself in impatient self-disparagement.

Not only are these weak episodes potentially tiresome for both storyteller and listener: allowance must continually be made for weakness in what is yet to come. The danger of representing something strong in the early stages of the narrative is considerable: it could only reduce some of what follows to anticlimax. Hence the need for more ellipsis: "Messieurs became completely drunk and performed horrors of such absolute filthiness that I should not be able to describe them without spoiling the less libertine tableaux I have yet to offer my readers" (I, 224).[n] In response to this constraint, Sade seems compelled to create a kind of narrative safety valve in the form of secret spaces: the private *cabinet* allotted to each of the *amis*, and, for most of the first part, the chapel (e.g., I, 155). Their existence permits libertine behavior of a kind that would be disproportionate in erotic intensity and perversity with the passions currently being rehearsed. The standard procedure

[j] Mais quels minces épisodes et quelle stérilité d'imagination!

[k] Son vit me parut très mesquin et toute sa personne assez chétive, et sa décharge fut aussi douce que son opération. / Il sort de sa culotte un petit membre vieux, pâle et ridé comme la divinité qu'il encense. [. . .] il perd deux ou trois malheureuses gouttes de sperme auxquelles il devait toute son extase

[l] un vit qui par sa petitesse incroyable ne vaut pas la peine d'un détail

[m] [Ils] convinrent qu'il leur fallait des scènes moins couleur de rose pour émouvoir leur vieille âme usée, et que toutes ces drôleries-là n'étaient bonnes que pour des jeunes gens.

[n] On s'y enivra complètement et l'on y fit des horreurs d'une saleté si complète que je ne pourrais les peindre sans faire tort aux tableaux moins libertins qu'il me reste encore à offrir aux lecteurs.

is for one of the libertines to gather up a group of victims and helpers, taking them with him into the *cabinet.* Before long, intense cries of pain and bellows of satisfaction can usually be heard, signaling the end of the episode. Here is just one example, involving Curval: "He flung himself into his cabinet, dragging Aline by the breast and calling on Sophie and Zelmire, the two girls from his seraglio, as well as Fanchon, to follow him. One cannot be sure precisely what he did there, but the loud cry of a woman was heard, and soon after, the bellowing that marked his discharge" (I, 249; cf. 197, 315, 324, etc.).[o] In an important sense, this is not an ellipsis. It takes (textual) time, and other activities are held up while it goes on. Yet it is no less dissonant in thematic terms for that. As Marcel Hénaff has argued in detail, it establishes within the novel an element of mystery, and thus acts as a problematic exception to the Sadian norm whereby the victim's body and the libertine project are made starkly visible. The general rule applies admirably to *Les Cent Vingt Journées:* "The program is the formula for Sadian time precisely because his narrative is not the dramatization and the artifice of revealing a mystery, but the arrangement of something already known, and its projection into successivity."[20] [p] The very existence of the *cabinet secret* might then be regarded as a sign of failure—"This offstage cabinet indicates first of all the failure of Sade's narrative to capture absolute horror"[q]—although Hénaff sees the (thematic) lapse as being saved, paradoxically, by its power to suggest something so radical as to be unshowable and untellable.[21] Certainly, this kind of suggestiveness is claimed, or hoped for, in a footnote to *La Nouvelle Justine:* "It is probably a mark of great art to leave these scenes covered with a veil; but how many avid, insatiable readers would like to be told everything! Yet, by the good Lord, if their desire was satisfied, what else would they have left to imagine?" (VII, 158n).[r] But one might well ask whether this is not a post hoc justification, and a mark of formal unease.

Something is certainly gained by the presence of secret spaces, but

[o] Il se jeta dans son cabinet, en entraînant par le sein Aline, et se faisant suivre de Sophie et de Zelmire, les deux filles de son sérail, et de Fanchon. On ne sait trop ce qu'il y fit, mais on entendit un grand cri de femme, et, peu après, les hurlements de sa décharge.

[p] Le programme est la formule du temps sadien précisément parce que le récit n'est pas la mise en scène et l'artifice de révélation d'un mystère, mais le déploiement d'un déjà connu, sa projection dans la successivité.

[q] Ce cabinet hors scène [. . .] marque tout d'abord l'échec du récit sadien à piéger l'horreur absolue.

[r] Il y a sans doute beaucoup d'art à laisser ainsi des scènes sous le voile; mais combien de lecteurs avides et insatiables désireraient qu'on leur dît tout! Eh, bon Dieu! et si on les satisfaisait, que leur resterait-il donc à imaginer?

at the expense, perhaps, of the empowering fiction of narrative mastery. The enigmatic pastimes are not simply maintained for the narrator's good pleasure: he is compelled to silence by what is not tellable *at this point* in the story. At a certain moment, Duclos suffers an occlusion of her capacity to observe what her sister does with clients in supposedly closed spaces: "They would shut themselves up together, and I do not know what they did in there, for my sister was never prepared to tell me, and they did not take up a position in the spot where I could have seen them" (I, 173).[s] We can only suppose that what went on there is too advanced to be told at this stage. Similarly, when the general narrator addresses his reader on the subject of the *cabinets,* it is to confirm his ignorance: "Aline displayed I've no idea what, for I have never been able to discover what went on in those infernal cabinets" (I, 315).[t] This is Sadian whimsy, no doubt, but the striking thing for a thematics of narrative power is that the narratorial voice is compelled to confessions of ignorance, and to another form of self-disparagement.

In the measuring of intensity, the narrative of *Les Cent Vingt Journées* finds itself struggling with delay as an awkward and irritating discipline. To put it simply, the narrator is continually required to restate the law "never the stronger before the weaker" in response to what might be called narrative temptation. Repeatedly, the reader is reminded apologetically of the "essential" laws that dictate the course of the story: "the laws essential to the interest of our story prevent us from describing it thoroughly" (I, 66).[u] Now these laws are not metaphysical ones. They are not even presented as generic. In fictive terms, they are the laws that the narrator has chosen to apply, precisely as the principle of his own mastery of time. The temporal order must in fact be both essential and something freely chosen. There is mention of "a thousand fresh horrors, each more extraordinary than the other, but which we are not yet able to describe to our readers because of the essential order we propose to follow" (I, 153).[v] In the name of this pact that the narrator has made with himself, the reader is reminded of, and politely held to, the same constraint. In *Les Cent Vingt*

[s] Ils s'enfermaient ensemble, et je ne sais ce qu'ils y faisaient, car jamais ma soeur ne me l'a voulu dire, et ils ne se plaçaient point dans l'endroit où j'aurais pu les voir.

[t] Aline montra je ne sais quoi, car il m'a toujours été impossible de découvrir ce qui se passait dans ces infernaux cabinets.

[u] les lois essentielles à l'intérêt de la narration empêchent que nous ne le peignions en entier.

[v] mille autres horreurs, toutes plus singulières les unes que les autres, mais que l'ordre essentiel que nous nous sommes proposé ne nous permet pas encore de peindre à nos lecteurs.

Journées, it is not, as it may sometimes appear in *Justine* or *La Marquise de Gange,* a matter of providence or destiny: the narrator is explicitly and impressively responsible for the way in which he unfolds his taxonomy of the erotic. Narrative time is worked out as a discipline requiring him to dwell on all sorts of minor activities resembling Crébillon's *divertissements:* "It is not yet time to allow myself energy-sapping pleasures; for the moment, we shall limit ourselves to chatting" (I, 70).[w]

The difficulty of measured narrative is felt most strongly, it seems, when the *amis,* caught up in urgent desire, fail to respect the contract that produced the whole situation of the novel. The *historienne* can call them to order in the name of the laws that they made themselves: "'Patience, Sire, patience,' said Duclos. 'Allow my stories to be told in the order you yourself dictated'" (I, 193).[x] Yet the narrator is continually required to *negotiate* his way out of the excessively "strong" situations they have created. Because of their (fictive) indiscipline, he is reduced to (feigned) apologies and regrets: "We deeply regret that we are not yet able to explain all this, but it is certain that these men, on the sly and before the appointed time, were indulging in things that had not been recounted, and in so doing they were acting in formal violation of the agreements they had set in place" (I, 308–09).[y] These irresponsible characters may be seen as both the scapegoats and the vehicles of an authorial failure, since Sade, as he reread his manuscript, felt the need to remind himself that he had moved ahead of his original plan:

> Remember to cover up better at the beginning what you are going to shed light on here. (I, 189)
>
> I have been too explicit about the toilet activities at the beginning; they must not be elaborated on until after the stories that speak of them. (I, 363)
>
> Said too much about active and passive sodomy; conceal that until the stories come to discuss it. (I, 363)
>
> Tone down the first part greatly; things develop too much in it. It cannot possibly be too weak and subdued. Above all, never have the four

[w] Ce ne sera point encore là le moment où l'on pourra se permettre des voluptés qui puissent énerver; il faudra encore s'en tenir au simple badinage.

[x] Patience, patience, monseigneur, dit Duclos, permettez que mon récit aille dans l'ordre que vous avez vous-même exigé.

[y] Nous sommes désolés de ne pouvoir pas encore expliquer tout cela, mais il est certain que ces messieurs, sous-main et avant que cela ne fût bien exactement permis, se livraient à des choses qu'on ne leur avait pas encore racontées, et en cela ils manquaient formellement aux conventions qu'ils avaient établies.

> friends do anything until it has first been recounted. You have not been careful enough about that. (I, 450)[z]

This may be an internal indication—in addition to the impressive circumstantial ones—as to why the text is unfinished. Perhaps the point had been reached, at the end of the first thirty days, where it was no longer possible to go on building intensity in a regular way for ninety more days. Most of the advanced horrors, in particular coprophagy, sodomy, and acts of cruelty, were already in full swing by the end of Part I.[22]

At times, the narrator of *Les Cent Vingt Journées* seems to bear the burden of delay lightly enough. He says simply, "this enigma will be explained" (I, 136),[a] or "what happens afterward will make this point clear" (I, 146).[b] At others, he speaks with uncomplicated *mauvaise foi,* blaming circumstances for the shape of his own project, precisely when that project was a denial of the power of circumstance:

> The reader will kindly allow us not to reveal what the president had done: circumstances do not allow us to do so. (I, 261)
>
> But since the manner in which they [the duke and the bishop] operated belongs to a class of procedures that circumstances compel us to keep hidden, we beg our readers to allow us to draw a curtain over it. (I, 286; cf. I, 303)[c]

Most remarkably, however, he enters into the fiction of narratorial discomfort as part of the rhetoric of politeness. The authorial "we" talks of being ill at ease, and asks the reader's pardon for leaving certain details "beneath the veil" (I, 91).

[z] Souvenez-vous de mieux voiler dans le commencement ce que vous allez éclaircir ici.

J'ai trop dévoilé les histoires de garde-robe au commencement; il ne faut les développer qu'après les récits qui en parlent.

Trop parlé de la sodomie active et passive; voilez-la, jusqu'à ce que les récits en parlent.

Adoucissez beaucoup la première partie: tout s'y développe trop; elle ne saurait être trop faible et trop gazée. Ne faites surtout jamais rien faire aux quatre amis qui n'ait été raconté, et vous n'avez pas eu ce soin-là.

[a] cette énigme s'expliquera.

[b] la suite nous expliquera tout ceci.

[c] Le lecteur trouvera bon que nous ne lui révélions pas ce que le président avait fait: les circonstances ne nous le permettent point encore.

Mais la manière dont ils avaient opéré étant encore du nombre de celles que les circonstances nous obligent de voiler, nous prions nos lecteurs de trouver bon que nous tirions le rideau.

It is almost poignant to witness the narrator's unhappiness: "We are unfortunately obliged, by the order we originally set for ourselves, to delay for some while longer the pleasure that the reader would doubtless take in learning the details of this religious ceremony" (I, 166).[d] At the very heart of his delaying action, we find him racked with the tension of it all, suffering under the tyranny of his own plan, plugging away at the construction of his own relentlessness: "We are in despair, for here the order of our plan prevents us from describing those lubricious punishments, but our readers should not hold it against us. They appreciate our inability to give them complete satisfaction at the present moment; but they can be sure that their time will come" (I, 171).[e]

This distress is, of course, a fiction of seduction. If Sade's narrator is to have all the skill of Duclos as a producer of pleasure in others, he must have that sense of "proportion" which allows her to espouse the patient's bodily rhythms. What Wolfgang Iser might have called the implied masturbation of *Les Cent Vingt Journées* is not particularly assured in its timing. Sade cannot just take hold of his readers, as an act of mastery. He has to keep hold of their attention, and "dare" to introduce them to new classes of passion: "there was even something more to it than tears, but we do not yet dare to say what it was" (I, 288).[f] The narrator cannot be sure of the libertine pact to the extent of taking it for granted, and he cannot depend on his fictive libertine friends to respect the proper discipline of a long-term series of orgies. The only way to tell time, in a powerfully measured way, is to intersperse it with shows of weakness. He must continually apologize and reassure, carrying on precisely the kind of seductive enterprise that measure is supposed to preempt. Only by sustained and patient negotiation can Sade maintain the textual space, and the narrative time, of tyranny.

[d] Nous sommes malheureusement obligé, par l'ordre que nous nous sommes prescrit pour les matières, de retarder encore quelque temps le plaisir qu'aurait sans doute le lecteur à apprendre les détails de cette cérémonie religieuse.

[e] Nous sommes désespéré de ce que l'ordre de notre plan nous empêche de peindre ici ces lubriques corrections, mais que nos lecteurs ne nous en veuillent pas. Ils sentent comme nous l'impossibilité où nous sommes de les satisfaire pour ce moment-ci; ils peuvent être sûrs qu'ils n'y perdront rien.

[f] il y avait même quelque chose de plus que des larmes, mais nous n'osons pas encore dire ce que c'était.

Chapter 6

Taking Sade Serially: *Les Cent Vingt Journées de Sodome*

He deals with thirty women a day and they all end up shitting [. . .][a]
—*Les Cent Vingt Journées*

Eroticism, we sometimes need to be reminded, is a serious business. Writers associated with the surrealist movement have often taken it upon themselves to do the reminding, none more eloquently than Robert Desnos: "Rabelaisian humor at its most repugnant, bawdiness that could hardly be further from love, and all that horrible funny business that common people call double entendre, blue jokes, or slap and tickle . . . generally constitute eroticism for schoolteachers and unrefined souls."[1] [b] Laughter, ribaldry, even smiling are frivolous, and therefore base and crude. They should not be allowed to contaminate the discourse of eroticism. Think how aggressively this is affirmed in the chilling invocation of Bataille's *Madame Edwarda:* "If you laugh, it is because you are afraid."[c] In the provocative intimacy of its *tutoiement,* this sentence functions as a ritual disqualification of readerly laughter. The one who laughs at *Madame Edwarda* is, in the same

[a] Il passe trente femmes dans sa journée et les fait toutes chier

[b] L'esprit gaulois dans ce qu'il peut avoir de plus répugnant, la paillardise la plus éloignée de l'amour et toutes ces horribles joies que le vulgaire nomme grivoiseries, bagatelles, légèretés. . . représentent en général l'érotisme pour les instituteurs et les âmes grossières.

[c] Si tu ris, c'est que tu as peur.

move, both excluded and denounced, by a kind of preemptive (psycho) analysis. The business of eroticism cannot proceed in the presence of the unworthy. Now the literary model for erotic gravity is always the marquis de Sade. Here is André Breton's judgment: "Indeed there is nothing more profoundly *serious* than [Sade's work], and one can gauge this by the fact that, in the midst of a civilized society, it continues to suffer exclusion, and be almost completely taboo."[2] [d] For Desnos, Sade makes other, earlier aristocrats of the erotic look vulgar. This is a comment on Brantôme: "Given the absence, in his time, of a writer who is able to conceive of love without smiling, he may be used as a base for the imagination of serious-minded people, but Sade has made us used to a far more elevated tone, and has relegated Brantôme to the bottom of the drawer."[3] [e]

What is it about Sade's work, exactly, that makes other writers of the erotic seem by comparison so despicably merry? In the first place, Sade—long before Bataille—ensures that laughter is excluded by decree from spaces of erotic intensity. One of the strictest rules governing the behavior of the prisoner-victims in *Les Cent Vingt Journées de Sodome* is the following: "The least display of mirth, or the least sign of disrespect or lack of submission during the debauch activities, shall be deemed one of the gravest of faults and shall be one of the most cruelly punished" (I, 73).[4] [f] The very elaboration of an erotic discipline depends on sustained and serious "attention." In the Société des Amis du Crime, where there is no separate class of victims, all members are still obliged during proceedings (rule no. 27) to "tone down laughter and conversations, that is, anything that is not in the spirit of libertinage or that tends to spoil it" (*Histoire de Juliette,* VIII, 444).[g] The most conventional notions of debauchery, or of the orgy, may not be appropriate here, for they do not correspond to the atmosphere of *calme* that strikes Juliette during her first evening in the Société: "All of this went on in a most orderly manner. [. . .] The most decent of acts would not have been carried out more calmly. And it was not

[d] Sans doute n'est-il au demeurant rien de plus *grave* que [l'œuvre de Sade] et cela dans la mesure même où en pleine société "civilisée" continue à peser sur elle le tabou d'une interdiction presque totale.

[e] En l'absence, à son époque, d'un écrivain qui conçoit l'amour sans sourire, il peut servir de base à l'imagination des esprits graves mais Sade nous a habitué à un ton autrement plus élevé et l'a relégué dans le tiroir aux poussières.

[f] Le moindre rire, ou le moindre manque d'attention, ou de respect et de soumission, dans les parties de débauche, sera une des fautes les plus graves et les plus cruellement punies.

[g] modérer les rires, les conversations, tout ce qui n'est pas enfin dans l'esprit du libertinage, ou tout ce qui y nuit

hard for me to realize, in this environment, that what man respects most in this world are his passions" (VIII, 458).[h] Sadian libertine order depends on silencing all that is disrespectful. Conversation as such is proscribed—and with it those distracting voices that echo from the *Ragionamenti* to Crébillon. But laughter is given first mention as a potential source of "harm." Were it to be heard, it could only be the symptom, perhaps the very form of a lack of application, of an inattentive attitude, or an unaligned body.[5]

Yet true gravity is not achieved merely by forbidding laughter, even if the threats that accompany its interdiction are as violent and immediate as in *Les Cent Vingt Journées.* The exclusion of the frivolous is achieved most resolutely, one must suppose, in the active pursuit of a serious purpose. We might well ask, then, how it is that Sade manages to convince Desnos, Breton, and others of his lofty erotic purpose. Or, to put it more narrowly and more mundanely: how does Sade make his claim to seriousness? There may be many answers to this question, but there is one that I think deserves consideration for its complexity and its very ambivalence: his practice of number.

Sade's relation to classical erotic number is complex. In *ars erotica,* we recall, number marks the completeness of a set of figures. It stands for a principle of inclusion whereby each position is called on to *faire nombre.* The geometrical numbers transmitted canonically are not, then, the product of some empirical procedure of measurement or counting. They are not the outcome of any inquiry, for they are not sums or totals, but the signs of a thematic order. Far from simply breaking with this tradition, like the radical modernist he is often said to be, Sade displays "respect" for it by his extensive use of foursquare numbers, multiplying them lavishly, it is true, but never fragmenting them or disturbing their geometry. Within the numbered space of eroticism, however, Sade, more than any of his contemporaries, develops a relentlessly temporal activity: that of counting. Counting should not be seen, in mere psychological terms, as an innocuous obsession, fit for an arithmomanic author deprived of normal social intercourse.[6] Nor should it be thought of as the statistical method needed to bring descriptive rigor, Kinseylike, to Elephantis and Aretino. Counting is most important here in philosophical terms. It may not have genuine explanatory power, but it constitutes a kind of ethical (and narrative) style. Less than a true method, it is the model for a method. A fiction

[h] Le plus grand ordre régnait au milieu de tout cela. [. . .] les plus décentes actions ne se seraient point passées avec plus de calme. Et je pus facilement me convaincre, en cette circonstance, que ce que l'homme respecte le plus dans le monde, ce sont ses passions.

of procedure, if you like, a way of moving through the world whereby the algorithm itself becomes thematic, as a rehearsal of sameness. Number is elaborated through time.

Counting can be said to pursue sameness because it enacts the triumph of abstraction. In dealing successively with the objects it meets, counting never fails to retrieve and affirm a determined order. For things, for people, for crimes to be counted, they must be taken as equivalent. Bataille sees the desire in Sade to count forms of cruelty—"enumerating to the point of exhaustion the possibilities for destroying human beings"[7] [i]—but Blanchot goes further in noting the cruelty of counting itself. In the eyes of the libertine, he says,

> She [the victim] does not exist by herself, she is not a distinct being, but a simple element that can be indefinitely substituted in an erotic equation.
>
> "All men are equal" means that, since no creature is worth more than any other, all are interchangeable, and each has meaning only as a unit in an infinite enumeration.[8] [j]

The pleasure of *le grand nombre* is mentioned explicitly in *Histoire de Juliette:* "variation and multiplicity are the two most powerful vehicles of lasciviousness. Fuck with the greatest possible number of men: nothing amuses and arouses the mind like a large number" (VIII, 127).[9] [k] No frivolous pleasure this: it is not a matter of playing with large numbers happened upon by chance, but of *reaching* them by a cumulative libertine practice. Here is a measure of Sade's seriousness: it can be found in the very seriousness of his measuring, in the seriality of his counting.

Sadian number involves not only the implacable progression of arithmetic but, parenthetically and paradoxically, in periods of great passion, the dizzying folly of multiplication. The one hundred twenty days of Sodom are counted out relentlessly, but some of the last days are marked by a calculation well suited to the dynamics of excess, the geometrical progression: "He flogs a girl nine days in a row, giving

[i] énumérer jusqu'à l'épuisement les possibilités de détruire des êtres humains

[j] Elle [la victime] n'existe pas par elle-même, elle n'est pas un être distinct, mais un simple élément indéfiniment substituable, dans une équation érotique.

Tous les hommes sont égaux, cela veut dire qu'aucune créature ne valant mieux qu'une autre, toutes sont interchangeables, chacune n'a que la signification d'une unité dans un dénombrement infini.

[k] la variation. . . la multiplicité, sont les deux plus puissants véhicules de la luxure. Foutez avec le plus d'hommes qu'il vous sera possible: rien n'amuse, rien n'échauffe la tête comme le grand nombre.

her a hundred lashes on the first day, and doubling it every day up to and including the ninth" (I, 382).[l] Violence is intensified by the multiplication of previous violence, so that each stage in the series becomes the basis for a further radicalization.[10]

In addition to the operations of counting and multiplying, numbers work phatically, so to speak. By their very presence in the text, they signify determinacy. *Les Cent Vingt Journées,* the book with the large number in its title, would be very different if it answered to such a title as *Les Journées de Sodome.* The latter could only be an interlude, framed in some general way perhaps by what preceded and followed, but not marked out with the same precision. As it is, the text seeks to carry our conviction, it seems, by sheer number of numbers. In two pages of text, it is possible to find no fewer than fourteen (14) numbers, being variously references to age, to the number of kisses exchanged, to the number of "discharges," and to the aerial distance traveled by ejaculated sperm (I, 312–13). As Marcel Hénaff says, numbers count in Sade as detail: "The variation and precision of the numbers is meant to introduce specific detail where storytelling only produces repetition. The demand for *detail* is explicitly stated in the text, either when the narrator/narratress seeks to respond to it, or when the audience calls out for it. But we should note that what is produced in reply to this demand are always figures, or at least measurable quantities."[11] [m]

We can understand the question of determinacy best, perhaps, by considering the one number in Sade that seems not to be determinate: the number *mille.* A thousand is the number of unspeakable events referred to by someone who intends not to (re)count them, as so often in the more modest or constrained narrations, such as *La Marquise de Gange* or the earlier versions of *Justine. Mille* is the number of *horreurs* that Justine cannot or will not tell—the inability to count being claimed by Luce Irigaray, incidentally, as proper to the feminine.[12] In the earlier stages of the *Cent Vingt Journées,* when certain erotic atrocities are being withheld from the reader, the appearance of *mille* is often a sign of this concealment. We are told, for instance, that "a thousand other horrors, a thousand other infamies accompanied and succeeded

[l] Il fouette une fille neuf jours de suite, à cent coups le premier jour, toujours en doublant jusqu'au neuvième inclus.

[m] La variation et la précision des chiffres entendent introduire le détail spécifique et inédit là où le récit ne reproduit que de la répétition. Cette exigence du *détail* on la trouve explicitement formulée dans le texte soit que le narrateur (ou la narratrice) se propose de la satisfaire, soit que les auditeurs la réclament; mais il faut bien remarquer que ce qui est avancé alors ce sont toujours des chiffres, ou du moins des quantités mesurables.

those" (I, 107),[n] or that someone pronounced "a thousand other invectives that I shall have occasion to relate to you during another passion, where they are the key element, rather than the minor accessory they happen to be in this instance" (I, 192–93).[o] The bishop talks of "a thousand and a thousand crimes" (I, 238),[p] but we have learned by now that

$$1{,}000 + 1{,}000 \doteqdot 1{,}000$$

because

$$1{,}000 \doteqdot \infty \doteqdot \text{any number.}$$

Les Cent Vingt Journées does not list a thousand perversions, but six hundred, that is, a very large, determinate number. In narrative terms, 600 (or 120) is very much more *telling* than a thousand.

As well as determinacy and seriality, Sade's numbers have an orderly, geometrical quality. Maurice Heine makes this observation about *Les Cent Vingt Journées:* "there is in Sade a rather mysterious harmony of numbers that it would be improper to disturb: it is not just by chance that the whole novel of the *Cent Vingt Journées* is constructed on a quadrangular base."[13] [q] The "mystery" of which Heine speaks ought to be familiar—and consequently a little less mysterious—to attentive readers of classical erotic literature, even if Sade's use of foursquare numbers is uncommonly intensive. What is more, Heine falls short of the mark in saying that the recurrence of such numbers is not a matter of chance: their presence provides the novel with an architectural principle—or at the very least, with an architectual theme—whose actual role seems to be to preclude the random or the unexpected. There are, of course, four *amis* forming the libertine group at Silling, and their number seems to be the common denominator of almost all calculations in the novel.[14] The numbers of people chosen to accompany them to Silling are such as to provide appropriately regular quantities of victims: "The number of subjects

[n] mille autres horreurs, mille autres infamies accompagnèrent et suivirent celles-là.

[o] mille autres invectives que je trouverai l'occasion de vous raconter dans une autre passion dont elles font le principal, au lieu qu'elles ne seraient ici qu'un très mince accessoire

[p] mille et mille crimes

[q] il y a chez Sade une harmonie des nombres assez mystérieuse et qu'il convient de ne point rompre: c'est mieux qu'un hasard, si tout le roman des *120 journées* s'édifie sur une base quadrangulaire.

was reduced to thirty-two in all, the storytellers included; to wit: four of that class, eight girls, eight boys, eight men endowed with monstrous members for the delights of passive sodomy, and four female servants" (I, 50).[r]

Now while the "reduction" mentioned here produces the final set of "characters" in the novel, it has only been attained by a process of the greatest severity, one that was inscribed in the methodology of the project, preshaping the referential world of France into the society of Silling. The preliminaries are themselves perfectly foursquare: "Four supper parties were held every week at four different country houses located at four different extremities of Paris" (I, 22).[s] The search itself is set up as a radical denial of empirical disorder: "Four accomplished procuresses to recruit women and a similar number of pimps to scout for men had as their sole duty to range throughout the capital and the provinces, bringing back everything that could satisfy their sensuality" (I, 22).[t] The four procurers and the four procuresses go out from the houses at (the?) four extremities of Paris, sending sixteen further procuresses into the "sixteen principal provinces" (I, 50) of what for modern readers can only be an archaic, prehexagonal France. They return with regular numbers of potential victims: "Each was to bring back nine subjects, which came to a total of one hundred forty-four girls, from which one hundred forty-four a choice of only eight was to be made" (I, 50).[15] [u]

It might be disturbing for the numerically anxious to note that there is an exception to this rule. For some unstated reason, to which I shall return in the next chapter, there is a group of six people (three cooks and three helpers) working in the kitchen at Silling, as is made clear in Sade's final summary:

Masters	4
Old women	4
In the kitchen	6

[r] On se réduisit à trente-deux sujets en tout, les historiennes comprises; savoir: quatre de cette classe, huit jeunes filles, huit jeunes garçons, huit hommes doués de membres monstrueux pour les voluptés de la sodomie passive, et quatre servantes.

[s] On faisait régulièrement ensemble quatre soupers par semaine dans quatre différentes maisons de campagne situées à quatre extrémités différentes de Paris.

[t] Quatre fameuses maquerelles pour les femmes et un pareil nombre de mercures pour les hommes n'avaient d'autres soins que de leur chercher, et dans la capitale et dans les provinces, tout ce qui, dans l'un et l'autre genre, pouvait le mieux assouvir leur sensualité.

[u] Chacune devait amener neuf sujets, ce qui faisait un total de cent quarante-quatre filles, et sur ce nombre de cent quarante-quatre, huit seulement devaient être choisies.

Storytellers	4
Fuckers	8
Boys	8
Wives	4
Girls	8
Total:	46

(I, 449)

This minimal disorder is, however, eliminated as a source of potential irritation in such a way as to produce what must count—*geometrically*—as a happy ending. Thirty people are tortured and killed, leaving the thoroughly regular number of sixteen—organized, compellingly, in four groups of four.

The foursquare is found, so to speak, at both ends of a process of Sadian brutality. It serves, as we have just seen, for the administration, the batching of victims. But most fundamentally, it serves to organize groups of *bourreaux* and, between them, spaces of torture. The victim finds herself in the middle of four men (I, 45), the middle being the theater of suffering produced by what Sade tends to refer to as a "circle of four":

> The four friends gathered in a circle, and in the middle the girl was put on show. (I, 51)
>
> The friends formed a circle around a pile of well-stuffed cushions arranged on the floor. The three girls [. . .] entered the ring formed by the friends' chairs. (I, 354)[v]

The same "figure" is found elsewhere in Sade: Justine, for example, experiences its cruel geometry in *Les Infortunes de la vertu* (II, 320). The Sadian rule, alluded to in *La Nouvelle Justine,* is that wherever four wicked people are gathered together, they are likely to achieve the fullness of villainy.[16] The circle thus formed is not the magic circle formed by a group of three. (The power of that circle is no doubt generated by its revolutions, by its constant tripping over: it is the circle of dancing witches.) The Sadian circle is a stable one, an unremitting frame that adds to the virtues of the foursquare those of perfect enclosure. Whatever dances are performed there must be *quadrilles*

[v] Les quatre amis formaient un cercle, au milieu duquel paraissait la jeune fille.
Les amis firent cercle autour d'une pile d'amples carreaux que l'on arrangea à terre. [. . .] les trois jeunes filles [. . .] passèrent dans la ceinture formée par les fauteuils des amis.

(see I, 91). The victim's space is, in the language of modern police surveillance, both "cordoned off" and "divided into squares."[w]

It might be observed that, while counting denies the specificity of each new instance, of each new instant, the practice of number helps to organize the world of the text as a space of memory, in which the different episodes are held together. In Bergson's sense, counting is a denial of time as radical successivity; it is an affirmation of the spatial.[17] In *Les Cent Vingt Journées,* an authorial voice makes just this sort of claim to the reader: "If we had not told everything and analyzed everything, how could we possibly have guessed what suits you best? It is up to you to take what you please and leave the rest; another reader will do the same; and little by little everything will find its true place. This is the story of a magnificent banquet, in which six hundred dishes offer themselves to your appetite" (I, 79).[x] Before being a meal, rather than being the "story" of a meal, this book is a menu. The counting of the available dishes helps to constitute what must be the essential paradigm of the text, namely the paradigm of the paradigmatic.

There are six hundred dishes, six hundred passions[18] in front of the reader, and "this table" (I, 80) that presents them is taxonomic as well as gastronomic. For a dish to appear in a certain place, it has to count, to *faire nombre* as part of a particular class (I, 281). What matters most are not the 600 (or 120) *courses,* as such, but the *spread. Les Cent Vingt Journées* claims to be the ultimate erotic buffet. And when Curval, one of the four *amis,* speculates about the daring that would be required to "divulge all the caprices, all the tastes, all the secret horrors to which men are subject when their imagination is fired up" (I, 276),[y] we are no doubt inclined to think, as readers, that we have already gauged the extent of this paradigm of vice. How many *caprices, goûts,* and *horreurs* would there be, all told? Not a thousand. Just about 600. So that when Maurice Blanchot says, "in Sade, everything is always in infinite quantities,"[19] [z] we know that he cannot mean it literally. Or at least, not numerically.

The passions thus deployed in their paradigmatic fullness are hardly

[w] bouclé/quadrillé

[x] Si nous n'avions pas tout dit, tout analysé, comment voudrais-tu que nous eussions pu deviner ce qui te convient? C'est à toi à le prendre et à laisser le reste; un autre en fera autant; et petit à petit tout aura trouvé sa place. C'est ici l'histoire d'un magnifique repas où six cents plats divers s'offrent à ton appétit.

[y] divulguer tous les caprices, tous les goûts, toutes les horreurs secrètes auxquels les hommes sont sujets dans le feu de leur imagination

[z] tout est toujours en quantité infinie chez Sade.

subject to analytical consolidation and reduction. We need only speculate for a moment about some disrespectfully Proppian reading of *Les Cent Vingt Journées:* how many erotic functions underlie this enormous diversity? Only a very few, no doubt. It happens occasionally, indeed, that a Sadian libertine lapses into a kind of prestructuralist pessimism that denies the satisfactions of number. Curval suggests that "there are only two or three crimes to commit in this world, [. . .] and when they are done, there is no more to be said. All the rest are inferior, and one ceases to feel anything" (I, 183).[a] Does he mean by this that the two or three crimes can generate 600 passions, or that the first 597 (or even 3/4 × 600 = 450) are unworthy of his attention? Dolmancé, in *La Philosophie dans le boudoir,* makes an analytical reduction for teaching purposes: "If, however, your Eugénie desires some analysis of men's preferences in the act of libertinage, we can examine them briefly by reducing these tastes to three: *sodomy, sacreligious fancies, and cruel ones*" (III, 443; Sade's emphasis).[b] Bressac, in *La Nouvelle Justine,* is trenchantly reductive, in a way that threatens to reduce the whole Sadian erotic buffet to a handful of recipes: "All our little immoral felonies can be reduced to a few sodomies, a few rapes, a few incests, and a few murders; our religious crimes can be reduced to a few blasphemies and profanations. Is there anyone here who can say that he has had enough of these paltry things?" (VII, 225).[c]

In *Les Cent Vingt Journées,* the dominance of the paradigmatic principle is nowhere more apparent than in the novel's time*table.* The events are planned to take place over four months, which supposes

$$4 \times 30 = 120 \text{ days.}$$

There is a problem with this, however. For the want of a more orderly world, Sade is obliged to follow the existing calendar. If four months are going to add up to 120 days (and no more), February must be included, and leap years must be avoided. Thus, when the period November to February is chosen, we have

$$30 + 31 + 31 + 28 = 120 \text{ days,}$$

[a] Il n'y a que deux ou trois crimes à faire dans le monde [. . .] et, ceux-là faits, tout est dit; le reste est inférieur et l'on ne sent plus rien.

[b] Si votre Eugénie pourtant désire quelques analyses des goûts de l'homme dans l'acte du libertinage, pour les examiner plus sommairement nous les réduirons à trois: *la sodomie, les fantaisies sacrilèges et les goûts cruels.*

[c] Tous nos petits forfaits immoraux se réduisent à quelques sodomies, quelques viols, quelques incestes, quelques meurtres; nos petits crimes religieux, à quelques

which is the closest approximation possible to a foursquare timetable. Furthermore, the number of weeks involved is taken to be 17 (i.e., 4 × 4 + 1). But even this already unsatisfactory situation—it should of course be 16 weeks—is aggravated by a hidden irregularity:

$$120 \text{ days} = (7 \times 17) + 1 \text{ day.}$$

Sade seems to have redrawn the map of France in order to make it foursquare, and is seeking to reshape the calendar in the same way. But we may note his failure to do this perfectly, with utter mastery. To dwell on the looseness of his calculations can indeed be a way for us to observe the resistance of the human world to his numerical enterprise. We can note with a kind of moral relief—and, dare I say it, a trace of a smile—that his relentlessness threatens at times to give way to puzzlement and irritation. Here is how it should have been:

4 months × 30 = 120 days
4 *historiennes* × 150 passions = 600 passions

$$\frac{600}{120} = 5 \text{ passions/day}$$

Complications arise, however, not just because of the intractability of the calendar, but because Sade wishes to maintain rhythmic variations in intensity. There are weekly *fêtes,* where particularly festive punishments, mock marriages, and ritual deflowerings occur. The need to make extra time for the festivities means that each such day "is an event that results in the recounting of only four passions" (I, 373).[d] Every time that a *fête* occurs, there must be narrative overtime on a working day, so that the extra passion can be recounted. Yet Sade often fails to make the proper compensating moves: he fails, so to speak, to measure the irregularity, so that we find him, at the end of the second, third, and fourth sections of his manuscript asking himself in his notes to find out why there are too many or too few passions.[20] In fact, to take but one example, there is one passion too many in the third quarter (I, 406)—the net result, by my reckoning, of no fewer than five (5) earlier errors:

blasphèmes, quelques profanations. Y en a-t-il un de nous ici qui puisse se dire suffisamment délecté de ces misères?

[d] c'est un événement qui fait que l'on ne conte que quatre passions.

Days 2 and 9 of this section should have 4 passions, not 5 (they are *fêtes*).
Days 6 and 11 should have 5, not 4.
Day 15 should have 5, not 6.

And that is only January. Little wonder that the narrow constraints of February should prove too much. Despite frequent extra narrations by Desgranges, we find Sade noting mournfully at the end of the fourth quarter that two passions are missing: "Check why these two are missing. They were all there in the original outline" (I, 443).[e] It is to be hoped, for Curval's sake, that the missing two are not the ones that he was waiting for.

At this point, Sade's enterprise seems threatened with some loss of seriousness. As a novelist whose writing foregrounds not only counting, but the most exact accountancy, Sade appears to have been found wanting. Just as the four experienced procuresses "kept themselves ready to give an exact account of these investigations" (I, 46),[f] so ought Sade to be fully accountable, if his numerical severity is to compel our respectful attention. Maurice Heine, in a preface to *Les Cent Vingt Journées,* asks us not to be too severe in our judgment: "one should not take him to task for the repetitions and oversights that are due to the unfinished nature of his work."[g] But this is just after Heine has described Sade himself as "pitiless."[21] It is true that we are dealing with an unfinished version of *Les Cent Vingt Journées,* but what really counts in the novel, what deserves to be counted seems already present, in the plan, in the notes, in the tables. Undeniably, Sade's marginal notes reveal a loss of efficiency: they show a wavering numerical tyrant whose sums do not add up. How can the conclusion of the novel be the most complex and intense of libertine passions when, by arithmetic definition, we know that we should have reached [Ultimate − 2]? All that might now be achieved, perhaps, is a kind of patchwork relentlessness.

It might seem here as if I hope to arrive at a heady deconstructionist moment in which we might perceive the self-defeating nature of Sade's artistic project. But I need not, indeed cannot, go so far. The very thematics of number has regularly driven us away from any rich notion of *différance* toward that of simple *différence.*[22] My modest proposal is that, in spite of its thematic show of arithmetical rigor, the novel does

[e] Vérifiez pourquoi ces deux manquent, tout y était sur les brouillons.

[f] se trouvaient en état de rendre un compte exact de toutes ces recherches

[g] on ne saurait donc lui tenir rigueur de redites et de négligences dues à l'inachèvement de son œuvre.

not respond satisfactorily to a careful *audit.* It might even, because of this discrepancy, be considered somewhat amusing . . .

Yet if we were to smile, perchance to laugh, we hardly need to be reminded what that would mean. It would be inane giggling, no doubt, or nervous tittering. It might rise with increasing confidence from lewd sniggers to broad guffaws. But it would only be read by relentlessly serious, authoritative critics as a symptom of our incomprehension. In failing to achieve the true Sadian perspective, we would have joined the grinning crowd of ignorants referred to by Desnos: "Whereas all his predecessors in the field of erotic literature had looked on 'it' with mocking smiles, irritating scepticism, or repulsive crudeness, Sade considers love and its acts from the point of view of the infinite."[23 h] Sade is committed to the infinite, we are told. But I have tried to suggest that it is his very attempt to count and recount the infinite that leads one to the brink of the risible. Did not Boris Vian once say in public, with unpardonable disrespect for the divine marquis, that "the dress rules and internal protocol of Durcet's chateau normally provoke people to outright laughter"?[24 i]

As if by a tacit recognition of this fragility at the hands of some vulgar "norm," admirers of Sade often insist from the outset on Sade's (black) *humor,* doing so in such a way as to preserve the utter seriousness of his work. Breton was perhaps the first to do this: Angela Carter certainly thinks so,[25] although Philippe Sollers thinks that he himself was.[26] Breton "defines" humor in such a way as to preserve much of the ambiguity deriving from the foreignness of the English word. Whatever humor is, it seems to be recognizable by its very vagueness: it has something sublime and elevated about it.[27] For Desnos, the knowledge of it is held out in the future: "this tragic humor whose definition is yet to be produced."[28 j] And who is its finest exponent, the darkest of black humorists, if not Sade? "Humor" is everywhere in his work:

> The very excesses of his imagination, to which he is led by natural genius and oriented by years in captivity, the wildly arrogant commitment he makes by always protecting his heroes from satiety, whether it be in pleasure or in crime, the concern he shows to seek infinite variation,

[h] Tandis que tous ses prédécesseurs en littérature érotique avaient vu 'la chose' avec un sourire goguenard, un scepticisme exaspérant ou une grossièreté repoussante, Sade considère l'amour et ses actes du point de vue de l'infini.

[i] Les rites du costume et les règlements intérieurs du château de Durcet provoquent normalement l'hilarité.

[j] cet humour tragique, dont la définition est encore à faire

albeit by ever-increasing complication, in the circumstances that are propitious for maintaining their folly, all these things are likely to give rise in the midst of his narrative to some scene that is manifestly outrageous, thereby providing the reader with some relief by suggesting that the author is not fooled.[29 k]

We know that the author *n'est pas dupe,* that his work is not laughable because it is so manifestly outrageous. This is, however, a worrying line of argument. Surely much of Sade's writing can be understood as an attempt to constitute—almost in the legalistic sense—a new set of libertine norms. What then is to count as outrageous, and at what point is the outrage such as to be identifiably humorous? Such hermeneutic considerations may well be, for Breton and Desnos, vulgar in themselves. Noble readers will respond to noble Sadian humor.

The notion of Sadian "humor" thus provides for an understanding of Sadian seriousness that is more or less compatible with a form of laughter. Not weak, vulgar laughter, of course. Not smiling: "there are no smiles in his work, but occasionally a tragic, sneering laugh that reminds one of the tragic laughter found in the Romantic *maudits.*"[30 l] To put it another way, black humor is likely to be characterized in part by the fact that it is not funny. Each reader, each critic who perceives it can thus talk about how imperceptible it is. Sollers first of all, of course, but before him, and after Breton and Desnos, we find Blanchot talking of "the imperceptible humor that is [. . .] proper [to Sade]."[31 m] From about the mid-1970s, a series of critics can be seen to discover Sade's humor, describing it each time as something previously neglected. Philippe Roger assures us that humor is everywhere in Sade:

Why do people so often fail to notice that Sade is a lighthearted author, in the way one can be when one tramples on the garden beds of an old society, in order to make room for a new way of talking, a young insolence, and a gay knowledge?

[k] Les excès mêmes de l'imagination à quoi l'entraîne son génie naturel et le disposent ses longues années de captivité, le parti pris follement orgueilleux qui le fait, dans le plaisir comme dans le crime, mettre à l'abri de la satiété ses héros, le souci qu'il montre de varier à l'infini, ne serait-ce qu'en les compliquant toujours davantage, les circonstances propices au maintien de leur égarement ont toute chance de faire surgir de son récit quelque passage d'une outrance manifeste, qui détend le lecteur en lui donnant à penser que l'auteur n'est pas dupe.

[l] nul sourire dans son œuvre, mais parfois un tragique ricanement qui fait penser aux rires tragiques des maudits romantiques.

[m] cet humour imperceptible qui [. . .] est propre [à Sade]

> His heroes do not laugh, they deride. But their laughter has been transferred to Sade's writing. Laughter builds up under Sade's pen, loads the text with irony, and saturates it with humor.[32] [n]

"Writing" (*écriture*) seems here to be the (modernist) name of that which is not found in any particular place in the text, because it is not really an aspect of content. Sadian laughter, for Roger and others, must be read not as thematic, but as somehow material. There is nothing to demonstrate, no structure to analyze, as Sollers shows when he refers broadly to the "underlying laugh"[o] in Sade. Either you "hear" the humor or you don't: "You either hear or you do not hear the mockery that passes through all the waste of situations, organs, suffering, spasms, and speeches."[33] [p]

My point here is not that there is no humor in Sade. There are certainly in *Les Cent Vingt Journées* incidents of a kind described as "very amusing,"[q] including an example of bedroom farce, where the duc de Blangis is drunk and tries to sodomize the still-virginal Sophie, having mistaken her for his companion, Aline. He soon transfers his rather blurred attentions to Zelmire, who sleeps in the same room. The young girls scream with fright and run around the room trying to avoid him. Help is slow to arrive, and confusion reigns (I, 272–73). "They laughed heartily all the next day over that nocturnal adventure,"[r] we are told (273). "They" (*on*) in this context is a relatively limited group, I suppose: it is unlikely that Sophie and Zelmire spent the day doubled up with laughter, if only because other poses were required of them. Later, we—or is it perhaps "they"?—all have another opportunity to laugh when Augustine serves milk for the duke's coffee through her anus: "They all laughed heartily at the joke, and each one requested milk for himself" (I, 293).[s] Julie, that most resourceful of women, knows how to stay out of the victim's role by sharing in the masters' laughter. Just after a session in which Augustine and Adélaïde have been made to cry out in pain, we learn that "she was

[n] Pourquoi le dit-on si peu: Sade est un auteur gai, comme on peut l'être quand on piétine toutes les plates-bandes d'une ancienne société, pour y camper une parole neuve, une jeune insolence, son gai savoir.

Ses héros ne rient guère, ils raillent. Mais leur rire est passé dans l'écriture. Il s'accumule sous la plume de Sade, charge le texte d'ironie, la sature d'humour.

[o] rire sous-jacent

[p] On entend ou on n'entend pas cette raillerie qui passe à travers le gaspillage des situations, des organes, des supplices, des spasmes, des discours.

[q] très plaisant

[r] On rit beaucoup tout le lendemain de cette aventure nocturne.

[s] On rit beaucoup de la plaisanterie, et chacun demanda du lait.

laughing madly" (I, 339).[t] Apart from these moments of local hilarity, there is little in *Les Cent Vingt Journées* that could be read as the textual mark of authorial humor. Such humor certainly exists, and is never more clearly identifiable than in certain footnotes. This one from *Histoire de Juliette* actually makes humor out of the very things I am discussing—and making fun of—in this chapter:

> The result was that these two upright individuals, if one leaves out the mouth, which does not produce a strong enough sensation to deserve to be counted, had been fucked until that point in time to the following extent: Clairwil one hundred eighty-five times, and Juliette one hundred ninety-two, counting both cunt and ass. We thought it appropriate to carry out this addition in order to save the trouble for all those women who might otherwise have broken off to do so. (VIII, 506n)[u]

Sade's apologists, without bothering to analyze such (relatively rare) examples of humor, have simply invoked the notion of preemptive authorial laughter. Sade is not to be laughed at by us as readers because *he* has always already laughed—blackly, tragically. It is for this reason, no doubt, that Sadian humor must be claimed by the critic from the outset, posited almost as a condition for reading the work. The proceedings of the Cerisy *Sade* bear as their epigraph a quotation from Sollers: "Everything Sade writes is humor."[34] [v] The very move of putting humor first is undoubtedly a way of rejecting what Philippe Roger, after Lacan, calls Sadian hagiography,[35] but it does have, despite claims made elsewhere in the colloquium's proceedings,[36] a most precisely *apologetic* function. We can ask, indeed, whether the claim to read all Sade's writing as humorous is not often apologetic in the humbly psychological sense of the word, rather than the dignified, rhetorical one.

To make the point more demandingly, one could say that the positing of Sadian humor serves to ensure that we will not laugh at Sade, but does so by admitting that his work cannot be taken seriously. Bataille is most quotable in this regard: "Let us be clear about this: nothing would be more pointless than to take Sade *literally*, seriously. From whatever side we approach him, he has already taken evasive

[t] elle riait comme une folle.

[u] De manière que ces deux honnêtes créatures, sans compter la bouche qui ne produit pas une sensation assez marquée pour être comptée, avaient été foutues jusque-là, Clairwil cent quatre-vingt-cinq coups, et Juliette cent quatre-vingt-douze, cela, tant en con qu'en cul. Nous avons cru devoir établir cette addition pour en éviter la peine aux femmes qui, sans cela, n'auraient pas manqué de s'interrompre pour la faire.

[v] Tout ce qu'écrit Sade est humour.

action beforehand."[37] [w] Imagine what would happen if we were to take Sade "seriously." As readers, we would be exposing ourselves to ridicule, says Marcel Hénaff: "To call him to account gravely is in fact to wind up involuntarily in his space. It means climbing onto the stage in the buffoon's role."[38] [x] What sort of literal-minded, numerical-minded reader would presume to call Sade to account? Chantal Thomas describes the typical plodder:

> His seriousness and his sustained incredulity (the other side of an unbending desire to believe) prevent him from seeing what sustains the written or cinematographic work, its fundamental nonreason. "Nobody with any sense," writes A. P. de Mandiargues, "can possibly believe that at the end of the novel Juliette could be capable of achieving pleasure once again on seeing her daughter Marianne subjected to every form of abuse, and then roasted by Noirceuil. Sade, as frenzied as he may have been, probably did not believe it was possible either.[39] [y]

Through the authoritative eyes of Mandiargues, the companion of Bataille, Breton, and Desnos, we can perceive the manifestly outrageous. And if we are not quite sure whether Sade was really serious about this murderous family barbecue, we can understand that taking it all seriously might lead to the worst. We might reject Sade utterly. We might even laugh at him.[40]

But seriously, folks . . . I want to return, without apology, to Sade's numbers. We may be quite uncertain whether they are dry calculations or marinaded in authorial humor, but they are sometimes amusing and certainly constitute much of the textual detail of *Les Cent Vingt Journées.* In his measurement of time, for example, Sade provides us, a little anachronistically, with a splendidly quantitative antidote to the Romantic instant: the foursquare division of the hour. The unit of time for noncopulative erotic activities is usually a quarter of an hour. This is the temporal scale of such pastimes as kissing, licking, and swallowing:

[w] Entendons-nous; rien ne serait plus vain que de prendre Sade *à la lettre,* au sérieux. Par quelque côté qu'on l'aborde, il s'est à l'avance dérobé.

[x] Lui demander gravement des comptes c'est se faire prendre involontairement dans son espace, c'est monter sur la scène mais dans le rôle du bouffon.

[y] Son sérieux et son incrédulité (envers d'un incoercible vouloir croire) l'empêchent de voir ce qui soutient l'œuvre écrite ou filmique, sa non-raison fondamentale. "Personne de sensé, écrit A. P. de Mandiargues, ne croira qu'à la fin du roman Juliette soit capable de jouir encore en voyant sa fille Marianne rôtie par Noirceuil après avoir subi tous les outrages, et Sade, si furieux fût-il, n'y croyait probablement pas."

He pumped his hole like that for a quarter of an hour. (I, 155)

He sucked my saliva for a quarter of an hour. (I, 207)

He kissed her on the mouth for a quarter of an hour. (I, 222)

He went on kissing her bottom for a quarter of an hour. (I, 240)[z]

Intensification is then produced, with arithmetic propriety, as measured extension. Unspeakable activities can last half an hour (i.e., two units): "they had gone on doing appalling things together for half an hour" (I, 243).[a] A whipping endures for three units: "Three quarters of an hour had gone by and I was still beating him" (I, 258).[b] And an epic bout of sucking, performed by the duc de Blangis, lasts for four units: "The duc sucked the lovely child's mouth for an hour" (I, 254).[c] Nothing lasts for 11 minutes, or 37, or 53.

Sadian number is never more narrowly erotic than when it measures itself against the human body.[41] The penis is, of course, the first object of attention. Pricks are subject, at times, to a qualitative evaluation that tends to favor both the enormous *and* the astonishingly small at the expense of the ordinary. Usually, they are discussed in strictly quantitative terms. The culminating *trait* in the first description of the duc de Blangis is "this member whose dimensions were an exact eight inches in circumference and twelve in length" (I, 29).[d] At the other end of the scale, within the group of the four *amis,* we have Durcet: "his prick is extraordinarily small: it is scarcely two inches round and four inches long" (I, 37).[e] Numerically sensitive readers will have noted with satisfaction that all of these penis measurements take the form of whole, even numbers. What the sexual giant and the sexual dwarf have in common, in Sade's world, are foursquare organs.

One of the reasons, one might surmise, for the geometrical exactitude of these measurements is that Sadian organs are never brought up against any sort of tape measure, rule, or vernier calipers. Whereas in Nerciat's *Les Aphrodites,* you will recall, Trottignac the virile Gascon

[z] Il [. . .] le gamahucha un quart d'heure de cette manière.

Il suça ma salive un quart d'heure.

Il la baise sur la bouche un quart d'heure.

Il lui baisait les fesses un quart d'heure.

[a] ils avaient fait tous deux ensemble des infamies une demi-heure de suite.

[b] Il y avait plus de trois quarts d'heure que j'y allais à tour de bras.

[c] Le duc [. . .] suça une heure la bouche de ce bel enfant.

[d] ce membre dont la taille était de huit pouces juste de pourtour sur douze de long

[e] son vit est extraordinairement petit: à peine a-t-il deux pouces de tour sur quatre de long.

is actually measured according to a (fictively) established procedure, being required to sustain weights on his erect penis (I, 111–12), Sade's characters never undergo mensuration as a narrative ordeal; they seem to be subject to a masterly *coup d'œil* that evaluates their quantity in a trice. As Marcel Hénaff says with nice humor: "At a more implicit level, one can deduce the pleasure of numeration from the fact that it would be thoroughly ridiculous to try to imagine the mensurative work supposed by the precise figures given in detailed description, unless we imagine the libertine with a compass in his eye . . . "[42] [f] Sade's arithmetic seems indeed to transcend the empirical, as if the length of the penis were counted or calculated, rather than actually measured.

There is more to Sadian virility than having a large, foursquare penis, of course. Not some masculine quality prized by Lawrence, Montherlant, or Hemingway, just the ability to ejaculate frequently and regularly within a given period of time: the duc de Blangis achieves up to 7 or 8 within a given erotic interval, and has done up to 18 per day. Such characters ejaculate frequently *and* copiously, of course, with measured quantities of sperm. Their ejaculate can be measured by volume, as in the case of Hercule, the first *fouteur* chosen for Silling (I, 58), but Sade seems to prefer, once again, to count out the units of production. He accounts for the pleasures of orgasm in terms of the number of *crachats*—"the vile man drowned them in sperm, projecting more than twenty thick spurts into my face in succession" (I, 328)[g]—or the number of *jets:* "he darted seven or eight streams of sperm onto her backside" (I, 339).[h] Yet these criteria—penis length, number of ejaculations, quantity of ejaculate, number of spurts within an ejaculation—do not quite exhaust the range of vital statistics that describe a Sadian hero like the duc de Blangis. There is also the matter of his receptive bodily *capacity:* he has been known to undergo fifty-five bouts of passive sodomy in one day (I, 30).

Sadian femininity is undoubtedly different from Sadian masculinity—but only in quantity. Instead of penis measurements, we have, in certain cases at least, clitoris measurement—the very large clitoris of a masculine woman being equal to a very small penis. Madame Champville has "a clitoris that protrudes more than three inches" (I,

[f] A un niveau plus implicite ce plaisir de numération se déduit du caractère inimaginable tant il est burlesque, du travail de mensuration que les indications chiffrées avec tant de précision supposent, sauf à prêter au libertin [. . .] un compas dans l'œil. . .

[g] le vilain homme les inonde de foutre en me lançant de suite plus de vingt crachats très épais au visage.

[h] il lui lâche sept ou huit jets de foutre sur le derrière.

48).[43] [i] Women have their own, relatively classical geometry, which is that of roundness. It is hardly remarkable that Adélaïde should have breasts that are very round (I, 41), but we are invited to focus admiringly on the *cul* of Constance, measuring thus its perfect geometricality: "Nothing could be more precisely round" (I, 39).[j] In *Histoire de Juliette,* attention is paid to the number of discharges achieved in a given time by the heroine and her companions,[44] but in *Les Cent Vingt Journées* the main preoccupation is with bodily capacity as gauged by orifice measurement. Like the penis, the vagina and the anus are noteworthy for their extremes: the painfully exquisite narrowness of Adélaïde (I, 41) or the cavernous, "volcanic" breadth of Thérèse and Fanchon (I, 61).

An area where Sade may perhaps be credited with opening up new territory to the erotic surveyor is the measurement of tongues. In *Histoire de Juliette,* we are told that six inches of tongue are inserted by Saint-Fond into a waiting orifice (VIII, 384), while in *Les Cent Vingt Journées,* we learn of lingual giants: "hurling himself at the old woman once again, he thrust his tongue at least a foot into her asshole and discharged like a madman" (I, 170; see also I, 208).[k] It is tempting, at the risk of overgeneralizing, to see signs of a numerical pattern here. To complete the range of tongue sizes, we would need to find a Sadian tongue (either that of a weak man or a strong woman) that measured three inches (i.e., one-quarter of a foot). Sade's arithmetic taxonomies may define, in principle, what has yet to be discovered in his novels.

Another area of Sadian calculation—one that tends to make the apologists rather uncomfortable[45]—is excremental measurement. This may indeed appear, at first glance, to be a domain that is resistant to sustained and serious endeavor. We have to be reminded, in particular, that Sade is utterly opposed to Rabelais in the nature of his preoccupations. Noëlle Châtelet writes: "But whereas there is so much happiness in Rabelais's grotesque scatology, Sade's overwhelms us with horror. Humiliating as a matter of principle and played out against a backdrop of suffering, it prevents any smiling, and is not even saved by the seductiveness of parody."[46] [l] Here again, we see the forward

[i] le clitoris saillant de plus de trois pouces

[j] Il était du rond le plus exact.

[k] se reprécipitant sur sa vieille, il lui enfonça sa langue dans le trou du cul au moins d'un pied et déchargea comme un furieux.

[l] Mais autant il y a de bonheur dans la scatologie grotesque de Rabelais, autant celle de Sade nous plonge dans l'horreur. Humiliante par principe et sur un fond perpétuel

defense strategy of Sadian apologetics. Marcel Hénaff, in turn, assures us that it is all done with "a kind of rasping humor";[47] [m] we are being reminded that Sadian shit is no laughing matter. Indeed, it is hardly matter at all, in the Bachelardian, phenomenological sense, since it is so utterly subject to formal enumeration and classification. Sade's scatology is largely a numerical practice of the turd.

The very move from counting and measuring organs to counting and measuring turds is itself a form of erotic intensification in Sade. As readers, we are compelled by the energy of the narration to move on from the by now routinely phallometric to the audaciously coprometric. And as we launch into the potentially revolting area of coprophagy, our sole reassurance may lie in the knowledge that Sadian accountancy is still working at something close to full efficiency. We begin the transition with simple fart counts: "Durcet was determined to have some farts from Augustine [. . .]. Happily, Augustine was prepared; she did nearly a dozen into the little financier's mouth" (I, 199).[n] It is a little surprising to learn that the number of farts was about a dozen, rather than the even dozen, although we can be confident that there were an even number. On a later occasion, we find a full-blown orgy of farting, where speed of oral consumption is matched only by the swiftness of the accountant: "one by one people came up to fart into their mouths. Duclos was responsible for counting and marking down the scores. Since there were thirty-six farters as against four swallowers [Note that this makes a farter/fartee ratio of 36:4, or 9:1], there were certain persons who received as many as one hundred fifty farts" (I, 316).[o] The figures are somewhat approximate, but if we suppose that these anal bounties were evenly shared among the four *amis*, the following calculations cannot be misleading:

$$4 \times \text{c. } 150 = \text{c. } 600 \text{ farts}$$

$$\frac{\text{c. } 600}{36} = \text{c. } 16 \text{ farts per farter [Note: } 16 \times 36 = 576\text{].}$$

There is every indication that the highly disciplined group has achieved something very close to quadrangular farting.

---

de souffrance, elle empêche tout sourire, pas même sauvée par la séduction de la parodie.

[m] une sorte d'humour grinçant

[n] Durcet voulut absolument faire péter Augustine [. . .]. Heureusement qu'Augustine était préparée; elle en fit près d'une douzaine dans la bouche du petit financier.

[o] l'on venait tour à tour leur péter dans la bouche; Duclos était chargée de compter et de marquer, et comme il y avait trente-six péteurs ou péteuses contre seulement quatre avaleurs, il y en eut qui reçurent jusqu'à cent cinquante pets.

Beyond fart counting—in the weakest possible, nontranscendental sense of "beyond"—we have turd counting. In *Les Cent Vingt Journées,* turds tend to appear in orderly groups and in predictable numbers, although once again the foursquare does not seem to reflect the empirical so much as respond to an abstract exigency, where the number is the shape of pleasure. "He liked to find four turds, without a single drop of urine in a commode's chamber pot" (I, 202).[p] And when the number is not fully stated, this seems to be because it is taken for granted that there must be four: "He took his place, pushed, and a turd landed there [. . . .]. He moved into position again, pushed out a second, then a third, each time with the same insertion ceremony. Finally, when it came to the last, [etc. . . .]" (I, 233).[q] So often in *Les Cent Vingt Journées,* the last and the fourth are the same thing. There may in fact be more than 4 turds: sometimes 8 or 10 (I, 201, 227), but there is never that indeterminate, undifferentiated, unspeakable substance that is so often designated scornfully in texts by other writers as *la merde.* Sadian turds, at their finest, achieve a remarkable perfection of form. At one point in *Les Cent Vingt Journées,* we find the Compleat Turd: "the most complete turd one could hope to find" (I, 216).[r] Later examples can only repeat the prodigy: "the most superb turd one could hope to find" (I, 293; see also I, 319).[s]

Sade's turd measurements, perhaps for the very reason that they appear narratively more intense, erotically more advanced than his phallometrics, seem not to attain the fullness of numerical precision. Their evaluation is often thoroughly quantitative, but usually takes the form of epithets, rather than raw figures. The turd is most visibly enormous when it is framed, presented, offered in a dish:

> Never in my life had I seen such a turd: all by itself it would have filled a deep salad bowl. (I, 213)
>
> An enormous turd filled the bowl. (I, 270)[t]

[p] Il voulait trouver quatre étrons sans une seule goutte d'urine dans le pot d'une chaise percée.

[q] Il se place, il pousse, un étron vient se poser [. . .]. Il se replace, en pousse un second, puis un troisième, et toujours à chaque la même cérémonie d'introduction. Enfin au dernier, [etc . . .].

[r] l'étron le plus complet qu'il fût possible de voir

[s] l'étron le plus superbe qu'il fût possible de voir

[t] De ma vie, je n'avais vu un tel étron: il remplissait à lui tout seul un très profond saladier.

Un enorme étron remplit le plat.

At one point in *Les Cent Vingt Journées,* we encounter the most detailed aesthetic and gastronomic order of these fecal objects, by what is effectively a meticulous denial of excrement as waste matter. The *vieux débauché* in question has a veritable turd cellar:

> a kind of wardrobe filled with pigeonholes, each of which housed a porcelain pot containing a turd. The old rake had made an arrangement with one of his sisters, who was abbess at one of the most important convents in Paris. That obliging girl, at his behest, every morning sent him crates full of the shit produced by her prettiest boarders. He filed it all according to a system, and when I arrived he ordered me to take such and such a number, which was in fact the oldest. (I, 227)[u]

Diligent auditors of *Les Cent Vingt Journées* may wish to calculate how many of the 600 "dishes" in the novel's great buffet may be found to contain offerings chosen from this range. Sade's daring may consist in tearing down the partitions between the kitchen, the chapel, the *garde-robe* (toilet), and the boudoir, but this can only have the most radical consequences for his erotic cuisine. As we read, are we not being entertained by an authorial *tastemerde* who has at his disposal a vast taxonomy of numbered turds?

In conclusion, we ought to consider what might be called Sade's final reckoning: that of torture and death. The most classically sadistic—and arithmetically undemanding—is that of the number of blows administered during a beating or whipping. We find a nicely graded set presented by Duclos, the first *historienne* in *Les Cent Vingt Journées,* as she works through a small set of passions centered on whipping:

> I myself dealt with a client on whose behind one had to lay one hundred carefully counted birch strokes. (I, 255)
>
> He had received at least two hundred lashes. (I, 256)
>
> Firstly, he required her to give him five hundred lashes, in front of everyone. (I, 260)[v]

[u] une espèce d'armoire toute remplie de cases ayant chacune un vase de porcelaine dans lequel était un étron. Ce vieux débauché était arrangé avec une de ses soeurs qui était abbesse d'un des plus considérables couvents de Paris. Cette bonne fille, à sa sollicitation, lui envoyait tous les matins des caisses pleines des étrons de ses plus jolies pensionnaires. Il rangeait tout cela par ordre, et quand j'arrivai il m'ordonna de prendre un tel numéro qu'il m'indiqua et qui était le plus ancien.

[v] j'en expédiai moi-même un, auquel il fallait appliquer cent coups de verges bien comptés sur le derrière.

Il avait reçu au moins deux cents coups de fouet.

Il se fit donner d'abord, devant tout le monde, cinq cents coups de fouet.

The measure of intensification here is (approximately) the one we have mentioned already: that of the geometrical progression, which drives on by the multiplication of excess. Thus, when we find further doubling—"an old veteran of Cythera who required more than a thousand lashes" (I, 262)[w]—the number 1,000 is actually reached by calculation and represents something arithmetically precise, as is suggested, oddly enough, by the qualification "plus de mille."

The mutilations carried out on Sade's characters involve more modest numbers, in proportion to their more drastic narrative impact. By narrative convention, the victim of a whipping is always able to heal, but the mutilations carried out on the minor characters of *Les Cent Vingt Journées* begin the final steps toward death: they lead eventually to the victims' disappearance from the story. Early mutilations involve the most finely measured brutality, being carried out slowly, carefully, and in appropriate numbers: "they pull out four of his teeth, cut off four of his fingers (always in fours, because each friend officiates in turn)" (I, 434; see also I, 439).[x] In the midst of this cruel fictional suffering, Sade maintains a geometrical fictional fairness. By a kind of unilateral version of the Talic law, each of the four *amis* is able to pull out a tooth, or cut off a toe. When Justine was being tortured, in *Les Infortunes de la vertu,* by Rodin and his associates, she underwent the same treatment: "one of them held on to me; the other performed the operation. They cut off a toe from each foot, sat me down, and each pulled out a tooth from the back of my mouth" (II, 310).[y] Demonstrably, at this point, Justine is 50 percent better off than the victims of Silling, but such calculations can only be made if one denies the quality of her suffering.

Sade's reckoning of cruelty includes yet another form of mensuration: we find the thematically tiresome allied with the morally outrageous in his counting of crimes. Durcet of the small penis has achieved a stunning quantity of evil:

> "Come on," said the duc. "Confess that on more than twenty occasions you have engineered the ruin of some poor folk, simply to satisfy the perverse tastes you have just admitted to."
>
> "More than twenty?" said Durcet. "More than two hundred, my friend. Without exaggeration, I could list more than four hundred families

[w] un vieux invalide de Cythère qui se faisait donner plus de mille coups de fouet

[x] on lui arrache quatre dents, on lui coupe quatre doigts (toujours par quatre, parce que chacun officie).

[y] l'un d'eux me tient, l'autre opère; ils me coupent un doigt à chaque pied, ils me rassoient, ils m'arrachent chacun une dent au fond de la bouche.

> reduced to beggardom, who would not be in that state today were it not for me." (I, 182)[z]

This is Durcet's own, privately generated subproletariat, his inverted version of the *deux cents familles* said to rule modern France, and ten times as many as the duc had guessed. The crimes of Clairwil, in *Histoire de Juliette,* are measured simultaneously on two scales, a daily round of routine viciousness and, parallel to this, or punctuating it, a series of capital offenses: "Her standing and her great wealth have always saved her from the gallows, but she has deserved execution on more than twenty occasions. In short, one could calculate her crimes by examining her daily acts, and the number of severe punishments she has deserved could be worked out by counting the number of days in her life" (VIII, 325).[a]

Crimes are not only gauged, however, by the risk factor, by an account of hypothetical punishments: their intensity can be measured more intimately and more erotically, as here in the case of Duclos. Having narrated a crime she committed in the past, she is questioned closely about its bodily effect on her:

> "Duclos," said the duc, "be truthful. Did you frig yourself? Did crime's precisely voluptuous sensation reach your organ of sensual pleasure?"
>
> "Yes, my Lord, I confess it did. As a result of it, I discharged five times that very evening." (I, 237)[b]

How big a crime, exactly? Five discharges worth, Sir. Duclos speaks to another woman of "a horror that will make you discharge for ten years!" (I, 280).[c] Not only does crime pay in Sade's novels, it goes on yielding interest of various kinds for years after the fact.

In addition to Durcet's reckoning of his own crimes, we find quite

[z] Avoue le fait, lui dit le duc, conviens qu'il t'est arrivé plus de vingt fois de faire ruiner des malheureux, rien que pour servir en ce sens-là tous les goûts pervers dont tu conviens ici.

Plus de vingt fois? dit Durcet, plus de deux cents, mon ami et je pourrais, sans exagération, citer plus de quatre cents familles réduites aujourd'hui à l'aumône et qui n'y sont que par moi.

[a] Son crédit et ses grandes richesses l'ont toujours sauvée de l'échafaud, mais elle l'a mérité vingt fois; c'est, en un mot, par ses actions journalières qu'on pourrait supputer ses crimes, et le nombre des supplices qu'elle a mérités s'évaluerait par celui des jours de son existence.

[b] Duclos, dit le duc, soi[s] vraie: te branlas-tu? La sensation fine et voluptueuse du crime atteignit-elle l'organe de la volupté?

Oui, monseigneur, je vous l'avoue; et j'en déchargeai cinq fois de suite dès le même soir.

[c] une horreur qui te fera décharger dix ans!

often in Sade attempts to calculate the lifetime achievements of a libertine. The duc de Blangis was to present such a count in the unfinished second part of the *Les Cent Vingt Journées:* "This will be the duc, who will admit to having devirginated more than fifteen hundred of them over a period of thirty years" (I, 368).[d] This is of course an invitation to Sadian pleasure at the great number of deflowerings, but it also gives us scope for analytical curiosity, and may lead to such calculations as the following:

$$\frac{1{,}500}{30} = 50 \text{ deflowerings/year} = 1/\text{week}.$$

The mental arithmetic is more difficult when one is required to effect a series of multiplications in order to reach the impressive numbers that mark the career of the true libertine. The narrator or the *historienne* tends to do most of it for us, however: "We used to go like that through three or four in the same evening, according to the number I had discovered, and we performed the same operations with all of them [. . .]. He was a man of about thirty, and I had his trade for more than ten years, during which time I made him discharge on more than two thousand coffins" (I, 322).[e] How many coffins in a lifetime, then? On another occasion, her calculations are advanced enough to provide us with a sense of where it all leads, as in the case of this committed coprophagist: "He deals with thirty women a day, and they are all required to shit in his mouth. He eats the turds produced by three or four of the prettiest ones. He repeats the bout five times a week, which means that he sees seven thousand eight hundred girls per year. When Champville encounters him, he is seventy years old, and has been in this business for fifty" (I, 371).[f] How many turds in a lifetime? (It might be objected that exact calculations are hindered by the relatively indeterminate daily turd count—*trois ou quatre*—but we should note that, in the previous example, Duclos was still able to carry out her multiplication.) Here is a scholastic, if not scholarly formulation of the problem: If a man eats 3 or 4 turds

[d] Ce sera le duc qui avouera en avoir depuis trente ans, dépucelé plus de quinze cents.

[e] Nous en allions courir comme cela trois ou quatre dans la soirée, suivant le nombre que j'en avais découvert, et nous faisions la même opération à tous [. . .]. C'était un homme d'environ trente ans, et j'ai eu sa pratique plus de dix ans, pendant lesquels je suis sûre de l'avoir fait décharger sur plus de deux mille cercueils.

[f] Il passe trente femmes dans sa journée, et les fait toutes chier dans sa bouche; il mange l'étron de trois ou quatre des plus jolies. Il renouvelle cette partie-là cinq fois de la semaine, ce qui fait qu'il voit sept mille huit cents filles par an. Quand Champville le voit, il a soixante et dix ans, et il y a cinquante ans qu'il fait ce métier.

per day, for five days a week, for fifty years, how many turds will he have consumed altogether? (Hint: Count "3 or 4" as 3.5 turds per working day. Calculators may be used.)

In a sense, this sort of unproblematical problem is exactly what the thematics of number leads to in *Les Cent Vingt Journées,* to more of the same: bigger and bigger numbers of things that are more and more horrible. We could conclude with this unfinished calculation as a mark of the minimal aperture, the false openness that shows in effect how there is no end to the counting, other than the end that has been inscribed in the first numbers mentioned—no end to the arithmetic other than the geometry. There need to be 4 friends, 4 turds, 120 days, 600 passions, and so forth, in order to stop the whole process from repeating itself indefinitely. The very compulsion to count seems rather laughable, really, but I cannot forget that Sadian number, for all its internal dynamism, is not, in the terms of his fiction, utterly disjunct from the human. In the very last passion of the fourth and final section, we read of a man who murders by numbers. He has "fifteen objects for his debauch, which is regularly executed every two weeks" (I, 444).[g] Not content with counting his victims in his head, or on paper, he actually brands each one with a number: "He touches, fondles, and scrutinizes them, sucks their mouths and has them shit one after the other into his mouth, but does not swallow. This operation is performed with dreadful seriousness. He brands each of them on the shoulder with a red-hot iron, imprinting a number that marks the order in which she will be dealt with" (I, 444).[h] The numbers involved here are undoubtedly smaller than those found in the great killing places of our own century, but it is the same dramatic encounter of the administrative and the physiological, the numerical and the fleshly. Number here is specifically opposed to flesh, brought up against it, imposed upon it. Numerical abstraction encounters the humanly concrete—marking, consuming, and destroying it.

However laughable Sadian number may sometimes appear, for its compulsive repetition or its manic self-confirmation, I cannot escape what Sade calls "the dreadful seriousness" of such representations as these. Only by taking them seriously can we see that Sade is not funny at all. Only by measuring what counting entails can we understand that his fiction is both laughable and hateful.

[g] quinze sujets pour sa passion qui s'exécute régulièrement tous les quinze jours

[h] Il les touche, il les manie, il les examine, les suce sur la bouche, et les fait toutes chier l'une après l'autre dans sa bouche, mais il n'avale pas. Cette première opération faite avec un sérieux effrayant, il les marque toutes sur l'épaule avec un fer rouge, au numéro de l'ordre dans lequel il veut qu'on les lui fasse passer.

Chapter 7

How Not to Be Murdered in Sadian Stories

Nothing and no one is as inconsistent as a libertine.

—*Les Cent Vingt Journées*[a]

Novelistic learning in the eighteenth century often takes place completely outside the classroom. Whatever the continuing prestige of the convent or the boudoir as places of graded erotic education, a great deal of what is valuable has to be learned through adventure, on the open road. Picaresque narrative shows the accumulation of worldly wisdom through a lifetime of inventive wandering. The young hero or heroine, having been initially exposed to danger by his or her lack of wealth and power, learns gradually to read the danger signs, and avoid the pitfalls. Within the tradition of erotic literature, worldly wisdom has long had a place, and it continues in a number of eighteenth-century novels to be of particular interest to a young woman choosing the life of a prostitute. The instruction provided by the older woman in Aretino or Pallavicino acted as a compendium of experience(s): narratively, worldly wisdom was served up as a set of anecdotal tricks. But now it is built up in time as one character's response to a succession of adventures. There exists, then, parallel to and yet intermingled with education narratives like *La Philosophie dans le boudoir, L'Anti-Justine,* and *Le Rideau levé,* a subgenre of picaresque

[a] Rien n'est inconséquent comme un libertin.

eroticism. Many texts, including even *L'Anti-Justine,* tend to move between the two kinds of narrative, alternating exposure to the outside world with an intimately demonstrative pedagogy. Movement through the world, for the chevalier de Faublas and many of his colleagues, can amount to movement from one bedroom to another—via a series of balconies, ladders, garden walls, and back alleys.

Thérèse philosophe presents, so to speak, a second-order narrative, wherein scenes of confession and instruction, closely administered by priests and relatives, give way, for the heroine, to the relation of an orphaned existence in Paris. Thérèse has been given a degree of formal erotic instruction by her confessor, but is dangerously lacking in worldly wisdom: "The lessons of Abbé T . . . had really opened my eyes to the role we should play in this world with respect to God and the laws of men; but I had no knowledge of the ways of the world. [. . .] Poor innocent that I was! How elementary my mistakes were!" (I, 165–166).[b] Getting beyond this relative innocence becomes Thérèse's vital concern for the next part of the story. Like a true picaresque narrator, she tells the whole story from the position of mature comfort. She is now no longer at risk. Similarly, the heroine of *Margot la ravaudeuse,* who was born into a poverty-stricken family with collective criminal tendencies, tells how she became a *catin* and a *fille de l'opéra.* With increasing skill, she attracted rich lovers and took full material advantage of them. At the time of telling, she lives a more simple existence, but can still speak from a position of health, comfort, and stability. *Illyrine,* too, is a story of exposure, especially through travel. At times, the heroine is obliged to use that standard technique of picaresque survival: running away (see, e.g., 51). For most of the story, as her narration continually reminds us, she is lost in "dissipation" (190). Eventually, however, she is able to find stability, *se fixer* as she repeatedly says. *Se fixer* here is both figurative and literal. In conventional erotic terms, it means finding a permanent lover: "setting my heart in place" (216);[c] "establishing myself with one single lover" (130).[d] In the simplest, spatial sense, it means no longer being on the road: "fixing my destiny" (39).[e] The "movement" toward maturity is a movement beyond adventure and travel, with their varied erotic experiences,

[b] Les leçons de l'abbé T. . . m'avaient bien dessillé les yeux sur le rôle que nous devons jouer ici-bas, eu égard à Dieu et aux lois des hommes; mais je n'avais aucune espèce de connaissance de l'usage du monde. [. . .] Pauvre innocente! Que je me trompais grossièrement!

[c] fixer le cœur

[d] me fixer à un unique ami

[e] fixer ma destinée

toward something like marriage. As the heroine looks for a faithful lover, she looks for immobility. "I had long favored change," says the narrator-heroine of *Félicia,* "but now I wanted to establish myself" (327).[f] In time, when narrative process has finally had its due, she will be able to settle down.

The starting point of Justine's and Juliette's story is very much the same as for Thérèse or Margot—or for that matter, Gil Blas: "the door of the convent was opened for them, the dowry placed in their hands, and they were left to become whatever they wanted" (VI, 33).[g] Dreadful freedom: this ought, by picaresque convention, to be the start of a series of "hard knocks" destined to school these two young women in the art of survival. Yet for Justine, the knocks take place without any effective schooling. That is what makes of her a kind of antiheroine for many modern readers. As Jane Gallop points out, she "never learns her lesson."[1] "Whatever happens," writes Jean Paulhan, "Justine is surprised by it. Experience teaches her nothing. Her soul remains ignorant, and her body more ignorant still."[2] [h] How can she be so lacking in the art of womanly self-defense? How can she continue to make the same mistakes, without learning from them? How can she wander from one trap to another without seeming to acquire even a glimmer of worldly wisdom? Susan Sontag describes her as lacking the necessary faculties for learning: "Pornography is mainly populated by creatures like Sade's Justine, endowed with neither will, intelligence, nor even, apparently, memory. Justine lives in a perpetual state of astonishment, never learning anything from the strikingly repetitious violations of her innocence. After each fresh betrayal, she gets in place for another round, as uninstructed by her experience as ever."[3] Justine's sexual virtue, which endures in some fashion through it all, seems unable to make any sort of tactical alliance with that most pedestrian of qualities, the essential picaresque virtue of prudence.

Prudence, it must be said, may be less valuable in Sade than in more conventional versions of the picaresque. *La Nouvelle Justine* is actually presented as a story that will teach the reader how to avoid the vicissitudes of life, by showing "the way one must walk along life's thorny pathway, in order to avoid the bizarre whims of fortune" (VI, 31).[i] But

[f] J'avais été partisan du changement, je souhaitais maintenant pouvoir me fixer.

[g] on leur ouvrit la porte du couvent, et on leur remit leur dot, en les laissant libres de devenir ce qu'elles voudraient.

[h] Quoi qu'il arrive, Justine s'étonne. L'expérience ne lui apprend rien. Son âme demeure ignorante, son corps plus ignorant encore.

[i] la manière dont il faut qu'il marche dans la carrière épineuse de la vie, afin de prévenir les caprices bizarres de [la] fortune

is the ability to *prévenir* adventure the same as prudent sidestepping, or is it not perhaps a kind of preemptive action, engineering the open road by straightening out the path and filling in the pitfalls? When Jérôme tells his own story of robbery and murder in *La Nouvelle Justine,* the lack of prudence appears to be a literally fatal flaw in those he deals with. His victims often go to their death with the accusation of rashness ringing in their ears. "Jeune imprudent," he says to Imbert just before killing him (VII, 61). "Homme imprudent," he says to Alberoni (VII, 11): "How could you have been so foolish as to confide both your mistress and your money to a man you do not know? Put down the money you have straightaway, and take with you to the depths of hell your eternal remorse for being so rash" (VII, 12).[j] When the punishment for imprudence is so swift and severe, no picaresque learning can occur. Remorse can only exist post mortem, in damnation. Clémentia, Jérôme's faithful accomplice, is killed with the same kind of rebuke: "O Clémentia! [. . .] how little you know the heart of libertines like me. How could you have not suspected the fate I had in store for you?" (VII, 46).[k] How could you fail to be distrustful? When dealing with libertines like me, you must be—should have been—constantly on your guard! One character, however, the experienced Delmas, is not a ready-made victim. He expects violence and treachery from Jérôme, so that when Jérôme steals in at night to murder him in bed with his mistress, Delmas is awake and prepared to defend himself. Yet, in spite of this, his shot misses Jérôme, and the final result is the same: "Hurling myself at the sleeping couple, I went to stab them a thousand times. But Delmas was wide awake, and seemed to be ready for anything. He shot at me, and missed. I rushed at him and stabbed him, together with the unworthy object of his desire. I left them swimming in their own blood" (VII, 51).[l] Delmas's mistress, Joséphine, in the same incident, takes even greater precautions by substituting another woman for herself (VII, 52–53), but she is nevertheless captured by Jérôme, imprisoned, and killed by him soon after (VII, 54). At some point, we must ask whether Jérôme's didactic accusation of imprudence has any point at all. There are careless characters

[j] Comment as-tu pu faire la bêtise de confier à la fois aux mains d'un homme que tu ne connais pas, et ta maîtresse et ton argent? Dépose promptement celui dont tu es chargé, et va porter au sein des enfers l'éternel remords de ton imprudence.

[k] O Clémentia! [. . .] que tu connais mal le cœur d'un libertin tel que moi, dès que tu ne t'es pas défiée du sort que je te préparais!

[l] Et tombant sur le couple endormi, je veux le percer de mille coups. Mais Delmas, éveillé, avait l'air de s'attendre à tout; il tire sur moi, me manque. Je me précipite sur lui; je le poignarde avec l'indigne objet de sa couche, et les laisse baignés dans leur sang.

and careful ones, but their fate at the hands of Jérôme is ultimately the same, and the path by which they reach death hardly any longer in one case than in the other.

The futility of prudence—its lack of narrative consequences—is acted out painfully by Justine during her enforced stay at the inn owned by the d'Estervals. Her role, as servant, is specifically to warn guests that they are in mortal danger just by staying at the inn overnight. Regularly and pointlessly, she counsels prudence in its most active form, calling on them to be vigilant at every moment. Yet this only adds to the pleasure of d'Esterval, as he demonstrates just before shooting them: "'Comrades,' said d'Esterval as he held his pistol to the throat of each of these men, 'you were warned. Why were you not on your guard?'" (VII, 98).[m] The repetitious cruelty of Justine's whole story lies in the reiteration of lessons that can never be learned. Most victims in *La Nouvelle Justine* fail in vigilance only once, if at all, and are immediately dispatched. Justine's doubtful privilege is to fail repeatedly, yet always be allowed to fail again. Survival, for her, is merely a reprieve, without being in any sense an overcoming of danger. She is just as exposed, on the road outside the château, at the time of her death, as she was at the picaresque beginning, outside the convent door.

What Justine should have done, or been, to avoid her fate is made quite clear by the existence of the pair of novels: she should have been like Juliette. We know that Juliette is a genius in the boudoir. Is she not an equally gifted learner on the road? Does she not apply her bodily and moral suppleness to developing defensive skills? Not really, says Maurice Blanchot, in a much-quoted remark: that is not the crucial difference between the two sisters. Rather than keeping her head down, and her clothing laced up, Juliette exposes herself to all sorts of horrors. She simply has the capacity, unlike Justine, to turn pain into pleasure:

> While attending to the sadness of the one, and the satisfaction of the other, people have failed to notice that the story of the two sisters is identical, that everything that happens to Justine happens to Juliette, and that they both go through the same ordeals. Juliette, too, is imprisoned, beaten, threatened with severe punishment, and endlessly tortured. Truly, hers is a horrible existence, but it so happens that her suffering gives her pleasure, and her torture brings delight.[4] [n]

[m] Camarades, dit d'Esterval en mettant le pistolet sur la gorge de chacun de ces hommes, on vous avait pourtant prévenus: par quel hasard n'étiez-vous pas sur vos gardes?

[n] Attentif seulement à la tristesse de l'une, à la satisfaction de l'autre, on a oublié de

Juliette's story, however, would not be so long and so successful, and would not even be told in the first person, if she confronted every possibility of suffering with a reckless determination to transform all danger into pleasure. In the early stages of her career as a prostitute, she turns around in time to see that the client who is about to sodomize her is visibly pox-ridden (VIII, 173). Later, she takes evasive action when her life appears threatened, successively, by Saint-Fond, Minski, and the pope. Convinced that Clairwil is plotting her death, she poisons her companion to save herself. "Prudence" might be too humdrum a word for such violent preemptive strikes as the murder of a faithful companion, but it is doubtless what Clémentia should have done to Jérôme, and it serves to remind us that there is a tactical dimension to Juliette's activity. From time to time, albeit fleetingly, she must take action to avoid becoming a victim.

There is in fact a broad thematic alternative to worldly prudence, one that we might not expect to find in the work of an "enlightened" philosopher like Sade: divine providence. Justine, in the first part of her story, avoids being raped on a number of occasions, and continues right to the end to escape death, even at the hands of comprehensively murderous villains. That she does so is not her own achievement, and certainly not the product of her learning. She is merely protected by something greater than herself, saved from rape so as to be further threatened, saved from death so as to be tortured. After Dubourg has ejaculated prematurely, and therefore failed to deflower Justine, he grudgingly acknowledges "the God or the Devil who protects this trollop" (*La Nouvelle Justine,* VI, 64).[o] Subsequently, when she is about to be penetrated by Cœur-de-Fer, the same anonymous god intervenes: "But a God moved to preserve Justine yet again from the misfortunes that awaited her; and nature, under the command of this God, whoever he is, frustrated the scoundrel's desires so cruelly at this point that his spirited member went soft at the peristyle of the temple" (*La Nouvelle Justine,* VI, 98).[p] On the occasion when Justine is raped by Saint-Florent, we are told that "the gods remained deaf to her cries. It is unimaginable how indifferent they are toward men"

---

remarquer qu'au fond l'histoire des deux sœurs était identique, que tout ce qui arrivait à Justine arrivait à Juliette, que l'une et l'autre traversaient les mêmes épreuves. Juliette aussi est mise en prison, rouée de coups, promise au supplice, torturée sans fin. Horrible existence que la sienne, mais voilà: ces maux lui font plaisir, ces tortures l'enchantent.

[o] le Dieu ou le Diable qui protège cette garce

[p] Mais un Dieu vint préserver encore une fois Justine des malheurs qui lui sont réservés; et la nature, aux ordres de ce Dieu, quel qu'il soit, trompa si cruellement ici les désirs du brigand, que son fougueux engin mollit au péristyle du temple.

(*La Nouvelle Justine,* VI, 106).[q] In the context of the first part of this story, their deafness seems to be no more than intermittent, however, for they—or he, or it—are soon back on the job again, defending the heroine against death at the hands of Saint-Florent: "But the unfortunate Justine, destined by the hand of heaven to go the full distance along the thorny path of misfortune, did not meet her death at such a young age" (*La Nouvelle Justine,* VI, 109).[r] When, imprisoned by Bressac, she is due to be killed, the same protection is again afforded her by "un dieu protecteur," for the sake of narrative fullness (*La Nouvelle Justine,* VI, 162).

Conversely, we may ask whether Juliette's worldly triumph is attributable entirely to her own personal qualities. She certainly does not believe so herself. When captured and imprisoned by Brisa-Testa's men, she does not spend her time planning an escape, but rather provides reassurance for her companions by stating some general principles. Elise shows in this dark moment that she knows how to keep the faith: 'There are,' you said to me, 'eternal laws in nature whereby crime triumphs and virtue is humiliated. I am relying completely on this immutable rule . . . Oh! my dear mistress, it will save our lives'" (IX, 209).[s] Nature here can apparently be relied on for something like providential support, in the cause of vice. As Brisa-Testa says in a moment of adversity: "Do not be afraid, my dear. Nature, which desires crimes, looks after those who commit them, and one is very rarely punished for having carried out its laws" (IX, 256).[t] And when, during a particularly daring enterprise, Clairwil expresses the fear of failure, recalling the deadly punishment that must follow, Juliette assures her that the very principle underlying their action will protect them: "You should calm down, Clairwil. Crime is fond of us and favors us in everything we do; I guarantee you that we will succeed" (IX, 409).[u] Crime does not merely pay here, it providentially guarantees a particular outcome. As a philosophy, it triumphs over Christian virtue, leaving us to wonder whether Juliette's

[q] les dieux furent sourds. On n'a pas d'idée de l'indifférence qu'ils ont pour les hommes.

[r] Mais la malheureuse Justine, destinée par la main du ciel à parcourir tout entière la route épineuse de l'infortune, ne devait pas succomber si jeune.

[s] Il est, m'avez-vous dit, dans les lois éternelles de la nature, que le crime triomphe et que la vertu soit humiliée; j'attends tout de cet immuable décret. . . Ah! ma chère maîtresse, il nous sauvera la vie.

[t] Cesse de craindre, ma chère; la nature, qui désire les crimes, surveille ceux qui les commettent, et l'on est bien rarement puni d'avoir exécuté ses lois.

[u] Mais calme-toi, Clairwil, le crime nous aime, il nous favorise; je t'en garantis le succès.

relative prudence and any local decisions she makes are not more like Justine's imprudence than might first appear to be the case. Both are transcended and trivialized by a higher narrative purpose.

In certain fictive places, such as the château at Silling or the monastery at Sainte-Marie-des-Bois, Sade establishes a highly regulated space, governed by the most punctilious libertinism. The form of tyranny that reigns there is characterized by its very refusal to be itself bound by rules. Omphale, who has been at Sainte-Marie-des-Bois for thirteen years, explains to Justine the practice of *la réforme,* the ritual murder of a victim chosen among the inmates. The choice is in no way predictable, she says: "What is more, nothing justifies the retirement. Age, or a change in appearance, makes no difference: caprice is their only rule" (*La Nouvelle Justine,* VI, 314).[v] The youngest may be killed almost immediately, and the oldest kept well beyond the time one might expect: "They will retire today the one they caressed the most yesterday, and keep for twenty years the one in whom they have lost all interest" (VI, 315).[w] The upshot of this, of course, is that there are no tactical options for those under threat. That, presumably, is the very definition of whimsical tyranny:

> Do not imagine that being very well behaved or extremely submissive will enable you to escape the fate that awaits you. I have seen women try to anticipate their every desire, attentively and thoughtfully, yet leave after six months. Others who were moody and uncooperative stayed around for years. It is useless, therefore, to advise those who have just arrived to adopt a particular kind of behavior: the sole motive of these monsters is their whimsical fancy: it breaks through all constraints and becomes the eternal law of their acts. (VI, 315)[x]

What could be the place of prudence when the final rule is that there should be no rules? How could Justine conceive of a self-defensive program, or set about actually *trying* to survive? The power of her

[v] Rien, au surplus, ne légitime cette réforme; l'âge, le changement des traits, rien n'y fait: le caprice est leur seule règle.

[w] Ils réformeront aujourd'hui celle qu'ils ont hier le plus caressée, et garderont vingt ans celles dont ils paraissent le plus rassasiés.

[x] N'imagine pas que la plus régulière conduite et que la plus extrême soumission puisse nous faire échapper au sort qui nous attend: j'en ai vu qui volaient au-devant de tous leurs désirs, qui les prévenaient avec le plus grand soin, et qui partaient au bout de six mois; d'autres, maussades et fantasques, végétaient ici des années. Il est donc inutile de prescrire à nos arrivantes un genre quelconque de conduite: la fantaisie, l'unique volonté de ces monstres, brise tous les freins et devient éternellement la loi de leurs actions.

masters is so sudden and capricious that she cannot learn to predict its effects, or avoid even its most drastic consequences. The old adage of survival is well known: when one is not master of the terrain, strategy must give way to tactics. That is why tactics are the standard measure of the picaresque hero(ine), the very *démarche* of his/her increasingly prudent movement through the world. In Sade, however, the preemptive violence of libertine tyrants is such as to take away even the time and space of tactics, submerging its victims in incalculable waves of misfortune.

Yet the principle of inconsistency is not applied in the most consistent manner. In *Les Cent Vingt Journées,* Julie, daughter of the duc de Blangis and wife of Curval, should be seen as a privileged victim. When Constance, the duc's wife, who is pregnant, speaks publicly of Curval's hatred of pregnancy, she does so partly to warn Julie not to fall into the trap: "if Julie were to listen to me, she'd watch out" (I, 168).[y] We do not know what Julie thinks of this sisterly advice, but Curval is enraged by it, precisely because it makes him appear predictable: "Bitch that you are, get it into your head that I have no need for reasons in order to kill a woman" (I, 169).[z] How, in the face of this determination not to be driven by a motive, can Julie possibly learn to stay alive? Yet stay alive she does—and not entirely by chance. The extraordinary thing is that Julie's survival seems to be achieved by the conjunction of fate and defensive politics.

"Fate," in *Les Cent Vingt Journées,* is not just broadly providential: it is narrowly arithmetical. Julie's chances of survival can in fact be calculated in quite precise fashion, given the difference between the number of people who travel to Silling and the number of those who eventually return. At the outset, the numbers are made up as follows:

4 masters
4 wives (including Julie)
4 storytellers
8 fuckers (including 4 "major" ones, identified by proper names)
8 girls
8 boys
4 old women/servants
6 in the kitchen (including 3 cooks and 3 helpers)
46

[y] et si Julie m'en croit, elle prendra garde à elle.

[z] Apprenez, garce que vous êtes, que je n'ai pas besoin de motif pour tuer une femme.

This number is eventually reduced by murder to sixteen, grouped in four sets of four. Now each of the final groups of four contains one member from the class of the *amis,* one *fouteur majeur,* and one *historienne,* exhausting each of those classes. In this way, twelve of the sixteen final places are occupied ex officio. The fourth place in each group is also occupied by a whole class, the cooks. Except that, by some aberration—*par quel hasard?*—there are only three cooks, and not four. The sense of this arithmetical discrepancy, I suggest, lies precisely in the survival of just one potential victim. As Noëlle Châtelet has pointed out, the kitchen staff are taboo during the goings-on at Silling,[5] but that does not prevent the eventual execution of the three servants employed there. Why, in any case, are there not four cooks and four helpers, if not so as to leave room for one survivor from all of the five classes of victims taken together (wives, minor fuckers, girls, boys, and servants)? Julie is the token spouse, the token daughter, the only one who makes it through. What does she do to deserve this?

The quick Sadian answer is that she cannot possibly "deserve" to survive: she can only be saved by masterly whim. But there are in fact indications in *Les Cent Vingt Journées* that Julie engages in defensive tactics. Any form of resistance on her part is unthinkable, according to the contractual understanding between her father and her husband: "We libertines need wives in order to have them as our slaves; as wives, they are more submissive than mistresses" (I, 20).[a] Yet Julie is not an ordinary spouse. She has qualities that distinguish her from her fellow victims. Not her beauty, of course, for that is the norm at Silling. Rather, the presence of one or two "flaws" in the midst of that beauty. The first of these is "the worst-adorned mouth, the foulest teeth, the habit of being so dirty about all the rest of her body, principally at the two temples of lubricity, that no other being, let me repeat it, no other being but the president [. . .] could have put up with Julie (I, 43).[b] What is the connection, exactly, between bodily hygiene and staying alive? The lack of hygiene seems at first glance to be a handicap for Julie, making her hard to accommodate, even for the other three *amis,* although it is finally the bishop, not Curval, who takes her into his group of four. Are we to consider Julie's story a confirmation of that well-loved narrative found in toothpaste commercials, wherein

[a] Nous autres libertins, nous prenons des femmes pour être nos esclaves; leur qualité d'épouses les rend plus soumises que des maîtresses.

[b] la bouche la plus mal ornée, les dents les plus infectes, et d'une saleté d'habitude sur tout le reste de son corps, et principalement aux deux temples de la lubricité, que nul autre être, je le répète, nul autre être que le président [. . .] ne se fût arrangé de Julie.

the woman loses the man's affections because she fails to clean her teeth properly? Presumably not: Julie's dirtiness is more profoundly natural than some simple "lack" of hygiene. Her dirtiness displays the indulgence of natural process about the orifices of her body. Her second flaw is thus closely related to the first: "To these faults Julie added a few others, although they were doubtless less unpleasant: she was a vast eater, she had a leaning toward drunkenness, little virtue, and I believe that, had she dared try it, whoredom would have held few terrors for her" (I, 43–44).[c]

Here, one quickly realizes, is a sister for Eugénie and Juliette, a woman of temperament. Furthermore, Julie has been brought up free of religious indoctrination: "She has never been given either principles or religion" (I, 81).[d] Clearly, she has all the qualities needed to become a libertine, and the process is already under way: "Brought up by the duc in a total abandon of principles and manners, she tended to adopt a whore's philosophy, and was probably suited to becoming a student of it all" (I, 44).[e] She is beginning to learn, but is *adopter assez* enough to guarantee her safety? Will she go on developing beyond this point until she achieves "subject" status? The issue is far from clear as the story unfolds, unless one sees all with the eyes of a master accountant. The problem is that the four *amis* are not reliably attracted to her. They seem to like the Justine type: "But, through yet another very curious effect of libertinage, it often happens that a woman who shares our faults appeals to us a great deal less in our pleasures than one who has nothing but virtues. The first resembles us, and we do not scandalize her; the second is terrified, and that is certainly one more source of charm" (I, 44).[f] How capricious of the *amis* not to be attracted to their own kind! Fortunately for the two most successful heroines, Juliette and Eugénie—notice that it *is* largely good fortune—they do not encounter that problem in their stories. Perhaps we should hesitate to call Julie's libertinage a problem, however. With an overall success rate for potential victims in *Les Cent Vingt Journées* of one in thirty-one, everything about Julie should be seen as helping her to survive.

[c] A ces défauts Julie en joignait quelques autres, mais moins désagréables sans doute: elle était très gourmande, elle avait du penchant à l'ivrognerie, peu de vertu, et je crois que si elle l'eût osé, le putainisme l'eût fort peu effrayée.

[d] On ne lui a jamais donné ni principes ni religion.

[e] Elevée par le duc dans un abandon total de principes et de mœurs, elle adoptait assez cette philosophie, et de tout point sans doute il y avait de quoi faire un sujet.

[f] Mais, par un effet encore très bizarre du libertinage, il arrive souvent qu'une femme qui a nos défauts nous plaît bien moins dans nos plaisirs qu'une qui n'a que des vertus: l'une nous ressemble, nous ne la scandalisons pas; l'autre s'effraye, et voilà un attrait bien certain de plus.

Julie has skills that are valuable at Silling. She rapidly learns the essential art of masturbating others: "she is beginning to frig like an angel" (I, 120).[g] From there, she goes on to bigger and better things of much the same kind: "There was as well another young person in the company [in addition to Duclos] who was beginning to make herself very amiable and to attract considerable attention: we are referring to Julie. She was already starting to show signs of imagination, debauchery, and libertinage" (I, 242).[h] To be *aimable* involves more than just manual skills, for Julie comes to act as a verbal intermediary, whispering a secret story to her father, for example (I, 97–98). And when Curval threatens to disturb the temporal order by his eagerness to deflower someone ahead of time, Julie is the one who takes the venom out of him: "Julie, who took charge of him for the whole night, brought him back the next morning as pliant as a reed" (I, 299).[i]

It would be misleading to infer from any of this that Julie was somehow safe from the beginning, training throughout the novel for a brilliant future as a libertine. We are told quite explicitly that she is not well suited to her husband, Curval. She is dirty, admittedly, but he is monumentally and systematically filthy: "Julie gained little by being with the president, whose prick, as we know, was extremely thick, and furthermore, however dirty she might be as a result of self-neglect, she could not begin to adapt to the debauched filthiness of the president, her beloved spouse" (I, 44).[j] *S'arranger* is exactly what Julie needs to do in the course of the story: she must survive by adapting, by finding her place, and it is not with Curval. Curval threatens her safety by the most routine domestic violence, throwing a plate at her "that would have split her head open if she had not dodged it" (I, 90–91).[k] Unlike those ritual victims who are held, or bound, or even nailed into position, Julie is still free to take evasive action, with the minimal tactic of a sideways movement of the body. Later, she goes much further in her resistance. After Duclos has described a passion that has as its distinctive feature shitting into a woman's mouth,

[g] elle commence à branler comme un ange.

[h] Il y avait aussi une autre créature dans la société qui commençait à se rendre très aimable et à y devenir très intéressante: c'était Julie. Elle annonçait déjà de l'imagination, de la débauche et du libertinage.

[i] Julie, qui s'en empara toute la nuit, le rendit le lendemain à la société aussi souple qu'un gant.

[j] Julie gagnait peu avec le président, dont on sait que le vit était fort gros, et d'ailleurs quelque malpropre qu'elle fût elle-même par négligence, elle ne s'arrangeait nullement d'une saleté de débauche telle qu'était celle du président, son cher époux.

[k] qui lui aurait fendu le tête si [elle] ne l'eût esquichée

Curval asks the duc to nominate someone with whom he can do the same thing. The duc volunteers his daughter: "By my faith, I recommend Julie, my daughter; she is right there at hand. You are fond of her mouth, put it to use."[l] At this, Julie does something quite radical: she objects. "Thank you for your advice," she complains. "What have I done to make you say such things about me?"[m] Rather than being punished for failing to obey instantly, she succeeds in avoiding this piece of erotic drudgery: "Why, since the idea upsets her," says the duc, "and since she's a good sort of girl, take Mademoiselle Sophie" (I, 227–28).[n] What Mademoiselle Sophie thinks is not recorded for posterity, but that is not the point. Julie has taken evasive action, and been excused for doing so because she is *une assez bonne fille*. In addition, she seems to become more explicit in defending not only herself, but the other victims. As the *historienne* Duclos finishes an evening set of stories, she is rebuked by the bishop for concluding with a particularly insipid passion. But Julie intervenes in Duclos's defense, advocating mildness in the name of all those who will soon be made to copy the model: "They'll allow us all to go to bed more peacefully, now that their heads are not full of those frightful ideas Mme Duclos started on a little while ago" (I, 324).[o] To speak in this way is not at all the same as being transformed into a libertine tyrant, like Juliette or Eugénie. Julie knows she is still very close to the victim's position. She knows how to say *nous* in the feminine plural.

Julie's story is not one of ritual alignment or regimental discipline: she conducts her own intrigue, and passes through a remarkable set of adventures without ever setting foot on the open road. The basis of her approach is to combine libertinage and political skill, each contributing to the other. She no doubt adopts libertine values because it is politic to do so, but is aware of the need for defensive political action precisely because she understands the murderous logic of Sadian libertinism. After a session in camera involving Curval, the duc, and a number of others, Julie returns unhurt thanks to her combination of philosophy and tactics: "Augustine appeared holding a handkerchief to her bleeding nose, while Adélaïde had one over her breast. As for Julie, always libertine enough and clever enough to get through any

[l] Ma foi, je vous conseille Julie, ma fille; elle est là, sous votre main, vous aimez sa bouche, servez-vous-en.

[m] Merci du conseil, que vous ai-je fait pour dire de telles choses contre moi?

[n] Eh! puisque cela la fâche, dit le duc, et que c'est une assez bonne fille, prenez mademoiselle Sophie.

[o] On nous laissera toutes coucher plus tranquilles, quand on n'aura pas dans la tête de ces vilaines idées que Mme Duclos avait entamées tout à l'heure.

situation without danger to herself, she was laughing hysterically and saying that if it had not been for her they would never have discharged" (I, 339).[p] Note, once again, that she claims credit for working as an intermediary of pleasure. A figurative and literal *branleuse* (masturbator), following and working with Duclos, she contributes to the rhythm of the masters' pleasure. "Politics," for Julie, despite the occasional courageous statement, is not reliably a matter of solidarity with the victims. More than anything, it consists in the search for one or more male protectors. The obvious choice for her is the *primus inter pares* of the four friends, her father the duc. Duclos has already cemented her position there, and Julie tries to stick with the two of them: "Astute enough to see that she stood in need of protection, clever enough to caress those very persons who may really have mattered little to her, she contrived to become Duclos's friend, trying thereby to achieve some favor in the eyes of her father who, she was well aware, had great influence over the others" (I, 242).[q] When Curval wanted to shit in her mouth, she said no, but she makes every effort to indulge the duc, working at bringing him to satisfaction: "Every time it was her turn to sleep with the duc, she joined in so well with Duclos, showing so much skill and consideration that the duc was always sure of obtaining delightful discharges whenever he used these two creatures to procure them" (I, 242).[r] Yet all her efforts with the duc come to naught. The politics of tyranny, and of the court intrigue it fosters, is such that she simply falls out of favor: "his enthusiasm for his daughter was waning prodigiously" (I, 242).[s]

This setback for Julie, typical of the narrative rhythm of adventure, is not the end for her, of course. She has at least made an ally of Duclos, who now provides secondary support: "perhaps without the help of Duclos, who consistently spoke up for her, she would never

[p] Augustine revint, ayant son mouchoir sur son nez, dont elle saignait, et Adélaïde un mouchoir sur le sein. Pour Julie, toujours assez libertine et assez adroite pour se tirer de tout sans danger, elle riait comme une folle, et disait que sans elle ils n'auraient jamais déchargé.

[q] Assez politique pour sentir qu'elle avait besoin de protection, assez fausse pour caresser ceux-mêmes dont peut-être elle ne se souciait guère au fond, elle se faisait amie de la Duclos pour tâcher de rester toujours un peu en faveur de son père dont elle connaissait le crédit dans la société

[r] Toutes les fois que c'était son tour de coucher avec le duc, elle se réunissait si bien à la Duclos, elle employait tant d'adresse et tant de complaisance, que le duc était toujours sûr d'obtenir des décharges délicieuses toutes les fois que ces deux créatures-là s'employaient à les lui procurer.

[s] il se blasait prodigieusement sur sa fille.

have been able to carry out her plans" (I, 242–43).[t] Here is the overall tactical picture, seen through Julie's eyes. It is her own exercise in accounting, a checklist of possible protectors:

> Her husband, Curval, was roughly of the same mind [as the duc], and although, by means of her impure mouth and kisses, she still managed to draw a few discharges out of him, disgust toward her was not far away in his mind: one might even have said that the fires of his hostility were fanned by her immodest kisses. Durcet had little interest in her, and she had not made him discharge even twice since the whole proceedings had begun. All that she really had left, then, was the Bishop. He indeed was fond of her libertine jargon, and judged her ass to be the world's finest. [. . .] She therefore concentrated her efforts in that direction, for she was resolutely determined to please, whatever the cost. Since she felt the extreme need for protection, she wanted to find someone. (I, 243)[u]

The desire to "please" is no doubt quite desperate, but Julie's efforts are carefully calculated, and precisely directed. Moreover, her judgment is sound: her place in the final sixteen will be in the bishop's group of four (I, 448). Before that happens, however, she will experience grave dangers. She is actually repudiated by Curval—"he repudiates Julie, who falls into the greatest discredit" (I, 394)[v]—although she is not completely bereft of support, either of the philosophical or the tactical kind: "her libertinage speaks strongly in her favor, however, and [. . .] the bishop protects her somewhat" (I, 394).[w]

This is the nadir of her fortunes, as she finds herself obliged to sleep in the stables (I, 397). Yet even as she is being pushed into this marginal position, she makes opportunities for sexual pleasure, thus displaying her temperament. She conducts an affair, outside the rules, with Hercule, a leading *fouteur*. When caught and reprimanded, she

[t] peut-être sans le secours de la Duclos, qui la soutenait de tout son crédit, n'aurait-elle jamais pu réussir dans ses vues.

[u] Son mari, Curval, en était à peu près au même point [que le duc], et quoique, par le moyen de sa bouche et de ses baisers impurs, elle obtînt encore de lui quelques décharges, le dégoût n'était cependant pas éloigné: on eût dit qu'il naissait sous le feu même de ses impudiques baisers. Durcet l'estimait assez peu, et elle ne l'avait pas fait décharger deux fois depuis qu'on était réunis. Il ne lui resta donc guère plus que l'évêque, qui aimait beaucoup son jargon libertin et qui lui trouvait le plus beau cul du monde. [. . .] Elle se cantonna donc de ce côté, car elle voulait absolument plaire, et à quelque prix que ce fût; comme elle sentait l'extrême besoin d'une protection, elle en voulait une.

[v] il répudie Julie, qui tombe dans le plus grand discrédit.

[w] son libertinage [la] soutient cependant et [. . .] l'évêque [la] protège un peu.

replies in the language of her masters, "libertinement." For her misdemeanor, she is whipped "extraordinarily"—extraordinary whippings are, after all, the norm at Silling—and then forgiven: "then, because they are fond of her, and also of Hercule, who has always been well behaved, they are pardoned and the incident regarded with amusement" (I, 383).[x] As Julie continues to grow in vice, she produces more unscheduled erotic events on the edge of the regimental celebrations. She is caught with one of the *historiennes:* "On that day Julie, who is becoming more libertine all the time, is discovered frigging herself with Champville" (I, 397).[y] Breaking the rules actually leads, by masterly caprice or by recognition of her progress as a pupil—or both—to her being better protected: "From that time on, the bishop affords her further protection, and admits her into his bedchamber, as the duc has Duclos, Durcet Martaine, and Curval Fanchon" (I, 397).[z] This is a much stronger position but not entirely a safe one, as the eventual disgrace (I, 423–24) and execution of Fanchon prove. Julie still has to go through the ordeal of a mock death. She is given a powder that causes the most violent symptoms, and believes that she has been poisoned. Her father's pleasure in this scene is great, but she recovers the same evening (I, 420). Here, quite specifically, is a simulacrum of the end Julie might so easily have known. Her survival is won by the narrowest of margins, and confirmed in extremis through acute suffering.

We might sigh with relief as Julie slumps into the last free *strapontin* out of Silling, but what have we really learned from her experience? Is it possible to infer from it a list of things for women characters to do in a Sadian world if they wish to avoid death, and are resigned to carrying out such erotic chores as being whipped or being forced to eat shit? Sade may have betrayed the (il)logic of libertinage by allowing just one character to struggle purposefully out of the victim's position. It may well be, on the other hand, that Julie's story of intrigue is so subtle and so fragile in its success as to be of little exemplary value. We know that she does a number of things right: she is temperamentally and progressively committed to libertine philosophy; she is an efficient manipulator and producer of pleasure in others; she practices the art of deceit, and is encouragingly unhygienic. Can it be said,

[x] puis, comme elle est aimée, ainsi qu'Hercule qui s'est toujours bien conduit, on leur pardonne et on s'en amuse.

[y] On surprend ce jour-là Julie, toujours plus libertine que jamais, se branlant avec la Champville.

[z] L'évêque la protège encore plus depuis lors, et l'admet dans sa chambre, comme le duc Duclos, Durcet Martaine, et Curval Fanchon.

however, that any woman with these qualities can overcome tyrannical caprice and attain survival? I think that the answer to this question is no, and that *Les Cent Vingt Journées,* as well as providing an exception to its own rule, discourages us from making any corollary rule about exceptions. It does so in a way I have not considered so far, by recounting the story of another young woman, also a potential victim, who has most of Julie's qualities and some other relevant ones, but finds herself becoming one of the most exposed and most cruelly treated of victims: the young Augustine.

Augustine is fifteen, and the oldest member of the group of *jeunes filles.* She does not shrink from her masters, but displays a natural eagerness for pleasure. She is referred to as "Augustine, whose sparkling, roguish eyes announced the most precocious temperament" (I, 130).[a] The proof of her temperament is produced experimentally by the duc: "Languedocian women have temperament, and Augustine was proof of that rule: fire leapt into her pretty eyes, she sighed, her thighs rose mechanically, and the duc was pleased to draw from her some young spunk that, in all likelihood, had never flowed before" (I, 131).[b] Just like a Provençal version of Eugénie de Mistival at the same age, one might think. Seen beside her roommate Zelmire, she provides the perfect contrast, for Zelmire is pious and melancholic. The A and the Z of natural desire, one might say, an alphabetical resolution of the Juliette-Justine pair. But Augustine's temperamental promise is not answered by libertine triumph, as in the case of Eugénie and Juliette, nor even rewarded with survival, as for Julie. How and why does she fail? It is not for lack of effort, certainly. She quickly learns the art of masturbating others, that sine qua non of successful Sadian womanhood, practiced so often even by Justine: "Augustine, Sophie, and Colombe could easily have been matched, for skill and nimbleness of wrist, against the capital's most celebrated friggers" (I, 184).[c] Eventually, Augustine emerges from this small group of girls as "the most famous frigger in the seraglio" (I, 312).[d] In the early stages of her learning, she has great difficulty acquiring another vital skill, that of farting on command. Her desperate efforts result only

[a] Augustine dont les yeux éveillés et fripons annonçaient le tempérament le plus précoce

[b] Les Languedociennes ont du tempérament; Augustine en fut la preuve: ses jolis yeux s'animèrent, elle soupira, ses cuisses s'élevèrent machinalement, et le duc fut assez heureux pour obtenir un jeune foutre qui coulait sans doute pour la première fois.

[c] Augustine, Sophie et Colombe auraient pu le disputer pour la légèreté et l'adresse du poignet aux plus fameuses branleuses de la capitale.

[d] la plus célèbre branleuse du sérail

in minimal compliance: "Strive as she might, [. . .] Augustine had been unable to make anything come out, [. . .] and the poor young thing was already in tears when a tiny fart finally emerged and satisfied [the duc]. He inhaled the aroma, and was highly pleased with this sign of docility from the pretty child of whom he was rather fond" (I, 172).[e] To be *aimée assez* would appear to put Augustine in much the same position as Julie, but their progress is not reliably parallel.

Augustine becomes quite outstanding in a number of ways in addition to masturbation. She now performs very successfully as a farter (I, 199), and even produces an exquisite turd on demand (I, 253). Her own erotic "discharge" seems to become more speedily responsive, a further sign that "the little minx" is "full of fire and temperament" (I, 313).[f] She almost wins a competition for the most beautiful bottom in the seraglio, failing only because her shape is perhaps a little too perfect (I, 333). Being too beautiful, too precocious, and too highly visible is in fact Augustine's fundamental "mistake." She is looked at by the duc and Curval much more often than, say, Julie—looked at with desire, indeed, but their desire is most dangerous when it is most intense. Aroused and yet not satisfied by one episode with her, the duc can be seen "casting furious glances at Augustine" (I, 131).[g] After her defeat in the best-bottom competition, Augustine appears the next day in a state of provocative disorder. This makes her "a thousand times more attractive,"[h] but provokes in Curval an urgent desire to deflower her ahead of time. Durcet has to intervene when he sees Curval "casting furious glances at Augustine" (I, 336).[i]

Whereas Julie is sometimes protected by being kept out of the way, as if to smuggle past the reader the anomalous fact of her survival, Augustine rises to ever greater prominence. On an evening when the person who was to serve as a "wife" for the duc, Adélaïde, has been unspeakably punished, Augustine replaces her in the wife's role (I, 303). Eventually, she replaces the duc's actual wife, Constance: "That evening the duc repudiates Constance, who falls into the greatest discredit [. . .]. Augustine is now treated as the duc's wife, and from then on performs only the wife's functions on the sofa and in the

[e] Augustine avait beau faire, beau s'efforcer, [. . .] rien ne sortit, et la pauvre petite pleurait déjà quand une vesse vint enfin [. . .] satisfaire [le duc]. Il respira, [. . .] content de cette marque de docilité du joli enfant qu'il aimait assez.

[f] la petite friponne/pleine de feu et de tempérament

[g] jetant des regards furieux sur Augustine

[h] mille fois plus intéressante

[i] lancer des regards furieux sur Augustine

toilets" (I, 383).[j] The duc clings to Augustine more and more (see, e.g., I, 308), but his grip is the grip of death. He is said, by another piece of libertine inconsistency, to be in love with her: "The duc devirginates Augustine, with whom he has been in love for a long time; he discharges three times in succession into her cunt" (I, 380).[k] Whatever "love" is in Sade, it is certainly not of the kind that suffereth long, for the duc now pushes with renewed vigor for Augustine to be put to death immediately: "He offers to pay two hundred louis into the common fund if the society will allow him to take her down into the cellars that very evening: his offer is refused" (I, 380).[l] Curval soon joins the duc in making such requests, each time alighting on Augustine as the one to be killed first (I, 382; see also I, 402). She has aroused in them not only furious looks, but a general *rage lubrique* (I, 397). The woman's role is to give pleasure, to aid and abet the rhythms of male discharge, but this young woman provokes the destructive wrath of the duc by somehow doing that too well. He is "more provoked than ever by Augustine, because she has made him discharge frequently" (I, 381).[m]

Augustine applies tactics that are not so different from those of Julie, but her efforts are ruined by her high visibility as an object of pleasure and a subject of pain. When unjustly accused of having washed herself, she tries to speak up in her own defense, and calls Duclos as a witness. The *historienne,* whose protection appears to be crucial for Julie, provides no support at all. Augustine persists energetically, but to no avail: "Augustine attempted to defend her thesis, and disputed the point with Duclos, but silence was imposed on her and, though she was perfectly innocent, her name was written down [on the punishment list]" (I, 319).[n] There is no point here in being assertive: the pleasure of punishing her, for the masters, is too great to be foregone. Late in the story, Augustine is found to be intriguing with one of the minor *fouteurs,* promising him sex in return for help to escape: "Augustine confesses that she was about to grant him what

[j] Le duc, ce soir-là, répudie Constance, qui tombe dans le plus grand discrédit [. . .]. Augustine passe pour femme du duc, et ne fait plus que les fonctions d'épouse au sopha et aux garde-robes.

[k] Le duc dépucelle Augustine, dont il est amoureux depuis longtemps; il lui décharge trois fois de suite dans le con.

[l] Il offre deux cents louis à la société pour la faire descendre au caveau dès le même soir: on refuse.

[m] plus animé que jamais contre Augustine, parce qu'elle l'a beaucoup fait décharger

[n] Augustine voulut soutenir sa thèse, et disputa contre la Duclos, mais on lui imposa silence, et elle fut inscrite [sur la liste des punitions], quoique parfaitement innocente.

he sought from her, in order to save herself from a place where she believes her life to be in danger" (I, 423).[o] This is a sound assessment of the threat, and a thoroughly picaresque way of avoiding it—worthy of Félicia or Margot, if not of Juliette—but it fails utterly. There is no trace here of the indulgence accorded to Julie: the young *fouteur* is beheaded and Augustine suffers the first of a long series of mutilations, by having two teeth pulled out (I, 423). This is the beginning of an excruciatingly protracted ordeal for her, spelled out in detail even in the text as it stands (see I, 423, 434, 435, 437–38). The final words on Augustine are words of praise, in recognition of her great erotic distinction: "Thus perished at the age of fifteen years and eight months one of the most heavenly creatures ever formed by nature's hand, etc. Her eulogy" (I, 438).[p] I observe simply that the *éloge* is not written out in Sade's notes, whereas the torture is. Her natural erotic talent is transformed into a propensity for great suffering.

My reading of the chances for feminine survival is itself a kind of thematic tactic, and a defensively ironic one at that. I have tried to find a pattern precisely where the masters affirm there is none, in the hope of earning some respite from the rule of their tyrannical narratives. Following Julie, I may have found a slight break in their discipline, an instance where they allow themselves to be seduced and perhaps deceived, to be momentarily the object of a woman's calculations rather than the unrelenting subject of their own counting. The pathetic story of Augustine's far too successful seduction of the duc shows, however, the brittleness of such tactics. It is (almost) pointless for a woman in the Sadian château to attempt to negotiate her way out of the victim's position, and wildly dangerous for her to seek full recognition as an object of desire. The most prudent thing is to run away, as Justine manages to do so often, and take her chances on the open road . . .

[o] Augustine avoue qu'elle était au moment de lui accorder ce qu'il demandait d'elle, pour se sauver d'un endroit où elle croit sa vie en danger.

[p] Ainsi périt à quinze ans et huit mois une des plus célestes créatures qu'ait formée la nature, etc. Son éloge.

III

THE TIME OF DESIRE

Chapter 8

Degrees of Virginity

Nothing in the world happens so quickly as the loss of virginity or the vanishing of illusion.

—Théophile Gautier, *Mademoiselle de Maupin*[a]

That virginity should be a recurring theme in erotic narrative is not difficult to understand. Admittedly, in *ars erotica,* virginity appeared to be of no particular interest. Initiation took place there precisely because girlhood, or innocence, or virginity, were due to end. The whole point of a rite of passage is to leave behind the rather indeterminate, nonerotic state of childhood, without turning back on it in any way. When virginity becomes a theme, however, and it does so quite regularly beginning in the latter part of the eighteenth century, it is always likely to be recuperated by erotic narrative. Far from being a simply transcendent virtue, and thus the exclusive property of moralistic or religious discourse, virginity becomes available for transformation. Nothing could be more precisely tellable, in the strict narratological sense, than the momentous occasion on which a "girl" becomes a "woman." That is why virginity ranks with "temperament" as one of the two sisterly givens of youthful femininity. Temperament we have already seen, in all of its narrative consequences, but virginity is of almost equal importance, if not for its rich promise, then for its remarkable vulnerability to change. The two qualities are not symmetri-

[a] Il n'y a rien au monde qui coule plus vite qu'une virginité qui s'en va et qu'une illusion qui s'envole.

cal, of course, any more than are Juliette and Justine. Virginity is a problematic, if attractive, theme for erotic narrative, since it takes on full significance only at the moment of its dramatic loss. The transformation may in fact fall short of the time required of a novel for the very reason that deflowering, by contrast with "flowering," is conventionally sudden and complete. Typically, where virginity is the embodiment of virtue, its loss is a tragic fall, precipitating the girl/woman from wholeness into defilement, from grace into hymenless perdition.

Virginity can, of course, be understood as an enduring condition, a lifelong moral and political option for women, as in some of Andrea Dworkin's writing. When Dworkin speaks of Joan of Arc, she invokes the image of an armed—indeed, an armored—virgin: "a woman untouched."[1] Yet the "woman untouched," as Dworkin would agree, is readily seen in stories as a woman yet-to-be-touched: not so much Joan of Arc as Lucretia. Repeatedly, girls who are intact are seen as having been left blank, so to speak, by their childhood, as they wait unknowingly to be marked by their first encounter with a male. Nancy Huston makes this point by contrasting the autobiographies of prostitutes with the stories of conventional pornography: "these women [prostitutes] are *marked* by their childhood. They do not just turn the page at the age of fifteen, leaving their past behind and coming out, virginal and corruptible, into the adult world."[2] [b] One might say that women characters are set up for narrative transformation by the virginity theme, their very purity being the obverse of—and therefore the prelude to—violent sexuality. Luce Irigaray asks the question "*What fantasy of a virgin-solid-closed-body to be opened with violence* underlies such a representation and such a practice of the sexual?"[3] [c]

There is some tension apparent here between the practice of gradation, as the time of narrative, and the dramatic violence of the sudden loss of virginity: between novelistic progression and tragic fall. As Simone de Beauvoir points out, the violence of deflowering consists precisely in its denial of a developmental process leading from girlhood to womanhood: "People talk of 'ravishing' a girl's virginity, of 'taking away' her flower. This deflowering is not the harmonious outcome of a continuous evolution: it is a break with the past, the start of a new cycle."[4] [d] But erotic narrative can only recount this singular

[b] ces femmes [les prostituées] sont *marquées* par leur enfance. Elles ne tournent pas la page à l'âge de quinze ans, laissant leur passé derrière elles pour émerger, vierges-et-corruptibles, dans le monde adulte.

[c] *Quel fantasme de corps-vierge-solide-fermé à ouvrir avec violence* sous-tend une telle représentation et une telle pratique du sexuel?

[d] On parle aussi de "ravir" sa virginité à une fille, de lui "prendre" sa fleur. Cette

event at the cost of its own essential duration. Long picaresque narratives can make room for the occasional Lucretia: *Gil Blas,* for example, has two of them, one ironic and one genuinely tragic.[5] Canonically erotic stories, however, need to be more focused and more insistent in their thematic development. A question for the novel might then be: how can the story of the loss of virginity be made to endure? In the first place, the answer may lie in telling the struggle to save virginity, whether it be ultimately successful or unsuccessful. Richardson's *Pamela* is exemplary in this regard, drawing its narrative vigor and its moral tone from the extraordinary capacity for resistance shown by the heroine. In strict narratological terms, it is a nonstory, since virtue is never transformed into vice. Or rather, it becomes a proper story by displacing the thematic focus of its narrative transformation as the heroine passes from the state of poor, virtuous servant to that of rich, virtuous lady. As Angela Carter points out, this outcome may be considered in much the same terms, since "all such fictional narratives of women that end in marriage could just as well end with death, because marriage means the death of the virgin."[6] Nonetheless, the fact remains that Pamela's "death" has been successfully negotiated, in both senses of that word, through the ritual of marriage. Framed now in a perfectly conventional way, Pamela's bodily change ceases to count as traumatic or precipitate, being no more than a comfortably discreet passage from maidenhood to womanhood.

Now it is undeniable that where virginity is shown to be assailed and defended, sexual behavior is in some sense at issue. Yet it should be equally clear that erotic narrative, insofar as it is genuinely narrative, cannot be sustained indefinitely as the successful defense of virtue. To put it another way, whatever erotic use value may be sought in the novel of virginity preserved, the latter ought not to be thought of as erotic narrative in the narrowly thematic sense. There is a paradox here that has, of course, been thoroughly domesticated by psychoanalysis: we can talk happily enough of an erotic blocking of the erotic story. In Bernardin de Saint-Pierre's *Paul et Virginie* (1788), for example, we find both the erotic promise (or threat), and its passionate denial. The novel contains in fact, in encapsulated form, the story of the virgin's disgrace. This is the story of Marguerite, the mother of Paul, whose irretrievable loss of virtue condemns her to the colonies: "She had therefore decided to leave forever the village in which she had been born, and hide her sin in the distant colonies, far from the

---

défloration n'est pas l'aboutissement harmonieux d'une évolution continue, c'est une rupture avec le passé, le commencement d'un nouveau cycle.

country in which she had lost the only dowry of a poor, honest girl: her reputation."[7] [e] The next generation is called upon to work out its destiny in specific opposition to this model, as Marguerite "endows" the novel's heroine with a name that is itself a narrative program: "Madame de la Tour asked me to join with her friend in giving a name to her daughter. Marguerite gave her the name Virginie. 'She will be virtuous,' said she, 'and she will be happy. I only met with unhappiness when I left the path of virtue.'" (209).[f]

This is the heroine's character, and the mark of her (anti)erotic destiny. She can either fulfill her essence or fall catastrophically beneath her moral station. Gratification lies close at hand, for she is promised in marriage to Paul almost from the time of her birth: "Their mothers were speaking of their marriage when they were still in their cradles" (213).[g] Is this the path of virtue? Certainly not, if it is taken prematurely. In any case, such a resolution is too close at hand, too quick for the interests of narrative. There is a danger that the novel will have no genuine plot, lapsing into the idyllic or collapsing into the incestuous.[8] As if in response to this formal requirement, Mme de la Tour seeks to gain time, exchanging a half-acknowledged present threat for a definite future promise:

> Madame de la Tour had given me to understand Virginie's condition, and her own desire to gain a few years in the young people's growth by keeping them well apart for a while. (276)
>
> Madame de la Tour was not sorry to take the opportunity of separating Virginie and Paul for a while, ensuring that they would one day be happy together. (280)[h]

Intrigue of this sort does not serve, however, to engage the characters in the complex negotiation of obstacles to union. It merely serves to prepare and delay the moment of tragedy.

[e] Elle s'était déterminée alors à quitter pour toujours le village où elle était née, et à aller cacher sa faute aux colonies, loin de son pays, où elle avait perdu la seule dot d'une fille pauvre et honnête, la réputation.

[f] Madame de la Tour me pria aussi de nommer sa fille conjointement avec son amie. Celle-ci [Marguerite] lui donna le nom de Virginie. "Elle sera vertueuse, dit-elle, et elle sera heureuse. Je n'ai connu le malheur qu'en m'écartant de la vertu."

[g] Déjà leurs mères parlaient de leur mariage sur leurs berceaux.

[h] Madame de la Tour ne m'avait pas caché l'état de Virginie et le désir qu'elle avait de gagner quelques années sur l'âge de ces jeunes gens en les éloignant l'un de l'autre.

Madame de la Tour n'était pas fâchée de trouver une occasion de séparer pour quelque temps Virginie et Paul, en procurant un jour leur bonheur mutuel.

It is the radical binarism of girlhood and womanhood entailed by Virginie's name that makes for the novel's sentimental intensity. If the somewhat contrived delay were simply to come to an end, something would no doubt be consummated that would be a denial of the heroine's essence. Only in dying is she able to achieve the virgin's salvation. At the point of climax, she cannot enter into the play of negotiation or seduction; she cannot be earthily pedestrian. All she can do is fall or ascend, such is the paradigmatic severity of virginal stories. True to herself, she refuses to take off her clothes for the sake of worldly survival, adopting in extremis an edifying position more worthy of Greuze than of Aretino: "and Virginie, seeing that death was inevitable, put one hand over her clothes, the other over her heart, and raising her serene gaze to the skies, took on the appearance of an angel who is heavenward bound" (345–46).[i] She goes down into the waters, in fact—"Oh fearful day! Alas! It was all swallowed up" (364)[j]—but only to rise the higher in the estimation of all who are watching. Beyond her death, she is allowed to speak with the words of the narrator, reminding us of her uncompromising stance: "I chose to give up my life rather than do violence to modesty. [. . .] Since that time, I have been beyond the reach of all the evils that frighten men [. . .]. I am as pure and as unchanging as a particle of light" (365).[k] Modesty or death: the narration of true virginity is defined by the refusal of any mediation.

In the middle of *Paul et Virginie*—for it does have some sort of middle, and not just a gap—we do find intimations of something more obscure. Innocence is both a given and a product of the story, its atmosphere and its climax. It is recognizable narratively by the absence of any psychological or moral event: "In this way the two children of nature continued to grow. No care had furrowed their brows, no intemperance had corrupted their blood, no unfortunate passion depraved their hearts" (263).[l] But in the heart of this eden, in the body of the virgin, appears a growing, adolescent disturbance: "However, for some time now Virginie had been disturbed by an unknown illness.

[i] et Virginie, voyant la mort inévitable, pose une main sur ses habits, l'autre sur son cœur, et levant en haut des yeux sereins, parut un ange qui prend son vol vers les cieux.

[j] O jour affreux! hélas! tout fut englouti.

[k] J'ai mieux aimé perdre ma vie que de violer la pudeur. [. . .] Aucun des maux qui effraient les hommes ne peut plus désormais m'atteindre [. . .]. Je suis pure et inaltérable comme une particule de lumière.

[l] Ainsi croissaient ces deux enfants de la nature. Aucun souci n'avait ridé leur front, aucune intempérance n'avait corrompu leur sang, aucune passion malheureuse n'avait dépravé leur cœur.

Her beautiful blue eyes were streaked with black; her skin was jaundiced; her body was subject to a universal languor. No longer did she bear serenity on her brow, or a smile on her lips. [. . .] She wandered everywhere in search of tranquillity, and could not find it anywhere" (266–68).[m] Desire has begun its work within, adding erotic color to Virginie's youthful complexion: "Her beautiful blue eyes were filled with melancholy. Her heart, agitated by the struggle against passion, gave a lively color to her complexion, and an emotional tone to her voice" (284–85).[n] The erotic storm that threatens to break here is suspended for a time when Virginie is sent away from the island when she has grown up. It is finally avoided only at the novel's denouement, precisely as Virginie is swept away by the tempest without. At last, she finds, not *du repos,* but *le repos,* being laid to rest in a definitively virtuous attitude. In response to such narrow thematic exigencies, the ending is happily tragic, both confirming the promise of virginity and averting the threat of a fall.

Whatever the dark secrets of *Paul et Virginie,* the novel quite properly marks itself off generically from the "licentious" novels of its time (see, e.g., 299–300). It seems to exploit the theme of virginity for the narrowness and the radicality of the narrative options made available, thereby precluding the deployment of any narrative of pleasure. To put it bluntly, *Paul et Virginie* shows the limitations, or the inconvenience of virginity as a theme for erotic narrative. Indeed, from a straightforwardly libertine point of view, virginity seems to require an explicit critique, in order to reject its narrative strictures. The whole notion deserves no doubt to be denounced "philosophically" as irrational prejudice, rather than being accepted and elaborated thematically. The point of a libertine critique would presumably be to narrow the gap between virginity and nonvirginity, denying the catastrophic binarism of virtue and vice. Brantôme had already made Lucretia the object of irony,[9] and Sade provides the philosophical denunciation in a thoroughly materialist harangue delivered to Justine by one of her captors: "How can a girl be so dull-witted as to believe that her virtue can possibly depend on the greater or lesser diameter of one part of her body? What conceivable difference can it possibly

[m] Cependant depuis quelque temps Virginie se sentait agitée d'un mal inconnu. Ses beaux yeux bleus se marbraient de noir; son teint jaunissait; une langueur universelle battait son corps. La sérénité n'était plus sur son front, ni le sourire sur ses lèvres. [. . .] [Elle allait] cherchant partout du repos, et ne le trouvant nulle part.

[n] Ses beaux yeux bleus étaient remplis de mélancolie; et son cœur agité par une passion combattue donnait à son teint une couleur animée, et à sa voix des sons pleins d'émotion.

make to men or to God whether this part is intact or spoiled?" (III, 54).[o] Much the same libertine point, in a milder form, is made in *Amélie de Saint-Far* (1802), a novel by Félicité de Choiseul-Meuse: "That dishonor is an illusion [. . .] and what you have lost amounts to so little that it would be madness to regret it."[10] [p] The message is plain enough: the loss of virginity is hardly worthy of being called an event. What the young woman is enjoined to do is to *forget* the classical story of the tragic fall, that of Lucretia. In *La Philosophie dans le boudoir,* Madame de Saint-Ange says to Eugénie: "Could you be so mad as to hope for immortality? Well then, my dear, it is by fucking that you will remain in the memory of mankind. The Lucretias are soon forgotten, whereas the Theodoras and the Messalinas lend themselves to life's sweetest and most frequently renewed conversations" (III, 417).[q] This is, in a sense, a phatically self-contradictory argument, since all of the classical proper names it mentions seem to be equally available for reference in the context. But the talk of forgetting may be read as an invitation to turn away from the theme. Alexandrine Durancy, the libertine woman in *Amélie de Saint-Far,* observes to the heroine that the cruel option, virginity or death, seems to break down in practice: "'Such big words for such little things,' Alexandrine went on, with all the marks of scorn. 'You act the role of Lucretia wonderfully well, but you are more prudent than she was: you are content just to declaim your lines'" (II, 59).[r] Why go on playing the role of Lucretia when one knows that losing one's virginity is unlikely to prove fatal?

Young heroines are called on to forget the theme of virginity precisely because no one manages to forget it completely. In both *Justine* (1791) and *Amélie de Saint-Far,* the libertine disparagement of virginity is addressed to a heroine whose preservation or loss of virtue is a constant focus of narrative interest. "Philosophical" comment helps to frame the virginity story rather than to dismantle it—deconstructing the theme, perhaps, but certainly not destroying it. For erotic narrative, virginity remains a fascinating object. Quite often, this fascination

[o] Comment une fille peut-elle être assez simple pour croire que la vertu puisse dépendre d'un peu plus ou d'un peu moins de largeur dans une des parties de son corps? Eh! qu'importe aux hommes ou à Dieu que cette partie soit intacte ou flétrie?

[p] Ce déshonneur est une chimère [. . .]; et ce que vous avez perdu se borne à si peu de chose que vous ne pourriez le regretter sans folie.

[q] Aurais-tu la folie de l'immortalité? Eh bien, c'est en foutant, ma chère que tu resteras dans la mémoire des hommes. On a bientôt oublié les Lucrèce, tandis que les Théodora et les Messaline font les plus doux entretiens et les plus fréquents de la vie.

[r] Que de grands mots pour de si petites choses, reprit Alexandrine avec les marques du dédain; vous jouez à ravir le rôle de Lucrèce; mais, plus prudente qu'elle, vous vous contentez de déclamer.

is enacted in a form of display, whereby something essentially intimate and temporal is able to be examined as a thing present in space. Before deflowering, there is the visible bodily flower, made available to the admiring gaze. In *L'Académie des dames,* Tullia sees Octavia's flower: "Oh the tender virgin! I can see a flower that will be preferred by anyone who sees it to all other flowers and their perfumes!"[s] Now to call virginity a flower is not so much to admire the hymen for itself: it is presumably to aestheticize the exciting narrative possibilities that the virginal state seems to afford. Julie, the heroine of another erotic novel by Choiseul-Meuse, has managed to preserve her flower, and her partner Caroline contemplates the precious rose with delight: "Her delicate hand opened the way slightly, and the latterday Sappho cried out with indescribable delight: 'She is a virgin! Good Lord, what a source of pleasure!'"[11] [t] If this kind of pleasure is to coexist with that of copulation, the question becomes: how can erotic narrative hold on to virginal beauty as potential and yet harness the energy of its transformation? Whereas Susanne, the instructor in *L'Escole des filles* (1660), had observed, "Virginity is a very beautiful thing in words and a very ugly thing in its effects" (167),[u] many later novels suggest that this is far too quick: virginity has to be considered in terms of its *discursive* effects. Inheriting the theme as part of a discourse of virtue, libertine narrative remains caught, in its attitude, between the critically dismissive and the indulgently exploitative.

A corrosive, and enduringly deconstructive, variant of the virginity theme can be found in Rousseau's *Julie, ou la Nouvelle Héloïse,* which undertakes what might be called a narrative reworking of the theme's very narrativity. The victim of passion, and of a lapse in moral rigor, Julie is precipitated into *l'ignominie:* "so it is that a moment's distraction ruined me forever. I have fallen into the abyss of ignominy out of which a girl can never return. I am alive, but only so as to suffer all the more."[12] [v] From these depths, one cannot rise again it seems, and Julie's subsequent life must be played out as infernal torment. She seems to live only to conjugate pragmatically defective verbs, writing to her cousin, for example, "You abandoned me, and I have perished!"

[s] Tendre vierge! je vois une fleur, qui, de quiconque la verra, sera préférée à toutes les fleurs et à tous les parfums!

[t] Sa main délicate entr'ouvre la rose, et la nouvelle Sapho s'écrie avec des transports de joie, impossibles à décrire: Elle est vierge! grand Dieu, quelle source de plaisirs!

[u] La virginité est une très belle chose en paroles et très laide en ses effets.

[v] c'est ainsi qu'un instant d'égarement m'a perdue à jamais. Je suis tombée dans l'abîme d'ignominie dont une fille ne revient point; et si je vis, c'est pour être plus malheureuse.

(58).[w] Yet this figurative death occurs when nine-tenths of the novel remain to be told, so that the very economy of Rousseau's text seems to establish the fall as something *lived,* something tellable in time. Instead of being regarded as catastrophically instantaneous, the fall appears to be analyzed in its dynamism. What the heroine sees, and fears most, is what we might call the seductive gravity of vice, whereby falling becomes a process, gathering its own momentum. The important thing, as with all drastically binary notions of virtue, is not to take the first step: "Oh! The first step, the hardest one to take, is the one at which I should have balked. How can I now expect to stop at the following ones? No, having taken that first step, I now feel myself drawn toward the abyss, and you can make me as unhappy as you wish" (15).[x] By an imaginative paradox, the abyss would thus be entered by degrees:

> For a while I was able to disguise my shame and yield by degrees so as to deceive myself. That was just pointless cleverness, flattering my vanity without saving my virtue! I see only too well now where the first sin leads. (15–16)
>
> Each defeat would thereby have prepared the next one; becoming accustomed to vice would have meant that I no longer saw the horror of it. (262)[y]

For Julie, the fall is strangely both a *fait accompli* and a continuing threat. The only tactic, for virtue, seems to lie in making sure that the fall is a singular, irreparable event. There must be no acceptance of a new kind of existence, no consolation of any sort. Moral grief must itself be kept "intact," and made to endure forever: "My sin is irreparable, and my tears shall never cease to flow. You who make them flow must ensure that you do not impair my just suffering. My only hope lies in making it last forever: the worst evil would be for me to be consoled. The lowest level of shame consists in losing not only innocence, but the sense of how dear innocence should be to us"

[w] Tu m'as abandonnée, et j'ai péri!

[x] Ah! le premier pas qui coûte le plus, était celui qu'il ne fallait pas faire; comment m'arrêterais-je aux autres? Non; de ce premier pas je me sens entraîner dans l'abîme, et tu peux me rendre aussi malheureuse qu'il te plaira.

[y] Je pouvais quelque temps déguiser ma honte, et céder par degrés pour m'en imposer à moi-même. Vaine adresse qui pouvait flatter mon amour-propre, et non pas sauver ma vertu! Va, je vois trop, je sens trop où mène la première faute.

Chaque défaite eût ainsi préparé la suivante; l'habitude du vice en eût effacé l'horreur à mes yeux.

(64).[z] What the heroine may achieve in this way, no doubt, is to make her loss present—"this fatal love that is the ruin of me" (64)[a]—refusing any therapeutic dulling of the memory, or any loss of moral acuity.

This moral agony is able to be sustained, becoming one of the key thematic elements in the novel, precisely because the heroine does not die when she might. Not dying, indeed, might be said to be a theme of this text, which resists quite self-consciously the tragic narrative program attendant upon virginal passion. Both Saint-Preux and Julie invoke the possibility of death as a source of fervor. "Would it not be a hundred times better to see each other for a single moment and then die?"[b] one says, while the other fantasizes about the *Liebestod:* "If someone breaks in on us, my plan is to hurl myself into your arms, wrap you closely in mine, and receive the death blow thus so that I shall never again have to be separated from you, more happy in death than in life" (96).[c] Dying together, especially for Saint-Preux, is a recurrent threat (see, e.g., 391). At one point indeed, the hero finds himself calling for the tragic story. Why did Julie not die, so that he could grieve her passing as unmitigated *loss,* and dream of an afterlife with her?

> "Why did she not die?!" I dared to cry out, swept away by my rage. Yes, that way I should have been less unhappy; I should have boldly thrown myself into suffering, and embraced her cold tomb [. . .]. I should at least have had the hope of going to join her there . . . But she is alive, she is happy . . . She is alive, and her life is my death, her happiness my torture. Heaven, having torn her away from me, has even denied me the sweetness of regretting her! . . . (466)[d]

The time for dying has now long gone, however. As Claire says to Saint-Preux, that should have happened after the climax of passion.

[z] Ma faute est irréparable, mes pleurs ne tariront point. O toi qui les fais couler, crains d'attenter à de si justes douleurs; tout mon espoir est de les rendre éternelles: le pire des maux serait d'en être consolée; et c'est le dernier degré de l'opprobre de perdre avec l'innocence le sentiment qui nous la fait aimer.

[a] cet amour fatal qui me perd

[b] Ne vaudrait-il pas mieux cent fois se voir un seul instant et puis mourir?

[c] Si nous sommes surpris, mon dessein est de me précipiter dans tes bras, de t'enlacer fortement dans les miens, et de recevoir ainsi le coup mortel pour n'avoir plus à me séparer de toi, plus heureuse à ma mort que je ne le fus de ma vie.

[d] Que n'est-elle pas morte! osais-je m'écrier dans un transport de rage; oui, je serais moins malheureux; j'oserais me livrer à mes douleurs; j'embrasserais sans remords sa froide tombe [. . .]. J'aurais au moins l'espoir de la rejoindre. . . Mais elle vit, elle est heureuse. . . Elle vit, et sa vie est ma mort, et son bonheur est mon supplice; et le ciel, après me l'avoir arrachée, m'ôte jusqu'à la douceur de la regretter!. . .

All that is left now is the *decline* of their love: "You stated yourself that one does not reach such heights of emotion twice in one's life, and that one ought to die after having felt them. My friend, that was the high point and, whatever fortune and love did for you subsequently, your passion and your happiness could only decline. That instant was also the beginning of your loss of favor" (235).[e]

La Nouvelle Héloïse works thus in the space between the theme of the tragic fall and that of the slow decline, purporting to tell the first, and generally working out its novelistic time in the telling of the second. For this reason, and as part of a thematic rewriting, such old lexical favorites of the virginity story as *perdre* and *perdue* come to have a range of meanings that tests their coherence to the limit. On one page of text, in a letter from Claire to Julie immediately following the "fall," we find three different usages of *perdre,* the first referring to the loss of virginity as a fait accompli ("if I had thought you were so close to your ruin"),[f] the second to the hypothesis of Julie's death ("I could not have borne to lose you without mortal despair"),[g] and the third to the possibility of her yet being definitively lost at some time in the future ("you must listen to me, or you will be lost")[h] (60). Between the different meanings of *perdue* lies the narrative space of *La Nouvelle Héloïse,* and the space in which it works out its morality. The famous warning to the virginal reader is that "the girl who, in spite of the title, dares to read a single page will be ruined" (4).[i] But what does ruined (*perdue*) mean, exactly? Julie has lost her virginity, an event which is only relatively momentous. She is not defined by this quality alone, as Claire points out:

> At this time, my dear, I must speak to you thus, and you must listen to me, or you will be lost: you have a thousand adorable qualities that can be maintained only by your self-esteem, and that would inevitably be destroyed by an excess of shame, and by the depravity that follows it. What you are really worth will depend on what you believe yourself to be worth.
>
> [. . .] Does one stain show in the sunlight? How many virtues do you have left, as against the one that has been damaged? (60–61)[j]

[e] Vous jugeâtes vous-même qu'on n'éprouvait point de pareils transports deux fois en la vie, et qu'il fallait mourir après les avoir sentis. Mon ami, ce fut là le comble; et, quoi que la fortune et l'amour eussent fait pour vous, vos feux et votre bonheur ne pouvaient plus que décliner. Cet instant fut aussi le commencement de vos disgrâces.

[f] si je t'avais crue si près de ta perte

[g] je n'aurais pu te perdre sans un mortel désespoir.

[h] tu dois m'écouter, ou tu es perdue.

[i] Celle qui, malgré ce titre, en osera lire une seule page est une fille perdue.

[j] A présent, ma chère, je dois te parler ainsi, et tu dois m'écouter, ou tu es perdue:

It is a matter, for the whole novel, of breaking the heroine's fall, and of braking against the dynamism of degradation.

In a sense, *La Nouvelle Héloïse* has something in common with libertine stories like *Justine* in the attention it gives to healing after sexual damage, for Julie and Saint-Preux are described eventually as recovering from their passion. The first thing said, as simple iteration of the virginity theme, is that there *is* no healing. These are "illnesses that cannot be healed" (59); "my sin is irreparable" (64).[k] But this affirmation of the impossibility of further change, and therefore of further narrative, is soon displaced by a question that becomes a focus of narrative interest for the rest of the novel: "but given that Julie, so pure and chaste, has nonetheless succumbed, how will she recover from her fall?" (138).[l] This is, so to speak, the mature question, asked by milord Edouard, as well as being the question of Julie's maturity. How will she continue, how will she grow, how will she heal from the fall itself? What is needed for recovery is time: long periods of separation, marriage to a wisely dispassionate husband, a disciplined life of charity and material devotion. This is not only the thematic moderation of *La Nouvelle Héloïse,* it is the very middleness of its narrative, the slow achievement of moral reparation and emotional repair:

> [Julie:] It is not true that my heart still feels the effects of its inner wounds. No, it is healed, I can feel it. I'm very sure of that. (300)
>
> [Saint-Preux:] How can I talk to you about my healing? It is in contact with you that I shall come to gauge it. Have I come back wiser than I left? I dare to think so, yet cannot affirm it. (310)[m]

Only after this story has been almost fully played out does the novel allow itself to return to the intensity of death and passion. Julie con-

---

car il reste en toi mille adorables qualités que l'estime de toi-même peut seule conserver, qu'un excès de honte et l'avilissement qui le suit détruirait infailliblement: et c'est sur ce que tu croiras valoir encore que tu vaudras en effet.

[. . .] Une tache paraît-elle au soleil? Combien de vertus te restent pour une qui s'est altérée!

[k] des maux que tu ne peux plus guérir/ma faute est irréparable.

[l] mais si Julie, pure et chaste, a pourtant succombé, comment se relèvera-t-elle après sa chute?

[m] [Julie:] Ce n'est pas, tu le sais, que mon cœur se ressente encore de ses anciennes blessures; non, il est guéri, je le sens, j'en suis très sûre.

[Saint-Preux:] Comment vous parler de ma guérison? C'est de vous que je dois apprendre à la connaître. Reviens-je plus libre et plus sage que je ne suis parti? J'ose le croire et ne puis l'affirmer.

fesses in extremis that she has never healed properly: "You thought I had fully recovered, and I thought I had too. Let us give thanks to the one who made this misconception last for as long as it was useful. Who knows whether, as I saw myself so close to the abyss, my head might not have begun to spin?" (564).[n] Yet it is now too late for a second fall, just as it was too late to contemplate death after she had begun to recover from the first. What novelistic time seems to ensure is that it is always too late for tragedy.

It is remarkable that Sade's *Justine* reworks the virginity story in much the same way as *La Nouvelle Héloïse,* referring continually to death as a radical path open to virtue, but sustaining the heroine's life as a form of unspectacular moral survival. If, as we are told in *Les Cent Vingt Journées,* "the most fortunate thing that can befall a woman is to die young" (I, 76),[o] then this might be the very definition of Justine's torture: not to be allowed the narrative short-circuit of early martyrdom. Repeatedly, Justine seems to call for the tragic option, saying that she would rather die than yield to vice:

> No, no. Dispose of my life if you must, but do not suppose that you will ever obtain from me the horror that you propose. (III, 86)
>
> You are a monster to dare so cruelly to take advantage of my circumstances in order to force upon me the alternatives of death or infamy. I shall be able to die if I must, but I shall die without guilt. (III, 290; cf. 233)[p]

Death here is not the unreal hypothesis that it may have been for Saint-Preux, but Justine, unlike Lucretia or Clarissa, can never achieve death on her own terms. All that might happen, in fact, is that she might find herself yielding to vice even in death. Not for Justine the saintly final baptism of Virginie, or even the partial drowning of Julie: all she can do, as she is locked into suffering, is to roll around the floor of her prison: "I threw myself to the ground, I made the walls ring with my cries, I struck my head against the stone floor, hoping

[n] Vous m'avez crue guérie, et j'ai cru l'être. Rendons grâces à celui qui fit durer cette erreur autant qu'elle était utile: qui sait si, me voyant si près de l'abîme, la tête ne m'eût point tourné?

[o] ce qui peut arriver de plus heureux à une femme, c'est de mourir jeune.

[p] Non, non: disposez de ma vie, s'il vous la faut, mais n'imaginez jamais obtenir de moi l'horreur que vous me proposez.

Vous êtes un monstre d'oser abuser aussi cruellement de ma situation pour me placer entre la mort et l'infamie; je saurai mourir s'il le faut, mais ce sera du moins sans remords.

to obtain a speedier death" (III, 305).[q] Death is not prompt, and Justine can only keep on rolling, being continually revived and used again as victim.

Yet even as this novel denies that the loss of virginity is (narratively and morally) equivalent to death, it continues to treat Justine's virginity as a kind of narrative capital. At some cost to verisimilitude, the story continues to maintain Justine intact, even as she is handled and soiled by her captors. As Béatrice Didier observes, "physical and moral rape is made all the more attractive by the victim's virginity, and that virginity gains its full value from having survived so many attacks."[13] [r] The need to keep Justine intact results, for example, in a kind of restrained pack rape, where some ingenuity is deployed in finding nondefinitive sexual acts. Ultimately, one of the band of thieves holding Justine captive seems to crack under the pressure of this formal narrative exigency, asking whether the difference between virginity and nonvirginity really ought to matter for villains like them: "'She has to go through with it,' one of them declared. 'It's not possible to relent now. Since when do you need proven virtue to belong to a band of thieves? Won't she be just as useful to us in a stained condition as a virgin would be?'" (III, 50–51).[s] These protests are of no more avail than Justine's own, such is the fate of the lesser villain, or the early libertine. The difference between *flétrie* and *vierge* may not matter philosophically, but structurally, for the narrative practice of *Justine,* it matters enormously.

Even when the great event occurs, when the heroine is assaulted and raped by Saint-Florent, the singularity and perhaps the definitive nature of the event are somehow attenuated by the fact that Justine had been knocked unconscious. She is able to infer what must have occurred, without experiencing directly the (supposedly) transforming presence of the male in her body: "Oh Madame, I have no idea what that man said or did after that, but the state I was in when I returned to my senses made me realize only too well to what extent I had been his victim" (III, 69).[t] It is still possible then for Justine, at

[q] Je me précipite à terre, je fais retentir la voûte de mes cris, je frappe ma tête contre les carreaux à dessein d'y trouver une mort plus prompte.

[r] Le viol physique et moral est plus séduisant grâce à la virginité de la victime; et cette virginité acquiert tout son prix d'avoir survécu à tant d'atteintes.

[s] Il faut qu'elle y passe, dit l'un d'eux, il n'y a plus moyen de lui faire de quartier: ne dirait-on pas qu'il faut faire preuve de vertu pour être dans une troupe de voleurs? et ne nous servira-t-elle pas aussi bien flétrie que vierge?

[t] Oh! madame, je ne sais plus ni ce que dit, ni ce que fit cet homme; mais l'état dans lequel je me retrouvai ne me laissa que trop connaître à quel point j'avais été sa victime.

a quite advanced stage of the novel, to speak of her *relative* purity, while measuring concessively the limited damage that has been done: "Whatever may have been my trials until that time, I had kept my innocence. Being merely the victim of attempts on the part of a few monsters, I was still able more or less to put myself in the category of decent girls. The fact was that I had never been really soiled except by a rape carried out five years earlier, and the traces of that had healed . . ." (III, 125).[u] Her confessor at the monastery of Sainte-Marie-des-Bois makes the same assessment: "One lone violation, friends, and that six years ago; she is therefore practically a vestal . . . and indeed, I give her to you as such . . . " (III, 131).[v] In *La Nouvelle Justine,* she is presented as a slightly used Lucretia: "Here is a Lucretia who bears on her shoulders the stigma of crime, yet at the same time has in her heart the naïveté of a virgin" (VI, 253).[w] Only now will her virginity be utterly destroyed—*anéantie* is the expression used in *Les Cent Vingt Journées* (I, 44). Severino compares the event to a shipwreck: "Was it not time that this proud virtue should be split asunder [*fît naufrage*]? Can one expect to be nearly a virgin at twenty-two years of age?" (III, 134).[x]

By contrast with that of Virginie, however, the story of Justine endures well beyond the *naufrage.* This is made possible by what might be called Justine's essential virginity, a quality undiminished by rape and torture. Whereas Lucretia affirmed and retrieved her eternal virtue only in death, Justine is apparently able to maintain hers in life—indefinitely. Dubois, at a late stage in the story, is making two victims available to a powerful master. One of them is a young girl, freshly abducted from a convent, but Justine, the other, need fear no comparison, such is the fullness of her moral virginity: "I am putting her into your hands today. You may prefer her to that pretty boarder from the Benedictine convent at Lyon whom you also desired, and who will be arriving at any moment. The latter has physical and moral virtue, whereas this one here has nothing but sentimental chastity,

[u] Quelles qu'eussent été mes peines jusques alors, au moins mon innocence me restait. Uniquement victime des attentats de quelques monstres, à peu de chose près néanmoins, je pouvais me croire encore dans la classe des filles honnêtes. Au fait, je n'avais été vraiment souillée que par un viol fait depuis cinq ans, dont les traces étaient refermées. . .

[v] Une seule attaque de viol, mes amis, et cela depuis six ans; c'est donc presque une vestale. . . en vérité, je vous la donne pour telle. . .

[w] Voici une Lucrèce qui porte à la fois sur ses épaules la marque du crime et dans le cœur toute la naïveté d'une vierge.

[x] N'était-il pas temps que cette fière vertu fît naufrage, et peut-on être encore presque vierge à vingt-deux ans?

but that virtue is part of her existence, and nowhere will you find a person more thoroughly filled with candor and honesty" (III, 276).[y] This is the thematic consecration of Justine's egregious failure to learn, the point at which her obtuseness becomes a kind of stubborn achievement.[14] Whatever its ultimate moral, or even political significance, Justine's original naïveté provides a principle of psychological fixity in the novel. As Ihab Hassan notes, "Nothing Justine ever does is too good to escape terrible chastisement, and no chastisement is too terrible to corrupt her goodness. It is a world of eternal fixity."[15] Her very inability, or refusal, to change is what enables Sade's narrative to rehearse its persuasive discourse and pursue its cruel exactions almost without end.

In this way, Justine is not only revived between episodes and made available again through healing, she is also lastingly *preserved* by, and as, innocence. Didier puts it succinctly: Justine can never heal from her virtue.[16] Yet even here, the picture is blurred somewhat with the passing of narrative time. In between passionate utterances that affirm her unequivocal choice of virtue against vice, Justine finds herself adapting, surviving by choosing something between the two. She would rather die than murder Bressac's aunt (III, 85–86); she would give her life a thousand times for love of the man himself (III, 78–79). Yet she decides not to confront her master, preferring to deceive him in the hope of avoiding the most drastic of crimes. Was it not a terrible thing to practice such deceptions, Bressac later asks as he is about to punish her. "By necessity placed between these two crimes, why did you choose the more abominable?" (III, 94).[z] The accused is convinced that she had chosen the lesser crime—"Alas, had I not chosen the lesser?" (III, 95)[a]—but it is precisely the very fact of such assessment that works to undo the radical program of virginity. More and more, with such monsters as Gernande and Roland, Justine applies herself to menial orgiastic tasks, always *à son corps défendant:* "I complied only when I could not do otherwise" (III, 209).[b] "What about the death option?" might be the harsh question asked of her by a thematic tradition of virtue. In an exceptional moment of despair,

[y] Je vous la livre aujourd'hui. Peut-être la préférez-vous à cette jolie pensionnaire du couvent des Bénédictines de Lyon, que vous avez désirée de même, et qui va nous arriver dans l'instant: cette dernière a sa vertu physique et morale, celle-ci n'a que celle des sentiments, mais elle fait partie de son existence, et vous ne trouverez nulle part une créature plus remplie de candeur et d'honnêteté.

[z] Nécessairement placée entre ces deux crimes, pourquoi as-tu choisi le plus abominable?

[a] Hélas! n'avais-je pas choisi le moindre?

[b] Je ne me prêtais que lorsque je ne pouvais faire autrement.

she actually asks the question of herself, suffering remorse at not having been a true Lucretia, "consumed by dreadful remorse at not having killed herself rather than act, albeit despite herself, as an accomplice to such frightful debauchery" (VII, 382).[c] Has she not fallen below the highest standard? The answer must be a little cloudy, for despite herself, despite her virginal essence, Justine turns away from the rigorous nonadaptation of Lucretia and Virginie. Insofar as she does so, she edges ever so slightly along the gentle downward path of vice.

What *Justine* does, so to speak, by compulsion, is to help shift attention from the anatomical to the cognitive dimension of virginity. Not that the heroine's innocence is actually a focus of narrative interest for Sade: it is merely a requirement of the story, taken for granted at every point. Other novels of the same period, or slightly later, continue the thematic shift by dwelling, aesthetically and erotically, on the quality of innocence. They begin to do this, in certain cases, by distinguishing between anatomical virginity (*pucelage*) and sublime sexual unawareness (being truly a *vierge*). In *La Secte des anandrynes* (1789), Mlle Sappho is checked prior to her admission to the novel's lesbian society, and the judge's verdict is: "she is intact [*pucelle*], on my honor, even if she is not virginal [*vierge*]" (17).[d] When invited to distinguish between the two states, Florence, in *Le Roman de Violette* (1883), does so with lyrical enthusiasm. Odette says to her: "Do you see any difference between a *vierge* and a *pucelle*?" (170),[e] and Florence replies: "Morally, there is an immense difference, dear heart. A *vierge* is a young girl who has never been touched by any mouth, never stroked by anyone's fingers, not even her own. The *vierge* is the innocent who has never experienced pleasure. The *pucelle* is simply one who, while touching herself and being touched by other men or women, has had the strength to keep her hymen's membrane intact" (171).[f] Instead of being conceived of as a form of nonbeing, or as a kind of undifferentiated, prenarrative condition, innocence is made to appear fascinating, and even relatively powerful. An elaborate example of this is *Amélie de Saint-Far, ou la Fatale Erreur* (1802), by

[c] devorée de l'affreux remords de ne s'être pas tuée, plutôt que d'avoir (quoique malgré elle) servi de plastron à d'aussi affreuses débauches

[d] elle est pucelle, sur mon honneur, si elle n'est pas vierge.

[e] Fais-tu donc une différence entre une vierge et une pucelle?

[f] Moralement, une immense, chère âme; la vierge est la jeune fille qu'aucune bouche n'a touchée, qu'aucun doigt, pas même le sien n'a effleurée; la vierge est l'innocente qui n'a jamais joui; la pucelle est tout simplement celle qui, au milieu de ses propres attouchements et de ceux des autres hommes ou femmes a eu la force de conserver intacte la membrane de l'hymen.

Félicité de Choiseul-Meuse.[17] Amélie grows up in a moral environment characterized by what we might call second-order innocence, where a woman's virtue is not considered a proper topic for discussion: "'People only go on praising a woman's virtue in that way,' said wise Rosa, 'when others have begun to cast doubt on it. Whether good or bad things are said about her, it is still offensive'" (I, 165).[g] Where sex is concerned, the heroine is "dans une parfaite ignorance" (I, 33), but it is the very perfection of this ignorance that makes her a worthy heroine. Amélie's radical innocence—her not knowing that she does not know—seems to require that she *not* bear a name like Virginie. Only her aunt has a virgin's name (Rosa): for Amélie herself, virginity must not even be an issue.[18]

How can innocence be characterized in stories, other than by the knowledge and the experience that it lacks? How can it be anything other than a nonevent? *Amélie de Saint-Far* begins to answer these questions, although it does not always do so with assurance. When Amélie is confronted—unwittingly, of course—with a redoubtable libertine opponent in Mme Durancy, one who is able to feign innocence, the narrator is moved to ask: "Why is it that vice is able to use the appearance and language of virtue? What advantages does innocence have, then? That of being easily seduced, and having fewer ways to give pleasure" (I, 38).[h] It is almost as if the narrator were driven to irony at this point by the dangers of naïveté, but there are clear indications in the story that innocence does not merely condemn the heroine to victimhood, as it did in *Justine*. Most notably, Amélie exercises a seductive charm, by her girlish babble and her playful caresses, that causes would-be seducers to lose their way. Charles, a seasoned rake, manages to deceive Amélie by hiding in her apartment and pretending to be her fiancé, Ernest. He is so charmed by Amélie's sweet nothings, however, that he delays the moment of deflowering, to the point where he runs out of time. "Charles, who thought he was assured of a night without interruptions, rather than hastening the decisive moment, yielded to the gentle pleasure of listening to charming confessions. Even though they were addressed to his rival, they delighted him by their naïveté and tenderness. He had only given

[g] On ne vante la vertu d'une femme, disait la sage Rosa, que lorsque d'autres ont commencé à la révoquer en doute, et soit qu'on en parle en bien ou en mal, c'est toujours lui faire un outrage.

[h] Pourquoi le vice peut-il employer l'air et le langage de la vertu? Quels sont donc les avantages de l'innocence? D'être plus facilement séduite, et d'avoir moins de moyens de plaire.

Amélie the simplest caresses, of a kind lavished on her a thousand times by Ernest" (I, 98).[i] Similarly, a more genuinely affectionate seducer, the duc de Nemours, begins to lose his sense of erotic purpose, wondering whether innocent, childlike pleasures may not be greater than those of sexual possession: "It seemed to him a dreadful thing to corrupt so much innocence, especially when he considered the boundless confidence Amélie had in him: her attitude toward him was open, friendly, and lively. She was so delightfully uninhibited with him that he sometimes doubted whether possessing her could possibly increase the pleasure he felt by her side" (II, 37).[j] These mature males are brought, for a time at least, under Amélie's seductive power, inveigled into intercourse with virtue.

Where innocence is rendered so utterly fascinating, it becomes narratively productive, allowing the story to delay the "fatal" moment of the fall. In fact, Amélie is not deflowered until two-thirds of the novel have past, surviving much longer than Julie in *La Nouvelle Héloïse*, and even longer than Justine. In the meantime, comments by a knowledgeable narrator, and the continued contact with characters of mature sexual awareness ensure that the story is not obliged somehow to mark time in some childlike pre-erotic paradise. Narrative interest, and even a certain form of tension or suspense, is generated as Amélie's innocence rubs up against the desire of others. Amélie is often all the more at risk because of her essential unawareness. Hers is not some frozen purity, but an outgoing, even enterprising exchange with those she loves. When she is strolling in the woods with her suitor Ernest, he experiences "une agitation extrême," while Amélie continues to arouse him without realizing it: "she made absolutely no attempt to defend herself, but aroused his desire further by her innocent caresses" (I, 83).[k] Amélie's strength and her weakness—what both protects her and puts her at risk—is not the absence of desire: that would be nonerotic or pre-erotic. It is rather that her own desire is perfectly hidden from her: "Amélie, entirely preoccupied by love, did not know

[i] Charles, qui se croyait assuré d'une nuit tranquille, au lieu de précipiter le moment décisif, s'était livré au doux plaisir d'entendre des aveux charmants, qui, quoique adressés à son rival, le transportaient par leur naïveté et leur tendresse; il n'avait fait à Amélie que de simples caresses qu'Ernest lui avaient prodiguées mille fois.

[j] Il lui semblait affreux de corrompre tant d'innocence, surtout lorsqu'il réfléchissait à la confiance sans bornes qu'Amélie avait en lui: elle lui montrait une amitié si franche, si vive, un abandon si délicieux, qu'il doutait quelquefois que sa possession pût augmenter le plaisir qu'il goûtait près d'elle.

[k] loin de chercher à se défendre, [elle] irritait encore ses désirs par ses innocentes caresses.

what risks she was taking, and shared all her lover's desires without realizing it" (I, 84).[l] The catastrophic event, for her, will therefore happen as a fall into self-knowledge.

This long-awaited dramatic moment occurs finally—as it should have—by mistake, and with the wrong man. While Ernest is far away in the colonies, the duc de Nemours becomes her constant, amorously avuncular companion. He has occasion to rescue Amélie from a fall into a pond, and presumably from a rather mundane version of the Virgin's Tragedy. Amélie is unhurt, but the duc himself passes out and turns cold. In her efforts to revive him, she lies on him and rubs him all over. This holistic therapy succeeds far too well in avoiding death, and Amélie finds herself deflowered without ever having known what was happening:

> The sharp pain caused by these cruel attempts put an end to her sweet intoxication. She had no idea what the duc was trying to do, and begged him in vain to cease his thrusting.
>
> [. . .] Finally, his efforts met with success, and he gained admittance to the place amidst the stream of blood he had drawn from her. (II, 50–51)[m]

That is, of course, the *fatale erreur* announced by the novel's title, but *whose* error is it, exactly? Can Amélie possibly be the subject of it, when the nature of her virginity is such as to exclude all capacity for moral judgment? We are told at one point that all the blame can be placed on her neglectful and sometimes malevolent guardian: "she alone was the cause of her sin, [. . .] she was persuaded beforehand that Amélie would fall into that final trap" (II, 52).[n] Yet we are also left to wonder whether innocence itself is not paradoxically responsible. At the very least, it seems that Amélie has been exposed to danger by being left without sexual instruction.

Such budding libertines as Nerciat's Félicia have a temperamental foreknowledge of pleasure that leads them to regard their virginity as onerous: Félicia is "guided completely by nature, and itching to

[l] Amélie, tout entière à l'amour, ignorait ce qu'elle avait à craindre, et partageait, sans le savoir, tous les désirs de son amant.

[m] Les vives douleurs que ces cruelles tentatives occasionnèrent à Amélie, suspendirent sa douce ivresse: elle ne concevait rien à la conduite du duc, et le suppliait en vain de suspendre ses coups.

[. . .] Enfin le succès couronna ses efforts, il entra victorieux dans la place à travers les flots de sang qu'il avait fait couler.

[n] elle seule était cause de sa faute, [. . .] elle était persuadée d'avance qu'Amélie tomberait dans ce dernier piège.

know its secrets to the full."[o] But Félicia is named for happiness, being called "belle Lucrèce" only in a kind of banter (83), as if to mark the absence of any tragic conclusion. Amélie, precisely by her virginal nature, seems to be deprived of erotic intuition, although not necessarily of natural capacity: she would appear to require some formal erotic tuition in order to enter the realm of conscious desire. Something like the ritual preliminaries found in the expounding of an *ars erotica* might perhaps be appropriate. But there is no solidarity with Durancy, the older woman who might have played the instructor's role in a more classical erotic text. Ernest, the fiancé, wonders whether it is his responsibility. He is about to spend two years in the colonies before returning to marry Amélie, but cannot bring himself to provide instruction before departing: "However, Ernest could not bring himself to discuss such a subject. He was afraid of arousing Amélie's imagination, and of not being able to teach her only the general principles. He considered that it would be highly dangerous, at the time of his departure, to initiate his beloved into the mysteries of Venus. After all, a fortification that has already been breached is much more difficult to defend against a daring enemy" (I, 137).[p] To initiate Amélie would be to make a breach in her innocence, to open up a passage between the closed world of innocence and that of sexual experience. Having once mapped the erotic, one could hardly fail to lead her in imagination down the paths of desire. The dangers of innocence are revealed ultimately by developments in the story, but, where innocence is so radical and so precious, the danger of instruction may be even greater. For the virginal Amélie, any such teaching is a form of violation.

So it is that Amélie's wondrously durable, yet perfectly fragile innocence finally evaporates at, or just after, the moment of organic penetration. While totally unable to sense danger in advance, she has the certain knowledge of disaster in retrospect: "As soon as she found herself alone, she realized the extent of her loss, and trembled at the thought of it" (II, 56–57).[q] Mme Durancy is unkind enough to read the symptoms of desire in Amélie's actions, pointing out that she seemed to be enjoying the experience at the time: "But what I cannot

[o] Toute à la nature, et brûlant de connaître à fond ses secrets

[p] Cependant Ernest ne peut se résoudre à traiter un semblable sujet; il craint d'enflammer son imagination [celle d'Amélie], et de ne pouvoir s'en tenir aux préceptes; il pense qu'il serait bien dangereux, au moment d'un départ, d'initier sa maîtresse aux délicieux mystères de Vénus; car une place à laquelle on a fait brèche, se défend plus difficilement contre un ennemi audacieux.

[q] Dès qu'elle fut livrée à elle-même, elle sentit toute l'étendue de la perte qu'elle avait faite, et sa situation la fit frémir.

understand is that you should put on such a show of regret for something you did with such good grace. I note, my dear, that you only cried afterward" (II, 58–59).[r] In response to this, Amélie can only reaffirm with bitterness the thematics of the fall: "How could I possibly have cried beforehand, Madame? [. . .] did I realize the indignity that lay ahead of me?" (II, 59).[s] Her virginity has been narrativized, much like Justine's, as the impossibility of seeing ahead. All she can do, to atone for the mistake she does not properly own, is to insist on looking back, consecrating the fall, so to speak, by her unbroken demonstration of grief, exactly in the manner of Rousseau's Julie, who sought to avoid all further contact with her lover "for fear that a second step toward disorder would irrevocably plunge her into it" (*La Nouvelle Héloïse,* 219).[t] When Durancy suggests to Amélie that she has now entered a different state, and should therefore speak and act differently, the reply is that there will only ever be one mistake: "There is no reason for my tone to change, Madame, since my feelings have not done so. I still do not know how I committed the first sin, although I do not seek to attenuate it. But henceforth, my conduct will prove that my heart was not culpable. I shall not see the duc again, my mind is made up" (*Amélie de Saint-Far,* II, 60).[u]

This is true postlapsarian morality. Only after the fall out of innocence can the knowing choice of virtue be made: the most terrible, most distressingly erotic thing would be to yield a second time. It might seem, in fact, that Amélie has already done this, immediately after the physical suffering of the first penetration: "soon she felt the stirrings of pleasure, nature claimed its rights, and sweet Amélie shared the duc's ecstasy, expiring at the moment when life was flowing from him" (II, 51–52).[v] But this is the pleasure that (conventionally) follows pain and, as such, the second part of a first event. Only in her experience of sensual *ivresse* does Amélie come to genuine erotic knowledge, and only then does she realize that she has lost her honor (II, 52). She had presumably long been acquainted with the diffuse

[r] Mais ce que je ne puis comprendre, c'est que vous affectiez tant de regrets pour une chose que vous avez faite de si bonne grâce; car, ma chère Amélie, vous n'avez pleuré qu'après.

[s] Eh! pouvais-je pleurer avant, madame? [. . .] savais-je l'affront qui m'était réservé?

[t] de peur qu'un second pas vers le désordre ne [l']y plongeât enfin sans retour

[u] Mon ton ne doit pas changer, madame, puisque mes sentiments ne le sont pas; j'ignore encore comment j'ai commis cette première faute, que cependant je ne cherche pas à atténuer; mais désormais ma conduite prouvera que mon cœur n'était pas coupable; je ne verrai plus le duc, j'y suis résolue.

[v] bientôt elle sentit l'aiguillon du plaisir, la nature exerça ses droits, et la tendre Amélie partagea l'ivresse du duc, qui la vit expirer au moment où il perdait la vie.

pleasures of bodily contact—sometimes called a *douce ivresse* (e.g., II, 50)—but now she reaches the climactic end of her childhood. Having been precipitated into moral adulthood, Amélie has two options that are decidedly less radical than death or honor. She can atone by a life of regret, or she can accept the reasoning of Durancy, who sets out what we might call the "what the heck!" option for fallen virgins. This was an argument put persuasively, if unsuccessfully, to Justine by Rodin's associate Rombeau: "I flung myself prostrate before my torturers, offered them my life, and asked them to preserve my honor. 'But given that you are no longer a virgin,' said Rombeau, 'what difference does it make? You will not be guilty of anything. We are going to violate you as you have been already, and there will not even be the least little sin to weigh on your conscience. You will have been ravished entirely by force'" (*Justine,* III, 123).[w] In Choiseul-Meuse's version of this, Durancy reminds Amélie that she is now a fallen woman and should behave accordingly: "Listen, my dear, I'm going to speak frankly. A young virgin may struggle determinedly, and may hesitate for a long time before yielding. Her virtue, whether sincere or not, makes her attractive, but a girl who has lost her rose only appears ridiculous when she puts on a show of prudery. Yesterday morning, these modest airs made you look utterly charming; today your tone must change because you have changed in yourself" (II, 60).[x] Approximately the same reasoning is used by Ernest, incidentally, after a first infidelity with Durancy: "As she finished saying this, Alexandrine had been flirting anew with her lover. Ernest's infidelity was complete: it was the thing itself, and not the number, that was criminal" (I, 119).[y] Faublas had already had the same kind of uncalculating thought apropos of a certain *marquise:* "what reason was there for not paying her another visit? It only added up to three rendezvous instead of two. How could the crime reside in the number?" (I, 144).[z] What does the

[w] Je me précipitai aux pieds de mes bourreaux, je leur offris ma vie, et leur demandai l'honneur.

Mais dès que tu n'es pas vierge, dit Rombeau, qu'importe? tu ne seras coupable de rien, nous allons te violer comme tu l'as déjà été, et dès lors pas le plus petit péché sur ta conscience; ce sera la force qui t'aura tout ravi.

[x] Tenez, ma bonne amie, je vous le dis franchement, une jeune vierge peut combattre avec fermeté, peut hésiter longtemps à se rendre; sa vertu, sincère ou non, intéresse toujours; mais une fille, après avoir perdu sa rose, n'est que ridicule en affectant de la pruderie. Hier matin, ces airs pudibonds vous allaient à ravir; aujourd'hui, il faut que votre ton change, puisque votre personne est changée.

[y] En achevant ces mots, Alexandrine fit de nouvelles agaceries à son amant; l'infidélité d'Ernest était complète, c'était la chose et non pas le nombre qui faisait son crime.

[z] quel inconvénient de lui faire encore une visite? Cela ne faisait jamais que trois rendez-vous au lieu de deux: le crime était-il dans le nombre?

number matter to them? Is there really any moral difference between one and two, or between two and three? They might as well go round again. After all, the male's erotic story is never so dramatically singular.

The struggle for such ex-virgins as Julie, Justine, and Amélie is partly a numerical one, as they attempt to preserve singularity against a powerful moral (and narrative) tendency affirmed by Sade: "rarely does one stop after the first offense" (*Justine,* III, 32).[a] Justine has her partially healed virginity torn apart by the monks at Sainte-Marie-des-Bois, and Julie soon yields a second time, actually anticipating and desiring her gift: "Oh charming place, happy place, you who in the past witnessed the repression of so many tender looks, and the stifling of so many ardent sighs; you who witnessed the birth and death of my first passion, for the second time you will see it triumph" (*La Nouvelle Héloïse,* 96–97).[b] Amélie resists longer, while continuing to see the duc: "she had finally forgiven the first attack on her, but she insisted that she would not tolerate a second" (*Amélie de Saint-Far,* II, 77).[c] Yet her resistance, with its implicit moral binarism, is being undermined by the gradualism of pleasure: "Amélie thus became used to receiving caresses that she would have found revolting, if the duc had not had the skill to win them from her by slow degrees" (II, 77).[d] Eventually, she does what residual virtue should never allow, yielding to the duc on a second occasion (II, 81). After this, she sees herself as truly fallen, in such a way that a certain form of moral agony is now disqualified: "When Amélie regained her senses, she was in the grip of agony, but she did not dare to give vent to her suffering. She had learned from her sad experience that she must avoid a second sin. Following the first, she could say that she was responsible for the others" (II, 81).[e] This is what proves that the mistake really amounted to a fall, and that there is no turning back—"once you are off the path of virtue, you cannot find a track leading back to it" (II, 81)[f]—

[a] il est rare de s'arrêter après un premier délit.

[b] Lieu charmant, lieu fortuné, qui jadis vit tant réprimer les regards tendres, tant étouffer de soupirs brûlants; toi, qui vis naître et mourir mes premiers feux, pour la seconde fois tu les verras couronner.

[c] elle avait enfin pardonné le premier attentat, mais elle persistait à n'en pas souffrir un second.

[d] Amélie s'accoutuma donc à recevoir des caresses qui l'auraient révoltée, si le duc n'avait eu l'adresse de les obtenir par de lentes gradations.

[e] Amélie, en recouvrant ses sens, fut saisie d'une douleur mortelle, mais elle n'osa pas l'exhaler; instruite par sa triste expérience, elle devait éviter une seconde faute; elle pouvait donc, après la première, dire qu'elle était responsable des autres.

[f] une fois écarté du sentier de la vertu, on ne trouve plus de route qui puisse y ramener.

but it is also what lays to rest the ghost of Lucretia. Henceforth, Amélie accepts her new condition, smuggling her moral grief through times of pleasure: "It would have been absurd to spend each day crying over the pleasures that gave her such delight, or disturb the duc's happiness with pointless regret. So she ceased shedding tears, or at least only cried in secret. The duc, who thought he had overcome her scruples, dated his triumph from that time" (II, 82).[g] Through inner conflict, Amélie achieves not so much maturity, or even richness of character, as a certain kind of beauty that makes her superior, not only to the unrepentant vice of Durancy, but perhaps even, in some undoubtedly erotic sense, to the innocent virgin she once was: "Were it not for her moral weakness, Amélie would have been superior to others of her sex. Yet she might have been more worthy of esteem without being more attractive. Unrepentant vice provokes horror and scorn, as we know, but rueful beauty, weeping bitterly over a fatal mistake, must be a touching sight for any sensitive heart" (II, 139–40).[h] The novel's conclusion, however, requires Amélie to *finir en beauté,* since she cannot sustain indefinitely the mixture of pleasure and grief. The story regresses, so to speak, to the old thematic program, confirming the prediction of the novel's title, avoiding ultimate degradation, and atoning for sin in the heroine's death (II, 140–41).

A rather different reworking of the virginity theme—a more sustained attempt to reclaim it for erotic narrative—occurs in *Thérèse philosophe.* Bois-Laurier, Thérèse's instructor in the tricks of the whore's trade, recounts her own career as a virgin prostitute: "I was a professional libertine, and I am still a virgin" (II, 1).[i] She has a most helpful congenital "defect," a *membrane nerveuse* that blocks her vagina and will not yield even to the most powerful thrusts (II, 2). Others might have had an operation to remedy the problem, but Bois-Laurier turns the problem itself into a narrative solution: "This defect, which appeared likely to put an end to my career in that shameful trade, was in fact my main reason for success" (II, 2–3).[j] She can engage in

[g] Il eût été trop ridicule de pleurer chaque jour les plaisirs dont elle s'enivrait, ou de troubler le bonheur du duc par des regrets superflus. Elle cessa donc de répandre des larmes, ou du moins elle ne les versa plus qu'en secret; le duc, qui croyait avoir vaincu ses scrupules, data son triomphe de ce moment.

[h] Amélie, sans sa faiblesse, l'eût emporté sur le reste de son sexe; mais, plus estimable alors, peut-être eût-elle été moins intéressante: si le vice orgueilleux cause l'horreur et le mépris, la beauté repentante, pleurant avec amertume l'erreur qui lui coûte la vie, doit émouvoir un cœur sensible.

[i] J'ai été une libertine de profession, et je suis encore pucelle.

[j] Ce défaut, qui semblait devoir être l'écueil de ma fortune dans ce honteux métier, en a été au contraire le principal mobile.

preludes to intercourse without fear of pregnancy or disease (II, 15–16). Five hundred men attempt to deflower her over a period of five years, assuming the most varied positions as they do so, without ever breaking through (II, 14). Feminine resistance here is not brittle or vulnerable. It is apparently submissive, but ultimately impenetrable—membranous, rather than armor-plated.

A second novel by Choiseul-Meuse, *Julie, ou J'ai sauvé ma rose* (1807), develops the virginity theme along similar lines, but without freakish anatomy, in a manner best described as tactically erotic. We know from the outset that this story cannot be tragic, since it is told in the first person by a reasonably contented, mature woman—in the manner of *Félicia* or *Illyrine*. In fact, the narrator-heroine's position seems to be defined by her specific refusal of any narrative of disgrace. Although her telling is seen to occur at the conventional time of repentance, she has always acted in such a way as to make repentance unnecessary: "Besides, despite my numerous frolics, I have always behaved in such a way as to forestall repentance; and now that I have reached the age at which people bewail their errors, my wise policy saves me from the stinging pain of remorse" (I, 28).[k] In the beginning, for this Julie as for Rousseau's, there was innocence, but of a kind less fragile than Amélie's: "despite my extreme innocence, I knew that virtue severely forbade certain freedoms, and I was utterly determined never to indulge in them" (I, 42).[l] The very imperfection of Julie's innocence lies in her awareness that there are certain limits to be observed and actively defended, even if she spends part of her youth wondering where these might be: "just what is this last favor that is so heady and so dangerous?" (I, 92).[m] Instead of giving herself up inattentively to social intercourse, as Amélie did, she is concerned to organize the space of her bodily virtue, finding or drawing the boundaries of her own power: "I want to know how far my power extends" (I, 92).[n] From the first, her virtue is measured tactically.

Julie understands early that her virginity is a treasure that must not be given away or plundered, but durably preserved:

> A prodigal son takes only the briefest time to spend the immense fortune amassed by his father, in the company of base relatives, and when he is

[k] D'ailleurs, malgré mes nombreuses folies, je me suis toujours conduite de manière à éviter le repentir; et maintenant que je suis arrivé à l'heure où l'on pleure ses fautes, ma sage politique me sauve des peines cuisantes du remords.

[l] malgré mon extrême innocence, je savais que la vertu défendait sévèrement de certaines libertés que j'étais bien résolue à n'accorder jamais.

[m] quelle est cette dernière faveur si enivrante et si dangereuse?

[n] Je veux savoir jusqu'où s'étend mon pouvoir.

> ruined, becomes the butt of their sarcasm and disdain. In the same way, a woman can listen only to the impulse of her heart, which leads her to make others happy, and fail to value the treasure she possesses. She can let herself be robbed of it by men who, in return for her favors, abandon her in her hour of remorse, and pour scorn on her. (II, 286)[o]

Vigilance, for Julie, does not consist, however, in some forward defense policy, but in a subtle and potentially seductive demarcation of the limit of maximum tolerance. Her virtue is not felt to be a treasure in the old sense, held fast and defended with severity for fear of being sacked and looted. It is rather a kind of narratively erotic *capital,* to be invested wisely in a life of pleasure. In broad terms, it is a matter for her of going down slowly: "I was doubtless born virtuous, and without the seducers who surrounded my childhood, I should always have remained so. It was only by slow gradations and with infinite difficulty that they managed to destroy that precious, rare quality: my virginal modesty" (I, 118).[p] As Julie goes down, she takes with her something of her virginal nature, as a principle governing the slow progress of virtue and vice. Her aunt is an irreproachable model of virtue, but the model is not taken as frozen or statuesque. Julie is content to be influenced by such virtue, and to apply it in her own life as a form of restraint: "She sought in a thousand ways to make me fond of virtue. Her example was more persuasive to me than her words: I listened meekly to her lessons, and they imprinted themselves so deeply on me that they have served ever since, if not to repress my passions, then at least to prevent me from yielding to them completely" (I, 26–27).[q] The strictness inherent in the theme of virginity is in fact tamed by an attentive erotic casuistry. In a manner reminiscent of Justine, Julie is able to note that her virginity, understood most narrowly, is still intact after a life of frivolity: "Regardless of how

[o] Semblables au jeune prodigue qui dépense en un moment, avec de vils parents, l'immense fortune amassée par son père, et devient, dès qu'ils l'ont ruiné, l'objet de leurs sarcasmes et de leurs dédains; telles, dis-je, les femmes, n'écoutant que l'impulsion de leur cœur, qui les porte à faire des heureux, et méconnaissant la valeur du trésor qu'elles possèdent, s'en laissent dépouiller par les hommes qui, pour les payer de ce bienfait, les abandonnent à leurs remords et les comblent de mépris.

[p] Sans doute, j'étais née vertueuse, et sans les séducteurs dont je fus entourée dès mon enfance, je l'aurais toujours été, ce ne fut que par de lentes gradations et avec des peines infinies, que l'on parvint à détruire en moi cette pudeur virginale, si précieuse et si rare.

[q] Elle cherchait par mille moyens, à me faire aimer la vertu; son exemple me persuadait encore mieux que ses paroles; j'écoutais ses leçons avec docilité; elles se gravèrent si fortement dans mon esprit, que depuis elles ont servi, sinon à réprimer mes passions, du moins à m'empêcher de m'y livrer entièrement

frivolous my conduct had been until that time, I remained strongly attached to virtue, and can make bold enough to say that I had never lost touch with it. According to my principles, honor lay only in that precious flower that I had so often been on the verge of losing, and that had become dear to me in keeping with the effort it had cost to preserve" (II, 124).[r] A key aspect of Julie's "daring" is the boldness with which she interprets the virginity theme. The flower becomes more precious because of the zeal with which it is defended, but it is, so to speak, an object to be cultivated, rather than an all-embracing, all-defining condition. Virginity is a narrow point of honor in a broad field of pleasure.[19]

Julie, ou J'ai sauvé ma rose tells of the virgin's project, rather than her destiny. There are no storms or drownings here: the heroine is always able to be the *subject* of virtue, the one who saves her own rose. For this, she undoubtedly requires some good fortune, of a kind that Justine rarely enjoys. There is a moment, for example, when Julie is bound, gagged, and abducted by an enemy of her father, in order to be used as a hostage. Her captor soon learns, however, that Julie's father has no proper love for her and cannot therefore be manipulated in that way (II, 88). As the ostensible villain loses his sense of malevolent purpose, Julie can begin to assert her own, erotic power: "seeing that I was in his power, I thought [. . .] it better to subjugate my master than to irritate him" (II, 89).[s] In another episode, she is in danger of falling, not into Justine's fate, but into that of her Rousseauian namesake, as she falters near the brink of passion. She loses her normal resolve, that is to say, her power, and can only note afterward, with relief, that she has been saved by good fortune: "When I had recovered my composure, I offered up thanks to my star for having preserved me from this most recent danger. It was the first time I had been prepared to yield and, for the first time, an obstacle that was both unforeseen and insurmountable had stopped me at the very edge of the precipice!" (II, 99).[t] "Fortunately," her lover develops a fatal illness,

[r] Quelle qu'ait été jusqu'alors la légèreté de ma conduite, je n'en étais pas moins attachée à la vertu, j'oserais même dire que je ne m'en étais pas écartée, puisque, d'après mes principes, l'honneur ne consistait que dans cette fleur précieuse que j'avais été si souvent sur le point de perdre, et qui m'était devenue chère à proportion de ce qu'elle m'avait coûté.

[s] me voyant en sa puissance, je crus [. . .] qu'il valait mieux subjuguer mon maître que de l'irriter.

[t] Lorsque j'eus recouvré mon sang-froid, je rendis grâces à mon étoile de m'avoir préservée de ce nouveau danger; c'était la première fois que je consentais à me rendre, et pour la première fois, un obstacle aussi imprévu qu'insurmontable m'avait arrêtée sur le bord même du précipice!

drawing Julie, in imagination, into the love-death dreamed of by Rousseau's Saint-Preux. She sees this as a climactic moment of passion—"At that fatal hour, I realized just how much love he had for me. I wanted to follow him to the grave" (II, 187)[u]—but it is the *man* whose death provides narrative relief. The heroine has time to convalesce, and resume her life as an erotic virgin, enhanced in her beauty by the assimilation of grief: "I no longer had the provocative gaiety that disarms opponents through charming conversation. It had been replaced by a sweet melancholy, but that made me all the more attractive" (II, 191).[v]

Julie's pleasure is repeatedly described as a properly narrative one: the delight of successfully conducted intrigue. Initially, she is inclined to avoid risks by the use of simple blocking tactics, feigning a migraine (I, 164–66) or simply changing lovers before the critical moment (I, 167). But such tactics are too radically prophylactic: they provide a degree of satisfaction without any quality of pleasure. Much more exciting and dangerous, much more productive in narrative and erotic terms, is Julie's practice, developed in the novel's second volume, of always saying yes and meaning no: "'I shall be doubly unique,' I said to myself. 'Men can win the ultimate favor from a woman without her ever saying yes, but I shall always refuse it, without ever saying no'" (II, 35).[w] At times, she provokes her would-be seducer to a premature conclusion: "I had never told him that he had to do without the most precious of my favors. But to compensate for this great loss, I increased his other pleasures a hundredfold. Made dizzy often with pleasure, he would lose, through an involuntary sacrifice, the necessary strength to attain further triumphs" (II, 180).[x] Most often, she defines regions of her body, with playful indulgence, as morally peripheral, giving them up gradually to the invader. By contrast with the drastically naked victim one finds in Sade, Julie is actually able to deploy her clothes as a barrier: "I arranged my clothes as best I could so that they could act as ramparts against Auguste's attacks and, in spite of

[u] C'est à cette heure funeste que je connus tout l'amour qu'il avait pour moi; j'aurais voulu pouvoir le suivre au tombeau.

[v] Je n'avais plus cette gaîté piquante qui fait rendre les armes tout en badinant. Une douce mélancolie l'avait remplacée; mais j'en étais plus intéressante.

[w] Je serai doublement unique, me disais-je, car on obtient d'une femme jusqu'à la dernière faveur, sans qu'elle ait jamais dit oui; et moi je refuserai toujours, sans avoir jamais dit non.

[x] Je ne lui avais jamais dit qu'il fallait renoncer à la plus précieuse de mes faveurs; mais pour le dédommager d'une si grande privation, je centuplais ses autres jouissances. Souvent enivré de volupté, il perdait, par un sacrifice involontaire, la force nécessaire pour cueillir de nouveaux lauriers.

his best efforts, he could not rid himself of that awkward barrier" (II, 125).[y]

In this way, the center of virtue is resolutely defended, though quite without any show of severity: "While the attack was lively, so was the defense. The enemy captured the outlying areas, but could not reach the citadel. Keeping faithfully to the plan I had drawn up, I defended myself only in a laughing manner. Every time, a kiss or some tender caress accompanied my refusal, which seemed to be made regretfully" (II, 39).[z] As the male attacks, his thrusts are adroitly parried: they are deflected and deferred from the singular object of his desire. The fall, as predictable outcome, is specifically avoided: "He wanted, so he said, to let me leave only when he had conquered me, but I threatened, if he kept me there any longer, never to come back. He relented, and I went away a thousand times happier than I had been on my way there. My triumph was greater even than I had hoped, and I was right to take pride in it, for I was surely the first woman to come out of that boudoir a virgin" (II, 40).[a] No matter what erotic intensity might have been found in dizzying passion, Julie prefers her tactical victories: "The greatest sensual delights could not have equaled the pleasure I took in defeating the expectations of those who envisaged a triumph over me" (II, 41).[b] Her pleasure is, in a sense, reflexive: it must correspond to the novel's feminine triumph over the oppressive theme of virginity.

Unlike some of her compulsively innocent predecessors, Julie has the benefit of precise instruction. This comes not from her (excessively) virtuous aunt, or from Céline, the (excessively) libertine woman who might have initiated her and in fact finally goes all the way down through degradation to "a death worthy of her life" (II, 242).[c] It comes instead as balanced advice from the man who is her first love, Adolphe. He introduces her to what might be called a postvirginal erotic art.

[y] J'arrangeai de mon mieux mes vêtements pour qu'ils me servissent de remparts contre les entreprises d'Auguste, qui, malgré tous ses efforts, ne put parvenir à se débarrasser de cette barrière incommode.

[z] Si l'attaque fut vive, la défense ne le fut pas moins. L'ennemi s'empara des alentours, mais il ne put parvenir jusqu'à la citadelle. Fidèle au plan que je m'étais tracé, je ne me défendais qu'en riant; et toujours un baiser ou quelque tendre caresse accompagnait le refus que je ne semblais faire qu'à regret.

[a] Il voulait, disait-il, ne me quitter qu'en vainqueur, mais je le menaçai, s'il me retenait encore, de n'y plus revenir. Il céda, et je m'en retournai mille fois plus gaîment que je n'étais venue. Mon triomphe surpassa mon espoir, et j'avais raison de m'en glorifier, car j'étais sûrement la première qui fût sortie vierge de ce boudoir.

[b] Les plus grandes jouissances n'auraient pu égaler le plaisir que je goûtais à déjouer les espérances de ceux qui se flattaient de triompher de moi.

[c] une mort digne de sa vie

The first thing to realize, says Adolphe, is that a strict notion of virtue could never be maintained by one such as Julie: at some point, she would inevitably yield to passion (I, 52–53). She must learn, rather, the art of prolonging pleasures—in the plural—so as to be able to refuse the last favor: "Give in to love, then, without seeking to provide pointless resistance. Enjoy all its small pleasures. Perfect, if you can, the art of prolonging sensual delights, of making them more lively and more dizzying. Bathe in a sea of voluptuousness, but have the courage to maintain enough composure, in the midst of sensual pleasure, to deny the last favor" (I, 53).[d] All the heroine's skill and subtlety go into extending the "first" pleasures to the point where the ultimate one is lost from view: "Happy the one who feels the value of these initial delights, and knows how to defer pleasure in order to make it more zestful: that is the art of enjoying pleasure to the full!" (II, 48).[e] The actual art of delay, as opposed to the discovery of a tactic, is perfected in the company of Camille, a much later partner who accompanies Julie through this stage of development: "Oh! How much progress I made, in the hands of this skillful master, in perfecting the art of pleasure! How Camille delighted in sensuality, how he savored each little caress, and gave full value to everything! He seemed to create new delights and varied everything, including kisses" (II, 47).[f] But the teacher here is episodic: it is Julie's erotic learning that gives the story its purpose, and her skill extends now to the point of deceiving the men who teach her. She often causes Camille to forget his narrowest desire, distracting and diverting him with a host of minor pleasures: "These initial caresses held so much interest for us that Camille often forgot while in my embrace that he had only half succeeded in his aims. But those moments of forgetting only heightened his rapture the more" (II, 49).[g] Another lover, Octave, is inveigled into lesser pleasures, seduced away from the normal seducer's role:

[d] Livre-toi donc à l'amour sans chercher à lui opposer une résistance inutile, goûtes-en tous les plaisirs; perfectionne, si tu peux, l'art d'en prolonger les jouissances, de les rendre plus vives, plus enivrantes; nagez dans une mer de délices, mais ayez le courage de conserver assez de sang-froid, au sein même de la volupté, pour refuser la dernière faveur.

[e] Heureux celui qui sent le prix de ces premières jouissances, qui sait différer le plaisir pour en augmenter la vivacité: c'est là vraiment savoir jouir!

[f] Ah! combien, sous ce maître habile, je me perfectionnai dans l'art de jouir! Combien Camille était voluptueux; comme il savourait jusqu'à la moindre caresse, et que de prix il savait lui donner! Il semblait créer de nouvelles jouissances, il variait tout jusqu'aux baisers.

[g] Ces premières caresses avaient pour nous tant d'attraits, que Camille oubliait souvent dans mes bras qu'il n'était heureux qu'à moitié. Mais ces moments d'oubli ne faisaient que redoubler ses transports.

"He was so utterly in love with me that he finally gave up hoping for the experience that, as he realized, he had desired in vain. In my embrace, he was happy to enjoy pleasures that were full of zest and variety. The idea of more complete bliss no longer interfered with his sensual delights" (II, 192–93).[h] Octave learns a range of sensual delights without experiencing *jouissance,* in the singular, as a definitive event.

By an eminently productive circularity, the heroine becomes more confident of elaborating her diffuse art precisely when she is sure of avoiding the final issue. Each "nonevent" proves to her that she can venture further without losing herself, being forward without being precipitate: "Reassured by my most recent successes, I yielded with less disquiet to the caresses of my charming Camille [. . .]. From moment to moment, I became less reticent. The voice of pleasure began to make itself heard in my heart, and I surrendered myself, in a kind of delirium, to Camille's frolics" (II, 45–46).[i] Success depends in fact on going as far as possible—and doubtless in as many directions as possible—without lapsing into the other state. Adolphe had warned Julie at the beginning of her career that this tactic would only work if it were never recognized as such: "but one thing that is no less necessary, and perhaps no less difficult, is to be so artful in your behavior that no one can guess your secret" (I, 55).[j] Art must hide artfulness, so that Julie's partner will not perceive the underlying resolve to withhold forever the "last favor": "you must use all the guile of which women are capable in order to persuade your lover that you are always on the point of giving in to him" (I, 55).[k] To this purpose, Adolphe calls upon her essential nature in its capacity to invent. Femininity must be exercised to the full as a fertile source of pleasurable distractions and narrative inventions: "fortunately women are richly resourceful, and I could compare with the most inventive of them" (I, 162–63).[l]

[h] Il m'aimait si éperdûment qu'il finit par renoncer à ce que l'expérience lui avait appris qu'il désirait en vain. Heureux de goûter dans mes bras des plaisirs aussi vifs que variés, l'idée d'une félicité plus complète ne vint plus troubler ses jouissances.

[i] Rassurée par mes derniers succès, je me livrai avec moins d'inquiétude aux caresses du charmant Camille [. . .]. A chaque instant je devenais moins farouche; la voix du plaisir commençait à se faire entendre à mon cœur, et je me livrais, avec une espèce de délire, à tous les jeux du folâtre Camille.

[j] mais une chose qui n'est pas moins nécessaire, ni peut-être moins difficile, c'est de mettre assez d'art dans ta conduite pour ne pas laisser pénétrer ton secret.

[k] il faut employer toute l'adresse dont les femmes sont capables, pour persuader à ton amant que tu es toujours à l'instant de te rendre.

[l] heureusement les femmes sont fécondes en ressources, et je ne le cédais jamais à la plus inventive.

One of Julie's great feminine triumphs is with a notorious Don Juan named Versac. This man is a plunderer of women's virtue, the great lover of Marseilles. She brings him under control, however, taking him slowly and playfully through all the preliminary stages. She teaches him the value of these things, reining in his impetuosity and satisfying his desire by allowing him to make a whole series of local "conquests" about her person: "Every little favor I gave him had doubled in price through the momentary resistance I had offered to his desires. Instead of the impetuosity Versac had shown at first, he came to delight in everything I yielded to him, and seemed to pay particular homage to each of his conquests" (II, 207).[m] Despite the sense of seductive urgency that had previously driven him from one yielding woman to another—"Of all men, Versac was the one who would respond most impatiently to being deprived of this" (II, 208)[n]—Versac is now bound to Julie by the quality of erotic activity that she is able to sustain with him. He is bound, it seems, because she is not: "I had not granted him the sole favor that, in my opinion, can actually commit a woman" (II, 274).[o]

At times, even as she narrates her triumph, Julie is subject to a certain nostalgia for the radical program that she has so skillfully avoided. Can the manifold *plaisirs* she has known be measured against the intense *jouissance* of sexual passion? She is generally inclined to think that her choice was the right one, for she may well be "the only woman who can boast of having tasted the pleasures of defeat a thousand times without ever being conquered! I could have known greater rapture, but it would have been briefer and less varied" (I, 46).[p] There are moments, however, when she dreams of that thrillingly conclusive experience she never knew, the "bonheur suprême," the "jouissance unique" (II, 97) that marks the singular intensity of an all-transforming eroticism: "I have known all pleasures, and never known satiety" (II, 283).[q] To choose moral freedom in the way she did was also to commit to a form of enduring ignorance. Now she will never know the heights of passion: "I am beyond the age of

[m] Mes moindres faveurs avaient doublé de prix par la résistance momentanée que j'avais opposée à ses désirs. Au lieu de l'impétuosité que Versac avait montrée d'abord, il savourait avec délices tout ce que je lui abandonnais, et semblait rendre un hommage particulier à chacune de ses conquêtes.

[n] Versac était sans doute de tous les hommes, celui qui supporterait le plus impatiemment cette privation.

[o] Je ne lui avais pas accordé la seule faveur qui, selon moi, puisse lier une femme.

[p] la seule femme qui puisse se vanter d'avoir goûté mille fois les plaisirs d'une défaite et de n'avoir jamais été vaincue! j'aurais pu connaître de plus grandes jouissances, mais elles eussent été plus courtes et moins variées.

[q] J'ai connu tous les plaisirs, et jamais la satiété.

pleasures, and I have never known the most intense of them! I have set aside prejudices and virtues, without ever having a clear idea of those sensual pleasures that are the lot and the justification of those who abandon themselves to their passions!" (I, 45).[r] What we might call Julie's greatest strategic achievement lies in her measuring the value of diffuseness against that of intensity: "I could give up the supreme rapture as long as I had the glory of resistance, but when one is deprived of triumph, one must at least encounter pleasure" (II, 107).[s]

There is some equivocation here with respect to the virginity theme. Adolphe gives to Julie the most serviceable piece of wisdom, but he also points out that this tactical knowledge is conditional upon her maintaining a form of virginal ignorance. The life of many pleasures, says Adolphe, can only be satisfying for one "who has never experienced that ultimate pleasure" (I, 53–54).[t] Effectively then, Julie's choice of an erotic career depends on her assessing the known against the unknown, negotiating available experience against unrevealed mystery. This is, of course, a logical impossibility, and what is presented as reasoned choice might appear, after all, to be mere consolation, the post hoc justification of a lifelong ersatz. There is hesitation about the edges of the triumph.

Julie, ou J'ai sauvé ma rose may be haunted by doubts about the heroine's fundamental option, but it usually manages to affirm the value of sustained erotic play over against the climactic intensity that leads to death: "The prize for voluptuousness should not be given to the one who is endowed with Herculean strength and dispassionately repeats sensual pleasure that kills you, but to the one who knows how to prolong enjoyment" (II, 49).[u] At almost every point, Julie's tactic does endow her with a capacity to manipulate, and it continues effectively to shape the story. Worthy of note, in this regard, is the place given to lesbianism in the novel, precisely because lesbianism will later appear as the central horror—the name of a kind of narrative malady—in *Gamiani* (1833).[20] Quite near the end of her story, Julie is driven to a lesbian encounter for tactical reasons. Having finally

[r] J'ai passé l'âge des plaisirs, et j'en ignore les plus vifs! J'ai mis de côté préjugés et vertus, sans avoir conçu les jouissances qui sont le partage et l'excuse de ceux qui s'abandonnent à leurs passions!

[s] Je pouvais bien renoncer à la félicité suprême lorsque j'avais la gloire de la résistance; mais lorsqu'on est privé du triomphe, il faut au moins trouver le plaisir.

[t] qui n'a jamais joui de ce dernier plaisir

[u] Ce n'est point à celui qui, doué d'une force d'hercule, répète, sans s'émouvoir, une jouissance qui vous tue, que la palme de la volupté doit être donnée, c'est à celui qui sait prolonger le plaisir.

failed to maintain the interest of Versac the Eligible, she fears that he will then turn to her rival, Caroline (II, 224). Now it happens that Caroline is known to have a taste for other women, so that Julie's new seductive task becomes that of binding Caroline to herself: "I determined to try all I knew in order to become the favorite of this latterday Sappho" (II, 225).[v] It all goes extremely well, and Julie is finally able to say: "I had gained my revenge on Versac, and subdued my greatest female enemy. What a triumph!" (II, 241).[w] But lesbianism is more than a simple incident in the plot. It becomes for the heroine an absorbing activity, one in which she seems to lose herself completely: "the light of pleasure shone in our eyes at the same time, and in our dizziness we lost even the memory of our existence" (II, 237–38).[x] This is her greatest triumph. Is it also the fullness of her erotic *Bildung*? Certainly Julie finds pleasure with Caroline far beyond that required by tactical duty: "not only was her sex not an obstacle to my impetuous desires: the novelty of this lively and unusual scene seemed to stimulate them all the more" (II, 264–65).[y] Without fear of any irretrievable slip, she can yield to the urgency of passion. She goes into the heart of mystery, but does so without precipitation, as she is led by her guide through all the steps of pleasure: "Caroline, whose desires no longer knew any bounds, took me through all the gradations of pleasure in order to give me satisfaction. I enjoyed in the one evening the unspeakable delights that I should only have known at the end of a long novitiate, were it not for the extraordinary passion that I inspired in her, and that led her to initiate me without delay into the most secret mysteries" (II, 269–70).[z] At this point, as if to mark the fact that the novel is drawing to an end, Julie actually speaks of attaining the "last" degree: "Caroline caused me to reach the last phase of pleasure" (II, 268).[a] Is this not the unavowed solution to the novel's

[v] Je résolus de mettre tout en œuvre pour être bientôt la favorite de cette moderne Sapho.

[w] Je me vengeais de Versac, et je soumettais ma plus grande ennemie; quel triomphe!

[x] l'éclair du plaisir brille en même temps à nos yeux, et nous perdons, dans l'ivresse qui le suit, jusqu'au souvenir de notre existence.

[y] non seulement son sexe n'était pas un obstacle à mes impétueux désirs; mais la nouveauté de cette scène piquante et bizarre semblait les aiguillonner encore.

[z] Caroline, dont les désirs ne connaissaient plus de frein, me fit passer, pour les satisfaire, par toutes les gradations du plaisir. Je goûtai dans la même soirée les jouissances indicibles que je n'aurais connues qu'après un long noviciat, si la passion extraordinaire que je lui avais inspirée ne l'avait portée à m'initier de suite aux plus secrets mystères.

[a] Caroline me fit atteindre le dernier période du plaisir.

thematic difficulties, the climax without a fall? So rich are these sensual delights that the narrator-heroine attains new heights of lyricism in a stylistic escalation to apostrophe: "Love! [. . .] lend me your burning colors, so that I can give a truthful description of that voluptuous scene" (II, 267–68).[b] These scenes are said to be the most *piquantes,* the most *bizarres,* the most *singulières* of any Julie has known. They are "a fertile source of pleasures and sensual delights, the breadth of which can only be appreciated through experience" (II, 270).[c]

Yet Julie's lesbian adventures are not allowed to be the actual conclusion of her story, whatever their promise in this regard.[21] While other women continue to be attracted to Caroline's secret society—"While they had been drawn in at first by simple curiosity, pleasure had later transformed a frivolous whim into a veritable need" (II, 270)[d]—Julie refuses to own any such "need," be it narrative or libidinal. Having threatened perhaps to choose lesbianism as the ultimate tactic, she pulls back, in her final maturity, to a more conventional, largely unmotivated trivialization of it: "Caroline is still in Marseilles; her taste for women has actually grown stronger over the years. I see little of her now, and I do not need to tell you that there has not been any relationship between us for a long time. Since I had had the courage to give up your sex, my own was not likely to cause me any great regret" (II, 282–83).[e] These words are spoken in a kind of picaresque wisdom, from the point of view of one who has now entered into erotic retirement, but they cannot effectively deny the relevance of lesbianism to the problems posed by the virginity theme. By its represented capacity to endure, it offers a strategic answer to the drastic suddenness of the fall.

By flirting so resourcefully, and for so long, with the dangerous theme of virginity, Choiseul-Meuse's text is constructing a feminine eroticism in narrative. Brutal deflowering, with its tragically destructive consequences, is deferred and deflected into a playful multiplicity of caresses. Measured intensification, marked as it is by numerical relentlessness, is countered by a calculated yielding of erotic terrain

[b] Amour! [. . .] prête-moi tes brûlants crayons, que je décrive avec vérité cette scène voluptueuse.

[c] une source féconde de plaisirs et de voluptés, dont l'expérience seule peut faire concevoir l'étendue

[d] Entraînées d'abord par un mouvement de curiosité, le plaisir avait ensuite transformé une légère fantaisie en un véritable besoin.

[e] Caroline est toujours à Marseille; son goût pour les femmes n'a fait que s'accroître avec les années. Je la vois peu maintenant; je n'ai pas besoin de vous dire que depuis longtemps il n'existe plus aucune liaison entre nous. Après avoir eu le courage de renoncer à votre sexe, le mien devait me coûter peu de regrets.

to the would-be invader. And all this is done by exploiting the equivocation of erotic narrative in its attempts to deal tellingly with virginity. On the home territory of the master pornographers, Julie not only plays for time in order to save her rose, but positively flourishes while so doing. She fashions her pleasure(s) out of resistance.

Chapter 9

On Being Erotically Disposed: Posture and the Modeling of Desire

I began on eroticism by talking about the impossibility of a radical beginning, and have pursued this study by insisting on the classically erotic. I have talked about that which is taken as known while being reworked as tradition. My "pursuit" has, of course, led me, as with any sustained line of questioning, to neglect other avenues of thematic inquiry, some of which might have appeared quite promising. Phenomenological critics of the Geneva school, from whom I rather distanced myself in the introduction, might well have asked: what about desire? Is it not the beginning of eroticism in subjective experience, the primary conception of an erotic object within the space of consciousness? Gaston Bachelard, Georges Poulet, or Jean-Pierre Richard might have begun by asking: what comes first in erotic experience? My response to their likely concern must be that beginnings (of desire or of history) are best understood as a construction of Romantically modernist narratives. Beginnings are associated, as Aristotle could remind us if we needed reminding, with middles (or climaxes) and endings. There is much to say about such narratives—and much that is relevant to a study of erotic literature, as I hope to show in a further volume[1]—but I want to insist for now on the *ongoing* value of a more classical thematics. Without doubt, phenomenology is well suited to the quasi-Romantic reading of Romantic texts. On the open face of virginal innocence, it can read the first flush of nascent desire. Yet to understand desire as radically new in this way, attempting to grasp it as it first appears, is to deny an older and apparently more durable "truth." This truth, more congenial to postmodern ears, is that the beginning of desire cannot be retrieved, that eroticism has always already begun.

Much erotic literature seems committed, as I think I have shown, to the notion that eroticism must be expressly taught. In the most classical writing, instruction is likely to be so formal as to be quite disconcerting for the subjectivist reader. "Is that what the pupils really desire in themselves?" such a reader might ask. Even when the pupil is blessed with a temperamental penchant for rapid learning, the same worries might arise. Is the particular focus of desire appropriate? Are its objects suited to, and fully embraced by, that particular subject? Does the learning process advance in an organic, authentic fashion? For these questions of subjectivity, classical erotic literature appears to have little or no regard: it simply makes them redundant, by constituting erotic behavior as a set of "attitudes." Faced with this tendency, modernists of various kinds can declare classical eroticism to be humanly inadequate or historically immature insofar as it ignores the "natural" spontaneity of desire in favor of a cultural discipline of the body.

The reflexivity that characterizes much erotic literature can be understood in these terms. It marks the canonically literary by phatic self-quotation, as I suggested at the outset, and by elaborating a self-conscious thematics. Often the characters in a story will have the opportunity to peruse sets of drawings or photographs representing erotic poses. More often still, they will hear stories recounting the experiences of others. Most commonly of all, the heroine or hero will be counseled and instructed by veteran exponents of the relevant techniques. In all of these cases, erotic art, typically *mise en abyme,* can be seen to have a double function: it serves to arouse desire, of course, spurring on the narrative, but it also gives a shape, in the most literal sense, to the action that will follow.

Time and again, reference is made not only to a preceding, but to a properly surrounding culture: one that is painted on the walls of the salon or boudoir. Representations of erotic poses thus constitute an environment, although not in the subtle ecological sense we might like to give to that word. Rather, they make up a decor that constrains and sustains erotic activity. Context here must be understood in a remarkably literal way, as a set of figures displaying the relative continuity of erotic art. The courtesan's apartment decorated by Restif's *Paysanne pervertie* (1784) is exemplary in every regard: "I have some paintings. They are not masterpieces, with the exception of my brother's works, which are of great worth, but they describe the passion I want to arouse, in all the attitudes, artistically graduated by me; and each one stands opposite a mirror that reflects it."[2] [a] Ursule's paintings have a precise erotic function, following a desired order, and marking an order of desire. Furthermore, the poses involved are not just presented pictorially; they are re-presented by mirrors. The classical decor figures the looking that is to take place within it. And when, despite the precision and the very closeness of the decor, a certain openness appears within the consecrated erotic space, it does so without any destructive breaking out, through the reflexive play of the decor itself. In Mirabeau's *Ma Conversion* (1783), we read: "one's gaze was lost in the distance formed by the mirrors and stopped only at the lascivious paintings, made more interesting by a thousand varied attitudes."[3] [b] As far as the eye can see, there are paintings and mirrors, and everything that meets the eye is a variation on what has already been seen. In the late but relatively classical *Le Roman de Violette* (1883), the heroine does her learning in a space that has both provocative sculptures—"the mantlepiece [had] ornamentation borrowed from models by Pradier, that charming sculptor, who would have made the statue of virtue itself look provocative"[c]—and endlessly reflecting mirrors: "standing exactly opposite each other, they [the mirrors] multiplied the painted tableaux to infinity" (19–20).[d] What better environment than this for a fifteen-year-old to read *Mademoiselle de Maupin* (60)? The decor "provokes" desire by in-voking a host of positions and actions. Sometimes, such spaces can be understood more philosophically, as in *Le Rideau levé,* where the heroine describes a libertine salon she enters for the first time, noting that its contents are equal to the works of Aretino (402). The moral effect of this room is powerfully atmospheric, in that it helps to liberate the characters from prejudice: "Those paintings, those sculptures, and the wines and liqueurs that we drank removed and dismissed from our minds any shadow of constraint: a voluptuous fever took hold of our senses; Bacchus and Madness were leading the dance" (402–03).[e] But what, one may ask,

[a] J'ai des tableaux: ce ne sont pas des chefs-d'œuvre, à l'exception de ceux de mon frère, qui ont beaucoup de mérite; mais ils peignent la passion que je veux exciter, dans toutes les attitudes, graduées avec art par moi-même; et chacun est en opposition avec une glace qui le reflète.

[b] la vue se perdait dans des lointains formés par les glaces et n'était arrêtée que par des peintures lascives que mille attitudes variées rendaient plus intéressantes.

[c] la cheminée [avait une] garniture [qui] était empruntée à des modèles de Pradier, ce sculpteur charmant, qui eût rendu provocante la statue de la vertu même

[d] parfaitement en face l'une de l'autre, elles multipliaient à l'infini les tableaux qu'ils représentaient.

[e] Ces peintures, ces sculptures, les vins et les liqueurs que nous avions pris écartèrent

is the quality of freedom thus attained, and what form of thoughtful "reflection" is possible when one is framed by such a decor? What kind of seductive constraint banishes all feeling of constraint?

On occasion, the practice of postural modeling may be seen as the obverse of enlightenment, indeed as a practice typical of oriental tyrants. In *La Secte des anandrynes,* there is a story told about the sultan of Turkey:

> They relate that the present great lord, when he wishes to set about producing an heir to the empire, has all his women brought together in a huge room in the seraglio built for the purpose and called for that reason the Room of the Tricks. The walls are painted with frescoes, and all the female figures, which are life-size, represent positions, attitudes, couplings, and the most lascivious groups. The sultanas take off all their clothes, mingle, embrace each other, and, beneath the gaze of the jaded despot, put into practice and diversify these models, which they surpass with their agility. When the sultan's imagination has been ignited by this spectacle, he feels his numb passion come to life again, takes his appointed place in the favorite's bed, and performs wonders. (116)[4] [f]

In this exotic place, the women have no choice but to follow the erotic imperatives inscribed in the Room of the Tricks. But we are not given time to dwell on any experience of constraint, for the passage tells the happy story of the sultan's transformation from a state where he is decadently *blasé* to one in which he can perform procreative miracles. The story has its own internal play of modeling, with the women of the harem being shaped by the wall paintings, and the sultan's desire being in turn modeled by the spectacle of theirs. In the fictive context, the telling of the story functions at yet another level as a model of modeling. When the images are reflected upon by the characters of *La Secte des anandrynes,* the play of reflection allows the exotic to be mirrored in the space of present intimacy, rewritten on the walls of libertine culture.

---

et chassèrent loin de nous jusqu'à l'ombre de la contrainte: le délire voluptueux s'empara de nos sens; Bacchus et la Folie menaient le branle.

[f] On raconte que le grand seigneur actuel, lorsqu'il veut procéder à la formation d'un héritier de l'empire, fait ainsi rassembler toutes ses femmes dans un vaste salon du sérail destiné à cet usage et appelé par cette raison la *pièce des Tours.* Les murs en sont peints à fresque et toutes les figures de femmes, de grandeur naturelle, y représentent les postures, les attitudes, les accouplements et les groupes les plus lascifs. Les sultanes se déshabillent nues, se mêlent, s'entrelacent, réalisent et diversifient, sous les yeux du despote blasé, ces modèles, qu'elles surpassent par leur agilité. Quand, l'imagination bien allumée par ce spectacle, il sent se ranimer ses feux engourdis, il passe dans le lit de la favorite préparée à le recevoir et opère des merveilles.

We should not be content here with merely finding *ars erotica* again, as *ars exotica,* with picking up yet another shard of this scattered, supposedly lost, but still diffusely present paradigm. The narrower and more immediate concern I have here does not concern the extent of such culture, or even its paradigmatic organization, so much as its workings—that is, a kind of thematic desire, even perhaps a desire for the thematic. How is it, I want to ask, that poses come to be adopted by the characters in erotic fiction? What kind of narrative event is constituted by the teaching and modeling of posture? My focus here is not just on erotic art as knowledge, then, but on how knowledge is received. In other words, this chapter and the next will be a study of postural *uptake.* Now to speak in terms of uptake is no doubt to open up the question of whether modeling takes time. Is it properly thought of as a thoroughly efficient form of seduction, with minimal delay between offer and acceptance, or rather as that which preempts the need for seduction? To put it in other, more precisely narrative terms, what quality of delay might there be, if any, in a given erotic narrative, between the prediction of some event, if such it be, and its fulfillment? What quasi-psychological space is filled or "fulfilled" by the accomplishment of an erotic pose?

"None!" say some of the most aggressive critics of erotic literature: the whole process, in their view, is essentially inhuman. Witness Steven Marcus: "The relations between persons set forth in such passages are in fact combinations. They are outlines or blueprints, diagrams of directions or vectors, and they must be read diagrammatically. They are, in other words, sets of abstractions."[5] Bruckner and Finkielkraut say much the same thing. For them, "porn is not obscene: it is abstract and structuralist. That is why it is so unstimulating."[6] [g] Could this be, after all, the long-sought solution of continuity, the quality whose presence or absence allows one to distinguish between high erotic art and base pornography? Clearly not, if so much classical erotic literature is also thoroughly given over to geometrical "abstraction." The fundamental issue, aesthetically and morally, politically and even psychologically, is the value of an "outline" for erotic action. Is it indeed the case that erotic art is inhabited by soulless structuralists? Might it not be that structuralists are better placed to understand the teaching of erotic knowledge because they are not preoccupied with soulful transcendence? When Steven Marcus writes of the "relations between persons" in literature, he may be failing to make room, in his readings

[g] le porno n'est pas obscène, il est abstrait, structuraliste (ce pourquoi il est si peu excitant).

of Victorian erotica, for a different notion of personhood, and notably for something that may be read as the vestige of a classical tradition, showing desire to be itself a kind of discipline.

None of this is meant to deny the ethical point that "modeling" and even "constraint" may well serve on occasion as polite names for violence inflicted on the bodies of others. Quite often in erotic narrative, the shape of a victim's body is imposed and held with no time, no space allowed her. When the preexistent model is imposed mechanically, that is surely a form of rape. The narrator-hero of Restif's *L'Anti-Justine* (1798), he of the kind heart and the inoffensive penis, borrows a mechanical chair that serves to "contain," as the text has it, the unsuspecting woman who sits in it. The chair takes hold of the victim and places her automatically in the optimal position: "Breathless, the pretty neighbor threw herself into the chair. Instantly, she was seized by the arms, one spring lifted up her skirts, and another spread her thighs apart. Another projected her cunt forward, and a third [*sic*] made her vibrate" (497).[h] Similar items of furniture lie in wait for women throughout eighteenth-century libertine stories. There is a *fauteuil à violer* in *Les Amours du chevalier de Faublas* that arouses indignation even in the dashing young hero.[7] Sade, as usual, provides the most elaborate and brutal of such devices. In the monastery at Sainte-Marie-des-Bois, there is a machine that holds victims in place for whipping, sixteen at a time. Its most ferociously useful function is that of stretching and spreading the victims to the absolute limit: "The sixteen girls, even the pregnant one, were attached to a highly ingenious machine: they were tied full-length to it, and a spring was used to spread their legs and thighs at will in addition to bending the upper parts of their bodies right down to ground level" (*La Nouvelle Justine*, VI, 272).[i] As if to outdo all other mechanical contrivances of the sort, this machine has a built-in positional variation: "When they were placed on their bellies, their backs and bottoms were prodigiously elevated [. . .]. When they were placed on their backs, their bellies, in turn, stuck out to bursting point" (VI, 272).[j] Minski the giant has a

[h] La jolie voisine, essoufflée, se jeta sur le diable de fauteuil. Aussitôt elle fut saisie par les bras, un ressort la troussa, et un autre lui écarta les cuisses. Un autre lui fit faire beau con, un troisième [*sic*] la fit osciller.

[i] Les seize filles, et même celle qui était grosse, furent attachées à une machine fort ingénieuse: là, liées tout de leur long, on faisait, au moyen d'un ressort, écarter leurs jambes et leurs cuisses à volonté et courber la partie supérieure de leur corps jusqu'à terre.

[j] Les y plaçait-on sur le ventre: alors, leurs reins et leurs fesses se trouvaient à une prodigieuse élévation [. . .]. Etaient-elles placées sur le dos: le ventre à son tour bombait au point de se crever.

machine for binding, spreading, and offering his victims for sacrifice (see *Histoire de Juliette,* VIII, 601–2). Bandole has a machine that acts vigorously and directly to produce softness, exposure, and plastic "receptiveness" in his victims: "In a specially prepared boudoir, there was a machine on which the woman, spread out and vigorously garroted, presented to the libertine her temple of Venus, to the fullest extent possible. He slipped into her; she did not move" (*La Nouvelle Justine,* VI, 226).[k] This is the point, Andrea Dworkin might say, at which pornography displays its truly manipulative nature: it grabs hold of women's bodies and positions them for rape. That seems incontrovertible, but the value of a detailed study like mine can hardly consist in reiterating such a judgment apropos of each new text. If there is something to be learned here for feminist critique, it must be in observing not just *that* women are raped in these stories, but *how* they come to be raped. I note, in particular, that women's bodies are likely to be violently positioned before being violently penetrated. That is why erotic modeling, for its complexity, deserves close attention, even if it is ultimately to be condemned.

Modeling, as ongoing cultural constraint, seems to entail an understanding of erotic learning as discipline, thus making a place for the mechanical in the heart of a domain often thought of as the privileged site of human spontaneity. Steven Marcus says, quite rightly, that "psychology is the mortal enemy of pornography" (22–23), but he neglects to add that pornography may well be the mortal enemy of psychology as he understands it. Let us consider the example of *Thérèse philosophe,* which is rewarding for the "philosophical" attention it pays to the whole question of modeling. The narrator-heroine, we remember, is a gifted learner, and an especially gifted imitator, noteworthy for her speed on the uptake. Here is an account of what happens when she first sees two people having sex: "Always the perfect imitator of whatever I saw, without pausing to think for a moment of my confessor's interdiction, I too pushed my finger inside. The slight pain I felt did not stop me from going on: I pushed as hard as I could, and reached the high point of sensual pleasure" (I, 134–35 emphasis).[l] Does she actually *decide* to copy the example that is before her? There is hardly time for that, since she does not take even an instant to

[k] Dans un boudoir préparé à cet effet, se trouvait une machine sur laquelle la femme, mollement étendue et vigoureusement garrottée, présentait à ce libertin le temple de Vénus au dernier degré possible; il enfilait; on ne bougeait pas.

[l] Toujours parfaite imitatrice de ce que je voyais, sans réfléchir un instant à la défense de mon Directeur, j'enfonçai mon doigt à mon tour; une légère douleur que je ressentis, ne m'arrêta pas, je poussai de toute ma force, et je parvins au comble de la volupté.

reflect: "It would be pointless, my dear Comte, for me to try to tell you what I was thinking of then: I felt nothing, because I felt too much. I found myself mechanically aping what I could see; my hand played the role of the priest's hand, and I imitated all of my friend's movements" (I, 134).[m] What went through her head is apparently unknown and unknowable. It is striking that she immediately found herself becoming an ape, in the sense that she aped what she saw. The power of desire is presumably such at this point that the young woman lapses spontaneously into bestially natural imitation. It is the mechanically natural that determines the alacrity of her response and makes her such a likely heroine for erotic narrative. Laure, the heroine of *Le Rideau levé,* appears more thoughtful than Thérèse, as she watches another woman masturbating: "Animated by this sight and instructed by the example, I imitated on my own [cavity] the movements I saw. I experienced a sensation unknown to me" (324).[n] She is, as we see, both *instruite* by the example and somehow compelled (*animée*) by it. The greatest heroines of erotic narrative, like Thérèse and Laure, appear to be those for whom every position serves as a model. They are not exactly like balls of *pâte à modeler,* as Nancy Huston claims in her critique of pornography:[8] it would be more appropriate to say that every model represented to them serves to trigger a desire to imitate, and an imitation of desire.

We must remember, of course, to talk of the natural/mechanical without launching into some anachronistic account of modeling as "behavior." The Desmond Morris approach would leave us with apes everywhere,[9] and no sense of the cultural dimension of erotic discipline. In that perspective, erotic art as such could only be denied or ignored, and its studied diversity recuperated as natural experiment or biologically driven spontaneity. What *Thérèse philosophe* proclaims is that postural modeling is a sustaining affirmation of erotic culture, for the heroine is both sexually aroused and called to "duty" by the sight of a group of paintings:

> With my imagination excited by the attitudes represented there, I pushed away the sheets and blanket and, without stopping to think whether my bedroom door was properly shut, I took it as my duty to imitate all the

[m] J'entreprendrais inutilement, mon cher Comte, de vous dire ce que je pensais alors: je ne sentais rien pour trop sentir. Je devins machinalement le singe de ce que je voyais; ma main faisait l'office de celle de l'Abbé; j'imitais tous les mouvements de mon amie.

[n] Animée par cette vue, instruite par l'exemple, j'imitai sur la mienne [la fente] les mouvements que je voyais. J'éprouvais une sensation qui m'était inconnue.

> postures I could see. Each figure inspired in me the feeling that the painter had imparted to it. Two athletes, who were on the left-hand side of the painting of the *Celebration of Priapus,* delighted and thrilled me by the conformity of taste between the small woman and myself. (II, 78–79)°

We are left to wonder about the *conformité de goût* that Thérèse finds between herself and the woman represented, for this similarity, this reflexive symmetry, is what allows the cultural to be natural, and the mechanical to be spontaneous. By a happy accident that occurs quite reliably in this type of narrative, youthful, "individual" desire is no more, but no less, than libertine, "social" taste. Indeed, one might well demonstrate a less anachronistic understanding of classical modeling by calling it *conformité de/du goût.*[10] What I hope to do here, however, is to go on working carefully between modern, more psychological notions of responsiveness and classical ones. I do not wish to be drawn into the dark mystery hinted at by Klossowski when he mentions the *mystérieuse conformité* of desired image and encountered one in *Le Bain de Diane.*[11] It will suffice for my purposes to examine the function of modeling, or rather the way in which this function delineates and exploits a thematic space. There is a particular place for modeling in erotic narrative—a place it is called upon to have and to hold as the marriage of constraint and desire, of force and seduction, of the mechanical and the natural. And the difficulty for modern readers of a humanist persuasion is to come to terms with this psychology of convenience.

If imitation were no more than the mechanical play of an erotic nature, modeling would hardly count as any sort of skill. *Conformité* would simply be a fact, mysterious or otherwise, and not an art. There would be no delay whatsoever, no discrepancy between the call and the response, no room for uptake. Yet we find in erotic fiction an enduring concern with accuracy. In *La Secte des anandrynes,* Mlle Sapho, in her first embrace with Mme Furiel, is sent back to the pictorial model in order to pay closer attention:

> Without uttering a word, filled with gratitude, I threw my arms around her neck and embraced her. "Oh! you foolish little thing! That is not

° L'imagination échauffée par les attitudes qui y étaient représentées, je me débarrassai de draps et de couverture; et sans réfléchir si la porte de ma chambre était bien fermée, je me mis en devoir d'imiter toutes les postures que je voyais. Chaque figure m'inspirait le sentiment que le Peintre y avait donné. Deux athlètes, qui étaient à la partie gauche du Tableau des *Fêtes de Priape,* m'enchantaient, me transportaient, par la conformité du goût de la petite femme au mien.

how it's done. Look at those two doves nuzzling amorously." As she said this, she made me look up to the arch above the niche where we were, with its ornamentation of floral sculpture. There, indeed, hung that lascivious couple, the symbol of tribadism. "Let us follow their charming example." And so saying, she slipped her tongue into my mouth. (24)[p]

The teacher, in this instance, seems to be the most actively affectionate of pedagogues, but the fundamental requirement is the same as with Sade's libertine martinets, who usually give their models in words. In both cases, in all cases, the pupil/victim must get it right. In Sade's fiction, nothing is more reprehensible than an inappropriate "attitude" on the part of the victim. Any fumbling or hesitation, any delay in assuming the pose are likely to provoke a display of impatient severity. In one of the stories narrated by Duclos in *Les Cent Vingt Journées de Sodome,* we are told how she herself, as a young prostitute, makes the mistake of facing the wrong way. She is rebuked for not covering her breasts, and thoroughly abused when she turns to face the client in order to apologize: "Hastening to cover them over, I approached him to beg his pardon, but seeing that I was about to show my front by the attitude I was going to adopt, he lost his temper a second time: 'But for God's sake! Can't you stay put?' he said, seizing my hips and turning me so that only my ass was visible to him. 'Stay that way, blast you! I don't care for your cunt any more than I do for your breasts: all that is needed here is your ass.' " (I, 162).[q]

We can recognize this narrow exigency, on the part of dominant libertines, as tyranny in the boudoir, the politics of intimacy exemplified most fully in Sade. Certain technical problems of position can be solved in a predictable way, by taking hold of the victim and forcing her into place (see, e.g., I, 132 and 160). High-precision work of the kind favored at Silling may simply require professional help. When, for example, the duc wishes to execute a tableau that has just been described, his great virility poses a problem. How is it to be done?

She [the victim] was placed in the attitude Duclos had just described, and the duc announced that he was going to discharge. But how was it

[p] Sans proférer une parole et pénétrée de reconnaissance, je me jette à son col et l'embrasse. "Oh! mais, petite imbécile, ce n'est pas comme cela qu'on s'y prend: voyez ces colombes qui se becquètent amoureusement": elle me fait en même temps lever les yeux vers le cintre de la niche où nous étions, garni d'une guirlande de fleurs en sculpture, où était, en effet, suspendue cette couple lascive, symbole de la tribaderie. "Suivons un si charmant exemple." Et en même temps elle me darde sa langue dans la bouche.

[q] Et m'empressant de les couvrir je m'approchai de lui comme pour lui demander

> going to be done? What Duclos had just related had been performed by a man incapable of an erection, and the discharge of his flabby prick could be directed wherever he wished. Such was not the case here: the fear-inspiring head of the duc's member had not the least inclination to lower the menacing stare whereby it threatened heaven above; it appeared necessary to find some way of placing the child above him. No one knew what to do, and the more obstacles were encountered, the more the duc fumed and blasphemed in his rage. Desgranges finally came to the rescue; nothing that pertained to libertinage was unknown to that old witch. She took hold of the child and placed her so skillfully upon her knees that, whatever the stance the duc might adopt, the end of his prick was bound to brush against her vagina. (I, 119)[r]

The old pimps, we see, do not just procure victims: their skilled labor helps to engineer positions in such a way that the master continues to enjoy some freedom of action.

There is more to recognize in Sade, however, than acts of violence, no matter how monstrous, that bring the victim to the master. What must also be seen is that the master's "imagination" does not simply exist as a dark and unpredictable source of capriciously new demands. His desire is apparently shaped and elaborated with the same punctiliousness as the body of his pupil. Throughout *Les Cent Vingt Journées*, for example, we see erotic modeling at work in the very particular kinds of self-discipline developed by the four *amis*. For it is not the case, of course, that the storytellers simply recount "passions" until the one hundred twenty days are used up. They rehearse in order four sets (and numerous subsets) of erotic activity, following as they do so an order agreed to beforehand, in the pact that brings the *amis* together at Silling. Yet even to put it this way is somewhat misleading, for there is no acknowledgment in the novel that the founding agree-

---

excuse, mais voyant que je lui montrais le devant par l'attitude que j'allais prendre, il s'emporte encore une fois: "Eh! restez donc comme on vous met, sacredieu, dit-il, en saisissant mes hanches et me replaçant de manière à ne lui représenter que le cul, restez comme cela, morbleu! On ne veut pas plus de votre con que de votre gorge: on n'a besoin ici que de votre cul."

[r] On la place dans l'attitude que Duclos venait de dépeindre, et le duc annonce qu'il va décharger. Mais comment faire? Ce que venait de raconter Duclos était exécuté par un homme qui ne bandait pas, et la décharge de son vit flasque pouvait se diriger où il voulait. Ce n'était plus le même ici: la tête menaçante du duc ne voulait pas se détourner du ciel qu'elle avait l'air de menacer; il aurait fallu pour ainsi dire placer l'enfant au-dessus. On ne savait comment s'y prendre, et cependant plus se trouvaient d'obstacles, plus le duc irrité sacrait et blasphémait. Enfin la Desgranges vint au secours. Rien de ce qui tenait au libertinage n'était inconnu à cette vieille sorcière. Elle saisit l'enfant et la plaça si adroitement sur ses genoux que, de quelque manière que se tînt le duc, le bout de son vit effleurait le vagin.

ment might be a chance "coming together" of eccentrics: it is, we are told, compellingly logical, and everything is done to shut out a sense of the whimsical or the arbitrary.

The "logic" of masterly desire at work in *Les Cent Vingt Journées* depends just as much on accurate modeling, and precise reflexivity, as does the training of pupils/victims. When Duclos begins to tell her stories, she has to be reminded on more than one occasion to pay close attention to detail if the *amis* are to respond. This is not, it should be quite clear, some kind of appeal to realism. To understand it thus would surely be anachronistic. It is rather a demand for the precise nuance, be it postural or material. Duclos, as storyteller, is being called on to get it right. After Curval has interrupted one of the early stories to say that he does not understand, Duclos adds significant detail, to the satisfaction of all: "'That's it, Duclos,' said Durcet, 'the president was right; I could not visualize a thing on the basis of your first telling, but now I can see how your man works'" (I, 97).[s] While Curval might have "failed" to understand, that was hardly a personal, psychological failure. It merely demonstrated the inadequacy of Duclos's telling, her failure to conform to a pattern that can be relied on to arouse the audience. She learns quickly enough, in fact, although a subsequent incident reminds her of the need for continuing narrative discipline. Curval simply requires to check a previously unspecified detail, and when he has done so declares: "Ah! Like that I can grasp it; but otherwise, I could hardly have understood at all" (I, 148).[t] What does it mean to *concevoir* or *figurer* the "passion" that has just been described, if not to imagine according to the given model and to know how to be aroused by it? When Curval says, as he does repeatedly, "Je conçois cela," this is an immediate prelude to requiring of those around and beneath him that they imitate, with him, what has just been narrated. When the storyteller gets it right, Curval is able to "get it," in the sense that he will be able instantly to desire according to the model, and imitate the model in his display of desire.[12]

Curval's "reflexibility"—his agility of desire—is remarkable even by the standards of his fellow libertines. Rather like the gifted junior female of *Thérèse philosophe*, but in the functionally opposite position of senior male, he shows himself to be a subtle, responsive imitator. To his quick sense of accuracy in the model corresponds the alacrity of his response. At times, there may be doubt as to whether the passion

[s] C'est cela, Duclos, dit Durcet, le président avait raison; je ne pouvais me rien figurer au premier récit, et je conçois votre homme à présent.

[t] Ah! comme cela je le conçois, mais je ne l'entendais guère autrement.

just recounted is fully able to be comprehended within libertine desire, but Curval always rises to the occasion, so to speak, responding with an expression of desire. Often he simply says, "Je conçois cela," or with infinitesimal delay, "Mais je conçois cela" (see, e.g., I, 194). At other times, he is challenged by his colleagues to respond. Durcet, for example, puts this question to him: "Now there's a quaint taste. Well, Curval, can you grasp that one?"[u] But the reply is unproblematic—"'Perfectly well,' said Curval" (I, 306)[v]—such is the swiftness and versatility of his desire. When the others reach the limit of their capacity to respond, Curval keeps on desiring: "'I knew that particular man,' said Curval. 'His existence and his tastes are as real as anything in the world.' 'Be that as it may,' said the bishop, 'I know something just as certain, and that is that I won't imitate him.' 'And why not, pray tell?' said Curval. 'I am convinced that it could produce a discharge.'" (I, 168).[w]

Curval's erotic character is precisely a certain absence of "character" in the modern, psychological sense. It is a capacity to mimic: "Curval [. . .] never heard anything that he did not desire to do" (I, 186).[x] To risk a kind of anachronism, his will to power, as erotic tyrant, is nourished and sustained by the most precise power to will. Within the group of the four *amis,* he is best thought of as the most accomplished modeler, rather than the most natural mimic. We must suppose that, in such "characters" at least, the "I" that conceives the particular *goût,* or the subject of an erotic passion, is the site of desire, and not its origin. The French reflexive verb does its reflecting admirably, as Durcet says: "All those excesses are perfectly conceivable [*se conçoivent*]" (I, 297).[y] And when Durcet exults at the identification/recognition of a particular nuance, declaring "that is how it must be done" (I, 197),[z] he bespeaks an essential truth of classical erotic modeling: the reflexive circularity linking the *il faut* of convention and conformity to the *il faut* of compelling desire. For the Sadian libertine, the capacity to understand all desires is the product of a lifelong discipline; "'I can understand that very well,' said Durcet. 'One needs only to be jaded to understand all these infamies. Sated libertines are inspired to execute

[u] Voilà un plaisant goût. Eh bien! Curval, le conçois-tu, celui-là?

[v] A merveille, dit Curval.

[w] "J'ai connu cet homme-là, dit Curval, son existence et ses goûts sont la chose du monde la plus sûre." "Soit, dit l'évêque, mais ce que je connais d'aussi certain que votre homme c'est que je ne l'imiterai pas." "Et d'où vient? dit Curval. Je suis persuadé que ça peut produire une décharge."

[x] Curval [. . .] n'entendait jamais rien qu'il n'eût envie de le faire.

[y] Tous ces excès-là se conçoivent.

[z] voilà comme il le faut

them unhesitatingly'" (I, 151).[a] The particularity of this discipline is simply that it involves a bodily commitment to the energetic and systematic practice of "excess."

Worth noting, in passing, is the rhetorical tension produced within *Les Cent Vingt Journées* by the practice of modeling. An oft-quoted invocation in the novel invites the reader to choose freely from a sumptuous buffet: "This is the story of a magnificent banquet in which six hundred different dishes offer themselves to your appetite. Are you going to eat them all? No, surely not, but this prodigious number extends the bounds of your choice" (I, 79).[b] We can readily see why this is a favored quotation for modernist readings of Sade, such as Philippe Roger's early essay. For Roger and others, this invitation "revolutionizes" the reader's role, leaving behind such banal, such "classical" concerns as the imitation of models:

> What is at stake for Sade, in going beyond pictorial description, is the entry of the reader's body onto this stage. The textual arrangement is conceived so as to allow the reader's desire to break in. The reader is the one who is invited to debauchery, and this is not done in a banal way, by proposing models, by urging him to copy in the familiar manner of erotic stories. Rather, this is an innovation that radically changes the classical relationship between book and reader, through the breaches Sade makes in his text, allowing the reader's body actually to invade the textual fortress.[13] [c]

My difficulty with such an enthusiastically modernist reading of *Les Cent Vingt Journées* is that it seems not to see how rhetorically defensive, how seductively duplicitous Sade's early invitation might be. The readerly freedom supposed by this appeal stands in contrast to the forms of disciplined erotic response inscribed thematically in the text. I have already tried to show in an earlier chapter that this is the "story" of

[a] Moi, je comprends tout cela, dit Durcet. Il ne faut qu'être blasé pour entendre toutes ces infamies-là; la satiété les inspire au libertinage, qui les fait exécuter sur-le-champ.

[b] C'est ici l'histoire d'un magnifique repas où six cents plats divers s'offrent à ton appétit. Les manges-tu tous? Non, sans doute, mais ce nombre prodigieux étend les bornes de ton choix.

[c] L'enjeu, pour Sade, d'un dépassement de la peinture, c'est l'entrée du corps du lecteur dans cette scène; le dispositif textuel est conçu pour permettre l'irruption dans son jeu du désir du lecteur. C'est bien à lui que s'adresse l'invitation à la débauche. Et cela, non pas, très banalement, en proposant des modèles, par ces incitations à la copie familières aux récits érotiques. Mais, en une innovation qui bouleverse le rapport classique du lecteur au livre, par les brèches que Sade ménage dans son texte pour que ce corps du lecteur investisse réellement la forteresse textuelle.

a meal, as the text says, and not simply a meal. The smorgasbord, for reasons of narrative successivity, tends to become a ceremonious *table d'hôte*. More to the point here, however, is that the passions recounted are presented as recipes. No one browses or samples at Silling. No one takes any of the dishes home. And absolutely no one "breaks into" the castle. Breaking in, in such stories as *Gamiani* (1833) or *L'Ecole des biches* (1868), becomes almost a cliché of erotic narrative. But not in Sade: fictions of eager self-service are thoroughly inappropriate in his case. It does not suffice even, within the story, that each taste should be merely repeatable in principle as recipe: each one must be experienced as a "passion," in the etymological sense, taken up and rehearsed by the audience. *Il le faut.* To pick through the novel's offerings, in the manner of the dilettante reader disingenuously supposed by the introduction, is in fact to refuse to be modeled by the text, thereby denying the form of understanding enacted in and exacted from the characters.

After all, understanding as modeling is a form of doing. In a world where the most general, philosophical forms of understanding seem hard to attain, what is left if not the erotic? "'Oh! What an enigma man is!' said the duc. 'Yes he is, my friend,' said Curval. 'That is what led a very witty individual to say that it is better to fuck a man than to understand him.'" (I, 299).[d] Curval might well have added, to articulate fully the hermeneutic discipline inscribed in *Les Cent Vingt Journées,* that for him at Silling, the difference between *comprendre* and *foutre* was minimal. He cannot hear (*entendre*) a passion without conceiving it, and he cannot conceive it without carrying it out, discharging his own *foutre* as he does so. This is how the libertine subject takes up pleasure as an attitude. Even the master can be the patient, if not the victim, of mechanical furniture compelling him to pleasure. Clairwil tries out a wondrous sofa in *Histoire de Juliette:* "'I do not believe,' said Clairwil as she settled down onto the seat quite naked, 'that it is possible to invent anything more extraordinarily lubricious. This position alone is arousing me . . . I am discharging just while taking my place here'" (IX, 373).[e] Her role, like that of Curval, is to *s'adapter:* to fit pleasurably into the pleasure that awaits her. "Sade se moque du désir," says Jean Gillibert, suggesting that the object of desire can only be unbearably

[d] "Oh! quelle énigme que l'homme!" dit le duc. "Oui, mon ami," dit Curval. "Et voilà ce qui a fait dire à un homme de beaucoup d'esprit qu'il valait mieux le foutre que de le comprendre."

[e] Je ne crois pas, dit Clairwil en s'adaptant bien nue sur ce siège, qu'il soit possible d'inventer rien de plus extraordinairement lubrique; cette seule position m'irrite. . . je décharge rien qu'en me plaçant.

deferred.[14] But modeling is what allows both object and subject to be disciplined. The process at its most developed ensures fully efficient responsiveness, whereby both desire and its objects are available on call, without hesitation or delay—or rather, with such precision and speed of delivery that the delay is almost imperceptible.

Classical modeling is able to be executed as fully as it is at Silling precisely because of the remarkably convenient arrangement of masters and victims. Indeed, to put it this way is a kind of (reflexive) tautology: modeling *is* an exercise in con-venience, in coming together. It practices what we might call an occasional eroticism—in the sense of occasional poetry—achieving and retrieving desire precisely where and when it is appropriate. It is, so to speak, a performance of desire. It is also, of course, a celebration of fortune, both of the wealth that makes possible such elaborate preparations, and of the good fortune whereby the four libertines are able to be friends in a quite particular Sadian sense. In the beginning, long before the action of *Les Cent Vingt Journées,* they had been brought together by their *conformité:* "For more than six years, these four libertines, united by the similarity [*conformité*] of their wealth and tastes, had been thinking of ways to strengthen their ties by means of alliances in which debauchery played a far greater role than any of the other motives that generally serve as a basis for such bonds. What they arranged was as follows" (I, 19–20).[f] The action of the novel is able to develop, then, because of this *con-formité,* but ongoing convergence is a key part of the action itself. The characters in this erotic narrative are shaped together.

There is doubtless, as Leo Bersani and Ulysse Dutoit suggest, a recognizable psychology of what I call *conformité* at work in what they call "mimetic sexuality."[15] Curval makes some striking statements which do seem to invite their kind of analysis, as when he says: "There's nothing that makes me discharge like a discharge" (I, 195).[g] Antonin, in *La Nouvelle Justine,* even declares a kind of libidinous allegiance to Ambroise: "I am terribly fond of Ambroise's mind [. . .]. For a long time now, [. . .] all my discharges have come from that fellow's ideas" (VII, 64).[h] The *narrative* significance of *conformité,* however, must not simply be ground up in the mill of a modern psychology. Narrative

[f] Depuis plus de six ans, ces quatre libertins, qu'unissait une conformité de richesses et de goûts, avaient imaginé de resserrer leurs liens par des alliances où la débauche avait bien plus de part qu'aucun des autres motifs qui fondent ordinairement ces liens; et voici quels avaient été leurs arrangements.

[g] Je ne connais rien qui fasse décharger comme une décharge.

[h] J'aime à la folie la tête d'Ambroise [. . .]. Il y a longtemps [. . .] que je ne décharge qu'après les idées de ce bougre-là.

conformité, understood simply enough, in a determinedly nonpsychological way, is that which "favors" a certain kind of action at a particular point in the story. "Fortune [. . .] favors all vices," we are told in *Les Cent Vingt Journées* (I, 25);[i] being with one's fellows "favors" emulation and display; having the victims line up and bend over favors the analytical comparison of bottoms (I, 333). In fact, erotic narrative continually has occasion to celebrate the remarkable postural convenience that libertines almost seem to deserve, such is the vigilance and the promptness of their desire. Time and again we read, as in *Tableaux des mœurs du temps,* "look . . . I could not be any better placed for you . . . " (81).[j] Or in *Histoire de Juliette:* "In this attitude, the victim presents in the most advantageous position the narrow, delicate part of her body in which the sword is to penetrate" (VIII, 134).[k] No position, we are told regularly, could be more superbly opportune: "Never was a tableau placed in such a favorable light, in view of my position" (*Thérèse philosophe,* 133).[l] At the formal meeting points of erotic narrative, mingled with the exclamations of pleasure, we can expect to hear cries of wonder that the objects of desire should be so accessible. Even at the conjuncture of Sadian violence, we find the same, oddly naïve delight that what was made to happen should indeed have happened so well: "Two servants came up to hold Sophie's legs and, had it been time to deflower her, never could she have displayed it to better advantage" (I, 119–20).[m] Really, things could hardly have turned out, or turned up, or been made to protrude better.[16]

It happens then that, when desire appears, it never does so inappropriately. Early in *Les Cent Vingt Journées,* we are told that the duc made an offer to Durcet whereby each would marry the other's daughter. This might, in another context, have appeared as a dastardly plot, or at least as a shameful avowal. As it happens—and this is always the way it happens in *Les Cent Vingt Journées*—Durcet is delighted to find that his friend's desires are the same as his: "Durcet, delighted by an overture that put him in a position where he could confess the feelings he too had conceived for Adélaïde, the president's daughter, accepted the duc as his son-in-law, provided he might become Curval's" (I, 20).[n]

[i] La fortune [. . .] favorise tous les vices.

[j] tiens. . . je ne peux pas mieux me présenter. . .

[k] En cette attitude, la victime présente dans la plus belle position l'étroite et délicate partie de son corps où doit pénétrer le glaive.

[l] Jamais tableau ne fut placé dans un jour [aussi] avantageux, eu égard à ma position.

[m] Deux servantes viennent contenir les jambes de l'enfant, et, eût-elle dû être dépucelée, jamais elle ne l'eût présenté plus beau.

[n] [Durcet,] enchanté d'une ouverture qui le mettait à même d'avouer les sentiments

Far from being put in an embarrassing position, the duc finds himself in just the right one. *Conformité* of the characters is what guarantees that avowal will never lead to exposure or betrayal. Confession is no more than a timely confirmation of already-shared desire.

The mounting erotic intensity so compellingly displayed in *Les Cent Vingt Journées* can be seen, from the point of view of the principal characters, as a *conformité* of rhythm. They begin with a shared program, but depend on continuing discipline in order to stay in time. Curval, especially, appears quite often to be straining at the leash, eager to move on to more vigorous pursuits. Yet he allows himself to practice restraint, being called back into line by his companions. At one point, he expresses the keen desire to "pop someone's virginity,"[o] but the other three argue that "since they too had equally powerful urges to break those laws, yet submitted to them all the same, he should imitate them, at least to indulge his comrades [*par complaisance*]" (I, 299).[p] Through the requirement to *se com-plaire,* the duty to imitate holds the narrative at the right level of intensity: it might be thought of as the characters' contribution to the narrative order. The opposite attitude, alluded to in the text, would appear to be unthinking *égarement* or even wild *abandon*—something yielded to by the duc in his youth: "From the time of his tender youth, the duc had abandoned himself unrestrainedly to the most shameful extravagances, and the most extraordinary ones" (I, 27).[q] Here and now, in the fictive present, the duc has learned to wear the bridle of discipline. He is becoming a model libertine. Throughout the story, it will still be necessary for him and his colleagues to respect the temporal order shaping the buildup of desire. Occasionally, as we have seen, they fail to do this accurately, and that is precisely the point at which, once again, modeling has to be mentioned explicitly. It can be the storyteller's role, at such moments, to call them to order, just as they had previously done to her in requesting further detail. Here is a rebuke delivered with ceremony by Duclos, reminding the friends that what they have just done is out of place:

> "Since these gentlemen are so fond of that kind of amusement," said our storyteller, "I greatly regret the fact that they were unable to restrain

qu'il avait également conçus pour Adélaïde, fille du président, accepta le duc pour son gendre aux conditions qu'il deviendrait celui de Curval.

[o] faire sauter un pucelage

[p] puisque eux, qui avaient pour le moins autant d'envie d'enfreindre ces lois, s'y soumettaient cependant, il devait les imiter au moins par complaisance.

[q] Le duc, dès sa plus tendre jeunesse, s'était abandonné sans frein aux égarements les plus honteux et les plus extraordinaires.

> their enthusiasm for a moment longer, for the effect of what I still have to relate to you this evening would, it seems to me, have come at a better time. Precisely what the honorable president declared to be lacking for the perfection of the passion I have just described was found word for word in the one that follows. I very much regret that he did not give me the time to finish." (I, 159)[r]

If the eroticism of narrative is to work properly, the participants cannot afford to be in the wrong "place" at the wrong time. They, too, must get it right.

Sadian modeling, which often does without the pictorial, is an exercise in the power of words. Texts like *Les Cent Vingt Journées* and *La Philosophie dans le boudoir* would provide a valuable corpus for a pragmatics of the fictive command. Orders are not merely given by the masters in response to, and as part of the program: they are actually recycled, one might say, distributed from one body of servants/victims to another, as each master echoes and conceives another's desire: "'Let it be done in the required manner,' said the Bishop. 'Come here, Rosette; you heard the order given to Fanny; do the same thing as she.' 'May the same order apply to you,' said Durcet to Hébé, who responded to his call. 'One must go with the fashion,' said Curval" (I, 224).[s] Many times, the command is hardly necessary, being foreshadowed and almost preempted by the convenient presentation of erotic opportunity. To verbs like *commander* and *ordonner* correspond in happy symmetry such other verbs as *offrir* and *présenter*, notably in sentences of the type:

	{offre}	{le cul}		{parfait}	{qui soit}
N	{ }	{ }	le plus	{ }	{ }
	{présente}	{le con}		{délicieux}	{du monde}

This is the domain of the well-shaped, well-positioned, thoroughly *apposite* orifice.

[r] Puisque ces messieurs aiment tant ces drôleries-là, dit notre historienne, je suis fâchée qu'ils n'aient pas encore un instant retenu leur enthousiasme, et l'effet en eût été mieux placé, ce me semble, après ce que j'ai encore à vous raconter ce soir. Ce que M. le président a prétendu qu'il manquait pour perfectionner la passion que je viens de conter se retrouvait mot à mot dans celle qui suivait. Je suis fâchée qu'il ne m'ait pas donné le temps d'achever.

[s] "Soit fait ainsi qu'il est requis," dit l'évêque. "Approchez-vous donc, Rosette; vous avez entendu ce qu'on ordonne à Fanny; faites-en autant." "Que ce même ordre vous serve," dit Durcet à Hébé, qui approche également. "Il faut donc se mettre à la mode," dit Curval.

As Gilles Deleuze suggests, however, the erotic power of Sadian words is of a particular kind: "In Sade, *Les Cent Vingt Journées de Sodome* is organized according to the stories that the libertines have asked the storytellers to recount; and no initiative on the part of the heroes, at least in principle, should anticipate what is told. The power of words is at its greatest when it commands the repetition of bodies."[17] [t] This power governs *repetition,* rather than invention at its most radical. It is predominantly a power to remind: "This passion having stimulated minds so well acquainted with that species of disorder and reminded them of a taste they all adored, they were not prepared to wait any longer before putting it into practice" (I, 164).[u] By a paradox germane to the process of modeling, the libertines are reminded with force of something to which they are well accustomed. Which is doubtless another reason why Sade does not often speak, as we might tend to, of desire. Taste as "custom" is what links different episodes of desire, putting present (Romantic) experience in its (classical) place, modeling it according to the already known.

At this juncture—or indeed well before it—someone could remark impatiently that the whole business of "modeling" is perfectly circular. Curval and the others respond with enthusiasm to what they hear, but they also have tight control over their storytellers, and doubtless the most precise foreknowledge of narrative events. They want to do what they are "told," certainly, but what they are told is surely what they already wanted to do in the first place. My point in response can only be that there is, for texts like *Les Cent Vingt Journées,* no "first place" of original desire, and that modeling is indeed circular, its narrative perfection being worked out in the self-confirming, self-conforming circle of planning and opportunity, power and good fortune.

[t] Chez Sade, *Les Cent vingt journées* s'organisent d'après les récits que les libertins se font raconter par les "historiennes"; et aucune initiative des héros, du moins en principe, ne doit devancer les récits. Car le pouvoir des mots culmine quand il commande la répétition des corps.

[u] Cette passion ayant échauffé des têtes si *accoutumées* aux désordres de cette espèce et leur *rappelant* un goût qu'ils encensaient si universellement, on ne voulut pas attendre plus longtemps pour la mettre en usage.

Chapter 10

Classical Poise: Thematic Modeling in *L'Image* and *Histoire d'O*

For all its circular perfection, erotic modeling has a broadly linear history, and that history appears to be the story of its gradual eclipse. As seen by post-Romantic moderns, the universal truth of eroticism is actually to be found, not in studied imitation or statuesque display, but in the shifting uncertainty that continually takes the human body from one attitude to another. Here is Alphonso Lingis's exposition of Emmanuel Lévinas: "Of course, someone cannot denude himself or herself without the light and the shadow molding the nudity and giving it form. But the carnal body does not hold its form; the erotic position is shifting and uncertain, is not a posture or an attitude. Its agitation is made of a continual formation and dissolve of poses."[1] The essence of the humanly erotic, we are told, is not the timely pose, but agitation itself. Desire is identified here as a principle of instability, manifesting itself in the very disturbance of form. The pose is epiphenomenal: nothing more than a holding up, and therefore potentially a denial, of human mobility. There is no existential time, it would seem, for the frozen attitude, and no room in authentically erotic life to dwell on postural models. Gilles Deleuze and Félix Guattari, in their glorifications of multiplicity—what they call "the multiple raised to the status of a substantive"[2] [a] see the pose as a kind of fixation, turning what ought to be incessant movement into stages, and therefore, no doubt, making "the body" available for the old geometry and the old

[a] le multiple élevé à l'état de substantif

accounting, rather than allowing it to enter into the new, ever-shifting geometry of the rhizome: "adopt the pose or follow the axis. Whether it is called the genetic stage or your structural destiny, they will break your rhizome" (22).[b] The very nature of libidinal multiplicity, as Deleuze and Guattari understand it, is that it should involve the continual displacement of countless "particles of desire" (48). Not sixteen attitudes or twenty-four tableaux, then, but "mille plateaux." The erotic position must no longer be classifiable or countable, for desire must be swept along in the dream (and the stream) of multiplicity: "One of the essential characteristics of the dream of multiplicity is that each element varies continually and changes its distance with respect to the others" (43).[c]

Yet it is still too early, even in this final chapter, to trumpet the victory of post-Romantic modernity over the old thematic ways. It will always be too early, in a sense, to declare classical eroticism thematically dead, for the history of its decay is also the story of its survival. In texts of the late eighteenth century, the self-sustaining closure of learning and desire certainly begins to be undone—without being shattered—by the notion that something can and should be added to the model. The most powerfully erotic imitation (or application) is then said to be accompanied by an extra quantity or quality taking it beyond the original. This supplement may be spoken of, classically enough, as a mark of refinement. Sade's characters certainly speak in these terms even as they are recognizing/conceiving a passion: "'Ah! By God,' said Curval, 'that's a delicious passion indeed, but it could be refined even more'" (I, 158).[d] By *raffiner,* they seem to mean repetition with a difference, where "difference" does not deserve to be spelled with an "a," being produced more or less regularly through technical variation. "Invention," in this context, is no great departure from the model, but a kind of multiplication within and around it: "They confined themselves that evening to mouth pleasures [following Duclos's stories] but invented a hundred manners of varying them" (I, 183).[e] *S'en tenir* ("to confine oneself") is a mark of discipline in this context: it signals a focus in the very elaboration of pleasures. The

[b] prenez la pose ou suivez l'axe, stade génétique ou destin structural, on cassera votre rhizome.

[c] Un des caractères essentiels du rêve de multiplicité est que chaque élément ne cesse pas de varier et de modifier sa distance par rapport aux autres.

[d] Ah! sacredieu, dit Curval, voilà une délicieuse passion, mais on pourrait encore la raffiner.

[e] On s'en tint ce soir-là aux plaisirs de la bouche mais on inventa cent façons de les varier.

supplement of erotic quality by which Sade's *amis* distinguish their pleasure from the one just presented is thus subject to a kind of thematic constraint. It is attained by quantitative or formulaic operations. Simply going on longer with a "taste" may be what makes the difference, as Curval suggests: "the man you are talking about definitely seems to have both my buttocks and my tastes, for I am utterly in favor of avoiding the bidet, but I prefer a longer delay beforehand" (I, 257).[f] Another possible way to do the same thing better is to do it with a superior class of victim, in this case a boy rather than a girl: "At this point Durcet, whom the story had inflamed, wanted like the old priest [in the story] to suck an asshole, but not that of a girl" (I, 133).[g] Generally, it is a matter of doing more and going further: "'Everything can be imagined,' said Curval, fondling Desgranges's buttocks. 'I am convinced one can go further still than that'" (I, 275).[h] *Aller encore plus loin,* in this situation, is not incompatible with the restraint of *s'en tenir.* It does not mean going on to other, stronger tastes, but rehearsing the topical passion with variations or embellishments, although these may include "later" things: "'Oh! As for that one, I can imagine it readily,' said Curval, 'and if I have to make confession to you, I have in fact done it a few times in my life. To be sure, I added a few episodes that it is too early to describe to you yet. Be that as it may, it is giving me a hard on'" (I, 323).[3][i]

As long as there is talk of refinement or improvement, thematic modeling continues to function. The Sade of *Les Cent vingt journées* still invites us to assess refinement, in remarkably quantitative terms, as a kind of erotic increment. The Mirabeau of *Ma Conversion* still speaks of refinement as well, although he may see it as an unspecified, perhaps incalculable improvement on the model(s): "Everything favored my gaze: the beauty of the light, its rays blurred by a diaphanous veil, which made the objects more tender for us, spring, its influence, Julie's innocence, my experience that allowed me to stimulate her so as to destroy her, and lascivious paintings that I explained to her in an even more lascivious manner" (*Œuvres érotiques,* 67; my emphasis).[j]

[f] il est bien certain que l'homme dont on parle a positivement et mes fesses et mes goûts, car j'approuve infiniment l'absence du bidet, mais je la voudrais plus longue.

[g] Ici Durcet, que ce récit venait d'enflammer, voulut, comme le vieil abbé, sucer le trou d'un cul, mais non pas celui d'une fille.

[h] Tout se conçoit, dit Curval en maniant les fesses de Desgranges; je suis persuadé qu'on peut aller encore plus loin que tout cela.

[i] Oh! pour celle-là, je la conçois, dit Curval, et s'il faut vous faire ma confession, c'est que je l'ai faite quelquefois dans ma vie. Il est vrai que j'y ajoutais quelques épisodes qu'il n'est pas encore temps de vous dire. Quoi qu'il en soit, elle me fait bander.

[j] Tout favorisait mes yeux. La beauté du jour, dont les rayons amollis par une gaze

Doing the *tableaux* better here means doing the standard patterns—the *figures imposées,* they are sometimes called in sports commentary—with greater or richer erotic style. What is most *lascif* is the compulsion to refine. That is precisely the kind of technical enthusiasm that goes on to produce something *plus lascif encore.* As long as passion, for all its dynamism, retains such points of reference, we are called on to locate the erotic supplement within a process of repetition-and-difference, modeling-and-invention.

There are high Romantic texts, however, that claim to sweep away all the old models, as their narratives work explicitly to undo that quasi-psychological mechanism whereby erotic literature perpetuates its themes, and affirms its thematic nature. In *Gamiani* (1833), for example, we find the classical tradition quoted only for memory's sake, summoned in order to be dismissed. Gamiani, the heroine, recounts her earlier life in a debauched convent, noting the infinite variety of erotic posture practiced by the nuns: "They did not restrict themselves to that [activity]: they varied things infinitely. Being deprived of men, we were in fact all the more ingenious at inventing extravagant things. All the priapic verse, all the obscene stories of antiquity and modern times were known to us. We had left them behind" (128).[k] The classical is present here as a point of reference, but it is more or less overcome by an immeasurable variety that is fundamentally other than finite classical variation. Fanny, Gamiani's partner and victim, recounts the moment of her transformation from innocent child into desiring adult, the moment at which she effectively *falls into* a certain number of indecent poses: "I lay down, spread my legs, and moved about in all directions. Without realizing it, I was taking up the most indecent poses" (93).[l] There is no conscious discipline here, no looking to a set of models, but rather a kind of unwitting, agitated "variety" whereby the erotic body twitches or writhes from one position to another. In *Gamiani,* the spectacle of desire is the essential focus of the story, and desire is seen best in the violent *movement* that takes the body from one position to another, provoking exclamations of horror and wonder

diaphane attendrissaient pour nous les objets, le printemps, son influence, l'innocence de Julie, mon expérience qui l'échauffe pour la détruire, des tableaux lascifs que je lui applique d'une manière plus lascive encore.

[k] Elles ne se bornaient point là: elles variaient à l'infini. Privées d'hommes, nous n'en étions que plus ingénieuses à inventer des extravagances. Toutes les priapées, toutes les histoires obscènes de l'antiquité et des temps modernes nous étaient connues. Nous les avions dépassées.

[l] Je m'allongeais, j'écartais mes cuisses, je m'agitais en tous sens. A mon insu, je formais les postures le plus indécentes.

at the frightening intensity of it all: "What a fire you have lit!" (84).[m] The heart of erotic drama is this dramatic outbreak of febrile symptoms. Twisting and arching the body, desire manifests itself in madness, drunkenness, and epileptic convulsion: "I suddenly felt a violent contraction and tension in all my limbs, followed by a dreadful, convulsive movement of the kind that generally goes with epileptic delirium . . . " (96).[n] In this disorder of the senses (116), there is no room for the classical order of desire. Fanny's death throes, when she is poisoned by Gamiani at the end of the story, take her in all directions, and through all positions almost in an instant: "a strange convulsion caused her to leap about in all directions" (138).[o] This violent temporal concentration, with its radical simultaneity of opposing movements, allows no time for corporeal modeling. Frenzy has no style.

Here, then, are the makings of a new thematics, and of a different kind of erotic narrative. Instead of modeling, we shall find the spectacle of desire "itself," instead of postural variations, the intensity of the sex act, instead of gradation, singular climax. When shaped by Romantic narrative, eroticism is likely to be conceived of as an imperious, ejaculatory force disturbing the temporal order, and manifesting itself in the rhythmic oscillation of frenzy and torpor. Of such things is modern pornography made, one might observe. Is this to say that a post-Romantic thematics of eroticism is somehow more "vulgar" than a self-consciously classical one? Are post-Romantic narratives less canonical than postclassical ones? To affirm that would be to overstate my point. Some modern erotic literature, in its claim to be distinct from vulgar pornography, depends on the prestige of what one could call canonical modernism, claiming legitimacy by association with Sade, and appealing to his work as revolutionary or diabolical. From the *divin marquis* canonized by the surrealists to Bataille, Klossowski, and Mandiargues a spark of fervor may be seen to pass. Erotic modernism can thus develop its own thematic norms, recounting the erotic event as a revolution of the self, and weaving discontinuity into narrative patterns. Whatever is gained in that way comes at some cost, since modernist eroticism is committed to narrating desire as radically spontaneous. For this reason, it must tend, as Gadamer might say, to obscure the tradition supporting its own thematics. Classical eroticism,

[m] Quel feu vous allumez!

[n] Je sentis tout à coup dans tous mes membres une contraction et une tension violentes, suivies d'un mouvement affreux et convulsif pareil à ceux qui accompagnent ordinairement les transports é[p]ileptiques. . .

[o] une étrange convulsion la fit bondir en tous sens.

by contrast, as I have tried to show throughout this study, is typically a form of literature that claims legitimacy through the very rehearsal of thematic closure.

In recognizing that modernist eroticism requires a separate study, I am not conceding that a Romantic account of this literary history is the only possible one. It is simply not the case, as I have already suggested by my discussion of such texts as *L'Ecole des biches* (1868) and *Le Roman de Violette* (1883), that classical eroticism comes to an end with *Gamiani.* Nor is it sufficient to say that there is a sprinkling of "late classical" works whose presence can be accounted for as historical regression or anachronistic whim. A number of twentieth-century erotic works that stand among the most prestigiously literary ones can be seen to achieve and consolidate their thematic position through the practice of a relatively classical narrative art.

L'Image (1956), now attributed by some to Robbe-Grillet,[4] foregrounds the question of its own literariness by thematizing distinctions of style and taste. According to Susan Sontag, both *L'Image* and *Histoire d'O,* which I shall consider subsequently, deserve to be recognized as literary:

> Both narratives have more to do with the "use" of erotic material than with the "expression" of it. And this use is preeminently—there is no other word for it—literary. The imagination pursuing its outrageous pleasures in *Story of O* and *The Image* is firmly anchored to certain notions of the *formal* consummation of intense feeling, of procedures for exhausting an experience, that connect as much with recent literary history as with the ahistorical domain of eros.[5]

Literary merit, for Sontag, depends on a kind of "anchoring," but that is merely what binds these two works to the broader intellectual projects of their own age. What she fails to recognize, even as she recognizes literariness, is that the domain of eros, too, has a historical dimension, and that its history is bound up in a circular way with the production of canonical erotic literature.

The narrator-hero of *L'Image* has the standing of an author, and not only because his name, Jean de Berg, is the same as the one on the novel's cover. He makes aesthetic judgments with confidence, declaring an erotic tableau to be well executed, although not in the very best taste: "I replied that it was indeed successfully done, although rather overladen with symbols, perhaps, in the best surrealist, Romantic tradition."[6] [p] The most refined taste, we infer, is opposed to the Romantic and the surrealist. And the best of taste presumably does not include such texts as the set of photographs shown to Jean by his friend Claire, for he recognizes them, with ironic condescension, as "the ones that were offered to sensitive souls in the very bookshop where I had met Anne" (53).[q] We must understand, through Jean, that these photographs are really not very good: they did not seem to him at the time to hold any "special interest" (53). Is it because they lack distinction? Where might the "special interest" of the story lie, if not in them?

At this point, *L'Image* may be seen to teeter on the brink. Will the authoritative literary voice dismiss these photographs as vulgar or will it take them into the literary domain as a classical *mise en abyme* of erotic art? The answer seems to be that the text seeks to accommodate images of the vulgar—the Romantic, the symbolic, the lurid—within a more classical thematic order. Jean de Berg admits to a desire that transcends (or forgets) good taste, when he describes a particular *image* as "very attractive, despite its exaggerated Romanticism" (62).[r] In this regard, the apartment occupied by Claire, for its very heterogeneity, represents the aesthetic space of the text. The living room is striking for its tranquil elegance, for its very "modern comfort and lightness,"[s] by marked contrast with "the dark, uncomfortable staircase, and the dilapidated condition of the building" (55).[t] Within the apartment, there is an "austere gothic bedroom" (65),[u] the decor of most of the photographs. The bedroom is referred to by the narrator, with his usual elegant reserve, as "that curious room" (109),[v] although it eventually takes on an oneiric function for him: "That night I had a dream. I found myself entering the gothic bedroom, which had now become much larger and higher. It resembled the church of my childhood" (119).[w] The notion of *conformité de goût* found in classical modeling is not, on the face of it, the most appropriate one here. When Jean wakes up, he smiles condescendingly at his own dream: "I woke up, smiling to myself at this dream with its allegorical air: it did not mean

[p] J'ai répondu que c'était en effet une réussite, quoique un peu trop chargée de symboles, peut-être, dans le meilleur goût de la tradition surréaliste et romantique.

[q] celles que l'on proposait aux âmes sensibles dans cette librairie où, précisément, j'avais rencontré Anne

[r] très attirante, malgré son romantisme exagéré

[s] le confort et la gaieté très moderne

[t] l'escalier sombre, malcommode, et la grande vétusté de l'immeuble

[u] austère chambre gothique

[v] cette pièce curieuse

[w] Cette nuit-là j'ai fait un rêve. J'entrais à nouveau dans la chambre gothique, plus vaste à présent, plus haute, ressemblant à l'église de mon enfance.

anything" (120).[x] But the aesthetic range of *L'Image,* the space of its stylistic play, abides in the very distance separating childlike gothic fantasy from refined elegance. The key question is: how can the novel accommodate the pornographic and still affirm its literariness?

In order better to perceive the novel's thematic classicism, let us forget for a moment the author and his framing aesthetic judgments. We shall not be able to forget him for long, in any case. We can then say that the novel is about the activity of modeling as carried out by Claire, a photographer: "Did I say that she was more or less an artistic photographer?" (16).[y] The *plus ou moins* is doubtless a reminder that Claire, as a woman, cannot coincide perfectly with a professional role—but this is part of what we are currently forgetting. The first thing to note is the continuing importance of an art of scenic arrangement. It is not just that theatrical scenes occur.[7] Much of the narrative interest lies in seeing the director actually at work. The object of Claire's art par excellence would appear to be something very like the classical tableau. When we first encounter her, she is looking at a group of other characters, "a group of three people, also standing, who were chatting not far from the window" (10).[z] What binds Claire to the group is not described as curiosity, or even as avid desire. Hers is the look of one who oversees events, and sees that they conform to her plan, "as if she were supervising the functioning of a scenario she had prepared, one not likely to cause her the least surprise" (13).[a] No erotic good fortune here, and no cries of wonder, it seems: just a perfect shaping of the action that somehow corresponds, in its clear definition, to Claire's own "inordinate beauty, [. . .] her excessive perfection" (13).[b]

The success of Claire's art as photographic director must depend on sureness of touch and timing. We do not understand exactly what is going on at the novel's opening cocktail, but we do see Claire later applying some finishing touches to the appearance of Anne, her "petit modèle" (16):

> Then she looked at her friend and bent toward her to arrange a lock of her hair, blond hair that shone like gold. (17)

[x] Je me suis réveillé, souriant moi-même de ce songe aux allures allégoriques, qui ne voulait rien dire.

[y] Ai-je dit qu'elle était plus ou moins photographe d'art?

[z] un groupe de trois personnes, debout également, qui causaient non loin de l'embrasure

[a] comme si elle était en train de surveiller la bonne marche d'un scénario mis au point par elle, qui ne risquait pas de lui procurer le moindre étonnement

[b] trop grande beauté, [. . .] son excès de perfection

> Claire bent backward again, to contemplate her handiwork from a little further away. She shook her head and screwed up her eyes, like a connaisseur evaluating a painting. (36–37)[c]

Sometimes, the model cannot get it right by herself, and the most energetic intervention is called for: "The young woman [Anne] began soaping herself once again. But Claire, judging that she was not doing it with enough conviction, took charge of her gestures, pointing to the places that needed scrubbing, showing the poses that had to be adopted (supposedly to make the task easier), the amplitude and the speed of each little brushing movement" (100).[d] It is indeed so much more *commode* when the model is taken through a whole series of poses in the bath, although the *commodité* does not have much to do with personal hygiene. Claire is visibly the agent, at this point in the story as elsewhere, of that particular narrative convenience with which we became familiar in the last chapter. Erotic art, *mise en abyme* in the text, is thus Claire's art: the set of six photographs (more or less, because a seventh is added) displayed and described in the novel's central chapter. That the title of the whole should invoke the notion of an image seems thoroughly appropriate, then, though the singular form of the noun is a little surprising. Certainly, the singular is more distinguished that the plural ("Les Photographies") found in the title of the central chapter, but it is not clear how the modern title stands for a classical thematics. The singular theme is not reliably achieved through a set of photos or a range of scenarios.

If we were determined to find some singularity of focus in order to fulfill the promise of the title, we might seek it in Claire's finest artistic production, namely her victim/lover, Anne. The first of the set of photographs, which are more or less all of Anne, shows a face that is *très réussi:* "The face, beneath the indistinct curls, was a great success: consenting eyes, lips apart, and a look that combined ingenuous charm with submissiveness" (56–57).[e] What is achieved here is

[c] Puis elle a regardé son amie et s'est penchée vers elle pour arranger une mèche de cheveux, des cheveux blonds et fins à reflets d'or.

> Claire a reculé le buste de nouveau, pour contempler son ouvrage d'un peu plus loin. Elle hochait la tête en plissant les paupières, d'un air de connaisseur qui apprécie un tableau.

[d] La jeune femme [Anne] a repris son savonnage. Mais Claire, ayant jugé qu'elle n'y mettait pas assez de conviction, s'est chargée de diriger ses gestes, indiquant les endroits qu'il fallait frotter, les poses qu'il fallait prendre (pour rendre censément la tâche plus commode), l'ampleur et la rapidité du moindre effleurement.

[e] Le visage, sous les boucles floues, est très réussi: les yeux consentants, les lèvres disjointes, un air mêlé de charme ingénu et de soumission.

double, and reflexively so. In the first place—or is it in fact the first?—this photograph is a fine illustration of the attitude of submissiveness. For this is the artist-photographer's task, to represent an attitude, and to pose her model "the better to illustrate her situation as defenseless prey" (102).[f] But underlying this representation, already in place before it, is a process of conditioning ensuring that the model will invest the pose with her own desire. Claire shows off her handiwork, her body work, with all the pride and condescension of a successful animal trainer: "It is all a matter of training, as with a dog! All that was needed was to caress her often in that position; now she cannot help but expect pleasure when she stands like that . . . " (76–77).[g] This is "dressage" in its narrowest cultural sense: the display of animal obedience as the trainer's artistic triumph.

Demonstrably then, the privileged object of modeling in *L'Image,* corresponding to its visibly active subject in Claire, is the person of Anne. Anne is at just the right age for erotic training, whatever that age might be exactly, because she is both child and woman: "From her whole person, in spite of her obvious extreme youth, there emanated the attractiveness of "the flesh," making her appear much more like a young woman than someone who answered to the ambiguous name of "girl." And yet, in her white dress, so light and simple, she looked like a child" (13).[h] Such difficulty of classification is not the revelation of her paradoxical character, or even the sign of enduring psychological mystery. It marks, rather, the space of narrative opportunity. Anne must not be thought of as flighty or seductively irresolute. She is simply going through a prolonged stage of development, more or less equivalent in length to the time span of the story. What makes her so like a *jeune fille* is her "attitude." She sits with knees together and hands joined in her lap: "Anne kept her upper body stiff, her legs tightly together, and her hands joined together and placed in her lap" (24; see also 16).[i] She curtsies, too, in the most orthodox fashion: "When she had drawn level with me, she executed her discreet curtsy, a little ceremoniously, like the ones that are taught to young boarders in religious institutions. And her voice was that of a well-behaved

[f] de façon à mieux illustrer sa situation de proie sans défense. . .

[g] C'est une question de dressage, comme pour le chien! Il a suffi de la caresser souvent dans cette posture; elle ne peut plus s'empêcher d'y attendre le plaisir. . .

[h] De toute sa personne, en dépit d'une extrême jeunesse évidente, émanait un attrait de "chair" qui la faisait bien plus concevoir comme une jeune femme, que sous la dénomination ambiguë de "jeune fille." Et pourtant, dans sa robe blanche, légère et simple, elle avait aussi l'air d'une enfant.

[i] Anne gardait le buste rigide, les jambes serrées, les mains jointes et posées sur les genoux.

pupil" (23).[j] Even as she moves through this constrained, undoubtedly constricted range, she displays a charming awkwardness that compels us to see her as becoming erotic, and erotically becoming: "graceful, filled with sweetness and reticence, with the movements of a timid ballerina whose charm was underlined by a slight touch of awkwardness" (14).[k] As with the heroines of Romantic virginity stories, Anne's body is caught up in narrative. Unlike them, however, she is undergoing a strict course in erotic deportment. When, during a day at the Bagatelle gardens, she is, so to speak, taken to visit that most traditional symbol of virginity, the rose, she accepts the literal *rapprochement* with herself, and follows Claire's instructions with a kind of meek thoroughness: "she [Claire] drew my attention to the girl, who went on steadily caressing the inside of the rose" (27).[l] Consistently, with no apparent effort of will, Anne is able to adopt the poses required, sustaining throughout an "application" to artistic-erotic duty as dictated by Claire. Consider her toilet training, for example. Refused permission to relieve herself on one occasion, she is able first to hold back, and then to urinate on command, in the presence of a strictly attentive audience (42–45).

At the "heart" of Anne's ongoing erotic activity then, as the guarantee of her bodily regularity, we find not seething inner desire, but the discipline of a model child:

> The girl did not protest; she lowered her eyes, blushing, with a charmingly submissive air. (29)
>
> The latter [Anne] had retrieved the discreet demeanor that became her as an object of lust. (40)
>
> As for the poor child, she showed exemplary docility, even if she was made to bear long, uncomfortable periods of standing, excessive penetrations, and the most spectacular overstretching of limbs. (101)[m]

[j] Une fois parvenue en face de moi, elle a exécuté son discret salut de cour, un peu cérémonieux, comme ceux que l'on apprend aux petites pensionnaires des institutions religieuses. Et sa voix était celle d'une élève sage.

[k] gracieuse, pleine de douceur et de réserve, mais avec des mouvements de ballerine timide, dont une pointe de gaucherie accentuait encore le charme

[l] elle [Claire] m'a désigné la jeune fille, qui continuait avec application à caresser l'intérieur de la rose.

[m] La jeune fille n'a pas protesté; elle a baissé les paupières, en rougissant, d'un air charmant de soumission.

Celle-ci [Anne], en même temps, avait retrouvé son maintien discret d'objet de convoitise.

Quant à la pauvre petite, elle se montrait d'une docilité exemplaire, même si on lui imposait de longues stations inconfortables, des pénétrations excessives, ou les plus spectaculaires écartèlements.

So it is that the notion of instinct comes to be effectively undone. When Claire and Jean enter while Anne is taking a bath, she immediately moves to adopt the "instinctive" pose of modesty: "Instinctively her palms with fingers spread slid toward her sex and her breasts, making some sort of an effort to hide them. But a steady look from her mistress was all it took to make her interrupt straightaway this reaction of modesty" (99).[n] The training given by Claire, as we see, goes against that instinct, but establishes and nurtures another, so that when Anne is trying on lingerie in front of a shop assistant, she adopts unthinkingly a submissive pose of the sort regularly required by her mistress: "Anne held her arms out from her body, so that she could be seen better. Instinctively, she had half-opened her mouth and moved her knees apart" (89).[o] There is no need for us to speculate here about competing theoretical accounts of what might cause Anne's behavior: the novel does not begin to pursue them, in any case. What matters infinitely more for the story is the convergence in Anne's body of two "natures"—the modest and the exhibitionist. We can note the ongoing thematic support given to erotic training by more reputable forms of discipline.

There are one or two moments when *L'Image,* in keeping with its broader aesthetic ambivalence, appears to entertain a kind of post-Romantic doubt about the whole modeling process. If Anne is so thoroughly childlike as to allow herself to be disciplined without question, so innocently submissive that she is always already acquiescing, not having the time or space to choose her attitude, then what might be the quality of her desire? Might she not be almost reduced to the materiality of some unconscious *pâte à modeler*? She is, after all, like putty in the hands of her mistress: "In this liquid element, her friend's body responded to every slight pressure, allowing itself to be turned this way and that, extended and folded, opened and shut with perfect softness and responsiveness" (101).[p] "Where is the evidence of desire here?" the would-be erotic confessor might ask. Avowal can in fact be forced from Anne's lips by Claire's inquisition, but Jean the narrator expresses doubt:

[n] Instinctivement, les paumes aux doigts écartés ont glissé vers le sexe et les seins, afin de les dissimuler tant bien que mal. Mais il a suffi que sa maîtresse arrêtât le regard sur elle, pour la faire aussitôt renoncer à ce mouvement de pudeur.

[o] Anne a écarté les bras du corps, pour qu'on la voie mieux. Instinctivement, elle avait entrouvert la bouche et disjoint les genoux.

[p] Dans cet élément liquide, le corps de son amie répondait à ses moindres impulsions, se laissant tourner et retourner, étendre et plier, ouvrir et fermer, avec une mollesse, une complaisance idéales.

"So you must have been happy, then? Seeing that everyone knew you were a little whore?" (Then more harshly:) "Go on then, answer!"

"Yes . . . I was happy . . . "

"Why were you happy?"

"I was happy . . . to show people . . . that I had been whipped . . . "

It was an almost imperceptible murmur. Was she repeating it without understanding, or did she really think that? (92–93)[q]

The child's catechistic utterances may be suspected of lacking authenticity, but they are soon borne out by an examination of the woman's body, by what Sade would call the "proof" of genital lubrication: "She's already moist, the little slut!" (93).[r] When Anne comes to utter cries of pleasure and pain, severe discipline can be said to be producing the marks of spontaneous avowal: "Now the girl uttered a little moan each time the whip cracked. The 'Ah' of pain resembled a lover's groan" (77).[s]

We are not told where Anne's cries have their source, nor invited to examine their substance: we are told what they "resemble." In this sense, *L'Image* has certain qualities of the *nouveau roman,* tending as it does to omit any exploration of character as psychological interiority. Desire is not sought as origin or cause of the action, but is distributed and displayed through the reflexive play of visible attitudes. Despite the first-person narration, we are invited to read desire as a dramatic modeling of one body by another. It ought to be remembered, of course—we have forgotten it long enough—that throughout *L'Image* Claire is *seen by Jean* to be modeling Anne. He it is, as narrator, who first (and last) describes Claire to the reader. Her pose, on the first occasion, has a suggestion of erotic openness about it: "She was standing with her arms out on either side of her body, grasping the upper railing of the balustrade, and leaning her back against it" (11).[t] Is Claire to fall back and open up, becoming the erotic object of the narrator-hero's gaze? Apparently not. She is beautiful, but not desir-

[q] "Tu devais être contente, dis? que tout le monde sache que tu es une petite putain? (Et plus durement:) Eh bien, réponds!"

"Oui. . . J'étais contente. . ."

"Contente pourquoi?"

"J'étais contente. . . de faire voir. . . qu'on m'avait fouettée . . ."

C'était un murmure à peine perceptible. Répétait-elle sans comprendre, ou bien le pensait-elle véritablement?

[r] Elle mouille déjà la petite garce!

[s] Maintenant la fille poussait un petit gémissement, chaque fois que claquait le fouet, un 'Ah' de douleur qui ressemblait à un râle d'amour.

[t] Elle avait les deux bras écartés de chaque côté du corps, tenant à pleines mains la barre supérieure du garde-fou, contre laquelle s'appuyaient ses reins.

able: "Claire was very beautiful, as I said, much more beautiful than her friend in the white dress. But in contrast to her friend, she had never caused me any sexual excitement" (13).[u] Jean suggests that her "excessive" beauty may be the reason for this, but it would seem more appropriate to the norms of this text to say that Claire generally fails to be desirable to Jean because she does not have a proper attitude, one that she holds, to which and in which she can be held. During a moment of abandon, he sees her "leaning right back in her armchair" (66),[v] in a classic pose of erotic availability. A moment later, however, she changes position suddenly: "but straightaway Claire regained her self-control. She got up abruptly out of her chair, executed a pirouette and once again appeared in her usual attitude: strict, rigid, and flawlessly beautiful" (66--67).[w] Claire may indeed be the embodiment of capricious, "feminine" mobility, but her twists and turns do not lead up the garden path of seduction. They merely disturb the order of desire, not allowing the time and space of its representation.

That Claire is a photographer can hardly guarantee her against being photographed: elementary Sartrian wisdom tells us as much. That she is a woman and more or less a photographer almost guarantees, in a reliably sexist world, that she will be actively observed in her professional role, and doubtless photographed in turn. So it is that Claire eventually comes to be photographed, and positioned within her own artistic production. As a late addition—and as an uneven erotic supplement—to the set of six photographs of Anne in various poses, she adds one that, Jean strongly suspects, is of herself: "Leaning right back in one of the small armchairs, a woman in a nightdress that had been pulled halfway up her belly was caressing the inside of her sex" (65).[x] This is a powerful prediction, and a precise narrative model for the end of the story. We begin to expect that Claire will finally make herself available, renouncing all willfulness, and becoming a model woman.

What lies in wait for the reader of *L'Image,* as a kind of predictable surprise, is Claire's finally coming to adopt the attitude of Anne. That ending is predictable, in fact, precisely because of the novel's lengthy

[u] Claire était très belle, ai-je dit, beaucoup plus belle que sa jeune amie à la robe blanche. Mais, à l'opposé de celle-ci, elle ne m'avait jamais causé d'émoi sensuel.

[v] renversée en arrière dans son fauteuil

[w] Mais Claire s'est reprise aussitôt. Levée elle-même brusquement de son fauteuil, elle a exécuté une virevolte et m'est apparue à nouveau dans son attitude de tous les jours: stricte, rigide, d'une beauté sans faille.

[x] Renversée dans un des petits fauteuils, une femme à la chemise de nuit relevée jusqu'à mi-ventre, se caressait l'intérieur du sexe.

and respectful quotation of the tradition of classical modeling, which entails that the one who supervises and directs feels compelled to adopt the attitude represented. In that sense, desire is not revealed in a moment, but played out in time, as thematic repetition. What is the "secret" pattern of Claire's desire, after all, if not the manifest one enacted by Anne? The poses are varied, certainly, but with a particular thematic insistence that almost precludes, for the reader, the possibility of genuine surprise. Instead of the Romantic notion of a dark inner lust reaching out suddenly to grasp at the future, we find here a reflexive and retrospective play of images held in memory:

> The girl was standing next to the column, in the same position in which Claire had put her in order to hide the stolen rose beneath her skirt. (56)
>
> The attitude, imposed by the present situation, was the one I had already had an opportunity to appreciate: open thighs, erect body, raised arms, half-open lips. Her large blue eyes shone with a deep, almost supernatural glow, taking us back several centuries, to the ecstasy of the Christian martyrs. (109)[y]

Memory, in the latter example, is personal and cultural at the same time, in quite the same way as Jean's dream links the gothic to his childhood. Desire is not merely avowed, but recognized and distributed as a kind of style throughout the already known. To remember is thus to desire again, and doubtless to desire better: "Even though I could now see the young woman from the front, I remembered the picture that represented her from behind: chained to the iron bed in a comparable position, her bottom striated by the whip. The memories of the photographs and of their torture gave full meaning to the waiting position in which she was presently holding the victim" (73).[z] Who gains the benefit of this erotic supplement? Anyone who has seen the photographs, anyone who is modeled as the subject of the desire they represent.

[y] La fille est debout, près d'une colonne, dans la même position que celle où Claire l'avait fait mettre pour cacher la rose volée sous sa jupe.

L'attitude, imposée par la circonstance, était celle que j'avais eu l'occasion d'apprécier déjà: cuisses ouvertes, corps bien droit, bras levés, lèvres disjointes. Les grands yeux bleus brillaient d'un éclat profond, quasi surnaturel, qui nous ramenait de quelques siècles en arrière, aux extases des martyres chrétiennes.

[z] Bien qu'apercevant la jeune femme de face, je me suis rappelé l'image qui la représentait par-derrière: enchaînée au lit de fer dans une posture voisine, les fesses striées par les coups de fouet. Le souvenir des photographies et de leurs supplices donnait toute sa valeur à la position d'attente où l'on maintenait à présent la victime.

In the fullness of narrative time, Claire comes to acknowledge before Jean the desire she has effectively rehearsed and displayed throughout the novel. She does so, of course, in the proper way, with hardly a moment's revelation of psychological interiority: "She only hesitated for a second. She knelt down in front of me on the sheepskin rug, and began to undo her garments, one by one, according to the ritual. She was wearing exactly the same lingerie as her model, and she too was without panties" (121).[a] The climactic fulfillment of modeling, in Claire's final attitude, is the perfect convergence of skill and desire: "I told her to embrace me. She did so with all the thoroughness, skill, and responsiveness one could wish" (123).[b] This is how Claire, the previously insubordinate and often aloof woman, is put in her place with respect to Jean—trapped, a psychoanalytically-minded observer might say, by her mimicry of male desire. Jean himself is positioned in symmetrically predictable fashion, finally standing tall as a model of male dominance. It is not as if his "heart" had previously been filled with feelings of frustration or powerlessness: he had simply been unable to sustain desire for Claire. Now that she holds a submissive attitude, however—finally getting it right—his desire rises to the occasion without the least difficulty, as he slaps her, bites and penetrates her in a stylistic variant of the treatment earlier meted out to Anne. On a previous occasion, Jean had allowed himself to be positioned by Claire's arrangement of Anne, taking his place in the tableau: "But I quickly realized that Claire could not be so ignorant as to fail to understand the irregularities to which she was exposing her friend by presenting her to me in this position. I took out my own sex, and reached out with it toward the prisoner's inclined face" (81–82).[c] At the end of the story, with the same swiftness, he is positioned by Claire's—or somebody's—modeling of Claire.

There is a remark on *L'Image* by J[ean] L[empert] in the *Dictionnaire des œuvres érotiques* that I find profoundly irritating. J.L. says that, at the end of the story, "one understands that Claire loved Jean without admitting it to herself; the real game is played between two people,

[a] Elle n'a hésité qu'une seconde. Elle s'est mise à genoux devant moi, sur le tapis en peau de mouton, et a commencé à défaire ses vêtements, un à un, suivant le rite. Elle portait du linge tout pareil à celui de son modèle. Elle n'avait pas de culotte, elle non plus.

[b] Je lui ai dit de m'embrasser. Elle y a mis toute l'application, l'adresse et la complaisance souhaitables.

[c] Mais, bien vite, j'ai pensé que Claire ne pouvait être assez ignorante pour ne pas avoir compris à quelles irrégularités elle exposait son amie en me l'offrant dans cette posture. J'ai dégagé mon propre sexe et l'ai tendu vers le visage penché de la prisonnière.

and all the rest is just images."[8] [d] Now this may not be simply wrong, and indeed it reflects well enough a certain crassly triumphant tone that can be heard in the final chapter. But it is remarkably insensitive to the kinds of thematic issues that I have been pursuing in this chapter. Certainly, the story ends with Claire's groans of avowal (124), but she comes already *dressed* confessionally (121). Her admission is a striking climax, but is also shown to be the final product of reflexive discipline. And the "couple" of hero and heroine does not stand over, as fundamental reality, against some collection of superficial or redundant images. The very subjectivity of Jean, Claire, and Anne is constituted by the play of postural images, in the circularity of memory and desire.

In keeping with the novels of Sade and his contemporaries, *L'Image* continues to rehearse the pleasures of narrative convenience. The *complaisance* shown by Claire in her final dealings with Jean is indeed both submissiveness and a form of coincidence. It consists, as the etymology suggests, in being "pleased-with"—with her partner, yes, undoubtedly, and with what he requires of her, but more particularly being pleased with (and in) the position or attitude that allows them to be partners. Most broadly, however, *L'Image* seems to settle indulgently into a tradition of erotic narrative, commenting reflexively on the ease with which it does so. The narrator regularly has occasion to note, in the most classical way, the convenience with which the erotic object presents itself to his gaze:

> Just above her waist, her two hands, which held the rolled-up material of her dress, were far enough apart to present a convenient sight for the viewer. (33)
>
> The photograph is taken from quite high up, so as to present her bottom in the most convenient position. (58)[e]

It is essentially a matter of technique in positioning the other, of course: "For greater convenience in lashing this soft flesh that lay at

[d] l'on comprend que Claire aimait Jean sans vouloir le lui dire, que Jean aimait Claire sans se l'avouer; la vraie partie se joue à deux, et tout le reste n'est qu'images.

[e] Juste au-dessous de la taille, ses deux mains, qui retenaient l'étoffe de la robe ramassée en rouleau, étaient assez écartées l'une de l'autre pour offrir à la vue un spectacle commode.

La photographie est prise d'assez haut, de manière à offrir les fesses à la vue dans la position la plus commode.

her mercy, Claire took her left hand away from the sex" (77).[f] "This system was quick and convenient" (79).[g] But the narration is not content to point out that Claire, as torturer, happily gets it right, for Jean's description moves invasively, in its evocation of comfort, into the very space of Anne's body. It transfers the epithet "comfortable": "The pubis itself was slightly prominent, and nicely cozy and round. It was small but comfortable" (33).[h] Where is comfort located here, exactly? Certainly not in Anne's subjective experience. If there is doubt about this, it is dealt with dismissively by Jean in conversation with a shop assistant, as Anne is trying on lingerie:

> "It's less convenient, isn't it?" I added.
> "For the wearer, sir, it's not at all uncomfortable."
> "No, I don't mean for the wearer! I'm talking about how difficult it is to see . . . and touch, too . . . "(87)[i]

Not comfortable for her, but for "us": Claire and Jean, and doubtless "the reader." Anne's role (and her narratively over-determined nature) is to be thoroughly convenient for desire.

The narratorial position in *L'Image* is thus, most often, an exercise in tranquil insolence. Whereas in Sade the question of the victim's comfort cannot arise, such is the swiftness and efficacity of violence, here we find a self-indulgent measurement of difference in comfort levels, a kind of postural smugness that allows Jean (and usually Claire) to hold that most bourgeois of attitudes, the sitting position, while Anne is standing, kneeling, or squatting before them. At Bagatelle, they have the good fortune to encounter two garden chairs "made out of iron, but comfortably shaped."[j] The masters' position is properly inscribed here, and all three can take their places:

> Claire settled into one of them and, pointing to the other, said:
> "Sit down, Jean." When she saw me hesitating, she added: "the little girl is to stay standing up." (30)[k]

[f] Afin de cingler plus fort et plus commodément les douces chairs abandonnées à sa merci, Claire a ôté sa main gauche du sexe.

[g] Ce système était rapide et commode.

[h] Le pubis lui-même était un peu saillant, bien douillet, dodu, petit mais confortable.

[i] "C'est moins commode, n'est-ce pas?" ai-je ajouté.
"A porter, monsieur, ce n'est pas gênant du tout."
"Non, pas à porter, bien sûr! C'est la vue que cela gêne. . . et la main, aussi. . ."

[j] en fer, mais d'un modèle confortable

[k] Claire s'est installée dans l'un et, me désignant l'autre:
"Asseyez-vous, Jean, me dit-elle. (Puis, comme j'hésitais:) La petite fille doit rester debout."

On other occasions, with unabashed insistence, the narrator refers to the furniture on which he and Claire are seated: "Claire and I had sat down again in the two small, well-upholstered chairs that faced the middle of the rug" (71).[l] If the reader were tempted, as with the garden seats, to suppose even a modicum of discomfort for Jean and Claire because of the firmness of the chairs or their relatively small dimensions, all such thoughts are to be banished: the position of sadistic voyeur really is elegantly restful. It even comes with refreshments: "during that time, we were quietly finishing off our glasses of orangeade" (111).[m] There is no question of writhing or thrashing about: one merely has to settle into the role.

While drinks are being served, Anne is of course required to maintain her pose of availability, although we are not privy to her exact feelings *within* the posture. Jean does note that she undergoes "long, uncomfortable periods of standing" (101),[n] and is subtle enough to read the signs of her fatigue in one of the photographs: "The upper body and thighs are erect, but the whole body is nonetheless slightly twisted to one side, because of the fatigue brought on by this position, and that makes one of the hips protrude further" (60).[o] The main thing to note, as always, is that it turns out rather well for the voyeur, since fatigue causes one of the model's hips to be more prominent. Any further attempt to gauge the quality of Anne's discomfort is bound to be defeated by the novel's point of view. All one could do, in solidarity with the victim, would be to discard the text, or denounce its "author."

No modern work in French is more likely to be called a literary classic of eroticism than *Histoire d'O* (1954). Pauline Réage's text shares with *L'Image* a certain canonical poise, as it positions itself thematically within a classical tradition. Neither text can be said to shrug off all modern requirements of psychological verisimilitude or credible character motivation. Rather, they seem to make room within the modeled pose for variation and intensity, and even for a degree of comfort. Not content to maintain a certain pose, or a certain style, they narrate the achievement of a more general "attitude" toward the erotic. They may even make room for a psychology of desire, but such "room" is a kind of reflexive decor, settled at the heart of the modeling process.

[l] Nous nous étions rassis, Claire et moi, dans les deux petits fauteuils bien rembourrés, tournées vers le milieu du tapis.

[m] Pendant ce temps, nous achevions tranquillement nos verres d'orangeade.

[n] de longues stations inconfortables

[o] Le buste et les cuisses se tiennent droits. mais tout le corps est légèrement tordu

The story of *Histoire d'O* is anything but an occasion for displays of unpredictable desire. Expression or avowal of desire does not occur with the suddeness of a Romantic outburst. It is in fact prepared and sustained by a process of postural modeling. It is opportune to recall here Foucault's claim—generally supported and, I trust, elaborated in my study—that there was a historical shift from the practice of something like an *ars erotica* to that of confession. The former, Foucault suggests, is imposed from above, while the latter wells up from below and bursts through the restraints which tended to hold it in: "Because of the power structure immanent in it, the discourse of avowal cannot come from above, as in *ars erotica,* by the master's sovereign will, but rather from below, like a word that is required or compelled, bursting open, by some imperious constraint, the seals of inhibition and forgetfulness" (*La Volonté de savoir,* 83).[p] Now it would be a grave mistake, in Foucault's terms, to see confession and *ars erotica* as incommensurate one with the other because one was held to be spontaneous and the other constrained. His point is that each of the two depends on a set of techniques, more or less symmetrically opposed, so that confession too can be seen as the object of a particular constructive attention. It comes at the end of a process that yields avowal as the instance of intimate truth. There is nothing to be gained, for Foucault, by separating voice from body, utterance from posture. Both expression and attitude are to be thought of as the products of discipline. Just as there is, or once was, an *ars erotica,* there is, so to speak, an art and a regimen of the "spontaneous."

In the same way and in much the same terms as Foucault's reworking of a historical distinction, we can read *Histoire d'O* as deconstructing the supposedly dramatic, revolutionary opposition between Romantic and classical eroticism. If we begin with Jean Paulhan's preface to the novel, as one is supposed to do, we can find there a triumphant exclamation that foregrounds the theme of confession in a rather crass way: "At last a woman who admits it! Admits what? What women have always denied (although never more than they do today), [. . .] that everything in them is sex, including their minds."[9] [q] The first

de côté cependant, à cause de la fatigue occasionnée par cette posture, ce qui fait saillir davantage une des hanches.

[p] Par la structure de pouvoir qui lui est immanente, le discours de l'aveu ne saurait venir d'en haut, comme dans l'*ars erotica,* et par la volonté souveraine du maître, mais d'en bas, comme une parole requise, obligée, faisant sauter par quelque contrainte impérieuse les sceaux de la retenue ou de l'oubli.

[q] Enfin une femme qui avoue! Qui avoue quoi? Ce dont les femmes se sont de tout

thing to say about this remark is that it is extraordinarily forgetful of traditional erotic literature, which repeatedly claims to speak the hidden truth of female desire, and to overhear its most intimate whispers. Furthermore, Paulhan's understanding of avowal would appear to be narrowly psychological. He supposes that the whole text functions as an admission of what this woman and doubtless all others really want deep down. At last, one of them voices the truth of desire that had been waiting inside them to be let out. Yet whatever Paulhan means here by *avoue* cannot be as subtle, or as precisely disciplined as the meaning supported by thematic tradition and (re)constructed in the course of *Histoire d'O*. O is in fact attentively surrounded by masters who wish to lead her to full confession. Sir Stephen is actually compared to a confessor for his practice of the art of questioning: "Sir Stephen began questioning again, with the firmness of a judge and the skill of a confessor" (151).[r] His questioning is meant to elicit a particular response, defined throughout by the masters themselves as the proper (or true) avowal. They know they can constrain O with the strictest violence, but the erotic supplement they require is that she actively desire the constraint: "Will you consent to take part in it? I am requesting you to do so, and I ask you for your avowal because it will commit you more than submissiveness, which I know you have already shown" (102).[s] The key point, for my analysis, is that they stipulate what will count as her *aveu*. They name it in advance: "What they wanted of her was not that she should obey an order, but that she should anticipate the orders, that she should declare herself to be a slave, and give herself up to them as such. That is what they called her avowal" (104).[t] What Paulhan ought to have said, displacing the adverb and therefore changing the meaning, was "une femme qui avoue enfin," for O's admission is the result of a long, severe discipline that produces the confessing self.

It is not by chance that reference is made in the story to nuns. They are more than pornographic bric-a-brac in the decor,[10] for they actually provide a postural model. On more than one occasion we find O thinking of them as she learns the art of kneeling: "She heard

---

temps défendues (mais jamais plus qu'aujourd'hui). [. . .] que tout est sexe en elles et jusqu'à l'esprit.

[r] Sir Stephen reprit ses questions, avec une fermeté de juge, une adresse de confesseur.

[s] Voulez-vous consentir à ý participer? Je vous en prie, et vous demande votre aveu parce qu'il vous engagera plus que votre soumission, dont je sais qu'elle est acquise.

[t] Ce qu'ils voulaient d'elle n'était pas qu'elle obéît à un ordre, c'était qu'elle vînt audevant des ordres, qu'elle se jugeât elle-même esclave, et se livrât pour telle. Voilà ce qu'ils appelaient son aveu.

someone saying that she must be made to kneel. That is what they did. She was very uncomfortable on her knees, and all the more so because she was forbidden to keep them together, and because the fact that her hands were tied behind her back made her lean forward. She was then given permission to bend slightly backward, half sitting on her heels in the way nuns do" (27; see also 81).[u] At the same time as she is undergoing this training, holding the ritual pose of religious confession, she is beginning to achieve a kind of inner tranquillity whose outward and visible sign can also be read on the faces of nuns: "That she should grow in dignity by being prostituted astonished her, but it was a matter of dignity, nonetheless. She was as if illuminated from within, and one could see in her the calm walk, the serene face, the imperceptible inner smile that one can detect in the eyes of female recluses" (70).[v] Is the modeling internal or external, spiritual or physical? The question makes no sense: it is both at once, such is the inward- and outward-reaching intensity of discipline. In her "mind," O maintains the most radical pose of submission, be it religious or otherwise. In response to certain commands, she experiences an "inner prostration": "The word 'open' and the expression 'open your legs,' when spoken by her lover, were laden with such excitement and power that she never heard them without a kind of inner prostration, a holy obedience, as if a god, and not he, had spoken" (82).[w] It would be trivial to say that O is open to suggestion: as her name suggests,[11] she seems to achieve the perfection of openness within her person. What is thus developed in the text is a compelling play of "abstract" and "concrete," whereby such notions as "openness" and "depth" continue to have an ancient spiritual function while being densely, even harshly corporeal.[12] O is learning to "open herself up," as the French has it, in every sense: "She thought to herself that the words to open up to someone, meaning to confide in them, had only one single meaning for her, a literal, physical, and indeed absolute one, since she opened

[u] Elle entendit qu'on disait qu'il fallait la mettre à genoux. Ce qu'on fit. Elle était très mal à genoux, d'autant plus qu'on lui défendait de les rapprocher, et que ses mains liées au dos la faisaient pencher en avant. On lui permit alors de fléchir un peu en arrière, à demi assise sur les talons comme font les religieuses.

[v] Qu'à être prostituée elle dût gagner en dignité étonnait, c'est pourtant de dignité qu'il s'agissait. Elle en était éclairée comme par le dedans, et l'on voyait dans sa démarche le calme, sur son visage la sérénité et l'imperceptible sourire intérieur qu'on devine aux yeux des recluses.

[w] Le mot "ouvre" et l'expression "ouvre les jambes" se chargeaient dans la bouche de son amant de tant de trouble et de pouvoir qu'elle ne les entendait jamais sans une sorte de prosternation intérieure, de soumission sacrée, comme si un dieu, et non lui, avait parlé.

up all the parts of her body that could be opened" (181).[x] By holding her body in a kneeling, open position, she becomes the one who must confess, who will confess, who is already confessing.

The modeling of O is exemplified in one particular pose, yet it is somehow more diffuse and more general. O is bent to the will of Sir Stephen and shaped by his every whim, but her angle of inclination and the outline of her shape are not always scrupulously recorded: "Since then, Sir Stephen had bent her to all his whims, fashioned her to his measure, and demanded of her the most outrageous favors [*complaisances*] as if they were a matter of course" (153).[y] What seems to matter most is the modeling itself, rather than the given, contingent model. The whole point appears to be the literal incarnation of a set of epithets, such that O becomes "still and silent, so bare and so available" (21).[z] Not just to be open, but to be *so* open, so readily bent and shaped, is the essence of her attitude. When she looks in the mirror, she sees not just one nuance in a range of poses, not one shape out of twenty-four, but the erotic and moral significance of her present "position": "Each time her gaze encountered the mirror, she saw herself to be open in this way" (23).[a]

One of the vectors of O's discipline is the limited but drastic movement summed up in the verb *basculer*. This tilting backward is achieved by Restif's and Sade's diabolical mechanisms. Unlike the virgin's tragically abysmal fall, the action of *basculer* amounts to a fall into some position of exposure:

> But suddenly she lost her balance and tipped over backward—held up by the arms of whom?—while her legs were opened and her lips gently moved apart. (27).
>
> The other man, [. . .] having tipped her forward over one of the arms of his chair—her raised skirt now offered him the full length of her thighs—took hold of her pudenda with his hand. (66–67; cf. 117, 150, 151, 184)[b]

[x] Elle songeait que le mot s'ouvrir à quelqu'un, qui veut dire se confier, n'avait pour elle qu'un seul sens, littéral, physique, et d'ailleurs absolu, car elle s'ouvrait en effet de toutes les parts de son corps qui pouvaient l'être.

[y] Sir Stephen depuis l'avait pliée à toutes ses fantaisies, l'avait façonnée à sa mesure, avait exigé et obtenu d'elle comme allant de soi les plus outrageantes complaisances.

[z] immobile et muette, si dénudée et si offerte

[a] Elle se voyait, ainsi ouverte, chaque fois que son regard rencontrait la glace.

[b] Mais, soudain elle perdit l'équilibre et bascula à la renverse, soutenue dans quels bras? pendant qu'on lui ouvrait les jambes et qu'on lui écartait doucement les lèvres.

L'autre homme, [. . .] l'ayant fait basculer en avant sur un des bras de son fauteuil—et sa jupe relevée lui offrait toute la longueur de ses reins—lui prit le ventre à pleine main.

The verb *basculer* is also used sometimes in a more figurative sense. To describe the workings of memory, for example: "she rocked [*basculait*] from memory into the present" (106).[c] We see, once again, that literal and figurative cannot be clearly opposed one to the other.

We can see too, from this last example, that memory has an interestingly complex function in the story. It appears, first of all, to provide the recognizably psychological dimension of training, so that O's disciplined position is a *remembered* attitude, causing her to be "gripped once again by the automatism of Roissy's rule" (238).[d] In addition, memory seems to serve here as a rather motley collection of images of submissiveness, each serving to provide a model for O from within her culture, her past experience, her youthful self. Nuns are, as I have suggested, the most frequently mentioned and presumably the privileged model. But images of them are mixed in with others in an apparently indiscriminate way. Here once again is the kneeling position: "She lifted up her chemise and kneeling, though seated on her heels, like Carmelites or Japanese women, she waited" (81).[e] Not only Carmelites or Japanese women, but an Egyptian statue can serve the same purpose: "O had bent her knees, sat on her heels, and placed her arms in her lap, like a statue from Egypt" (191–92).[f] Elsewhere, it is the image of a woman friend "leaning right back in the leather chair of a hotel room" (119),[g] or a sixteenth-century etching representing a husband beating his wife (109), or a statue O had seen as a child in the Luxembourg gardens (185). For Sadian modeling, these quite different passions would need to be classified and rehearsed with precision, but in *Histoire d'O* they are valued only as fleeting contributions to, or reinforcements of O's general attitude. This is refinement as *opposed to* discrimination, refinement as the ongoing (re)production of a certain, strictly immanent *quality*. Rather than a (classical) process of variation and multiplication, we find a honing-down, or a stylization. A bodily abstraction, so to speak, of the model's essence. Instead of being regularly available on cue, as narrative convenience, desire is oriented and developed throughout the story. It can be sustained as a kind of reflexive quest, and perfected as an attitude of openness.

Modeling in the novel is symbolized, if you like—but also specifically

[c] elle basculait du souvenir dans le présent.

[d] reprise par l'automatisme de la règle de Roissy

[e] Elle releva donc sa chemise, et à genoux, mais assise sur les talons, comme sont les carmélites ou les Japonaises, elle attendit.

[f] O, les genoux pliés, était assise sur ses talons et avait posé ses bras sur ses genoux, comme une statue d'Egypte.

[g] renversée dans le fauteuil de cuir d'une chambre d'hôtel

applied and enforced—by the kind of costume worn by O and her fellow "recluses." Typically, the costume combines tightness and exposure, the *serré* and the *ouvert:* The costume was similar to theirs: over a very rigid corset, severely bound at the waist, and a starched linen petticoat, there was a long, full-skirted dress whose bodice left the breasts, raised up as they were by the corset, more or less exposed, and scantily veiled by lace" (33).[h] The same kind of outfit—essentially—is worn by Jacqueline, the model photographed by O: "she was wearing an enormous silk dress [. . .] that [. . .] spread out at the hips and hugged her tightly at the waist. Its framework outlined the shape of her bust" (90).[i] The *épanouissement,* the blooming, expansion, or self-expression to which the woman's body is both invited and compelled is thus the unqualified avowal of its desire to be contained, its absolute openness to constraint.

That is the subtle difference, the essential discrepancy between Sadian rigor and the bondage that occurs in *Histoire d'O*. Sade's victims are transfixed, riveted to the spot with fear, sometimes literally enchained or impaled: "my companion's thighs were spread to the greatest possible degree, and attached to large items of furniture so that they could not change position [*varier*]" (*Les Cent Vingt Journées de Sodome,* 160).[j] On the other hand, O is always bound in such a way that some movement is still possible: "with the exception of her hands, which would always be fixed just above her head, she would therefore be able to move, and see the blows coming" (30).[13] [k] She is bound "more or less tightly" (37),[l] the *plus ou moins* being precisely the margin of her freedom: "the chain [. . .] only allowed her the freedom to take two steps forward" (75).[m] Sade's tyranny is devastatingly preemptive, rigidly precluding any maneuvering on the victim's part. Réage's, on the other hand, allows just enough play in the constraint for the victim to oscillate: "O swung to and fro in pain along the wall at the end of

[h] Le costume était semblable au leur: sur un corset très baleiné, et rigoureusement serré à la taille, et sur un jupon de linon empesé, une longue robe à large jupe dont le corsage laissait les seins, remontés par le corset, à peu près à découvert, à peine voilés de dentelle.

[i] elle portait une immense robe de soie [. . .] qui [. . .] s'épanouissait aux hanches, la serrait à la taille, et dont l'armature dessinait la poitrine.

[j] les cuisses de ma compagne étaient dans le plus grand écartement possible, et fixées à de gros meubles pour qu'elles ne pussent varier.

[k] sauf les mains qu'elle aurait tenues un peu au-dessus de la tête, elle pourrait donc bouger, et voir venir les coups.

[l] plus ou moins étroitement

[m] La chaîne [. . .] ne lui laissait que la liberté de faire deux pas en avant.

her chain, groaning in the dark" (48);[n] "swinging on her chain, she stood unsteadily on her bare feet" (144).[o] So it is that while O suffers she is able to twist and turn within the space of her suffering: "She twisted and turned so frantically to escape the biting of the leather thongs that she almost seemed to be revolving in front of the post, for the small chain that held her in place was long and a little slack, though solid" (31).[p] She is at "liberty" or at "leisure" to struggle in periods of great pain:

> The suffering would not all be inflicted on her at once. She would have time to shout, struggle, and weep. (30)
>
> O was struggling with all her might; she thought the straps were going to tear her. (196, cf. 71, 106)[q]

Effectively, the mechanical freedom built into O's tightly constrained play is what allows her, involuntarily, to aggravate—or should it be "enhance"?—her own suffering: "the rump was therefore wide open beneath the rope below her waist, and it only exposed itself all the more by its attempts to dodge the blows" (32).[r] Movement will never be unbridled here, nor will it result in any net displacement. It will never degenerate into the wild convulsions of *Gamiani*. Even at moments of intense suffering—never more tightly than at those moments—O is contained by masterly discipline, arranged in the very shape of proper womanly struggle, held fast against shapeless writhing and deliquescent agony.

By allowing such play *within* the heroine's position, the novel leaves open a space to be traversed and transformed by narrative. In a sense, the struggling can and must go on indefinitely as a "leisure" activity, or as a pleasurable exercise in "vanity": "she struggled in his [René's] grip, for the pleasure of feeling weaker than him, and at his mercy"

[n] O gémissante oscillait de douleur le long du mur, au bout de sa chaîne, dans le noir.

[o] balancée par la chaîne, elle chancelait sur ses pieds nus.

[p] Elle se tordait avec une telle frénésie pour échapper aux morsures des lanières qu'elle tournoyait presque sur elle-même, devant le poteau, car la chaînette qui la retenait était longue et donc un peu lâche, bien que solide.

[q] Tout ne lui serait pas infligé à la fois, elle aurait le loisir de crier, de se débattre et de pleurer.

O se débattait de tout son pouvoir, elle crut que les sangles la déchireraient.

[r] cette croupe offerte qui se tendait sous la corde au-dessous de sa taille et ne s'offrait que davantage en voulant se dérober.

(235).[s] In another sense, however, the space left for O is exactly the space of effort, of her work. While "more or less" bound and shaped, she must learn to *se conformer* more perfectly to these constraints, practicing locally the kind of sustained discipline deployed by Sade's heroes throughout the duration of the one hundred twenty days: "she would need to be constantly attentive in order to comply [*se conformer*] with this discipline" (82).[t] At the end of the long process, in *Histoire d'O,* lies the achievement of immobility as moral and postural perfection, rather than its imposition as absolute denial of freedom. Even after the first stay at Roissy, "what was especially striking was the perfection of her stillness" (88).[u]

It becomes clear at this point in our reading that the psychological elements of *Histoire d'O* in no way undo the theme of modeling. The story is actually about the desire for modeling, as much as it is about the modeling of desire. It is even demonstrably about the existential choice of bodily constraint. O is not free to wander around, or to propose any sort of action, but she is free to struggle and, in some drastic sense, to leave. René says as much to her: "He said to her that from that time forward she should not see herself as free. Except that she was free not to love him any more, and to leave him straightaway. But if she loved him, she was in no way free" (81; cf. 103).[v] This stops short of denying the most basic Sartrian tenets and allows us to see O's action as the enactment of a free, existentially responsible choice. O comes more and more in fact, as her desire shapes itself, to loathe freedom as an imposition: "The problem was that René was leaving her free, and she hated her freedom. Her freedom was worse than any chain" (138).[w] She can only rejoice in being branded, because her scars will bind the future to the past: "these marks meant that she could not cheat" (153).[x] What would it mean to cheat, if not to heal too well and thus spoil the shape of her life by choosing radically against that which she had previously chosen?

As the novel draws toward a conclusion, O appears finally to have approached the desired attitude so closely that she may be eliminating

[s] elle se débattait entre ses mains [celles de René] pour le plaisir de se sentir plus faible, et d'être à sa merci.

[t] il lui faudrait pour se conformer à cette discipline un constant effort d'attention.

[u] ce qui frappait surtout était la perfection de son immobilité.

[v] Il lui dit tout d'abord qu'il ne fallait pas qu'elle se crût libre désormais. A cela près qu'elle était libre de ne plus l'aimer, et de le quitter aussitôt. Mais si elle l'aimait, elle n'était libre de rien.

[w] C'est que René la laissait libre, et qu'elle détestait sa liberté. Sa liberté était pire que n'importe quelle chaîne.

[x] ces marques faisaient qu'elle ne pouvait tricher.

the space of discrepancy and struggle. She looks forward with confidence to the stage where there will be no delay whatsoever in her response. Not that she will have needed to learn that particular alacrity of desire, that swiftness to assume the pose which characterize both master and victim in Sade: "From now on there would be no more hiatus, no time-out, no remission. The one you are waiting for, because you are waiting for him, is already present, and already the master" (148).[y] It will simply be the case that her master's will is always already present, inscribed indelibly in her body, achieved with perfection in her open, empty "self."

Comparison with Sade must remind us at some point that nothing has so far been said, apropos of *Histoire d'O,* of that particular reflexivity of master and victim that seemed so often to be a part of thematic modeling, whether in Sade or in *L'Image. Histoire d'O* is in fact remarkably discreet about the master's role, in keeping with its continual narrative focus on the victim's position, and on the narrow circle of her movements. It is as if the telling were complicitous with O's attitude, obeying the rule of Roissy that seems not to allow the observation of male character: "you must never look one of us in the face" (35–36).[z] We do glimpse from time to time, as O must, a certain reflexivity, a play of equivalence that allows René as her first master to give way to Sir Stephen, precisely because Sir Stephen plays the role better: "In Sir Stephen he had found the strict master that he himself could not manage to be" (145).[a] What is denied us, almost teasingly so, is any clear view of a masterly position, if there is one, or any hearing of the master's confession of desire. Sir Stephen, in particular, seems continually on the point of revealing something like love to O, but can only allude to it, or whisper it in fragments (see, e.g., 122, 142, 156, 157, 177, 211). On one such occasion: "O suspected that this brutality [Sir Stephen's] was directed at himself as much as at her, and recalled only the end of the sentence: a man who loved her. What other avowal did she want?" (159).[b] It is patent that no symmetrically disciplined avowal of desire will be forthcoming from the male.

It does happen that the attitude of one character is mirrored in that of another, but this is something that goes on between women—

[y] Désormais, il n'y aurait plus d'hiatus, de temps mort, de rémission. Celui qu'on attend, parce qu'on l'attend, est déjà présent, déjà maître.

[z] vous ne devez jamais regarder un de nous au visage.

[a] En Sir Stephen, il avait trouvé le maître rigoureux que lui-même ne savait pas être.

[b] O douta si cette brutalité [celle de Sir Stephen] ne s'adressait pas à lui autant qu'à elle, et elle ne retint que la fin de la phrase: un homme qui l'aimait. Quel autre aveu voulait-elle?

or rather, between images of women. O's employment, before she gives it up to work at becoming a true woman of leisure, is as a fashion photographer, more or less like Claire, in *L'Image:* "O worked for the fashion section of a photographic agency. That meant that she executed, in the studio where posing went on for hours, photographs of the strangest and most beautiful girls, chosen by the designers to display their creations" (87–88).[c] This would seem to provide the perfect narrative opportunity for her to take her place in a chain of command, helping to shape young women in the image of submissiveness, rather like Sade's Saint-Ange or Mirabeau's Laure (*Le Rideau levé*). Yet there are a number of reasons why this does not happen in the way we might expect, and all of these reasons are thematic restrictions contributing to the narrow refinement of the notion of modeling in *Histoire d'O.*

First, it is not given to O, in her job, to "conceive" poses in any inventive way. She does not vary or multiply them, apparently: she merely "executes" photographs. Second, the models with whom she deals, notably Jacqueline, while professionally trained to hold attitudes, are not effectively modeled without *and* within, as O is. Clearly, the text is drawn toward the theme of modeling here, preferring to use an anglicism in order to speak of Jacqueline's "job as a mannequin, or as they say after the Americans, as a model" (170),[d] and then continuing to use the more compelling term: "her irregular job as a model" (175).[e] But for all her relevant training, or perhaps because of it, Jacqueline does not seem to have the inner posture, the finely molded desire that she might have observed in O herself. Her stillness, and her silence, are "false": "He [René] would come, she kept saying to herself, and it would be for him that Jacqueline, falsely still and falsely silent, would look up for a second, with her eyes like cold water that did not look directly at you. No one would need to teach her anything: neither keeping silent, nor leaving her hands open and her arms by her side, nor half tilting her head back" (138).[f]

The third effective restriction on modeling between women is

[c] O travaillait dans le service de mode d'une agence photographique. Ce qui voulait dire qu'elle exécutait, dans le studio où elles devaient poser durant des heures, les photos des filles les plus étranges et les plus jolies, choisies par les couturiers pour parer leurs modèles.

[d] métier de mannequin, ou comme on disait à l'américaine, de modèle

[e] son métier intermittent de modèle

[f] Il [René] viendrait, se répétait-elle, et ce serait pour lui que Jacqueline, faussement immobile, faussement muette, lèverait une seconde ses yeux d'eau froide qui ne regardaient pas en face. A elle, personne n'aurait besoin de rien apprendre: ni à se taire, ni à laisser ses mains ouvertes le long d'elle, ni à renverser la tête à demi.

marked as a quite specific ban on the type of pedagogical lesbianism that characterizes much erotic writing prior to the eighteenth century. Jacqueline's young sister Natalie, at fifteen, has reached the right age according to tradition for initiatory exercises in the art of love. She has the desire to emulate, "the admiration, impatience, and keenness" (229)[g] of, say, Chorier's Ottavia, and is eager to learn from and with O. But contact between them is expressly forbidden: "But Sir Stephen forbade O to teach her caresses of any sort, not even to embrace her on the mouth or let herself be kissed by her. He intended that Natalie should reach Roissy without having been touched by anyone's hands or lips" (228).[h]

O will not be allowed to present herself as exemplary, or undertake any teaching program based on her skills. For there must be no hierarchy, only the radical dualism of master and slave. Thus, when O does serve quite dramatically as a model for a young woman, it is because she is pointed to by a man. This is indeed the end of the story of O, if not exactly its climax: the acting out of a scene in which O merely holds her shape—as athletes sometimes say of themselves—and thereby serves a didactic purpose. As she sits naked and masked on the fringe of the commander's party, with her chain and her branded flesh, she can be approached and used as a model victim/lover. A young couple sits down next to her, and the man begins to carry out a demonstration, directing his lover's touch: "He took her hand, and forced her to caress O's breasts, which quivered at the touch of the cool hand. He made her touch O's pudenda, and the ring, and the hole through which the ring passed. The girl obeyed silently, and when the boy said that he would do the same thing to her, she did not flinch. But even as he took advantage of O in this way, using her as a model and an object for demonstration, not once did he speak to her" (250).[i] O is restricted, indeed powerfully disciplined to being no more than her bodily attitude. The fulfillment of her narrative destiny is as an image for others, a statue or a photograph in their memory, a kind of template for erotic servitude. In being so disposed,

[g] l'admiration, l'impatience et l'envie

[h] Mais Sir Stephen interdit à O de lui apprendre la moindre caresse, de l'embrasser fût-ce sur la bouche, et de se laisser embrasser par elle. Il entendait qu'elle [Natalie] arrivât à Roissy sans avoir été touchée par les mains ou les lèvres de qui que ce fût.

[i] Il lui prit la main, la força de caresser les seins d'O, qui frémit sous la légère main fraîche, et de toucher le ventre d'O, et l'anneau, et le trou où passait l'anneau; la petite obéissait en silence, et lorsque le garçon lui dit qu'il lui en ferait autant, elle n'eut pas un mouvement de recul. Mais même en disposant ainsi d'O, et même en la prenant ainsi comme modèle, ou comme objet de démonstration, pas une seule fois on ne lui adressa la parole.

and so disposed of, she may seem to achieve the ultimate refinement, a kind of transcendent erotic condition whereby the attitude is available to be taken up by others as the style of their desire.

Like *L'Image, Histoire d'O* thematizes comfort, although in a manner that is less insolently offensive, precisely because it is more complex, pursuing as it does a dialectic of comfort and discomfort. Kaja Silverman makes the point that O "never experiences hunger, sleepiness, poor health or discomfort of any sort except in so far as it is induced by her captors."[14] Is this to say that O is protected from social adversities of the kind that afflict, say, Sade's Justine? She is sometimes tortured in such a way that to speak of "discomfort" would itself be a form of insolence, but she clearly does have, while imprisoned, a kind of atmospheric comfort. In particular, while she is sensitive to cold (87), she is never made to suffer in that regard for her lack of warm underwear. There are thick blankets of fur on her bed at Roissy (44), radiators in the cell where she is punished (75), and heating, in Sir Stephen's car, that flows along her legs (98). Within this material comfort, with its velvet blindfolds (73) and its warm silk sofas (192), she suffers quite acute discomfort of a postural kind. The kneeling position really hurts—"she was very uncomfortable on her knees" (27)[j]—at least until she is able to refine the pose and learn to be at home in it. She is bound up at Roissy in a finely made costume whose very tightness produces paradoxical comfort: "At the same time, the waist was extremely tight, making the pudenda protrude and the back curve right in. The strange thing is that this framework was very comfortable and, up to a point, restful. One had to stand up very straight in it, but it made one aware, for some reason, perhaps by contrast, of the freedom, or rather the availability of those parts that were not compressed" (57).[k] For one who knows how to inhabit the role perfectly, there is comfort to be found at the heart of the severest constraint.

I began my discussion of modeling by asking a question about beginnings, but was only able to continue by giving that question up. One has to be reminded, in reading erotic literature produced before the Romantic period, of the ongoing nature of desire. This is why it is appropriate to talk in terms of the classical, even apropos of Sade,

[j] Elle était très mal à genoux.

[k] En même temps, la taille s'étranglait, ce qui faisait saillir le ventre et cambrer profondément les reins. L'étrange est que cette armature était très confortable, et jusqu'à un certain point reposante. On s'y tenait bien droite, mais elle rendait sensible, sans qu'on sût très bien pourquoi, à moins que ce ne fût par contraste, la liberté ou plutôt la disponibilité de ce qu'elle ne comprimait pas.

Mirabeau, and their contemporaries. They describe in fact a process in which the object of desire is already given in culture, and in which the subject is called upon for the appropriate response. Recognizing this, I have sought nonetheless to ask what kind of quasi-psychology occurs classically as a by-product, what quality of desire is required to ensure that the thematically proper response will in fact occur. It has thus been possible, in the midst of tradition, to discern a responsiveness that seems to be almost the essence of "character" in such erotic narrative. This is what Georges Poulet might have called, had he ever been able to endure all these exercises in unfreedom, a *cogito* of obedience. At the heart of disciplined continuity, we found the punctuality of desire, in both senses: its happening at a particular point in time and its doing so quite regularly, arriving on time at the crossroads, being there when it was needed by the narrative.

It has been helpful, I suggest, to read classical modeling as a form of training that effectively denies the radical newness of romantic lust, and the wildly unpredictable nature of its outcomes. We have been able to follow the working of a material discipline that preempts, so to speak, the radical duality of body and mind, holding the body in place, and affirming that desire must follow. The great dichotomies of Romantic discourse—spiritual and material, natural and artificial, individual and social—are precluded by the affirmation of *conformité de goût* as that which enables and sustains erotic action. For modern texts such as *Histoire d'O* and *L'Image,* to retrieve and consolidate this tradition is thus to partake of its authority. *Histoire d'O* and *L'Image* do not just quote some of the same themes: they actually rehearse in a comparable way the thematic nature of desire, with its echoing commands and its reflexive, circular compulsion. They represent the very workings of desire as bound up in literary tradition.

Conclusion

Michael Perkins, in *The Secret Record: Modern Erotic Literature,* claims to discover erotic literature as a hitherto untouched field for critical study. Because such writing has been "neglected," he says, "the instructive processes of public appraisal and literary criticism have not been available to it." Perkins is constructing here a historical narrative to describe the development of criticism, and that narrative is itself a good old virginity story. By a dizzily unself-conscious *mise en abyme,* erotic literature is said to be young, innocent, and potentially thrilling: "Erotic writing is therefore peculiarly virginal, for in the absence of these reactions there are no standards by which its real achievements can be measured. Erotic writing is strong because it is read innocently and weak because its readers have no criteria by which to judge it. [. . .] What is the difference between good and bad erotic writing and how is one to distinguish between the two?"[1] It is hard to imagine how any critical opinion could be more radically opposed, or any approach more utterly foreign to the argument I have been making in this book. Perkins sees an exciting new opportunity for critical judgment to mold this maidenly body of texts into a canonical shape: my point is that erotic literature is available for criticism only because it always already has a shape, and indeed some sort of place in the canon.

At times, that place can appear relatively uncontentious. Emile Henriot took it for granted, and made it more comfortably familiar, when he spoke of the "second shelf," coining a phrase that continues in modern critical use.[2] As he devoted an indulgent series of essays to the "livres du second rayon," Henriot supposed that the books of which he spoke were not merely packed away in boxes, or lying in piles on the floor, or even hidden under pillows. They were, and doubtless still are, aligned on a shelf, in their own discreet section of the library. The authors' names, in Henriot's list of "irréguliers et libertins" include many of those I have been referring to in this study: Brantôme, Crébillon fils, Godard d'Aucour, Nerciat, Restif, Laclos, and Vivant Denon.[3] But the criteria for their admission to the critic's second shelf are in fact double, not to say ambiguous. It is not hard, after all, to see why libertine writers are irregular by definition, yet "irregularity" is a quality that signifies resistance to categorization, and need not manifest itself only as libertinism. Henriot's list of names recognizes this implicitly by including a dozen or so authors whose work could not be considered part of any tradition of eroticism. Important here, however, is that those authors are said to belong in the one group as "menus conteurs," "légers moralistes," "amuseurs," and "libertins" (8). While these writers may lack the true genius proper to "les écrivains de premier plan" they are often more precise in their observation of life (8). Eroticism is thus dealt with in passing by being subsumed under an aesthetic category, so that the *literary* irregularity found in Crébillon, Nerciat, and their colleagues can be attributed to their practice of particular forms of description. For Henriot's transhistorical humanism, libertine/irregular writing is distinguished by its (perhaps excessive) detail and by the narrow focus of its descriptive attention. Any eroticism that may occur can thus be seen as stemming from a forgivable overindulgence in the art of realism. There is an underlying principle that regulates and domesticates irregularity.

Henriot represents the proper reader of libertine works as one who responds in a measured way. There are, admittedly, some rather offensive things in Nerciat's *Le Diable au corps,* for example, but the challenge of irregularity can be dealt with readily enough by "a reader who is curious, but sane enough to put everything in its place, and not exaggerate its importance" (281).[a] Moderation in all things appears to be the key—even at times when one may be indulging in excesses. Maintaining aesthetic (and moral) order, for Henriot, means putting *Le Diable au corps* where it really belongs. It is a matter of enjoying the work, and then carefully putting it away where it is no longer in

[a] un lecteur curieux, mais désintéressé et assez sain d'esprit pour voir toute chose à sa place sans s'en exagérer l'importance

full view, on the lower shelf. Yet no matter how serenely such works are put in their place, no matter how determined the critic may be to defuse any dramatic tension surrounding the event of their exclusion, the business of distinction, in Bourdieu's sense,[4] cannot be carried out with total ease. If every work on the second shelf were both aesthetically inferior and socially improper, then all would be well enough. Yet from time to time, these twin criteria fail to coincide. Of Nerciat's *Félicia,* Henriot feels compelled to say: "I shall always regret the fact that half a dozen passages with a little too much detail should have condemned this book to the shelf of forbidden masterpieces" (296).[b] Were it not for these few momentary lapses of tact, *Félicia* would presumably occupy a place alongside other masterpieces. As it is, however, the work must remain "forbidden." Comparably, Vivant Denon's *Point de lendemain* is no doubt to be thought of as condemned despite—or because of?—being a "frivole chef-d' œuvre" (382) or a "léger chef-d'œuvre" (276). Between the peccadillo of frivolity and the punishment of canonical interdiction, there is a strange disproportion, such that the partial exclusion of such fine writing can only be accepted with regret.

In this way, the second shelf appears more or less to reconcile the functions of accommodation and exclusion. *Félicia* and *Point de lendemain* can be thought of, in Henriot's terms, as masterpieces that might almost have claimed a place on the highest shelf, yet have somehow slipped to the level below, by an unhappy accident of authorial misjudgment. In that rather facile sense, the second shelf can be thought of as a kind of safety net: when works have failed to be canonical highfliers, they are still saved from oblivion with its support. To put it most simply, the second shelf is hardly more than a gathering place for narrowly failed masterpieces. The paradox, in the context of my study, is that Henriot affirms the relative coherence of his second shelf, through an aesthetic or cognitive style shared by its denizens, without remarking directly on the eroticism that might be said to bind many of the works together. There is no discussion of any thematic network, or of any generic tendency to mutual reinforcement. Even as Henriot gestures toward a problematic subcanon of irregular eroticism, he leaves unanswered some rather pressing questions. How are we to understand the paradox of exclusion and accommodation? What is the nature of canonical marginality?

[b] Je regretterai toujours que pour une demi-douzaine de passages trop circonstanciés l'auteur ait condamné son livre au rayon des chef-d'œuvres défendus.

The extent of the difficulty here becomes clear as soon as one mentions the great name unspoken in Henriot: that of Sade. Sade is not light, frivolous, or amusing, and does not belong on the second shelf. Indeed, Henriot does not begin to negotiate a place for him, presumably because he is so utterly beyond the pale as not to attract the nicely ambivalent blend of condemnation and indulgence that supports the second shelf. Where eroticism of the kind found in Nerciat or Vivant Denon is considered as impropriety, then propriety must only be a matter of degree. Such excesses as Nerciat's are forgivable precisely because they can be seen as mere irregularities. There seems to be no common measure between these passing indelicacies and Sade's systematic obscenity. Yet it can hardly be denied that Sade's work, too, must have a place somewhere, if only in recognition of its widespread historical influence. To follow Henriot is to locate Sade at an infinite distance from his close contemporaries, Nerciat and Restif.

James Hulbert, in a 1988 study, considers Sade as an exemplary figure in the French literary canon. Indeed, as Hulbert goes on to point out, the very fact of taking Sade as exemplary has itself been part of the historical process of canon formation.[5] In the first instance, Sade was generally declared to be anathema to a civilized society. Later, he was saved by radicals in the name of his very accursedness, being transformed by revolutionary decree from the diabolical to the "divine." Frances Ferguson suggests, no doubt correctly, that it was often possible for twentieth-century writers like Klossowski, Blanchot, and Bataille to consider Sade's writings as "fossil remains" saved from destruction by chance, and uncompromised by "historical baggage." Sade's texts, she says, "have become icons of a cultural heritage especially valuable for being one that we have very nearly been denied. With the preciousness of narrowly averted scarcity and possible extinction, they have functioned as central illustrations of the argument that censorship and repression violate a text's right to cultural transmission, a public's right to receive a canonical legacy as broad and diverse as possible."[6] This is, I am sure, an accurate reflection of the way in which Sade has been read as ahistorically modern, but it is still very much, as Ferguson herself suggests, bound up with the processes of canon formation. Nancy Miller describes the twentieth-century "discovery" of Sade's work as "an exemplary instance of the political ambiguities of what used to be called 'critical fortunes,'"[7] and Lucienne Frappier-Mazur calls it a "magnified example" of canon formation.[8] Whether reviled or exalted, Sade's work has long been a privileged—

not to say, a canonical—object of canonical dispute. Hunted down by some and held up in defiance by others, it has never been able to nestle quietly on Henriot's second shelf.

The ambivalence of canonical exclusion/inclusion is such that it seems to require ever more complicated shelving arrangements. Jules Janin, in an article that helped to consecrate Sade's notoriety in the first part of the nineteenth century, located Sade's work on a mysterious "hidden shelf": "Make no mistake about it, the marquis de Sade is everywhere. He is in all the libraries, on a mysterious, hidden shelf that one can always uncover. His is one of those books that is normally placed behind Saint John Chrysostom or Nicole's *Treatise on Morality*, or Pascal's *Thoughts*."[9] [c] These books lurking in the depths of the library must be a kind of uncountable supplement to the standard works of the canon. Yet there are indications that, in the course of the nineteenth century, Sade's presence became less diabolically ubiquitous and more precisely, more canonically localized. As if to reflect a certain rational progress in cataloguing the erotic, Rachilde's *Monsieur Vénus* (1884) has a libertine heroine whose library groups separately the books that Henriot was later to describe and those that Janin saw, or feared he might see, lurking behind every famous edifying work. Rachilde's heroine has a private library with hundreds of books on show, including the likes of Boccaccio and Brantôme, while in the center of this display stands a closed, ivory-incrusted chest, with crimson velvet shelves. This is her own private collection of "unspeakable works" (*ouvrages inavouables*).[10] She appears to devote one shelf—let us call it the second—to the more polite, or longer established, libertines, and a private case to the Sades.

Holding all these books together in a homogeneously canonical space is doubtless beyond the skill of any cabinetmaker. We must be content to note the metaphorical tensions produced between the two most common ways of relating erotic literature with respect to—and more or less within—the canonical library. Mediating between the two, however, in the French context, is the notion of the *enfer*. The *enfer* is of course both a specific place—a set of shelves in the national library—and a domain of accursedness. It can be the object of routine cataloguing, but also bears the mark of a collective denunciation. By its double nature, this space accommodates the frivolous and the unspeakable, housing irregularities and obscenities side by side. In-

[c] Car ne vous y trompez pas, le marquis de Sade est partout; il est dans toutes les bibliothèques, sur un certain rayon mystérieux et caché qu'on découvre toujours; c'est un de ces livres qui se placent d'ordinaire derrière un saint Jean Chrysostome ou le *Traité de morale* de Nicole, ou les *Pensées* de Pascal.

deed, where exclusion from public display also means inclusion in the *enfer,* or the Reserve, or the Private Case, it is possible to maintain the mechanisms of canon formation—ivory and velvet—while systematically inverting the aesthetic and moral values that normally guide them. When Mandiargues is called upon to identify modern erotic literature, he enters fully into this double game, replying authoritatively with a list of great works, and closing his list with a sacred formula. The works listed are:

Apollinaire, *Les Onze Mille Verges*

Louÿs, *Trois Filles de leur mère*

Bataille, *Histoire de l'œil*

Aragon, *Le Con d'Irène*

Genet, *Le Miracle de la rose* and *Pompes funèbres*

Anon., *L'Anglais décrit dans le château fermé*

Réage, *Histoire d'O*

Noël, *Château de Cène*

de Berg, *L'Image*

Guerre, *Les Dix Japonais*

Louvre, *Les Trigynes*

Pierre, *Qu'est-ce que Thérèse?*

"Voilà," says Mandiargues. "These are the modern books of hell that I include in paradise. Beyond them, unless I have forgotten one or two, there is no salvation!"[11] [d] That *L'Image* and *Histoire d'O* are included should hardly surprise us: the canon exists, in part, as a guarantee against surprise. But what is most striking here is the ritual practice of exclusion: "Hors de ceux-là, [. . .] pas de salut!" Clearly, being in "hell" and being in paradise are approximately equivalent, for the *enfer* of erotic literature is no place of primitive chaos. Its constituent works are not in limbo: they are harmoniously disposed and properly identified, just like their heavenly counterparts.

Infernal canonicity, I have tried to show, is both confirmed and

[d] Voilà les modernes livres d'enfer que je mets en paradis. Hors de ceux-là, à quelque oubli près, pas de salut!

produced by an ongoing thematics. Not simply the presence in a range of texts of some thing called eroticism, but the intertextual working of a certain order that helps to determine what will count as a theme. It might be said, in summary, that I am pointing both to the inadequacy and to the usefulness of Henriot's "shelf" metaphor. This is the best answer I can give to a set of demanding and highly relevant questions formulated by Lucienne Frappier-Mazur, who asks: "can one speak of a 'marginal canon' of works often widely read by major writers but not belonging to the academic institution? [. . .] What is the relation of low to high literature, which actually overlaps that of pornographic to erotic?"[12] Belonging on the shelf, durably taking a place in the literary set, depends on a complex play of exclusion and inclusion. Pornography, at its most base, is unproblematically excluded. Unlike Sade or Bataille, it is not accursed. Its authors are not infamous: merely despised or grubbily anonymous. Its works, as we know, are published in paperback and delivered in plain brown wrappers, for immediate consumption. They have almost no shelf life.

Canon formation has been highlighted and problematized in recent critical debate by considerations about the exclusion of women writers from the canon. James Hulbert points out that Sade, in his "Idée sur les romans," was "himself one of the first propounders of a canon of novels."[13] Joan De Jean and others, as noted earlier, locate decisive moments of academic canonical legislation at about the same time as Sade.[14] But what is the relationship, if any, between the equivocal inclusion/exclusion of erotic literature like that of Sade and the apparently more tranquil neglect of, say, Riccoboni? Or rather, since that question is too vast in scope for a study such as mine—especially at a time when it is seeking to arrive at a conclusion—what can be said about the place of women authors within the erotic (sub)canon? Answering even this question is no simple matter. The first problem is that traditional erotic literature appears to see women as the privileged sources of sexual knowledge. They it is who are represented as teachers, learners, and, most generally, utterers of venereal talk. Is this representation a vestigial recognition of what was once an autonomous feminine ritual? Is it a fictive convenience whereby women are made to give voice to a sexual nature imputed to them by men? Our thematic history has left us wavering between these two accounts, as if the slippage itself were somehow closest to an explanation.

Claudine Brécourt-Villars, in her anthology of women's erotic texts from 1799 to 1984, objects vigorously to the canonical closure of standard erotic literature, saying that it is closed against women writers. She notes the repetition of canonical themes, with its "obsessive hell,"[e] and suggests that the received list of authors' names functions effectively to exclude most literature produced by women. She could almost be speaking here of Mandiargues's list, but that is simply a reminder to us that Mandiargues is not expressing a narrowly personal opinion:

> It is true that those who reduce the space of literary eroticism in this way support their claims by mentioning only a few titles—always the same ones—of masculine works that are acknowledged [*consacrées*] but limited in number, and whose reputation depends solely on the author's name! That was the case for Sade who, for generations, obsessed people who could not even gain access to his work. Among our contemporaries, people often cite Georges Bataille, Pierre Klossowski, André Pieyre de Mandiargues, Alain Robbe-Grillet, sometimes Michel Leiris and, here and there, where women are concerned, works like *Emmanuelle* and inescapably—despite its quality—the solitary *Histoire d'O*.[15 f]

"What about other works produced by women?" asks Brécourt-Villars, pointing to Choiseul-Meuse, Pougy (*Idylle saphique*), Colette, Wittig, and dozens more.

Here is a further site, then, for the struggle of canon formation and reformation. To what extent is the exclusion of women part of the constitutive dynamics of the erotic canon? Can works written by women now be added to the second shelf, without disturbing the arrangement currently in place? The first answer to these questions would appear to be implicit in the analysis of Choiseul-Meuse's and Réage's work conducted in this book. Choiseul-Meuse, in particular, makes thematic room for herself: she contributes to the undoing of certain classical themes, and to the elaboration of feminine erotic tactics, but she does so in a way that engages—subversively—with canonical themes. Pougy and Wittig, as I have tried to show elsewhere,[16] are writing in a very different thematic context, involving a modernist thematics of narrative time. Their work, like that of Colette, Gaëtane, and others, deserves to be studied as "erotic literature," but

[e] enfer obsessionnel

[f] Il est vrai que ceux qui réduisent ainsi l'espace de l'érotisme littéraire n'évoquent, pour fonder leurs assertions, que quelques titres—toujours les mêmes—d'œuvres masculines consacrées, mais circonscrites, dont la réputation repose seulement sur le nom de l'auteur! Ce fut le cas de Sade obsédant des générations qui n'eurent même pas accès à son œuvre. Pour les contemporains, on cite volontiers: Georges Bataille, Pierre Klossowski, André Pieyre de Mandiargues, Alain Robbe-Grillet, éventuellement Michel Leiris et, çà et là, pour les femmes, des œuvres comme *Emmanuelle* et encore et toujours—en dépit de sa qualité—la seule *Histoire d'O*.

the notion of erotic literature then requires a newer thematics, a polemical relation with the modernist canon, and a substantially renovated library shelf.

As if to preempt any such renovation, Alexandrian, as literary historian, seems committed to denying female authorship to any of the hundred erotic classics he identifies with confidence.[17] Of Choiseul-Meuse, we are told that "this countess, like many society ladies playing at being bluestockings [. . .], had her books written by ghostwriters" (252; cf. 276–77).[g] Liane de Pougy's *Idylle saphique* was "written by her usual ghostwriter, Henri Albert" (260).[h] Réage is merely a mask for Jean Paulhan: "*Histoire d'O* was imagined by Paulhan himself" (276);[i] and Emmanuelle d'Arsan's work, it is "whispered," was written by her husband (279). The denial of women's writing in Alexandrian's history is so systematic as to be almost comic—as if the same voices were always whispering in his ear. Yet all this leaves us to wonder about what is at stake between, for example, Brécourt-Villars and Alexandrian, as the one struggles to include women writers within the field of erotic literature and the other works to preserve a homogeneously masculinist domain. For antipornographic feminists like Andrea Dworkin, the most straightforward polemical strategy would no doubt be to concede Alexandrian's claims by saying that no woman could be authentically complicitous with such themes. For others, like Luce Irigaray perhaps, the issue of feminine authorship might be seen as something of a distraction from the real work (and the real play) of an enunciative construction of the feminine. Part of the achievement of a text such as Wittig's *Le Corps lesbien* is no doubt to disturb the very possibility of the woman's confessional voice as heard from Aretino to *Histoire d'O*.

In recognizing the difficulty of pursuing the same old thematics apropos of Wittig, for example, I am marking the limits of my own study. Attention to the classically erotic has been the strategy I have followed from the outset, and a strong point is made, I think, by showing a degree of traditional continuity from the *Ragionamenti* to *L'Image*. I have in fact refused to tell the story of erotic literature as a great modern narrative. Classical eroticism was not guillotined at the end of the eighteenth century, and did not deserve to be. Nor did Sade's release from the Bastille unleash on the world a totally unprecedented set of sexual themes. It remains true nonetheless that

[g] cette comtesse, comme bien des femmes du monde jouant les bas-bleus [. . .], faisait écrire ses livres par des "nègres."

[h] écrit par son "nègre" habituel, Henri Albert

[i] *Histoire d'O* a été imaginée par Paulhan lui-même.

modernism, from the nineteenth century onward, tends to reshape the erotic to its own narrative purpose. Discontinuity itself takes on narrative significance, as the symptom, or the product, of desire. The beginning, the middle, and the end become significant moments in the rise and fall of intensity. Notions like "the sex act," "orgasm," and narrative climax take their place in a highly narrativized thematic order, superseding both the paradigmatic spread of *ars erotica,* and the incrementally progressive syntagm characteristic of many eighteenth-century stories. From Musset's *Gamiani* (1833) to *Le Corps lesbien* (1973), this modernist thematic is developed and reworked, bridging over Bataille and Klossowski, with their powerful reinterpretations of Sade. But that, as they say, is another story, and can be told in another place.

Apropos of modernist eroticism, I should say that I believe it, too, can be helpfully studied as a tradition, in approximately Gadamerian terms. On the face of it, there is every indication that the institutions of canonicity function just as powerfully around and within modernist erotic literature as they do around the more classical kind. The "classics" of modernist eroticism, as listed by Mandiargues, or even in the augmented list put forward by Brécourt-Villars, require a reading that is sensitive to their status. The difference is that modernism is an antitraditional tradition, affirming its revolutionary strength by breaking with the past, yet at the same time drawing its rhetorical power from an already-established revolutionary discourse. The surge of spontaneous desire and the radical discontinuity at the heart of erotic experience function thematically even as they are said to be utterly singular. Spontaneity, rupture, and the unprecedented are themselves powerful themes, and constraining narrative shapes. The distinctive thing about classical erotic literature is that it is systematically more reflexive about its own canonicity. It deserves to be studied first, not as the early, inferior phase of a great historical narrative, but because it presents an edifying object for study. Here, better than elsewhere, are manifest both the broadly cultural and the narrowly thematic nature of the erotic.

Notes

1. Erotic Literature as a Field of Study: Canonical Thematics

1. Storm Jameson, "The Retreat from the Pleasure Principle," *The Case against Pornography*, ed. David Holbrook (London: Stacey, 1972) 209.

2. Susan Griffin, *Pornography and Silence: Culture's Revenge against Nature* (London: Women's Press, 1981) 1–2.

3. Audre Lorde, "Uses of the Erotic: The Erotic as Power," *Take Back the Night: Women on Pornography*, ed. Laura Lederer (New York: William Morrow, 1980) 297.

4. Steven Marcus, *The Other Victorians: A Study of Sexuality and Pornography in Mid-Nineteenth Century England* (London: Weidenfeld and Nicolson, 1966) passim.

5. Bradley Smith, *Les Maîtres de l'art érotique au XXe siècle* (Paris: Julliard, 1980) 8.

6. P. B. Gobin, "L'Erotisme et la fête: Bataille, Leiris, Vailland," *Mosaic* 1, no. 2 (1969), 88.

7. J.-M. Lo Duca, *Histoire de l'érotisme* (Paris: Pygmalion, 1979) 7.

8. Milan Chlumsky, "Esthéticité, érotisme et pornographie," *Erotiques* (Paris: 10/18 Inédit, 1978) 207.

9. Joan Hoff, "Why Is There No History of Pornography?" *For Adult Users Only: The Dilemma of Violent Pornography*, ed. Susan Gubar and Joan Hoff (Bloomington: Indiana University Press, 1989) 27.

10. See also Pierre Bourdieu, *La Distinction: Critique sociale du jugement* (Paris: Minuit, 1979) passim.

11. Cf. Joan De Jean, "Teaching Frenchness," *French Review* 61 (1988), 398, and John Guillory, "The Ideology of Canon-Formation: T. S. Eliot and Cleanth Brooks," *Critical Inquiry* 10 (1984), 195.

12. Angela Carter, *The Sadeian Woman and the Ideology of Pornography* (New York: Harper and Row, 1980) 17.

13. Andrea Dworkin, *Pornography: Men Possessing Women* (London: Women's Press, 1981) 10. For other attempts to undo the distinction, see Ellen Willis, "Feminism, Moralism, and Pornography," and Ann Snitow, "Mass Market Romance: Pornography for Women is Different," both in *Powers of Desire,* ed. Ann Snitow, Christine Stansell, and Sharon Thompson (New York: Monthly Review Press, 1983) 84 and 268 respectively. The following writers on eroticism all reject the distinction on logical or methodological grounds: John Alfred Atkins, *Sex in Literature I: The Erotic Impulse in Literature* (London: Calder and Boyars, 1970) 9; Maurice Charney, *Sexual Fiction* (London: Methuen, 1981) 2; Alexandrian, *Histoire de la littérature érotique* (Paris: Seghers, 1989) 8.

14. Gloria Steinem, "Erotica and Pornography: A Clear and Present Difference," *MS,* November 1978, 54.

15. Diana E. H. Russell, "Pornography and Violence: What Does the New Research Say?" *Take Back the Night,* 218–19.

16. De Jean, "Teaching Frenchness," 398.

17. Robert von Hallberg, "Editor's Introduction," *Critical Inquiry* 10 (1984), iii–iv.

18. De Jean, "Teaching Frenchness," 403, speaks of repetition: "the importance of repetition in canon formation must never be underestimated. Critics-pedagogues most often just reiterate the judgments of others." Von Hallberg, however, in his "Editor's Introduction," iv, does speak briefly of "emulation." Richard Ohmann, while tracing circuits of power and commercial influence at work in canon formation, also points to thematic regularities at work in canonical modern fiction ("The Shaping of a Canon: U.S. Fiction, 1960–1975," *Critical Inquiry* 10 [1984], 212–19).

19. Hans-Georg Gadamer, *Truth and Method* (New York: Seabury Press, 1975).

20. See Peter Cryle, "Réflexions thématiques sur la théorie littéraire: Gadamer 'contre' Iser," *Texte* 3 (1984), 119–39, and "Sur la critique thématique," *Poétique* 64 (November 1985), 505–16.

21. Denis Hollier, *La Prise de la Concorde: Essais sur Georges Bataille* (Paris: Gallimard, 1974) 251–52. In Gadamerian terms, genre can be understood as that which allows us to know what to do with a text from the past. Typically, the canon functions through the articulation of genre and theme.

22. Atkins, *Sex in Literature,* I, 103.

23. Erling Eng, "Psyche and Longing, Mourning and Anger," *Facets of Eros: Phenomenological Essays,* ed. F. J. Smith and Erling Eng (The Hague: Nijhoff, 1972) 80.

24. Simone de Beauvoir, *La Force de l'âge* (Paris: Gallimard, 1960) 144.

25. Horst Robert Glaser is quoted in *Erotiques,* special issue of *Revue d'Esthétique* (1978) (Paris: 10/18 Inédit, 1978) 209, on the same point: "Setting up a category called 'erotic literature' that, because it referred directly to the sexual in its content, would be separated from other kinds, considered to be non-erotic, would not only amount to a revival of the old aesthetics of content in an even more refined costume, but would also be ignoring the sexualization that has become established in the meantime throughout the whole field of aesthetics."

26. Roland Barthes, *Le Plaisir du texte* (Paris: Le Seuil, 1973) 56; Barthes's emphasis.

27. This is what Barthes himself recognizes when he says in *Le Plaisir du texte,* 88: "The text of *plaisir* is not necessarily the one that relates pleasures; the text of *jouissance* is never the one that recounts a particular sensual delight."

28. Michel Foucault, *Histoire de la sexualité I: La Volonté de savoir* (Paris: Gallimard, 1976) 77, 78.

29. Henry Spenser Ashbee is the author of *Bibliography of Prohibited Books* (New York: Brussel, 1962), Louis Perceau of *Bibliographie des romans érotiques au XIXe siècle* (Paris: Fourdrinier, 1930), and Pascal Pia of *Les Livres de l'enfer* (Paris: Coulet et Faure, 1978).

30. J.-Cl. Lattès has published a series under the name "Les Classiques interdits," and Fayard one entitled "L'Enfer de la Bibliothèque Nationale."

31. Anon., *Le Roman de Violette* (Lisbon: Da Boa-Vista, 1870) [Brussels, 1883] 60–61.

32. Friedrich Carl Forberg, *Manuel d'érotologie classique,* trans. Alcide Bonneau (Paris: I. Lisieux, 1882) 2 vols.

33. Nicolas Chorier, *Les Dialogues de Luisa Sigea sur les arcanes de l'amour et de Vénus, ou Satire sotadique de Nicolas Chorier,* trans. Alcide Bonneau (Paris: I. Lisieux, 1882) 4 vols., I, ixxxii.

34. Suetonius, *Vie de Tibère,* trans. Henri Ailloud (Paris: Livre de Poche, 1966) 43. Robert Graves's version, in *The Twelve Caesars* (Harmondsworth: Penguin, 1957) 131, has: "The inmates of the establishment would know from these exactly what was expected of them." Richard Lewinsohn talks in comparable terms about the mural illustrations in the lupanars of Pompeii. See his *A History of Sexual Customs* (New York: Harper, 1958) 71.

35. Anon., "Priapée, III," in Forberg, *Manuel d'érotologie,* I, 9 n. 4.

36. Pierre de Brantôme, *Les Dames galantes* (Paris: Garnier, 1965) 27.

37. David Fairweather Foxon, *Libertine Literature in England, 1660–1745* (London: Book Collector, 1964) 5. Lucienne Frappier-Mazur puts it more carefully when she says: "The genre as such begins to appear in the sixteenth century and slowly follows the evolution of the novel." Frappier-Mazur, "Marginal Canons: Rewriting the Erotic," *Yale French Studies* 75 (1988), 112 n. 2.

38. Morse Peckham, *Art and Pornography: An Experiment in Explanation* (New York: Basic Books, 1969) 288. Wayland Young locates a beginning just one stage later, in Chorier's text, of which he says: "it is an epochal work in the sense that it is the first book (I think) which contains nothing but sex from

start to finish. [. . .] There is nothing else, and within the demarcated field, nothing is left out. It is the first work of rigid [*sic*] specialization, and thousands of later works have done no more than ring the changes on it." Young, "In Despite of Christendom," *The Perverse Imagination: Sexuality and Literary Culture,* ed. Irving Buchen (New York: New York University Press, 1970) 94.

39. *Les Sonnets luxurieux du divin Pietro Aretino* (Paris: I. Lisieux, 1882) 3, tells us that the sonnets were composed on (*sopra*) the postures.

40. It is hard for modern readers to ignore the fact that erotic literature since the late eighteenth century has been dominated by the reputation of another "divine" author: the marquis de Sade.

41. Lewinsohn, *A History of Sexual Customs,* 157.

42. Félix Nogaret, *L'Arétin français, suivi des Epices de Vénus* (Versailles: Aux dépens des fermiers généraux, n.d.) 8.

43. Pietro Aretino, *Les Ragionamenti, ou Dialogues du divin Pietro Aretino,* trans. Alcide Bonneau (Paris: I. Lisieux, 1882) I, v–vi.

44. See the note on this by Alcide Bonneau in his introduction to Forberg, *Manuel d'érotologie,* I, 17 n. 8.

45. See the note on this by Jean Hervez in his introduction to Pidansat de Mairobert, *La Secte des anandrynes* (Paris: Bibliothèque des curieux, 1920) xxix n. 1.

46. Louis Perceau, introduction to Nogaret, *L'Arétin français,* 7.

47. Foxon puts it much better when he speaks of the "dialogue between an older and a younger woman" as "one which remained the norm for at least 150 years," in *Libertine Literature,* 25.

48. See Perceau, introduction to Nogaret, *L'Arétin français,* 8.

49. Ferrante Pallavicino, *La Retorica delle puttane* (Cambrai: n.p., 1642) E9.

50. From *Stances* by Pierre Motin (1566–1610), in *La Poésie érotique,* ed. Georges Pillement (Paris: Régine Deforges, L'Or du temps, 1970) 51.

51. Diane Griffin Crowder, "Amazons and Mothers? Monique Wittig, Hélène Cixous and Theories of Women's Writing," *Contemporary Literature* 24 (1983), 123.

52. Elaine Marks, "Lesbian Intertextuality," *Homosexualities and French Literature: Cultural Contexts/Critical Texts,* ed. G. Stambolian and E. Marks (Ithaca and London: Cornell University Press, 1979) 357.

53. See Marks, "Lesbian Intertextuality," 359–60.

54. Renée Vivien, *Une Femme m'apparut* (Paris: A. Lemerre, 1905) 91: "She [Lorély] was the divine priestess. And I, the faithful disciple, was the soul chosen among all others to adore her eternally."

55. Lo Duca, *Histoire de l'érotisme,* 472.

56. Abbé Du Prat, *Vénus dans le cloître, ou la Religieuse en chemise* (Paris: Lattès, 1979) 141–43.

57. Anon., *Thérèse philosophe* (Geneva: Slatkine, 1981) II, 74.

58. Andréa de Nerciat, *Mon Noviciat, ou les Joies de Lolotte* (Paris: n.p., 1932) 15–16.

59. Anon., *L'Escole des filles, ou la Philosophie des dames,* ed. Pascal Pia (Paris: Cercle du livre précieux, 1959) xii.

60. Anon., *L'Escole des filles,* xlvii, 57.

61. Jean-Baptiste Louvet de Couvray, *Les Amours du chevalier de Faublas* (Paris: Chez les marchands de nouveautés, 1910) I, 49.

62. Anon., *Thérèse philosophe,* II, 3ff.

63. Félicité de Choiseul-Meuse, *Julie, ou J'ai sauvé ma rose* (Hamburg and Paris: Chez les marchands de nouveautés, 1807) I, 129.

64. Anon., *L'Ecole des biches, ou Mœurs des petites dames de ce temps* (Erzerum: Chez Qizmich-Aga, 1880 [1868]) 25.

2. Conversation and Confession: The Secrets of Femininity

1. Lucien de Samosate, *Lucius ou l'âne, suivi des Dialogues des courtisanes,* ed. Gilbert Lély (Paris: Lattès, 1979) 9.

2. Alexandrian, in his *Histoire de la littérature érotique* (Paris: Seghers, 1989) 120, affirms that "Pallavicino takes up the Aretine tradition while modernizing it." Just where Pallavicino's relative "modernity" might lie is not made clear.

3. Pietro Aretino, *Dialogues,* trans. Raymond Rosenthal (New York: Stein and Day, 1971) 145.

4. When Morse Peckham states, in *Art and Pornography* (New York: Basic Books, 1969) 291, that "Aretino's dialogues were modeled on the dialogues of classical philosophy and literature, specifically Lucian," he can hardly be wrong. My point is simply that any process of "modeling" is not reflected in the play of a rich thematic antecedence.

5. Anon., *La Putain errante, ou Dialogue de Madelaine et de Julie* (Paris: n.p., n.d. [1791]) 10–11.

6. See Maurice Béalu, preface to Du Prat, *Vénus dans le clôtre* (Paris: Lattès, 1979) x: "The future author of *La Religieuse* drew his inspiration from it." To talk of "inspiration" is undoubtedly to ignore the dynamics of tradition, but Béalu's comment does at least make a thematic link.

7. Diderot, *Œuvres romanesques* (Paris: Garnier, 1962) 350–51.

8. Pidansat de Mairobert, *La Secte des anandrynes* (Paris: Bibliothèque des curieux, 1920) 38.

9. Mirabeau, *Le Rideau levé, ou l'Education de Laure,* in *Œuvres érotiques* (Paris: Fayard, 1984) 309.

10. Félicité de Choiseul-Meuse, *Entre chien et loup* (Hamburg and Paris: Chez les marchands de nouveautés, 1809) I, 2.

3. Number and Singularity

1. David Foxon, *Libertine Literature in England, 1660–1745* (London: Book Collector, 1964) 23 n. 11.

2. Foxon, *Libertine Literature,* 23, notes: "By the late seventeenth and early

eighteenth century sets of twenty-four and thirty-six erotic plates are regularly referred to and associated with Aretino's name, but they have no relation to the original series."

3. Forberg, *Manuel d'érotologie classique* (Paris: I. Lisieux, 1882) I, 17.

4. Anon., *La Putain errante, ou Dialogue de Madelaine et de Julie* (Cologne: n.p., n.d.). Catalogued in the Bibliothèque Nationale as Enfer 597.

5. Anon., *La Putain errante, ou Dialogue de Madelaine et de Julie* (Paris: n.p., n.d. [1791]). B.N. catalogue, Enfer 754.

6. Félix Nogaret, *L'Arétin français* (Versailles: Aux dépens des fermiers généraux, n.d.). B.N. catalogue, Enfer 463.

7. Anon., *Les Quarante Manières de foutre* (Cythère: Au Temple de la volupté, 1790). B.N. catalogue, Enfer 756.

8. Restif de la Bretonne, *L'Anti-Justine*, in *Œuvres érotiques* (Paris: Fayard, 1985) 352.

9. Anon., *Les Dames de maison et les filles d'amour* ([Paris:] Cour de la Sainte-Chapelle, Chez le concierge, n.d. [c. 1830]) 37.

10. Andréa de Nerciat, *Mon Noviciat, ou les Joies de Lolotte* (Paris: n.p., 1932) 200.

11. Sade, *Œuvres complètes,* 15 vols. (Paris: Pauvert, 1986–87) VI, 215. Parenthetical references to Sade in the text are to this edition.

12. Mirabeau, *Erotika Biblion,* in *Œuvres érotiques* (Paris: Fayard, 1984) 533.

13. See, e.g., Sade, *La Philosophie dans le boudoir,* III, 468: "Augustin, Dolmancé, and the chevalier cry out in unison. The fear of being monotonous prevents us from evoking expressions that are always the same at such moments."

14. Cf. Steven Marcus, *The Other Victorians* (London: Weidenfeld and Nicolson, 1966) 81: "The need for variety is itself monotonous, and the mechanical monotonous variety of both compulsive sexuality and pornography is one of their chief common characteristics." Here is a comparable remark by George Steiner: "the plain truth is that in literary erotica as well as in the great mass of 'dirty books' the same stimuli, the same contorsions and fantasies, occur over and over with unutterable monotony." Steiner, quoted in *Perspectives on Pornography,* ed. Douglas A. Hughes (New York: Macmillan, 1970) 101.

15. Claude Godard d'Aucour, *Thémidore, ou Mon Histoire et celle de ma maîtresse* (Paris: Offenstadt, 1907) 79.

16. Jean-Charles Gervaise de Latouche, *Histoire de dom Bougre, portier des Chartreux* (London: n.p., 1788) I, 13.

17. "I have left five hundred louis with a notary for the person who is able to teach me a passion I do not know, and plunge my senses into delights I have not yet enjoyed." Sade, *La Philosophie dans le boudoir,* III, 459–60.

18. Louis-Charles Fougeret de Montbron, *Margot la ravaudeuse* (Hamburg: n.p., 1800) 51–52. Clinchetel is described in an authorial footnote as a "painter who was once very famous in Paris for his obscenities."

19. Barthes sums it up a little too quickly when he says that Sade, in *Histoire de Juliette,* puts a scornful stroke through all the "érotiques antérieurs" that make up a particular monk's library. The fact is that the works mentioned

by name are among the most canonical ones—*Portier des Chartreuux, L'Académie des dames, L'Education de Laure,* and *Thérèse philosophe*—although it is certainly true that all but *Thérèse philosophe* are criticized for not knowing how to be thoroughly immoral (see Sade, *Histoire de Juliette,* VIII, 481).

20. Alfred de Musset, *Gamiani,* in *L'Erotisme romantique,* ed. J.-J. Pauvert (Paris: Carrere, 1984) 125.

4. Toward the Learner-Centered Boudoir

1. Ferrante Pallavicino, *Alcibiade enfant à l'école* (Amsterdam: Chez l'ancien Pierre Marteau, 1866) 15.

2. Philippe Ariès, *L'Enfant et la vie familiale sous l'ancien régime* (Paris: Plon, 1960) 155–56.

3. Cf. Stephen Heath, *The Sexual Fix* (London: Macmillan, 1982) 11: "The idea that the sexual is some naked and primordial realm of individual human being is itself a cultural representation."

4. Jean-Charles Gervaise de Latouche, *Histoire de dom Bougre, portier des Chartreux* (London: n.p., 1788) I, 13.

5. Suzanne Giroux de Morency, *Illyrine,* in *L'Erotisme Directoire,* ed. Claudine Brécourt-Villars (Paris: Garnier, 1983) 65.

6. Anon., *Le Tartuffe libertin, ou le Triomphe du vice* (Cythère: Chez le gardien du temple, n.d.) 79.

7. Andréa de Nerciat, *Félicia, ou Mes Fredaines* (Paris: Le Livre de Paris Hachette, 1976) 53. "I was already learned and resigned to all that my genius might demand of me."

8. Marcel Hénaff, *Sade: L'Invention du corps libertin* (Paris: P.U.F., 1978) 53.

9. Translations of *La Philosophie dans le boudoir, Les Cent Vingt Journées de Sodome,* and *Justine, ou les Malheurs de la vertu* often follow those of Autryn Wainhouse and Richard Seaver in Sade, *Justine, Philosophy in the Bedroom, and Other Writings* (New York: Grove Weidenfeld, 1990), and *The 120 Days of Sodom and Other Writings* (New York: Grove Weidenfeld, 1987).

10. Nancy K. Miller, "*Juliette* and the Posterity of Prosperity," *L'Esprit Créateur* 15 (Winter 1975), 414–15.

11. Roland Barthes's discussion of this occurs in *Sade, Fourier, Loyola* (Paris: Seuil, 1971) 30, and is quoted in Miller, "Juliette," 415.

12. Maurice Blanchot, *Lautréamont et Sade* (Paris: U.G.E., 1967) 69–70.

13. Franco Moretti, *The Way of the World: The Bildungsroman in European Culture* (London: Verso, 1987) 48.

14. Maurice Blanchot, *Sade et Restif de la Bretonne* (Paris: Complexe, 1986) 60–61.

15. Elizabeth Abel, Marianne Hirsch, and Elizabeth Langland, eds., *The Voyage In: Fictions of Female Development* (Hanover, N.H.: University Press of New England, 1983) 7.

16. Quoted in Miller, "Juliette," 413.

17. David Williams, "Another Look at the Sadean Heroine: The Prospects for Femininity," *Essays on French Literature* 13 (1976), 30.

18. On *Histoire de Juliette* as bildungsroman, see: Miller, "Juliette," 413; Béatrice C. Fink, "Food as Object, Activity, and Symbol in Sade," *Romanic Review* 65 (March 1974), 102; and Fink, "Ambivalence in the Gynogram: Sade's Utopian Woman," *Women and Literature* 7 (Winter 1979), 25. For a dissenting opinion, see Hénaff, *Sade,* 25, 161. Lucienne Frappier-Mazur describes *Histoire de Juliette* as a "veritable caricature" of the progression of a bildungsroman in *Sade et l'écriture de l'orgie* (Paris: Nathan, 1991) 102.

19. Restif de la Bretonne, *L'Anti-Justine,* in *Œuvres érotiques* (Paris: Fayard, 1985) 347.

20. Pauline Réage, *Histoire d'O* (Paris: Pauvert, 1975) 32–33, 69.

21. Pierre Louÿs, *Trois Filles de leur mère* (Paris: Pauvert/Compagnie, 1988) 77.

22. Mirabeau, *Le Rideau levé, ou l'Education de Laure,* in *Œuvres érotiques* (Paris: Fayard, 1984) 362.

5. Measured Pastimes, Graded Narratives

1. Crébillon fils, *Les Egarements du cœur et de l'esprit,* in *Romanciers du XVIIIe siècle,* ed. René Etiemble (Paris: Gallimard, 1960–65) II, 84.

2. Cf. this comment by Etiemble, in his preface to *Romanciers du XVIIIe siècle,* II, xv: "The admirable thing, or rather one of the admirable things, about this book is that such a tight, concentrated intrigue (lasting two weeks) should give the happy illusion of interminable delay. Those who produce learned dissertations on temporality, on time and the novel, should sit down on Madame de Lursay's sofa in order to reflect on this miracle: that the most 'classical' novel, moreover, a psychological one, not at all 'new,' and perfectly fast-moving, should have made such a long time out of two weeks."

3. Denis Diderot, *Les Bijoux indiscrets* (Paris: Garnier-Flammarion, 1968) 98.

4. Cf. Patrick Wald Lasowski, *Libertines* (Paris: Gallimard, 1980) 27: "The marquis de Sade condemns Crébillon with violence, seeing in his *petits-marquis* only 'hypocrites,' pale, emotionless seducers, lacking any inspiration, and 'cloaking their immoralities in unprincipled cynicism.'"

5. Peter Brooks, *Reading for the Plot: Design and Intention in Narrative* (Oxford: Clarendon Press, 1984) 107–8.

6. Suzanne Giroux de Morency, *Illyrine,* in *L'Erotisme Directoire,* ed. Claudine Brécourt-Villars (Paris: Garnier, 1983) 76.

7. In *Mon Noviciat,* too, Félicité recovers from smallpox, although in a more conventional manner (see 237).

8. John Alfred Atkins, *Sex in Literature* (London: Calder and Boyars, 1970) I, 78, notes the general absence of pregnancy and menstruation in erotic literature. The "cult of sterility," he suggests, extends beyond Sade's work (75–78).

9. On the narrative significance of feminine laughter, see Angela Carter, "Alison's Giggle," *The Left and the Erotic*, ed. Eileen Phillips (London: Lawrence and Wishart, 1983) 54.

10. *L'Escole des filles* (Paris: Cercle du livre précieux, 1959) actually contains an explanation of why laughter is impossible at the moment of ejaculation: "The soul is pulled downward by the force of pleasure, as if torn from its seat by the great attention it gives to the desired union of the two bodies that occurs at this place here." Since the soul is no longer free, it can no longer reason, and thus no longer produce laughter, which is both a property of reason and an effect of freedom" (138).

11. The comtesse tells the story of an orgy with a group of monks that ends with the appropriate punctuation: "this monkish gallantry marks a pleasant ending, accompanied by bursts of laughter, to the lively scene that has just occurred" (V, 103).

12. Marcel Hénaff, *Sade: L'Invention du corps libertin* (Paris: P.U.F., 1978) 142–43. "Rather than attaining the height of pleasure, it is urgent not to wait for it," adds Hénaff (143). ["Plus que de jouir, il est urgent de ne pas attendre sa jouissance."]

13. Hénaff, *Sade*, 58–59.

14. Dubourg, for example, is actually too well prepared to rape Justine: "Unfortunately, he is frigged, very skillfully, as a preliminary. Alas! The same incident that occurred the first time happens again on this occasion" (*La Nouvelle Justine*, VI, 63).

15. Cf. *Les Cent Vingt Journées*, I, 35: "Curval, who was only irritated by the growing number of refusals, did not know what tack to follow in order to subject her to his libidinous caprices, until it struck him that by simply having the father broken he could lead the daughter to his bed." "Irritation" is not a vague general condition, like an itch. It can be measured in *doses:* "He found in this episode alone, he said, the full dose of irritation needed to condemn the person to death" (*La Nouvelle Justine*, VII, 45).

16. Leo Bersani and Ulysse Dutoit, "Merde alors," *October* 13 (Summer 1980), 28.

17. Joan De Jean, *Literary Fortifications: Rousseau, Laclos, Sade* (Princeton: Princeton University Press, 1984) 297.

18. Cf. Hénaff, *Sade*, 61: "*Les Cent Vingt Journées* explicitly attempts to classify [the possibilities] and aims to be the repertoire of all possible variations on these basic passions. What makes narrative time progress, then, is not the accumulation of signs and the gradual clearing up of the mystery; it is rather the necessity of completing the program that works through the bodies. You could almost say that it is only done for ease of exposition, as the simplest way of linearizing the taxonomy, by acting it out as a lived, believable story."

19. Chantal Thomas, *Sade, l'oeil de la lettre* (Paris: Payot, 1978) 60.

20. Hénaff, *Sade*, 159.

21. Hénaff, *Sade*, 90–91.

22. Cf. Vera Lee, "The Sade Machine," *Studies on Voltaire and the Eighteenth Century* 98 (1972), 216, on *Les Cent Vingt Journées:* "Another drawback in Sade's

use of intensification is that the author is usually too impatient to be able to start in a stage whisper and build up to a high pitch. What can astonish us after the excesses of the first few pages?"

6. Taking Sade Serially: *Les Cent Vingt Journées de Sodome*

1. Robert Desnos, *De l'érotisme considéré dans ses manifestations écrites et du point de vue de l'esprit moderne* (Paris: Cercle des Arts, n.d.) 37.

2. André Breton, *Anthologie de l'humour noir* (Paris: Pauvert, 1972) 39; Breton's emphasis.

3. Desnos, *De l'érotisme*, 37.

4. Marcel Hénaff, *Sade: L'Invention du corps libertin* (Paris: P.U.F., 1978) 186, quotes the same passage, with this comment: "There is no joking, at Silling, about the duty to produce, nor is there any joking about servicing libertinage."

5. It might indeed be, for Hélène Cixous, a form of bodily production, rejecting that phallocratic accountancy of the feminine that is only able to compute what woman "lacks." But Sade moves as if to preempt feminine physiological resistance, leaving us only with abstraction. All we can consider here, in fact, is the (abstract) possibility of laughter. On femininity and laughter, see Cixous, "The Laugh of Medusa," *New French Feminisms: An Anthology*, ed. Elaine Marks and Isabelle de Courtivron (Amherst: University of Massachusetts Press, 1981) 245–64.

6. Raymond Jean calls Sade an *arithmomane* in *Un Portrait de Sade* (Arles: Actes Sud, 1989) 10.

7. Georges Bataille, *La Littérature et le mal* (Paris: Gallimard, 1967) 135.

8. Maurice Blanchot, *Lautréamont et Sade* (Paris: U.G.E., 1967) 46, 47.

9. Vera Lee, "The Sade Machine," *Studies on Voltaire and the Eighteenth Century* 98 (1972), 215, observes: "Numbers count, because for Sade numbers are at least as exciting as size or duration." Annie Le Brun, *Soudain un bloc d'abîme* (Paris: Pauvert, 1986) 288–89, takes it upon herself to be indignant about the failure of Sade criticism in general to perceive the relationship between repetition and accumulation.

10. The same dynamic is found in Belmor's arithmetical fantasy for expanding corruption to a global level, presented in *Histoire de Juliette;* see VIII, 542.

11. Hénaff, *Sade*, 34; Hénaff's emphasis.

12. Cf. Luce Irigaray, *Ce Sexe qui n'en est pas un* (Paris: Minuit, 1977) 206: "Luminous, we are. Without one or two. I have never been able to count. Up to *tu*. We would be two in their calculations." When "they" do their sums, they practice the enumeration (*dénombrement*) of women (*Ce Sexe*, 95). It seems clear enough that $1{,}000 \neq 1{,}003 - 3$.

13. Maurice Heine, "Lettre ouverte à Luis Bunuel," *Lectures de Sade*, ed. Françoise Laugaa-Traut (Paris: Armand Colin, 1973) 203.

14. Cf. Béatrice C. Fink, "Food as Object, Activity, and Symbol in Sade," *Romanic Review* 65 (March 1974), 99, where *Les Cent Vingt Journées* is described as having "a spatial mechanism operated in symphonic fashion in patterns of four (four parts, four months, four master libertines, four historians, four inches, etc. . . .)."

15. The following should be clear to most readers:

$$16 \times 9 = 144$$
$$144 = 12 \times 12$$
$$\frac{144}{18} = 8$$

It was not clear, apparently, to Autryn Wainhouse and Richard Seaver who somehow came up with the number 153 at this point in their translation (Sade, *The 120 Days of Sodom and Other Writings* [New York: Grove Weidenfeld, 1987] 223). Sade would have pointed out instantly that 153 = 9 × 17, hardly the stuff of which geometrical perfection is made. There is other evidence of numerical insensivity (or tampering) in the same translation: a twelve-inch-long tongue is shortened to six inches (349) and an hour-long sucking session reduced by half (445). There seems to be a lack of awareness on the part of these translators of the thematic nature of Sadian number, not to mention their tendency to attenuate certain excesses, and thus to make Sade less outrageous.

16. Justine herself seems to be able to effect this calculation. She observes: "There will be four of you gathered together, four scoundrels of the vilest sort . . . Horrible deeds will be done" (*La Nouvelle Justine,* VII, 161).

17. Henri Bergson, *Les Données immédiates de la conscience* (Paris: P.U.F., 1963) passim.

18. It seems more appropriate to use Sade's preferred term here, rather than that of "perversion." As Pierre Klossowski observes, "The term perversion in its pathological sense does not exist in Sade. His terminology in this field remains that of moral psychology, that is the *examination of conscience* developed by the casuists." Klossowski, *Le Philosophe scélérat,* in *Sade mon prochain, précédé de Le Philosophe scélérat* (Paris: Le Seuil, 1967) 28; Klossowski's emphasis.

19. Blanchot, *Lautréamont et Sade,* 45.

20. Martin Pops, "The Metamorphosis of Shit," *Salmagundi* 56 (Spring 1982), 40–41, notes the pathos of self-contradiction here, and finds a counting error: "Sade's unfinished manuscript is itself beset with confessions of vulnerability. There is a self-addressed note after the first part entitled 'Mistakes I Have Made'—like rueful mirth, a touching acknowledgment that, even amid hundreds of sadistic exempla, the harshest masters of all are consistency and verisimilitude. The outline of the second part seems to list 151 torments instead of the requisite 150. 'Find out why there is one too many,' Sade asks himself, for he has inadvertently and comically omitted passion number 69

[see I, 374, for confirmation of this], just as Sadian libertines exclude *soixante-neuf* from their sexual repertoires."

21. Maurice Heine, preface to *Les Cent Vingt Journées de Sodome,* in Sade, *Œuvres complètes* (Paris: Cercle du livre précieux, 1966–67) XIII, xv.

22. I say this in spite of Philippe Roger's broad claim, in his earlier work on Sade, to add the quality of difference to Sadian quantity: "The episodes of sensual pleasure, in their endless return, do not all come down to the same thing, any more than the episodes of *Justine,* in Sade's writing, just tell the same things when they relate them *again.*" Roger, *Sade: La Philosophie dans le pressoir* (Paris: Grasset, 1976) 111; Roger's emphasis.

23. Desnos, *De l'erotisme,* 79–80.

24. Boris Vian, "Utilité d'une littérature érotique," *Ecrits pornographiques* (Paris: Bourgois, 1980) 39.

25. Angela Carter, *The Sadeian Woman and the Ideology of Pornography* (New York: Harper and Row, 1980) 36; cf. 122.

26. "I believe that I was one of the first to say that, contrary to a massively held general view, everything Sade wrote was humorous." Philippe Sollers, "Sade, encore," *Le Monde,* 13 February 1987, 20.

27. Breton, *Anthologie de l'humour noir,* 16. Cf. his quotation of Valéry, 13.

28. Desnos, *De l'erotisme,* 78.

29. Breton, *Anthologie de l'humour noir,* 50.

30. Desnos, *De l'érotisme,* 80.

31. Maurice Blanchot, *Sade et Restif de la Bretonne* (Paris: Complexe, 1986) 46.

32. Roger, *Sade: La Philosophie dans le pressoir,* 189. Cf. also Jean, *Un Portrait de Sade,* 299: "It is deeply regrettable that so many commentators have shown no sensitivity to this humor." Annie Le Brun, *Sade, aller et détours* (Paris: Plon, 1989) 123, speaks of "the kind of joy that is so particularly Sadian."

33. Sollers, "Sade, encore," 20.

34. Centre culturel international de Cerisy-la-Salle, *Sade: Écrire la crise* (Paris: Belfond, 1983) 11. The quotation is from Philippe Sollers's "Lettre de Sade," *Tel Quel* 61 (Spring 1975), 20.

35. Philippe Roger, "Le Protocole," in Centre culturel, *Écrire la crise,* 14: "We have managed to bring off one thing at least: freeing Sade from the monological incantation typical of so many Sadians—'all hagiographers,' as Lacan said."

36. Cf. Michel Camus, who speaks of "taking Sade out of the ghetto he is kept in by his detractors and his apologists." Camus, "L'Impasse mystique du libertin," in Centre culturel, *Ecrire la crise,* 270.

37. Georges Bataille, *La Littérature et le mal* (Paris: Gallimard, 1967) 128; Bataille's emphasis.

38. Hénaff, *Sade,* 325. Cf. what he says on 326: "It has to be admitted that it is terribly easy to take Sade 'seriously,' and therefore pass judgment on him in the tribunal of the Referent."

39. Chantal Thomas, *Sade, l'œil de la lettre* (Paris: Payot, 1978) 38. The

quotation from Mandiargues is drawn from a preface in Sade's *Œuvres complètes* (Paris: Cercle du livre précieux, 1966–67) XIX, 14.

40. Annie Le Brun is conscious of struggling to be free of Bataille's modernist dialectic in order to take Sade seriously: "That is when it seemed to me vital that we begin to *take literally* those things in Sade that successive generations have sought to keep only as a dead letter." Le Brun, *Soudain un bloc d'abîme,* 16; Le Brun's emphasis. Le Brun's reading of Sade is in fact an admiring one, without being concerned to head off critical irony. Other critics who are not locked into the apologetic mode are able to speak more narrowly and more convincingly of particular instances in Sade of authorial irony, *désinvolture,* or *dérision.* See Béatrice Didier, *Sade: Essai* (Paris: Denoël/Gonthier, 1976) 96; Jane Gallop, *Intersections: A Reading of Sade with Bataille, Blanchot, and Klossowski* (Lincoln: University of Nebraska Press, 1981) 87; Lucette Finas, "L'Increvable Féminin dans *Faxelange, ou les Torts de l'ambition,*" and Andreas Pfersmann, "L'Ironie romantique chez Sade," both in Centre culturel, *Écrire la crise,* 18 and 89–93 repectively. Lucienne Frappier-Mazur has most to say about the question, noting in her study *Sade et l'écriture de l'orgie* (Paris: Nathan, 1991) 75, that Sade's humor implies a certain distance between the libertine and himself, but it does not neutralize the vehemence of what he says. A more careful *study* of Sade's humor as such can be found on pp. 151–56 of Frappier-Mazur's work, although her premises are quite different from mine.

41. Cf. this observation by Hénaff, in *Sade,* 33: "Having been cut up into pieces, displayed, and mechanized, the Sadian body is also subject to accountancy. There are always precise figures to state the quality of the organs used, the quantity of bodies mobilized, and the size of the orgy accomplished."

42. Hénaff, *Sade,* 35. There is an indication in *Histoire de Juliette* that these dimensions are sometimes a matter of *reputation:* "Noirceuil has, as you know, a member that is seven inches in circumference and eleven inches long" (VIII, 176).

43. In *La Nouvelle Justine* (VII, 95), Madame d'Esterval is described as having "a clitoris that is three inches long, with a thickness proportionate to its length."

44. See, e.g., *Histoire de Juliette,* VIII, 99: "ten times in a row the little hussy swooned with pleasure in my embrace. I thought that she would melt away into spunk."

45. Gilbert Lély's expression of distaste has been commented on by others. In his preface to Sade's novel, Lély writes: "So it is that in *Les Cent Vingt Journées de Sodome,* verisimilitude is often disturbed by a gratuitous climax involving a particularly hideous deviation that could readily have been replaced by other nuances of an essentially erotological nature." Lély, preface to *Les Cent Vingt Journées* (Paris: U.G.E., 10/18, 1975) I, 13–14. This regretful comment can only count as a lame apology, but it has at least the merit of being explicit—something Marcelin Pleynet considers a rarity in Sade criticism. Coprophagy, says Pleynet, is what really threatens to make Sade unreadable,

and commentators are remarkably discreet on the subject. Pleynet, "Sade, des chiffres, des lettres, du renfermement," *Tel Quel* 86 (Winter 1980), 29. Marcel Hénaff produces a strong critique of Lély's laughable reticence: "the most hilarious thing about this text is the horrified, sententious distance taken [by Lély] in dealing with what is in fact Sade's most vigorous and rigorous piece of daring." Hénaff, *Sade,* 219–20; cf. Laugaa-Traut, *Lectures de Sade,* 213.

46. Noëlle Châtelet, "Le Libertin à table," in Centre culturel, *Ecrire la crise,* 77–78.

47. Hénaff, *Sade* 226.

7. How Not to Be Murdered in Sadian Stories

1. Jane Gallop. *Intersections: A Reading of Sade with Bataille, Blanchot, and Klossowski* (Lincoln: University of Nebraska Press, 1981) 109.

2. Jean Paulhan, "Préface," in Sade, *Les Infortunes de la vertu,* Folio ed. (Paris: Gallimard, 1970) 22.

3. Susan Sontag, "The Pornographic Imagination," *Perspectives on Pornography,* ed. Douglas A. Hughes (New York: Macmillan, 1970) 150. Cf. Angela Carter, *The Sadeian Woman and the Ideology of Pornography* (New York: Harper and Row, 1980) 50: "she passes from the cruel hands of one master to another and her innocence is so perfect it precludes any advance knowledge of the strength and malice of her adversaries."

4. Maurice Blanchot, *Lautréamont et Sade* (Paris: U.G.E., 1967) 38–39.

5. Noëlle Châtelet, "Le Libertin à table." in Centre culturel international de Cerisy-la-Salle, *Sade: Écrire la crise* (Paris: Belfond, 1983) 67–68.

8. Degrees of Virginity

1. Andrea Dworkin, *Intercourse* (London: Secker and Warburg, 1987) 107.

2. Nancy Huston, *Mosaïque de la pornographie* (Paris: Denoël/Gonthier, 1982) 200; Huston's emphasis.

3. Luce Irigaray, *Ce Sexe qui n'en est pas un* (Paris: Minuit, 1977) 199; Irigaray's emphasis. Cf. also 210: "There is, *just between us,* no break between the virgin and the nonvirgin. No event that would make women of us. Long before your birth, you touch yourself, innocently. The sex of your/my body is not given to us by an operation. By the action of a power, a function, or an organ. Without any particular intervention or manipulation, already you are woman"; Irigaray's emphasis.

4. Simone de Beauvoir, *Le Deuxième Sexe* (Paris: Gallimard, 1949) II, 131–32.

5. Alain-René Le Sage, *Gil Blas de Santillane,* in *Romanciers du XVIIIe siècle,* ed. René Etiemble (Paris: Gallimard, 1960–65) I, 506, 1169.

6. Angela Carter, "Alison's Giggle," *The Left and the Erotic,* ed. Eileen Phillips (London: Lawrence and Wishart, 1983) 58.

7. Jacques-Henri Bernardin de Saint-Pierre, *Paul et Virginie* (Paris: Livre de Poche, 1974) 203–5.

8. On the question of plotting and delay, see Peter Brooks, *Reading for the Plot* (Oxford: Clarendon Press, 1984).

9. Pierre de Brantôme, *Les Dames galantes* (Paris: Garnier, 1965) 183: "Lucretia did not do the same thing, for she did not taste the pleasure, even though she was asked by a noble king. In this, she was doubly foolish, in not giving in to him on the spot, and in killing herself for so little."

10. Félicité de Choiseul-Meuse, *Amélie de Saint-Far, ou la Fatale Erreur* (Brussels: Gay et Doucé, 1882) II, 53.

11. Félicité de Choiseul-Meuse, *Julie, ou J'ai sauvé ma rose* (Hamburg and Paris: Chez les marchands de nouveautés, 1807) II, 267. In *Trois Filles de leur mère,* by Pierre Louÿs (Paris: Pauvert et Compagnie, 1988) 20, we find such display as a form of female exhibitionism: "With the immodesty of youth, she spread her thighs wide, held them apart with both hands, and opened up her flesh . . . My surprise was all the greater because the boldness of her pose hardly prepared me for such a revelation.

'Virginity!' I exclaimed.

'A beautiful one at that!'"

12. Jean-Jacques Rousseau, *Julie, ou la Nouvelle Héloïse* (Paris: Garnier-Flammarion, 1967) 59.

13. Béatrice Didier, "Introduction," in Sade, *Les Infortunes de la vertu,* Folio ed. (Paris: Gallimard, 1970) 67.

14. Annie Le Brun, *Soudain un bloc d'abîme* (Paris: Pauvert, 1986) 282–83, sees Justine's attitude as an absolute refusal to be persuaded to a libertine view of the world.

15. Ihab Hassan, "Sade: Prisoner of Consciousness," *The Perverse Imagination: Sexuality and Literary Culture,* ed. Irving Buchen (New York: New York University Press, 1970) 47.

16. Didier, "Introduction," 60.

17. Alexandrian, *Histoire de la littérature érotique* (Paris: Seghers, 1989) 252, claims that these texts were not really written by Choiseul-Meuse. He may be correct in this, but it is striking to me that, as historian, he takes every opportunity to argue against women's authorship of erotic texts. Liane de Pougy and Emmanuelle d'Arsan are treated in the same way, without any documentary evidence in support of the claims made.

18. When the young Violette is first asked by Christian, the narrator-hero of *Le Roman de Violette,* whether she is a virgin, she replies virignally: "A virgin? What does that mean?" For Christian, there could be no clearer reply: "The tone of her reply left no doubt" (16). Later in the story, she comes to ask of her own accord: "Well, what is it to be a virgin?" (47). By this time, she has developed a form of sexual curiosity, and shortly afterward her virginity is lost: "By learning what virginity was, poor Violette had lost hers" (53).

19. It is in this that Robert Desnos identifies the novel's the novel's moder-

nity. Desnos, *De l'érotisme considéré dans ses manifestations écrites et du point de vue de l'esprit moderne* (Paris: Cercle des arts, n.d.) 71: "this is a novel that, for the first time, gives a modern description of flirting. In that regard, the work is of considerable interest."

20. See Peter Cryle, "Gendered Time in Erotive Narrative: Finishing Power vs. Staying Power," *Romanic Review* 83 (1992), 131–48.

21. Lucienne Frappier-Mazur, "Marginal Canons: Rewriting the Erotic," *Yale French Studies* 75 (1988), 120, writes: "As early as 1807, *Julie, ou J'ai sauvé ma rose* ends on a lesbian episode." This may be strictly correct, but I am suggesting that it is a rather misleading summary.

9. On Being Erotically Disposed: Posture and the Modeling of Desire

1. For a first attempt at this, see Peter Cryle, "Enunciation and Ejaculation: The Poetics of Climax," *Style* 24 (Summer 1990), 187–200.

2. Restif de la Bretonne, *La Paysanne pervertie* (Paris: Garnier-Flammarion, 1972) 380.

3. Mirabeau, *Ma Conversion, ou le Libertin de qualité,* in *Œuvres érotiques* (Paris: Fayard, 1984) 57.

4. The allusion is shared with, or mirrored by Mirabeau, in his *Erotika biblion,* in *Œuvres érotiques,* 533: "The sultan enters this room where the mutes have made everything ready. He squats down in one corner, looking at floor level so as to see the attitudes from a favorable angle. He smokes three pipes, and while he is doing so, the perfection of Asia's production appears naked in this room. They copulate first of all following the painting of Helen the beautiful, then mingle and vary the groups and positions whose models are provided for them by the walls, surpassing the models by their agility."

5. Steven Marcus, *The Other Victorians: A Study of Sexuality and Pornography in Mid-Nineteenth Century England* (London: Weidenfeld and Nicolson, 1966) 277.

6. Pascal Bruckner and Alain Finkielkraut, *Le Nouveau Désordre amoureux* (Paris: Seuil, 1977) 154.

7. There is some discussion of such machines in Henri Lafon, "Machines à plaisir dans le roman français du XVIIIe siècle," *Revue des Sciences Humaines* 58 (1982), 111–21. Lafon takes examples from both *Faublas* and *L'Anti-Justine* (116).

8. See Nancy Huston, *Mosaïque de la pornographie* (Paris: Denoël/Gonthier, 1982) 60.

9. I refer, of course, to the author of such works as *The Naked Ape: A Zoologist's Study of the Human Animal* (London: Jonathan Cape, 1967).

10. The ambiguity of the French seems productive at this point. We need to think both of the way in which a general phenomenon of taste can be relied on to occur throughout a given social space (*conformité du goût*), and of the

similarity which serves to link particular manifestations of it (*conformité de goût[s]*).

11. Pierre Klossowski, *Le Bain de Diane* (Paris: Gallimard, 1972) 31: "Can we expect to find in a painting what may happen to us? There would need to be a mysterious similarity [*conformité*] between the image and our unpredictable intentions. Unless the image exercises such persuasive force on us that we are compelled to encounter it in our everyday space."

12. It should be clear that my work here is at cross purposes with that of Leo Bersani's "Representation and Its Discontents," *Allegory and Representation,* ed. Stephen J. Greenblatt (Baltimore: Johns Hopkins University Press, 1981) 145–62. Bersani uses Sade's definition, in *Les Cent Vingt Journées,* of desire in response to representation in order to contribute to a general theory of desire. I am continually deflecting and deconstructing the question of desire "as such," and thereby refusing to accept the premises of a psychoanalytic study. To put it in Foucault's terms, I am contributing not to the modernist undoing and reformulation of *scientia sexualis,* but to the archaeological reconstitution and hermeneutic revaluation of a classical *ars erotica.*

13. Philippe Roger, *Sade: La Philosophie dans le pressoir* (Paris: Grasset, 1976) 119. Annie Le Brun, *Sade, aller et détours* (Paris: Plon, 1989) 44, also talks of Sade the liberator: "That is another aspect of Sade's genius, inventing something quite new in the area of pedagogy, at a time when others are establishing techniques for animal training that are still making cretins out of us two centuries later." But what kind of education other than *dressage* is envisaged, for example, when Verneuil gives his son Victor over to Bressac, saying: "Concentrate on correcting his weaknesses; introduce him to our principles; automatize his soul, and make him loathe women" (*La Nouvelle Justine,* VII, 299)?

14. Jean Gillibert, "Sade, sadiste, sadique," preface to *Les Cent Vingt Journées,* in Sade, *Œuvres complètes* (Paris: Cercle du livre précieux, 1966) XIII, lxxiii.

15. See Leo Bersani and Ulysse Dutoit, "Merde alors," *October* 13 (Summer 1980), esp. 24.

16. That is presumably why, as Alexandrian reminds us, erotic spaces in Nerciat's *Les Aphrodites,* are furnished with *avantageuses.* These are not postural traps, like the machines mentioned earlier, but, one might say, devices providing support, both for bodies and for narrative. They are especially conceived to favor "the sex act." Alexandrian, *Historian de la littérature érotique* (Paris: Seghers, 1989) 175.

17. Gilles Deleuze, *Présentation de Sacher-Masoch* (Paris: Minuit, 1967) 17–18.

10. Classical Poise: Thematic Modeling in *L'Image* and *Histoire d'O*

1. Alphonso Lingis, *Libido: The French Existential Theories* (Bloomington: Indiana University Press, 1985) 61.

2. Gilles Deleuze and Félix Guattari, *Capitalisme et schizophrénie, Mille plateaux* (Paris: Minuit, 1980) 10.

3. Here is Juliette picking her way through a series of less interesting variations before alighting on one that is genuinely tellable: "Fifteen or sixteen others with the same taste, although they were in good health, had their way with me in the next month, with varying numbers of singular episodes, before I was sent to a man whose details in the act of sodomy are bizarre enough for me to have to recount them to you" (*Histoire de Juliette,* VIII, 174).

4. Claudine Brécourt-Villars, in her *Ecrire d'amour: Anthologie de textes érotiques féminins (1799–1984)* (Paris: Ramsay, 1985) 32, invites us to some anagrammatic play: "Jean de Berg marks, in reality and without equivocation, an unexpected phallic emergence—the name can obviously be read as an anagram of 'Je bande!' [I have a hard-on]. The two extra letters 'R' and 'G' display, most probably, the initials of Robbe-Grillet himself."

5. Susan Sontag, "The Pornographic Imagination," *Perspectives on Pornography,* ed. Douglas A. Hughes (New York: Macmillan, 1970) 146; Sontag's emphasis.

6. Jean de Berg, *L'Image,* préface de P[auline] R[éage] (Paris: J'ai lu, 1986) 37.

7. Cf. Leo Bersani, *A Fugure for Astyanax: Character and Desire in Literature* (Boston: Little, Brown, 1976) 292.

8. *Dictionnaire de œuvres érotiques: Domaine français* (Paris: Mercure de France, 1971) 237.

9. Jean Paulhan, "Le Bonheur dans l'esclavage," preface to Pauline Réage, *Histoire d'O* (Paris: Pauvert, 1975) v.

10. I say this in order to resist a judgment made by Susan Sontag in "The Pornographic Imagination," 147–48: "most of the action is removed to more familiar if less plausible territory: that conveniently isolated château, luxuriously furnished and lavishly staffed with servants, where a group of rich men congregate [. . .]. In short, the novel comes equipped with some of the creakiest items in the repertoire of pornography." In appealing for a reading of *Histoire d'O* as classical, I cannot, of course, prove that these things are not clichés, but I am suspicious of what appears to me to be a modernist refusal to read themes thematically.

11. Here is a rather heady list of thematic associations from Maurice Charney's *Sexual Fiction* (London and New York: Methuen, 1981) 69: "'O' obviously stands for 'open,' but the anonymous name, like a discreet character in an eighteenth-century novel, also has meanings. O is the conventional symbol of eternity, the snake with its tail in its mouth, which has neither beginning or end. The O of the marriage ring symbolizes everlasting love, a circle that is lifted out of time and mortality. O is the hole, the cunt, female sexuality, which is either the eternal circle or an emptiness—zero—waiting to be filled. O is an exclamation of rapture, an emotive word for physical pleasure, at orgasm. O is the tabula rasa, the empty white sheet of all women's experience on which Pauline Réage's novel is being written, since O only exists through the words of *Story of O.*"

12. After her branding, O expects that "she would be returned to Sir Stephen more openly and deeply a slave than she had imagined possible" (198). In this thematic context, *ouvertement* and *profondément* are puns.

13. On the one occasion where a more Sadian image of fixity is used, there is still a striking difference: "O was attached to the sofa like a butterfly by a pin, a long pin made of words and looks piercing the middle of her body and pressing her bare, attentive thighs against the warm silk" (102). She is not nailed to the spot, but attached, like a beautiful object, to a beautiful (and comfortable) background.

14. Kaja Silverman, "*Histoire d'O:* The Construction of a Female Subject," *Pleasure and Danger,* ed. Carol S. Vance (Boston: Routledge and Kegan Paul, 1984) 331.

Conclusion

1. Michael Perkins, *The Secret Record: Modern Erotic Literature* (New York: Morrow, 1976) 11.

2. See for example, Michel Camus, "Introduction générale," *L'Enfer de la Bibliothèque Nationale* (Paris: Fayard, 1985–88) V, 9, 11.

3. Emile Henriot, *Les Livres du second rayon, irréguliers et libertins* (Paris: "Le Livre," 1926).

4. See Pierre Bourdieu, *La Distinction* (Paris: Minuit, 1979) passim.

5. James Hulbert, "The Problems of Canon Formation and the 'Example' of Sade: Orthodox Exclusion and Orthodox Inclusion," *Modern Language Studies* 18 (1988), 122.

6. Frances Ferguson, "Sade and the Pornographic Legacy," *Representations* 36 (Fall 1991), 2.

7. Nancy K. Miller, "Authorized Versions," *French Review* 61 (1988), 406.

8. Lucienne Frappier-Mazur, "Marginal Canons: Rewriting the Erotic," *Yale French Studies* 75 (1988), 112.

9. Jules Janin, from an 1834 article in *La Revue de Paris,* quoted in Jean-Pierre Jacques, *Les Malheurs de Sapho* (Paris: Grasset, 1980) 47.

10. Rachilde, *Monsieur Vénus* (Paris: Flammarion, 1977) 83–84.

11. André Pieyre de Mandiargues, *Le Désordre de la mémoire: Entretiens avec Francine Mallet* (Paris: Gallimard, 1975) 174–75.

12. Frappier-Mazur, "Marginal Canons," 112–13.

13. Hulbert, "The Problems of Canon Formation," 122.

14. See Joan De Jean, "Teaching Frenchness," *French Review* 61 (1988), 398–404.

15. Claudine Brécourt-Villars, *Ecrire d'amour: Anthologie de textes érotiques féminins (1799–1984)* (Paris: Ramsay, 1985) 16. The phrase "en dépit de sa qualité" is ambiguous. It no doubt implies a positive judgment about *Histoire d'O,* but then leaves us to wonder whether all the other works in the list are actually to be considered inferior to Réage's.

16. Peter Cryle, "Gendered Time in Erotic Narrative: Finishing Power vs. Staying Power," *Romanic Review* 83 (1992), 131–48.

17. See Alexandrian, *Histoire de la littérature érotique* (Paris: Seghers, 1989) 9: "The whole of European erotic literature can be reduced to a hundred or so masterpieces in Greek, Latin, French, Italian, English, and German. When you have studied those, all the rest seems to be only repetition or attenuation: these authors established the laws of the genre." Whether the distinction is made in the breezily "liberated" manner of Alexandrian, or with the quiet solemnity of Mandiargues, the canonical product appears to be much the same.

Bibliography

The bibliography contains the following subsections:

1. Specialized Bibliographies

Ashbee, Henry Spencer. *Bibliography of Prohibited Books (With Bio-biblio-iconographical and Critical Notes on Curious, Uncommon and Erotic Books by Pisanus Fraxi).* New York: Brussel, 1962.

Ashbee, Henry Spencer. *Forbidden Books of the Victorians,* ed. Peter Fryer. London: Odyssey Press, 1970.

Haight, Anne Lyon. *Banned Books: Informal Notes on Some Books Banned for Various Reasons at Various Times and in Various Places.* New York: R. R. Bowker, 1970. 3d ed.

Kearney, Patrick J. *The Private Case: An Annotated Bibliography of the Private Case Erotica Collection from the British Museum Library.* London: Gay Landesman, 1981.

Perceau, Louis. *Bibliographie des romans érotiques du XIXᵉ siècle.* Paris: Fourdrinier, 1930. 2 vols.

Pia, Pascal. *Les Livres de l'enfer: Bibliographie critique des ouvrages érotiques dans leurs différentes éditions du XVIᵉ siècle à nos jours.* Paris: Coulet et Faure, 1978. 2 vols.

2. Dictionaries and Glossaries

Brécourt-Villars, Claudine. *Petit Glossaire raisonné de l'érotisme saphique (1880–1930).* Paris: Pauvert, 1980.

Guiraud, Pierre. *Dictionnaire érotique: Dictionnaire historique, stylistique, rhétorique, étymologique de la littérature érotique.* Paris: Payot, 1978.

Guiraud, Pierre. *Les Gros Mots.* Paris: P.U.F., 1975.

Le Pennec, Marie-Françoise. *Petit Glossaire du langage érotique au XVIIᵉ et XVIIIᵉ siècles.* Paris: Borderie, 1979.

Wedeck, Harry E. *Dictionary of Erotic Literature.* New York: Citadel Press, 1962.

3. Literary Works

[Editions given are the most recent and widely available, wherever more recent editions exist. The date of first publication is given at the end of each entry, except in the case of collected works.]

3a. *Anonymous Works and Works of Doubtful Authorship*

Bigarrures: Coiro-pygo-glotto-chiro-phallurgiques, ed. Béatrice Didier. Geneva and Paris: Slatkine, 1981 (1800).

Le Cabinet satyrique ed. Fernand Fleuret and Louis Perceau. Paris: Fort, Librairie du bon vieux temps, 1924 (1618) 2 vols.

Les Dames de maison et les filles d'amour. [Paris:] Cour de la Sainte-Chapelle, Chez le concierge n.d. (1830).

L'Ecole des biches, ou Mœurs des petites dames de ce temps. Erzerum: Chez Qizmich-Aga, 1880 (1868).

L'Escole des filles, ou la Philosophie des dames, ed. Pascal Pia. Paris: Cercle du livre précieux, 1959 (1660).

Les Leçons de la volupté, ou Confession générale du chevalier de Wilfort. Brussels: Gay et Doucé, 1882 (1758).

La Putain errante, ou Dialogue de Madelaine et de Julie. Paris: n.p., n.d. (1791). Also Cologne: n.p., n.d. (1531).

Quarante Manières de foutre, dédiées au clergé de France. Cythère: Au temple de la volupté, 1790 (1790).

Le Rideau levé, ou l'Education de Laure [attributed to Mirabeau and included in his *Œuvres érotiques* (see below); also attributed to Sentilly]. Paris: Lattès, 1980 (1786).

Le Roman de Violette. Lisbon: Da Boa-Vista, 1870 (Brussels, 1883).

Sapho, ou l'Heureuse Inconstance, par Madem . . . The Hague: A. Troyel, 1695 (1695).

Les Tableaux vivants, ou Mes confessions aux pieds de la duchesse. Amsterdam: n.p., 1870 (1870). 2 vols.

Le Tartuffe libertin, ou le Triomphe du vice. Cythère: Chez le gardien du temple, n.d. (1845).

Thérèse philosophe. Geneva: Slatkine, 1981 (1748).

Vénus dans le cloître, ou la Religieuse en chemise [attributed to Jean Barrin, or to François de Chavigny de la Bretonnière, under the pseudonym of l'abbé Du Prat], ed. Marcel Béalu. Paris: Lattès, 1979 (1682).

3b. *Literary Works Listed by Author Names*

Aretino, Pietro. *Dialogues* [*Ragionamenti*]. Trans. Raymond Rosenthal. New York: Stein and Day, 1971.

Aretino, Pietro. *I Ragionamenti.* Rome: Frank, 1911 (1534–39).

Aretino, Pietro. *Les Ragionamenti, ou Dialogues du divin Pietro Aretino.* Trans. Alcide Bonneau. Paris: I. Lisieux, 1882. 6 vols.

Aretino, Pietro. *Les Sonnets luxurieux du divin Pietro Aretino.* Trans. [Alcide Bonneau]. Paris: I. Lisieux, 1882 (1524).

Bataille, Georges. *Madame Edwarda.* Paris: U.G.E., 1973 (1941).

Baudelaire, Charles. "Pièces condamnées tirées des *Fleurs du mal.*" *Œuvres complètes.* Paris: Gallimard, Pléiade, 1975 (1857). 150–55.
Berg, Jean de. *L'Image.* Paris: Minuit, 1956 (1956).
Berg, Jean de. *L'Image.* Préface de P[auline] R[éage]. Paris: J'ai lu, 1986 (1986).
Berg, Jeanne de. *Cérémonies de femmes.* Paris: Grasset et Fasquelle, 1985 (1985).
Bernardin de Saint-Pierre, Jacques-Henri. *Paul et Virginie.* Paris: Livre de poche, 1974 (1788).
Bouchard, Jean-Jacques. *Les Confessions d'un perverti.* Paris: Cercle du livre précieux, 1960 (c. 1650).
Brantôme, Pierre de Bourdeille, seigneur de. *Les Dames galantes,* ed. Maurice Rat. Paris: Garnier, 1965 (1666).
Capellanus, Andreas. *On Love,* ed. P. G. Walsh. London: Duckworth, 1982 (c. 1185).
Choiseul-Meuse, Félicité de. *Amélie de Saint-Far, ou la Fatale Erreur.* Brussels: Gay et Doucé, 1882 (1802). 2 vols.
Choiseul-Meuse, Félicité de. *Entre chien et loup.* Hamburg and Paris: Chez les marchands de nouveautés, 1807 (1807). 2 vols.
Choiseul-Meuse, Félicité de. *Julie, ou J'ai sauvé ma rose.* Hamburg and Paris: Chez les marchands de nouveautés, 1807 (1807). 2 vols.
Chorier, Nicolas. *Les Dialogues de Luisa Sigea sur les arcanes de l'amour et de Vénus, ou Satyre sotadique de Nicolas Chorier.* Trans. Alcide Bonneau. Paris: Lisieux, 1882 (1655). 4 vols.
Crébillon fils. *Les Egarements du cœur et de l'esprit.* Paris: Gallimard, 1977 (1736).
Crébillon fils. *Le Sopha.* Paris: U.G.E., 1966 (1748).
Crébillon fils. *The Sofa: A Moral Tale.* Trans. Bonamy Dobrée. London: Folio Society, 1951.
Crébillon fils. *Tableaux des mœurs du temps dans les différents âges de la vie.* Paris: Lattès, 1980 (1750).
Diderot, Denis. *Les Bijoux indiscrets,* ed. Antoine Adam. Paris: Garnier-Flammarion, 1968 (1748).
Diderot, Denis. *La Religieuse. Œuvres romanesques,* ed. Henri Bénac. Paris: Garnier, 1962 (1760).
Diderot, Denis. *Memoirs of a Nun: La Religieuse.* London: Routledge, 1928.
Eluard, Paul, and André Breton. *L'Immaculée Conception.* Paris: Editions Surréalistes, 1930 (1930).
Fougeret de Montbron, Louis-Charles. *Margot la ravaudeuse.* Hamburg: n.p., 1800 (1750). 2 vols.
Gaëtane. *Histoire d'I.* Paris: Filipacchi, 1974 (1974).
Gautier, Théophile. *Lettre à la présidente. Voyage en Italie, 1850.* Naples: Imprimerie du musée secret du roi de Naples, 1890 (1890).
Gautier, Théophile. *Mademoiselle de Maupin.* Paris: Bibliothèque Charpentier, 1919 (1835).
Gautier, Théophile. *Mademoiselle de Maupin.* Trans. Paul Selver. London: Hamish Hamilton, 1948.
Gervaise de Latouche, Jean-Charles. *Histoire de dom Bougre, portier des Chartreux, écrite par lui-même.* London: n.p., 1788 (1741). 2 vols.

Giroux de Morency, Suzanne. *Illyrine, ou l'Ecueil de l'inexpérience. L'Erotisme Directoire,* ed. Claudine Brécourt-Villars. Paris: Garnier, 1983 (1799).
Godard d'Aucour, Claude. *Thémidore, ou Mon Histoire, et celle de ma maîtresse.* Paris: Offenstadt, 1907 (1745).
Klossowski, Pierre. *Le Bain de Diane.* Paris: Gallimard, 1980 (1956).
Louvet de Couvray, Jean-Baptiste. *Les Amours du chevalier de Faublas.* Paris: Chez les marchands de nouveautés, n.d. [c. 1910] (1793). 2 vols.
Louÿs, Pierre. *Trois Filles de leur mère.* Paris: Pauvert, 1988 (1913).
Lucien de Samosate. *Lucius ou l'âne, suivi de Dialogues des courtisanes,* ed. Gilbert Lély. Paris: Lattès, 1979 (2nd century).
Mairobert, Pidansat de. *La Secte des anandrynes: Confession de mademoiselle Sapho.* Paris: Bibliothèque des curieux, 1920 (1789).
Mirabeau. *Œuvres érotiques.* Paris: Fayard, 1984.
Monnier, Henry. *Deux Gougnottes.* Partout et nulle part [Brussels]: n.p., 1864 (1864).
Musset, Alfred de. *Gamiani, ou Deux Nuits d'excès. L'Erotisme romantique,* ed. J.-J. Pauvert. Paris: Carrere, 1984 (1833).
Nerciat, Andréa de. *Les Aphrodites, ou Fragments thali-priapiques pour servir à l'histoire du plaisir.* N.p.: n.p., 1925 (1793). 2 vols.
Nerciat, Andréa de. *Le Diable au corps, œuvre posthume du très recommandable docteur Cazzone, membre extraordinaire de la joyeuse faculté phallo-coïto-pygo-glottonomique.* N.p.: n.p., 1803 (1803). 6 vols.
Nerciat, Andréa de. *Félicia, ou Mes fredaines.* Paris: Livre de Poche Hachette, 1976 (1775).
Nerciat, Andréa de. *Mon Noviciat, ou les Joies de Lolotte.* Paris: n.p., 1932 (1792).
Nogaret, Félix. *L'Arétin français, suivi des Epices de Vénus,* ed. Louis Perceau. Versailles: Aux dépens des fermiers généraux, n.d. (1787).
Ovid. *The Art of Love* [*Ars amatoria*] *and Other Poems.* Cambridge, Mass.: Harvard University Press, 1979 (1st century).
Pallavicino, Ferrante. *Alcibiade fanciullo a scola.* Geneva: n.p., 1642 (1642).
Pallavicino, Ferrante. *Alcibiade enfant à l'école.* Amsterdam: Chez l'ancien Pierre Marteau, 1866.
Pallavicino, Ferrante. *La Retorica delle puttane.* Cambrai: n.p., 1642 (1642).
Pougy, Liane de. *Idylle saphique,* ed. Jean Chalon. Paris: des femmes, 1987 (1901).
Rachilde. *Monsieur Vénus.* Paris: Flammarion, 1977 (1884).
Réage, Pauline. *Histoire d'O.* Paris: Pauvert, 1975 (1954).
Réage, Pauline. *The Story of O.* Paris: Olympia Press, 1954.
Restif de la Bretonne, Nicolas-Edmé. *Œuvres érotiques.* Paris: Fayard, 1985.
Restif de la Bretonne, Nicolas-Edmé. *La Paysanne pervertie, ou les Dangers de la ville.* Paris: Garnier-Flammarion, 1972 (1784).
Restif de la Bretonne, Nicolas-Edmé. *Pleasures and Folies of a Good-natured Libertine* [*L'Anti-Justine*]. Trans. Pieralessandro Casavini. Paris: Olympia Press, 1955 (1798).
Reveroni Saint-Cyr, Jacques-Antoine de. *Pauliska, ou la Perversité moderne, mémoires récentes d'une Polonaise.* Paris: Deforges, 1976 (1798).

Rousseau, Jean-Jacques. *Julie, ou la Nouvelle Héloïse,* ed. Michel Launay. Paris: Garnier-Flammarion, 1967 (1761).
Sade. *Les Cent Vingt Journées de Sodome.* Paris: U.G.E., 10/18, 1975 (1785).
Sade. *Les Infortunes de la vertu.* Paris: Gallimard, 1970 (1787).
Sade. *Justine, Philosophy in the Bedroom, and Other Writings.* New York: Grove Weidenfeld, 1990.
Sade. *Œuvres complètes.* Paris: Cercle du livre précieux, 1966–67.
Sade. *Œuvres complètes,* ed. Annie Le Brun and Jean-Jacques Pauvert. Paris: Pauvert, 1986–87. 15 vols.
Sade. *The 120 Days of Sodom and Other Writings.* Trans. Autryn Wainhouse and Richard Seaver. New York: Grove Weidenfeld, 1987.
Vatsayana. *The Kama Sutra,* ed. W. G. Archer. Trans. Sir Richard Burton and F. F. Arbuthnot. London: Allen and Unwin, 1963. (2d–4th century)
Vian, Boris. *Ecrits pornographiques, précédés de: Utilité d'une littérature érotique.* Paris: Bourgois, 1980.
Vivant Denon. *Point de Lendemain.* Paris: Desjonquières, 1987 (1777).
Vivien, Renée. *Une Femme m'apparut.* Paris: A. Lemerre, 1905 (1905).
Wittig, Monique. *Le Corps lesbien.* Paris: Minuit, 1973 (1973).

3c. *Anthologies and Collections*

Béalu, Marcel, ed. *La Poésie érotique de langue française.* Paris: Seghers, 1971.
Brécourt-Villars, Claudine, ed. *Ecrire d'amour. Anthologie de textes érotiques féminins (1799–1984).* Paris: Ramsay, 1985.
Brécourt-Villars, Claudine, ed. *L'Erotisme Directoire.* Paris: Garnier, 1983.
L'Enfer de la Bibliothèque Nationale., vols 3–6, *Œuvres anonymes du XVIIIe siècle;* vol. 7, *Œuvres anonymes du XVIIe siècle.* Paris: Fayard, 1985–88.
Etiemble, René, ed. *Romanciers du XVIIIe siècle.* Paris: Gallimard, Pléiade, 1960–65. 2 vols.
Forberg, Friedrich Carl, ed. *Manuel d'érotologie classique* [*De figuris Veneris*]. Trans. Alcide Bonneau. Paris: I. Lisieux, 1882. 2 vols.
Pauvert, Jean-Jacques, ed. *Anthologie historique des lectures érotiques.* Paris: Ramsay, 1980–83. 3 vols.
Pauvert, Jean-Jacques, ed. *L'Erotisme Second Empire.* Paris: Carrere, 1985.
Pillement, Georges, ed. *La Poésie érotique.* Paris: Régine Deforges, L'Or du temps, 1970.
Robert, Raymonde de. *Contes parodiques et licencieux du XVIIIe siècle.* Nancy: Presses Universitaires de Nancy, 1987.

4. Historical Studies of Eroticism and Erotic Art

Alexandrian, *Histoire de la littérature érotique.* Paris: Seghers, 1989.
Alexandrian. *Les Libérateurs de l'amour.* Paris: Le Seuil, 1977.

Angenot, Marc. "Pornographie fin de siècle: Le Polisson, le leste, le grivois et le pimenté." *Cahiers pour la littérature populaire* 7 (1986): 38–54.

Ariès, Philippe. *L'Enfant et la vie familiale sous l'ancien régime*. Paris: Plon, 1960.

Ariès, Philippe. *Western Sexuality: Practice and Precept in Past and Present Times*. Trans. Anthony Forster. Oxford: Blackwell, 1985.

Atkins, John Alfred. *Sex in Literature I. The Erotic Impulse in Literature*. London: Calder and Boyars, 1970.

Atkins, John Alfred. *Sex in Literature II. The Classical Experience of the Sexual Impulse*. London: Calder and Boyars, 1973.

Battacharyya, Narendra Nath. *A History of Indian Erotic Literature*. New Delhi: Munshiram Manoharlal, 1975.

Bold, Alan, ed. *The Sexual Dimension in Literature*. London: Vision, 1982.

Bonnet, Marie-Jo. *Un Choix sans equivoque: Relations amoureuses entre les femmes, XVIe—XXe siècle*. Paris: Denoël, 1981.

Bremmer, Jan. ed. *From Sappho to Sade: Moments in the History of Sexuality*. London: Routledge, 1989.

Brissenden, Robert F. *Virtue in Distress: Studies in the Novel of Sentiment from Richardson to Sade*. London: Macmillan, 1974.

Burnett, Anne Pippin. *Three Archaic Poets: Archilochus, Alcaeus, Sappho*. Cambridge, Mass.: Harvard University Press, 1983.

Calverton, V. F. *Sex Expression in Literature*. New York: Boni and Liveright, 1926.

Campion, Léo. *Le Cul à travers les âges*. Paris: S.O.S. Manuscrits, 1981.

Cazenobe, Colette. *Le Système du libertinage de Crébillon à Laclos*. Oxford: Voltaire Foundation, 1991.

Charney, Maurice. *Sexual Fiction*. London: Methuen, 1981.

De, Sushil Kumar. *Ancient Indian Erotics and Erotic Literature*. Calcutta: Mukhopadhyay, 1959.

Desai, Devangana. *Erotic Sculpture of India: A Socio-Cultural Study*. New Delhi: Tata McGraw-Hill, 1975.

Foster, Jeannette H. *Sex Variant Women in Literature: A Historical and Quantitative Survey*. London: Frederick Muller, 1958.

Foucault, Michel. *Histoire de la sexualité I: La Volonté de savoir*. Paris: Gallimard, 1976.

Foucault, Michel. *Histoire de la sexualité II: L'Usage des plaisirs*. Paris: Gallimard, 1984.

Foucault, Michel. *Histoire de la sexualité III: Le Souci de soi*. Paris: Gallimard, 1984.

Foucault, Michel. *The History of Sexuality*. Trans. Robert Hurley. New York: Vintage Books, 1986.

Foucault, Michel. *Les Mots et les choses*. Paris: Gallimard, 1966.

Foucault, Michel. *The Order of Things: An Archaeology of the Human Sciences*. (Trans. anon.) New York: Pantheon Books, 1971.

Fowlie, Wallace. *The Clown's Grail: A Study of Love in Its Literary Expression*, N.p.: Norwood, 1977.

Foxon, David Fairweather. *Libertine Literature in England, 1660–1745*. London: Book Collector, 1964.

Furber, Donald, and Anne Callahan. *Erotic Love in Literature: From Medieval Legend to Romantic Illusion.* Troy, N.Y.: Whitston, 1982.

Gillett, Charles Ripley. *Burned Books: Neglected Chapters in British History and Literature.* Fort Washington, N.Y.: Kentucket Press, 1964.

Goldberg, Rita Bettina. "Female Sexuality and Eighteenth-Century Culture in England and France: Richardson and Diderot." Ph.D. diss., Princeton, 1979.

Goldfarb, Russell M. *Sexual Repression and Victorian Literature.* Lewisburg: Bucknell University Press, 1970.

Goodden, Angelica. *The Complete Lover: Eros, Nature, and Artifice in the Eighteenth-Century French Novel.* Oxford: Clarendon Press, 1989.

Goulemot, Jean-Marie. *Ces Livres qu'on ne lit que d'une main: Lecture et lecteurs de livres pornographiques au XVIIIe siècle.* Aix-en-Provence: Alinéa, 1991.

Hagstrum, Jean H. *Sex and Sensibility: Ideal and Erotic Love from Milton to Mozart.* Chicago: University of Chicago Press, 1980.

Harari, Josué. *Scenarios of the Imaginary: Theorizing the French Enlightenment.* Ithaca: Cornell University Press, 1987.

Henriot, Emile. *Les Livres du second rayon, irréguliers et libertins.* Paris: "Le Livre," 1926.

Jacques, Jean-Pierre. *Les Malheurs de Sapho.* Paris: Grasset, 1980.

Lafon, Henri. "Machines à plaisir dans le roman français du XVIIIe siècle." *Revue des Sciences Humaines* 18 (1982): 111–21.

Lascault, Gilbert. *Alphabets d'Eros.* Paris: Galilée, 1976.

Lewinsohn, Richard. *A History of Sexual Customs.* Trans. Alexander Mayce. New York: Harper, 1958.

Lo Duca, J.-M. *Histoire de l'érotisme.* Paris: Pygmalion, 1979.

Loth, David. *The Erotic in Literature: A Historical Survey of Pornography As Delightful As It Is Indiscreet.* New York: Julian Messner, 1961.

Marcadé, Jean. *Eros Kalos: Essay on Erotic Elements in Greek Art.* Geneva: Nagel, 1962.

Marcus, Steven. *The Other Victorians: A Study of Sexuality and Pornography in Mid-Nineteenth Century England.* London: Weidenfeld and Nicolson, 1966.

Maupertuis, Alexandre. *Le Sexe et le plaisir avant le christianisme: L'Érotisme sacré.* Paris: CELT, 1977.

Moureau, François, and Alain-Marc Rieu. *Eros philosophe: Discours libertins des lumières.* Paris: Champion, 1984.

Nelli, René. *L'Erotique des troubadours.* Paris: U.G.E. 10/18, 1974.

Pastre, Geneviève. *Athènes et le péril saphique: Homosexualité féminine en Grèce ancienne.* Paris: Les Mots à la bouche, 1987.

Perrin, Noel. *Dr. Bowdler's Legacy: A History of Expurgated Books in England and America.* London: Macmillan, 1970.

Pintard, René. *Le Libertinage érudit dans la première moitié du dix-septième siècle.* Paris: Slatkine, 1983.

Roger, Philippe. "L'Imaginaire libertin et le corps 'spectaculeux.'" *Revue de l'Université de Bruxelles* 3–4 (1987): 53–60.
Roy, Bruno, ed. *L'Erotisme au moyen âge.* Montréal: Aurore, 1977.
Van Ussel, Jos. *Histoire de la répression sexuelle.* Paris: Laffont, 1972.
Wald Lasowski, Patrick. *L'Ardeur et la galanterie.* Paris: Gallimard, 1986.
Wald Lasowski, Patrick. *Libertines.* Paris: Gallimard, 1980.
Wald Lasowski, Patrick. *Syphilis: Essai sur la littérature française du XIX*[e] *siècle.* Paris: Gallimard, 1982.

5. Eroticism and Sexuality in General

Allen, Suzanne. *L'Espace d'un livre.* Paris: Gallimard, 1971.
Barthes, Roland. *Fragments d'un discours amoureux.* Paris: Le Seuil, 1977.
Barthes, Roland. *Le Plaisir du texte.* Paris: Le Seuil, 1973.
Barthes, Roland. *The Pleasure of the Text.* New York: Hill and Wang, 1975.
Bataille, Georges. *La Littérature et le mal.* Paris: Gallimard, 1967.
Bataille, Georges. *La Part maudite.* In *Œuvres complètes.* Paris: Gallimard, 1970–88. VII, 17–179.
Baudrillard, Jean. *De la séduction.* Paris: Galilée, 1979.
Baudrillard, Jean. *Seduction.* Trans. Brian Singer. London: Macmillan, 1990.
Becker, Raymond de. *The Other Face of Love.* Trans. Margaret Crosland and Alan Daventry. London: Neville Spearman, 1967.
Bersani, Leo. *A Future for Astyanax: Character and Desire in Literature.* Boston: Little, Brown, 1976.
Bersani, Leo. "Representation and Its Discontents." *Allegory and Representation,* ed. Stephen J. Greenblatt. Baltimore: Johns Hopkins University Press, 1981. 145–62.
Bruckner, Pascal, and Alain Finkielkraut. *Le Nouveau Désordre amoureux.* Paris: Le Seuil, 1977.
Buchen, Irving, ed. *The Perverse Imagination: Sexuality and Literary Culture.* New York: New York University Press, 1970.
Chasseguet-Smirgel, Janine. *Ethique et esthétique de la perversion.* Paris: Champ Vallon, 1984.
Deleuze, Gilles. *Présentation de Sacher-Masoch: Le Froid et le cruel, avec le texte intégral de la Vénus à la fourrure.* Paris: Minuit, 1967.
Deleuze, Gilles, and Félix Guattari. *Capitalisme et schizophrénie. Mille plateaux.* Paris: Minuit, 1980.
Desnos, Robert. *De l'érotisme considéré dans ses manifestations écrites et du point de vue de l'esprit moderne.* Paris: Cercle des arts, n.d.
Eaubonne, Françoise d'. *Eros minoritaire.* Paris: Balland, 1970.
Elsom, John. *Erotic Theatre.* London: Secker and Warburg, 1973.
"Eros and Literature." Special issue of *Mosaic* (1968) (Winnipeg).

"Erotiques." Special issue of *Revue d'Esthétique* (1978). Paris: 10/18 Inédit, 1978.
Etiemble, René. *L'Erotisme et l'amour.* Paris: Arléa, 1987.
Fiordo, Richard. "*Tales from the Smokehouse:* A Rhetorical Enquiry into Erotic Didactics." *Semiotica* 60 (1986): 1–27.
Gass, William. *A Philosophical Enquiry: On Being Blue.* Boston: Godine, 1975.
Hanson, Gillian. *Original Skin: Nudity and Sex in Cinema and Theatre.* London: Stacey, 1970.
Heath, Stephen. *The Sexual Fix.* London: Macmillan, 1982.
Hollier, Denis. *La Prise de la Concorde: Essais sur Georges Bataille.* Paris: Gallimard, 1974.
Kroker, Arthur, and Marilouise Kroker (eds.). *Body Invaders: Sexuality and the Postmodern Condition.* London: Macmillan, 1988.
Le Brun, Annie. *Les Châteaux de la subversion.* Paris: Pauvert/Garnier, 1982.
Le Brun, Annie. *A distance.* Paris: Pauvert/Carrere, 1984.
Lingis, Alphonso. *Excesses: Eros and Culture.* Albany, SUNY Press, 1983.
Michelson, Peter. *The Aesthetics of Pornography.* New York: Herder and Herder, 1971.
Morin, Violette, and Joseph Majault. *Un Mythe moderne: L'Érotisme.* Paris: Casterman, 1964.
Nobile, Philip (ed.). *The New Eroticism: Theories, Vogues, and Canons.* New York: Random House, 1970.
Peckham, Morse. *Art and Pornography: An Experiment in Explanation.* New York: Basic Books, 1969.
Perkins, Michael. *The Secret Record: Modern Erotic Literature.* New York: Morrow, 1976.
Phillips, Eileen (ed.). *The Left and the Erotic.* London: Lawrence and Wishart, 1983.
Pieyre de Mandiargues, André. *Le Désordre de la mémoire. Entretiens avec Francine Mallet.* Paris: Gallimard, 1975.
Pops, Martin. "The Metamorphosis of Shit." *Salmagundi* 56 (Spring 1982): 26–61.
Smith, F. J., and Erling Eng. *Facets of Eros: Phenomenological Essays.* The Hague: Martinus Nijhoff, 1972.

6. Pornography and Censorship

Bos, Mary, and Jill Pack. "Porn, Law, Politics." *Camerawork* 18 (1980): 4–5.
Burns, Alan, ed. *To Deprave and Corrupt: Technical Reports of the US Commission on Obscenity and Pornography.* London: Davis-Poynter, 1972.
Copp, David, and Susan Wendell, eds. *Pornography and Censorship.* Buffalo, N.Y.: Prometheus Books, 1983.
Fryer, Peter. *Private Case: Public Scandal.* London: Secker and Warburg, 1966.

Griffin, Susan. *Pornography and Silence: Culture's Revenge against Nature.* London: Women's Press, 1981.
Hawkins, Gordon, and Franklin E. Zimring. *Pornography in a Free Society.* Cambridge: Cambridge University Press, 1988.
Holbrook, David, ed. *The Case against Pornography.* London: Stacey, 1972.
Hughes, Douglas A., ed. *Perspectives on Pornography.* New York: Macmillan, 1970.
Huston, Nancy. *Dire et interdire. Eléments de jurologie.* Paris: Payot, 1980.
Hyde, Harford Montgomery. *A History of Pornography.* London: Heinemann, 1964.
Marcus, Steven. "Pornotopia." *Encounter* 27, no. 2 (1966): 9–18.
Marcuse, Ludwig. *Obscene: The History of an Indignation.* Trans. Karen Gershon. London: MacGibbon and Kee, 1965.
Stoehr, Taylor. "Pornography, Masturbation, and the Novel." *Salmagundi* 2 (1966): 28–56.
Young, Wayland Hilton. *Eros Denied.* London: Transworld, 1968.

7. Eroticism and Gender

Abel, Elizabeth, Marianne Hirsch, and Elizabeth Langland, eds. *The Voyage In: Fictions of Female Development.* Hanover, N.H.: University Press of New England, 1983.
Bartkowski, Frances. "Toward a Feminist Eros: Readings in Feminist Utopian Fiction." Ph.D. diss. University of Iowa, 1982.
Beauvoir, Simone de. *Le Deuxième Sexe.* Paris: Gallimard, 1949. 2 vols.
Beauvoir, Simone de. *The Second Sex.* Trans. H.M. Parshley. New York: Knopf, 1952.
Brown, Beverley. "A Feminist Interest in Pornography: Some Modest Proposals." *m/f* 5–6 (1981): 5–18.
Carter, Angela. *The Sadeian Woman and the Ideology of Pornography.* New York: Harper and Row, 1980.
Cixous, Hélène. "The Laugh of the Medusa." *New French Feminisms: An Anthology,* ed. Elaine Marks and Isabelle de Courtivron. Amherst: University of Massachusetts Press, 1980. 245–64.
Cornillon, Susan Koppelman. *Images of Women in Fiction: Feminist Perspectives.* Bowling Green, Ohio: Bowling Green University Popular Press, 1973.
Dardigna, Anne-Marie. *Les Châteaux d'Eros, ou les Infortunes du sexe des femmes.* Paris: Maspero, 1980.
Didier, Béatrice. *L'Ecriture-femme.* Paris: P.U.F., 1981.
Dobay Rifelj, Carol de. "Cendrillon and the Ogre: Women in Fairy Tales and Sade." *Romanic Review* (1990): 11–24.
Dworkin, Andrea. *Intercourse.* London: Secker and Warburg, 1987.
Dworkin, Andrea. *Pornography: Men Possessing Women.* London: Women's Press, 1981.

Evans, Martha Noel. *Masks of Tradition: Women and the Politics of Writing in Twentieth-Century France.* Ithaca: Cornell University Press, 1987.

Fink, Béatrice. "Ambivalence in the Gynogram: Sade's Utopian Woman." *Women and Literature* 7 (Winter 1979): 24–37.

Gallop, Jane. *The Daughter's Seduction: Feminism and Psychoanalysis.* Ithaca: Cornell University Press, 1982.

Gallop, Jane. *Intersections: A Reading of Sade with Bataille, Blanchot, and Klossowski.* Lincoln: University of Nebraska Press, 1981.

Gubar, Susan, and Joan Hoff, eds. *For Adult Users Only: The Dilemma of Violent Pornography.* Bloomington: Indiana University Press, 1989.

Hans, Marie-Françoise, and Gilles Lapouge. *Les Femmes, la pornographie, l'érotisme.* Paris: Le Seuil, 1978.

Hunt, Lynn Avery, ed. *Eroticism and the Body Politic.* Baltimore: Johns Hopkins University Press, 1991.

Huston, Nancy. *Mosaïque de la pornographie.* Paris: Denoël/Gonthier, 1982.

Irigaray, Luce. *Ce Sexe qui n'en est pas un.* Paris: Minuit, 1977.

Irigaray, Luce. *Passions élémentaires.* Paris: Minuit, 1982.

Irigaray, Luce. *Speculum de l'autre femme.* Paris: Minuit, 1974.

Irigaray, Luce. *Speculum of the Other Woman.* Trans. Gillian C. Gill. Ithaca: Cornell University Press, 1985.

Irigaray, Luce. *This Sex Which Is Not One.* Trans. Catherine Porter with Carolyn Burke. Ithaca: Cornell University Press, 1985.

Jardine, Alice. "Pre-texts for the Transatlantic Feminist." *Yale French Studies* 62 (1981): 220–36.

Kappeler, Susanne. *The Pornography of Representation.* Minneapolis: University of Minnesota Press, 1986.

Kuhn, Annette. *Women's Pictures: Feminism and Cinema.* London: Routledge and Kegan Paul, 1982.

Lederer, Laura, ed. *Take Back the Night: Women on Pornography.* New York: William Morrow, 1980.

Marks, Elaine. "Lesbian Intertextuality." *Homosexualities and French Literature: Cultural Contexts/Critical Texts,* ed. G. Stambolian and E. Marks. Ithaca: Cornell University Press, 1979. 353–77.

Miller, Nancy K. "*Juliette* and the Posterity of Prosperity." *L'Esprit Créateur* 15 (1975): 413–24.

Miller, Nancy K., ed. *The Poetics of Gender.* New York: Columbia University Press, 1986.

Millett, Kate. *Sexual Politics.* Garden City, N.Y.: Doubleday, 1970.

Moi, Toril. *Sexual/Textual Politics: Feminist Literary Theory.* London: Methuen, 1985.

Scholes, Robert. "Uncoding Mama: The Female Body as Text." *Semiotics and Interpretation.* New Haven: Yale University Press, 1982. 127–42.

Snitow, Anne, Christine Stansell, and Sharon Thompson eds. *Powers of Desire.* New York: Monthly Review Press, 1983.

Steinem, Gloria. "Erotica and Pornography: A Clear and Present Difference." *MS,* November 1978, 53–54, 75.

8. The Canon

Bourdieu, Pierre. *La Distinction: Critique sociale du jugement.* Paris: Minuit, 1979.

Bourdieu, Pierre. *Distinction: A Social Critique of the Judgement of Taste.* Trans. Richard Nice. Cambridge, Mass.: Harvard University Press, 1984.

Critical Inquiry 10, no. 1 (1983) special issue, "Canons," ed. Robert von Hallberg.

Ferguson, Frances. "Sade and the Pornographic Legacy." *Representations* 36 (Fall 1991): 1–21.

French Review 51, no. 3 (1988), special issue.

Gadamer, Hans-Georg. "The Eminent Text and Its Truth." In *The Horizon of Literature,* ed. Paul Hernadi. Lincoln: University of Nebraska Press, 1982, 337–47.

Gadamer, Hans-Georg. *Philosophical Hermeneutics.* Trans. David E. Linge. Berkeley: University of California Press, 1976.

Gadamer, Hans-Georg. *Truth and Method.* Trans. Garret Barden and John Cumming. New York: Seabury Press, 1975.

Hulbert, James. "The Problems of Canon Formation and the 'Example' of Sade: Orthodox Exclusion and Orthodox Inclusion," *Modern Language Studies* 18 (1988): 120–33.

Yale French Studies 75 (1988), special issue, "The Politics of Tradition," ed. Joan De Jean and Nancy K. Miller.

9. Narrative

Barthes, Roland. *S/Z.* Paris: Le Seuil, 1970.

Barthes, Roland. *S/Z.* Trans. Richard Miller. New York: Hill and Wang, 1974.

Brooks, Peter. *Reading for the Plot: Design and Intention in Narrative.* Oxford: Clarendon Press, 1984.

Moretti, Franco. *The Way of the World: The Bildungsroman in European Culture.* London: Verso, 1987.

10. Author Studies

10a. *Sade*

Barthes, Roland. *Sade, Fourier, Loyola.* Paris: Le Seuil, 1971.

Barthes, Roland. *Sade, Fourier, Loyola.* Trans. Richard Miller. New York: Hill and Wang, 1976.

Beauvoir, Simone de. *Faut-il brûler Sade?* Paris: Gallimard, 1955.

Bersani, Leo, and Ulysse Dutoit. "The Forms of Violence." *October* 8 (1979): 17–29.

Bersani, Leo, and Ulysse Dutoit. "Merde alors." *October* 13 (Summer 1980): 23–35.
Blanchot, Maurice. *Lautréamont et Sade.* Paris: U.G.E., 1967.
Blanchot, Maurice. *Sade et Restif de la Bretonne.* Paris: Complexe, 1986.
Bonnet, Jean-Claude. "La Harangue sadienne." *Poétique* 13 (1982): 31–50.
Breton, André. *Anthologie de l'humour noir.* Paris: Pauvert, 1972.
Brochier, Jean-Jacques. *Le Marquis de Sade et la conquête de l'unique.* Paris: Le Terrain Vague, 1966.
Centre aixois d'études et de recherches sur le dix-huitième siècle. *Le Marquis de Sade.* Paris: Colin, 1968.
Centre culturel international de Cerisy-la-Salle. *Sade: Écrire la crise.* Paris: Belfond, 1983.
DeJean, Joan. *Literary Fortifications: Rousseau, Laclos, Sade.* Princeton: Princeton University Press, 1984.
Delon, Michel. "La Copie sadienne." *Littérature* 69 (1988): 87–99.
Didier, Béatrice. *Sade: Essai.* (Paris: Denoël/Gonthier, 1976.
Fink, Béatrice C. "Food as Object, Activity, and Symbol in Sade." *Romanic Review* 65 (March 1974): 96–102.
Fink, Béatrice C. "Sade and Cannibalism." *L'Esprit Créateur* 15 (1975): 403–12.
Flake, Otto. *The Marquis de Sade, with a Postscript on Restif de la Bretonne.* London: Peter Davies, 1931.
Frappier-Mazur, Lucienne. *Sade et l'écriture de l'orgie.* Paris: Nathan, 1991.
Hackel, Robert J. *De Sade's Quantitative Moral Universe: Of Irony, Rhetoric, and Boredom.* The Hague: Mouton, 1976.
Heine, Maurice. "Préface de l'édition de 1931" [of *Les Cent Vingt Journées de Sodome*]. In Sade, *Œuvres complètes.* Paris: Cercle du livre précieux, 1967. XIII, xi-xv.
Hénaff, Marcel. *Sade: L'Invention du corps libertin.* Paris: P.U.F., 1978.
Ivker, Barry. "On the Darker Side of the Enlightenment: A Comparison of the Literary Techniques of Sade and Restif." *Studies on Voltaire and the Eighteenth Century* 79, (1971): 199–218.
Jean, Raymond. *Un Portrait de Sade.* Arles: Actes Sud, 1989.
Klossowski, Pierre. *Sade mon prochain, précédé de Le Philosophe scélérat.* Paris: Le Seuil, 1967.
Laborde, Alice M. *Les Infortunes du marquis de Sade.* Paris and Geneva: Champion-Slatkine, 1990.
Laborde, Alice M. "Sade: L'Érotisme démystifié." *L'Esprit Créateur* 15 (1975): 438–48.
Laborde, A. M. *Sade romancier.* Neuchâtel: La Baconnière, 1974.
Lacan, Jacques. "Kant avec Sade." *Ecrits II.* Paris: Le Seuil, 1971.
Lacombe, Anne. "*Les Infortunes de la vertu,* le conte et la philosophie." *L'Esprit Créateur* 15 (1975): 425–37.
Laugaa-Traut, Françoise, ed. *Lectures de Sade.* Paris: Armand Colin, 1973.
Le Brun, Annie. *Sade, aller et détours.* Paris: Plon, 1989.
Le Brun, Annie. *Soudain un bloc d'abîme.* Paris: Pauvert, 1986.

Lee, Vera. "The Sade Machine." *Studies on Voltaire and the Eighteenth Century* 98 (1972) 207–18.
Lély, Gilbert. "Introduction." In Sade, *Les Infortunes de la vertu.* Paris: U.G.E., 1968.
Lély, Gilbert. "Le Marquis de Sade et Rétif de la Bretonne, auteur de l'*Anti-Justine.*" In Sade, *Œuvres complètes.* Paris: Cercle du livre précieux, 1966–67. 483–87.
Lély, Gilbert. "Le Marquis de Sade et Rétif de la Bretonne." *Mercure de France* 331 (1957): 364–66.
Mercier, Roger. "Sade et le thème des voyages dans *Aline et Valcour.*" *Dix-Huitième Siècle* 1 (1969): 337–52.
Michael, Colette V. *Sade: His Ethics and Rhetoric.* New York: Peter Lang, 1989.
Pleynet, Marcelin. "Sade, des chiffres, des lettres, du renfermement." *Tel Quel* 86 (1980): 26–37.
Riffaterre, Michael. "Sade, or Text as Fantasy." *Diacritics* 2 (Fall 1972): 2–9.
Roberts, David. "Is de Sade Funny? or, The Prison of Parody." In Pavel Petr, David Roberts, and Philip Thomson, *Comic Relations: Studies in the Comic, Satire and Parody.* Frankfurt: Lang, 1985. 227–37.
Roger, Philippe. *Sade: La Philosophie dans le pressoir.* Paris: Grasset, 1976.
Sollers, Philippe. "Lettre de Sade." *Tel Quel* 61 (Spring 1975): 14–20.
Sollers, Philippe. "Sade dans le texte." *Tel Quel* 28 (Winter 1967): 38–50.
Sollers, Philippe. "Sade, encore." *Le Monde,* 13 February 1987: 20.
Thomas, Chantal. *Sade, l'œil de la lettre.* Paris: Payot, 1978.
Tort, Michel. "L'Effet Sade." *Tel Quel* 28 (Winter 1967): 66–83.
Williams, David. "Another Look at the Sadean Heroine: The Prospects for Femininity." *Essays on French Literature* 13 (1976): 28–43.

10b. *Restif*

Brahimi, D. "Restif féministe? Etude de quelques 'contemporaines.'" *Etudes sur le XVIIIe siècle* 3 (1976): 77–91.
Lafarge, Catherine. "*Les Délices de l'amour* de Restif de la Bretonne: Attaque efficace contre Sade?" *Studies on Voltaire and the Eighteenth Century* 153, (1976): 1245–53.
Poster, Marc. "Patriarchy and Sexuality: Restif and the Peasant Family." *The Eighteenth Century. Theory and Interpretation* 35 (1984): 217–40.
Revue des Sciences Humaines 212 (1988), special issue on Restif.

10c. *Crébillon*

Sgard, J. "La Notion d'égarement chez Crébillon." *Dix-huitième siècle* 1 (1969): 241–49.
Sturm, Ernest. *Crébillon fils et le libertinage au XVIIIe siècle.* Paris: Nizet, 1970.

10d. *Nerciat*

Ivker, Barry. "The Paramaters of a Period-Piece Pornographer, Andréa de Nerciat." *Studies on Voltaire and the Eighteenth Century* 98 (1972): 199–205.

10e. *Réage*

May, Charles E. "Sex, Submission, and the Story of O." *Carleton Miscellany* 16 (1977): 22–32.

Ostrovsky, Erika. "A Cosmogony of O." *Twentieth-Century French Fiction: Essays for Germaine Brée,* ed. George Stambolian. New Brunswick, N.J.: Rutgers University Press, 1975. 241–51.

Silverman, Kaja. "*Histoire d'O:* The Construction of a Female Subject." *Pleasure and Danger,* ed. Carole S. Vance. Boston: Routledge and Kegan Paul, 1984. 320–49.

Index